Up
Against
The Wall,
Mother...

UP AGAINST THE WALL, MOTHER...

On Women's Liberation

Elsie Adams

Mary Louise Briscoe

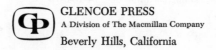

GLENCOE PRESS
A Division of The Macmillan Company
Beverly Hills, California

Contents

A note on our title   *ix*

Introduction   *xi*

Part One: The Traditional View of Women   1

The Second Sex   3

The Creation and the Fall, from *Genesis*   4

A Jewish Prayer   8

The Unclean Woman, from *Leviticus*   9

Catholic Teaching on Women   10   W. B. FAHERTY

Some Psychical Consequences of the
Anatomical Distinction between the Sexes   15   SIGMUND FREUD

The Womanly Image: Character
Assassination through the Ages   25   PAULA STERN

Woman-as-Object   33

Woman in the Elizabethan Sonnet: Poems by Spenser
and Shakespeare   34

The Victorian Woman   37   ANONYMOUS

On Playboys and Bunnies   38   H. M. HEFNER

In Memoriam: *Sex and the Single Girl*   40

Princess Grace Turns Forty   40   WILLIAM B. ARTHUR

Achieving Womanhood   44   WILLIAM H. GRIER
AND PRICE M. COBBS

The Bride of Frankenstein   54   EDWARD FIELD

Woman-as-Enemy   57

Tickets, Please   58   D. H. LAWRENCE

Faustine   69   ALGERNON CHARLES SWINBURNE

from *The Mill on the Floss*   74   GEORGE ELIOT

from *S.C.U.M. Manifesto*   **75**   VALERIE SOLANAS

Common Women   **78**   PHILIP WYLIE

from *Lyistrata*   **96**   ARISTOPHANES

The Eternal Feminine   103

The Goddess, from *The Golden Ass*   **104**   APULEIUS

True Woman—Herself   **107**   DANTE GABRIEL ROSSETTI

from *Riders to the Sea*   **108**   JOHN MILLINGTON SYNGE

Three Poems   **111**   ROBERT GRAVES

Karintha   **112**   JEAN TOOMER

Part Two: The Nature of Woman   115

Who Is She?   117

from *The Subjection of Women*   **118**   JOHN STUART MILL

Political and Civil Status of Women as
   of January 1, 1969   **133**   U.S. DEPARTMENT OF LABOR

The Matriarchal Myth   **144**   EVE MERRIAM

"X" Doesn't Equal "Y"   **154**   ASHLEY MONTAGU

Three Sexual Myths Exploded   **161**   RUTH AND EDWARD BRECHER

The Myth of the Vaginal Orgasm   **167**   ANNE KOEDT

Psychology Constructs the Female, or The Fantasy
   Life of the Male Psychologist   **176**   NAOMI WEISSTEIN

Part Three: Adjustment For Survival   193

The "Better Half"   195

The Monogamous Family   **196**   FREDERICH ENGELS

The Problem that Has No Name   **207**   BETTY FRIEDAN

from *Main Street*   **222**   SINCLAIR LEWIS

To Room Nineteen   **229**   DORIS LESSING

The Mother   **257**   GWENDOLYN BROOKS

Man and Wife   **259**   ANNE SEXTON

Communes: A Footnote
   for the Future   **260**   MARY LOUISE BRISCOE

The Working Woman 263

Women in the Labor Force 263   U.S. DEPARTMENT OF LABOR

On Day Care 268   LOUISE GROSS AND PHYLLIS MAC EWAN

The Morning Half-Life Blues 275   MARGE PIERCY

from Mrs. Warren's Profession 277   BERNARD SHAW

The Invisible Bar 284   CAROLINE BIRD

Fail: Bright Women 302   MATINA HORNER

Her Story 309   NAOMI LONG MADGETT

from A Room of One's Own 310   VIRGINIA WOOLF

Part Four: Toward Freedom 323

Sojourner Truth: On Women's Rights 325   FRANCES D. GAGE

from A Doll's House 328   HENRIK IBSEN

The Changing Women 335   STAN STEINER

One Woman's Lib 348   JOAN JONES

On Sisterhood 350   DANA DENSMORE

Women of Lesbos 353   MARTHA SHELLEY

On Celibacy 358   DANA DENSMORE

Abortion: Women, Men, and the Law 362   WILLIAM LAFFERTY

Man's Role in Women's Liberation 375   MARY LOUISE BRISCOE
     AND ELSIE ADAMS

Bibliography 385

Organizations 386

Journals, Press and Bookstores 386

General Bibliography 389

Women of Lesbos   **476**   MARTHA SHELLEY
On Celibacy   **481**   DANA DENSMORE
Abortion: Women, Men, and the Law   **485**   WILLIAM LAFFERTY
Man's Role in Women's Liberation   **498**   MARY LOUISE BRISCOE
                                                AND ELSIE ADAMS

Topics for Further Study   *509*

Topics for Literary Study   *511*

Bibliography   *513*
     Organizations   *514*
          Journals, Press and Bookstores   *514*
General Bibliography   *517*

A note on our title

The title of our book is intentionally ambiguous. On the most obvious level, it echoes the threat that has become a part of militant black rhetoric. The threat was first expressed in Leroi Jones' poem *Black People*, and it constitutes the dénouement of a Black Panther Party film: "Up against the wall, motherfucker. This is a stick-up. We've come for what's ours." It is the oppressed talking to the oppressor—black to white, or, in our book, woman to man. Deliberately drawing on the analogy between white oppression of black and male oppression of female, our title is a warning to those who have kept woman down: She is ready to take what has been stolen from her—that is, control of her own life.

On another level, the title serves not as a command but as a description of woman's place: she has been pushed up against the wall by a culture that defines her as inferior and prescribes roles (especially the wife-mother role) for her, thus giving her little or no choice about what she can do with her life. As the selections in "The 'Better Half'" make abundantly clear, marriage and motherhood often result in frustration, even desperation, for the woman. Mother is literally driven up against the wall. Our goal is to liberate woman so that she can be free to choose her own life style.

Introduction

Women are oppressed. They are oppressed today and have been oppressed throughout the history of Western civilization. In our culture, they are viewed as the descendants of a creature who was brought into being as a kind of sexual second thought and who is responsible for man's fall from paradise. (Perhaps as a punishment for Eve's sin of disobedience—to a male god—women are expected to find total human fulfillment in marriage and motherhood.) Women have been traditionally enslaved by this partly religious, partly cultural, partly biologic view and, because all of Western history, its concomitant myths, its art, and a good deal of its science have served to reinforce it, they still are.

Although their status as an inferior ("the weaker vessel"; "the second sex") or as an object (the body beautiful; the body bountiful) is clearly subordinate to that of men, women have often found themselves put on pedestals and literally worshipped for supra-human—and dehumanizing—attributes. This paradox of subjection venerated has, in turn, widened the distance between the sexes and brought about the myth of the Mystery of Woman, which is a direct adjunct to the equally pernicious myth of Woman-The-Enemy, because it is a particular property of mysteries to both fascinate and terrify. Then, too, either from guilt at the subservient roles they have prescribed for women or because of the occasional instances when women have struck back out of resentment at being so rigidly type-cast, men have come to fear that woman, in any of her several stereotyped guises, may destroy them: as the virago who makes their life a continuous misery, or as the *femme fatale* lusting for blood, or as Mommy perverting their minds and mutilating their bodies. Most Western myth-makers, however, have preferred to create a more comfortable illusion of woman in which she appears as the embodiment of sensual loveliness, spiritual beauty, and moral principle. According to this less apocalyptic definition, woman is abused, she suffers, but she endures.

The traditional views of woman are a product of a male-dominated, male-created culture, and only within the last century have men or women begun challenging them. John Stuart Mill, writing on *The Subjection of Women* a century ago, expressed an opinion that still prevails among partisans of women's rights: "What is now called the nature of woman is an eminently artificial thing." When most people speak of "the nature of woman," they are speaking of woman as she has been defined by custom. The result is that knowledge about the physiology, psychology, and history of woman is still (pardon the expression) in an embryonic stage. This is not to say that woman is, as romantics believe, an enigma, mysterious and incomprehensible; it is simply an admission that so few attempts have been made to disentangle the reality from the myths that no one knows what woman really is.

Most women know what they are *not*: They are not goddesses or beauty queens. They know that to serve as a model of spiritual and physical beauty requires a lifetime of hiding the self from view; cosmetics and costume pass as the self, but they are forms of pretense and hypocrisy that mask woman's psyche. The editors of this book do not know whether woman is, as Bernard Shaw says, merely a "man in petticoats," or, as Ashley Montagu believes, physically and psychically superior to males, or, as tradition has it, inferior to them. We do know that if anything is to be learned about the nature of woman, it will have to be ascertained by women *and men* who have liberated themselves from culturally determined (i.e., male-dictated) assumptions and prejudices.

And we also know that the roles traditionally assigned to women result in psychological strain, creative waste, and social evils. Nora Helmer's pretending to be her husband's "little lark" in *A Doll's House* while faced with real financial problems and anxiety over the additional problem of protecting her husband's male ego or Carol Kennicott's desperately trying to "make something" of her life in *Main Street* point up the acute though sometimes inarticulate dissatisfaction with life felt by many women forced into the confines of the wife/mother role. We refer anyone who still believes that Nora's problems were solved at the end of the nineteenth century or that Carol's ended in the 1920's to the dissatisfaction Betty Friedan documented in 1963. What she rediscovered in *The Feminine Mystique* was that the woman who, according to the values of our culture, had made it—the middle-class woman with the security of husband, children and home—was ravaged by "a problem that has no name." And it is the same problem that beset Ibsen's Nora and Lewis' Carol Kennicott: a feeling that a woman's life has to be "more than this"; that, contrary to the prevailing view, the roles of housewife and mother do *not* in and of themselves lead to fulfillment but to frustration. Friedan supplies abundant examples of the "successful" wife and mother who is nevertheless dissatisfied with life; to these every observant woman can add examples from her own experience. We know of a college graduate with a devoted husband, six children, a comfortable home, who invariably watches soap operas on TV. When asked how someone as well-educated as she could possibly watch afternoon television, she answered, "I need to cry a little every day." Now, this is not someone who dislikes her husband and children, nor is she a woman lacking in intellectual and spiritual resources. She loves to cater to her husband's wishes; she likes to play games with her children. She bakes her own bread, makes her own curtains, decorates her house, plans imaginative parties; she is devoutly religious. But she also has to cry a little every day.

Unfortunately, the solution to the woman's problem is not as simple as slamming the door on the doll's house. As a general rule, the working woman, like her housewife sister, has an equally unsatisfactory life comprised of low wages, boring work, and slim chances of advancement. In her work she typically serves others: typing, clerking, cleaning, mechanically performing mechanical tasks for which she is paid much less than a man receives for doing the same job (if, indeed, a man will do the same job). Furthermore, statistics show that most working women are also housewives; so what in fact happens is that the working woman has two jobs—worker (badly paid labor) and housewife/mother (unpaid labor). In short, except for a few exceptional women who, in spite of incredible obstacles, either by luck or grit or both, have found satisfying and rewarding jobs, women in the labor force are oppressed. As Marge Piercy says in *The Morning Half-Life Blues*, "each day ... opens like a can and is empty."

Women are programmed to fail: It isn't "ladylike" to be intelligent and ambitious. In her essay *Fail: Bright Women*, Matina Horner observes, "A bright woman is caught in a double bind. In testing and other achievement-oriented situations she worries not only about failure, but also about success. If she fails, she is not living up to her own standards of performance; if she succeeds, she is not living up to societal expectations about the female role." The creative potential of women is systematically discouraged not only by social attitudes toward "woman's place" but also by the denial to women of money and time. On the latter point, John Stuart Mill notes (after a woman had pointed it out to him) that "Everything a woman does is done at odd times." If she is married, the home and family occupy her major time while writing or reading or thinking is sandwiched into her spare time. Furthermore, she usually has no place of her own. Though the house is her province, no part of it is exclusively hers. Hence Virginia Woolf insists that a creative woman must have what most women do not have: a room of her own—as necessary as money if she is to be independent and free. Equal demands might be made for all women; Sinclair Lewis understood this when he had his housewife heroine of *Main Street* demand from her husband a separate income for maintaining the household, and a separate room, to which she could retire for reading and thought.

Given their oppression in our culture, what can women do? They can do what they have always done: diet, dress, and spend money and time on cosmetics and coiffure in order to attract and keep a man; they can serve as symbols of moral rectitude and spiritual perseverance, and, incidentally, invite martyrdom at the hands of men; if the pressures of conforming to stereotyped roles becomes too great, they can become nags and shrews. Or they can, as more and more women are doing, rebel.

Rebellion—the focus of the present Women's Liberation movement—is the theme of this book; rebellion against the traditional definitions of woman; against male assumptions about her function in society; against her systematic exploitation as sex object, wife, mother, and worker; against the gigantic brainwashing that serves in place of her education and which begins so early that, by the time she is five years old, she understands and accepts the fact that certain jobs are closed to her ("I want to be a nurse. I like to take care of people." "Why not be a doctor?" "Men are doctors. Women are nurses.") and that housework and mothering are her destiny ("I play with my dolls. I wash them, dress them, cook for them, serve them meals, take care of them when they are sick. Johnny builds houses and drives trucks and goes fishing.") The rebellion is manifested in the hundreds of Women's Liberation groups that are springing up around the United States; by the increasing militancy of women asking for equal rights under the law and human dignity in the eyes of their fellow men/women; by the gradual (though often begrudging) admission of women to jobs previously held only by men; by the institution of Women Studies in schools and colleges, and by the widespread media concern with tracing, explaining, analyzing, patronizing, ridiculing, but nevertheless *talking about* Women's Liberation.

The present drive towards women's liberation is rooted in the feminist movement of the nineteenth and early twentieth centuries. But the lesson of that movement was that women's suffrage and legal reform are not enough. For its success, democracy requires an enlightened electorate, and women got the vote but not the enlightenment. Hence women as voters have tended to be a conservative force, historically casting their ballots and exercising their influence against their own liberation. Often they do not exercise their basic rights, do not vote for other women, do not like to work for women bosses, and prefer to take courses from male instructors. They have preserved the status quo—even, or especially, on the woman question. The Women's Liberation movement hopes to accomplish the enlightenment that legal reform did not effect: It aims at educating, or re-educating, women to their nature and roles. In order to do this, it questions the traditional views, asking that women become a radicalizing force, destroying old assumptions, shaking the foundations of a chauvinist society which, in its demand for dominance abroad and at home, is wrecking the world with its superior/inferior, master/servant, powerful nation/weak nation, big man/little woman obsession.

That women are ready for this re-education is evident from the proliferation of Women's Liberation groups during the past few years. In 1966 Betty Friedan founded the National Organization for Women (NOW) which focuses on problems of job discrimination, constitutional inequities, and minority group exploitation. Tactically it makes use of court action and lobbying and has around 35 chapters coast to coast. Within the last two years, other, more militant groups have formed as women in the New Left came to realize that even if a revolution came about tomorrow women would still be oppressed. As radical women began analyzing the sick desire for dominance—one nation over another, the white race over the black—they came to see that, on matters pertaining to the man-woman relationship, radical males joined hands with their liberal and conservative sexist brothers. Women's caucuses were formed within radical groups and were received with either laughter or hostility or downright condescension, as in the case of a 1967 SDS (Students for a Democratic Society) resolution which consisted of a series of "Whereas" clauses defining the need for personal (and hence women's) liberation, followed by a "BE IT RESOLVED, BABY" clause providing for workshops and "projects" (sewing circles? baking contests?) on Women's Liberation. It was not a Kiwanis or Junior Chamber of Commerce member who said, when a woman stood to speak on Women's Liberation, "Take her off the stage and fuck her." The hostile and degrading comment, reflecting the traditional view of woman as object, as brainless, ineffective, irrelevant, etc., occurred at a radical meeting and was made by a radical. Therefore, women in and out of the radical movement have begun directing their energies and talents to the cause of their own freedom. As a recent Women's Liberation paper proclaims, "I ain't fighting in no man's war."

Women's groups independent of male-dominated radical groups have developed, with diverse aims and tactics. WITCH (Women's International Terrorist Conspiracy from Hell) uses guerilla theater to call attention to social institutions which exploit women; the Redstockings (New York) feature consciousness-raising "therapy" sessions for women; S.C.U.M. (The Society for Cutting Up Men), which can be characterized as the terrorist wing of the movement, aims at the destruction of all males; the Daughters of Bilitis, a national Lesbian organization, wants to change laws pertaining to homosexuality. *Time* Magazine reported in 1969 that there were 50 Women's Liberation groups in New York; 35 in the San Francisco Bay Area; 30 in Chicago; 25 in Boston. But the movement is not limited to large cities. In February, 1969, women from nine Southern states attended workshops at a conference sponsored by the Southern Student Organizing Committee. The Commission on the Status of Women is demanding an end to sex discrimination in Kansas laws. Though this Commission opposes the "silly groups" (e.g., the bra burners), its position has militant overtones. According to its spokeswoman, "As long as things proceed reasonably, Kansas women are going to be non-violent." (But what if legislators continue to laugh at women's efforts and things do not "proceed reasonably"?) Milwaukee, Wisconsin, has at least four Women's Liberation groups, and the NOW chapter recently held a sit-in at an all-male section of a downtown restaurant. The Women's Liberation Front of Hawaii held its first rally on April 13, 1970. And so it goes—literally coast to coast, in large and small cities, reaching thousands of women who are becoming more and more vocal and militant.

One of our foremost demands is for an end to "sexism," the exploitation of woman as sexual object and the concomitant failure to recognize her humanity. The primary targets thus far have been beauty contests, bridal fairs, and printers of pornography. Women's Liberation groups protested the Miss America Pageant in 1968 and 1969—"Welcome to the Miss America Cattle Auction." In 1968, a live sheep was crowned in guerilla theater depicting the pageant; in 1969, a Women's Liberation "plant" made the finals of the contest and tried to seize the microphone. The union of commerce and marriage at bridal fairs is often attacked by Women's Liberation leafleting, speeches, and guerilla theater. The Feminists of New York go one step farther and protest at marriage license bureaus. Women's liberation groups forced a pornography printer in San Francisco to withdraw his publication. And an *ad hoc* committee to protest discrimination in the newspaper industry in Washington, D. C. has as one of its charges the publication of sexist and condescending news stories. Such protests, scattered and uncoordinated, are indicative of one of the major aims of Women's Liberation: the freeing of woman from sexual exploitation so that she will no longer be, like Edward Field's monster-woman in *The Bride of Frankenstein*, "just another body to be raped."

A woman's right to govern her own body, including her right to determine if and when she will bear children, is another major demand of Women's Liberation. Women's groups have argued, marched, lobbied for liberalization of existing birth control and abortion laws. For example, on March 28, 1970, 45 women's liberation groups in New York supported a demonstration by People to Abolish Abortion Laws, which is asking for laws providing for free abortions on demand. When New York liberalized its abortion law in April 1970, Governor Rockefeller admitted that women's liberation groups had been influential in bringing about the new law (which does *not*, however, provide for free abortions on demand). Women also demanded to be heard during the January 1970 Senate Subcommittee hearing on the birth control pill; Women's Liberation of Washington, D.C. disrupted the hearing, protesting against the use of women by doctors and the drug industry as part of an experiment. They also objected to the absence of women on the panel before the committee. The latter protest is significant—heretofore women have simply not been consulted in matters pertaining to their lives; the laws governing them, the advice given them, the education offered them all derive from the male. It is not unusual for a panel on birth control or abortion to be all male; and, until women began to protest it, no one considered this inappropriate.

The fight for equal protection under the law is a continuing struggle. Since the first Women's Rights Convention in Seneca Falls, New York, in 1848—which demanded an end to the "absolute tyranny" of men over women and asked specifically for laws enabling a woman to vote, to own property, to defend herself against abuses in marriage, to obtain guardianship of her children, to earn a living in the professions, and to attend college—progress has been slow. Admittedly, women now have most of the legal rights outlined by the Seneca Falls Convention, but the change in attitudes requisite for genuine equality has not come about. The final complaints of the Convention concerning the double moral standard, the assignment of traditional roles to women, and the education of women to submissive roles can stand today:

> [Man] has created a false public sentiment by giving to the world a different code of morals for men and women, by which moral delinquencies which exclude women from society are not only tolerated, but deemed of little account in man.
>
> He has usurped the prerogative of Jehovah himself, claiming it as his right to assign for her a sphere of action, when that belongs to her conscience and to her God.
>
> He has endeavoured, in every way that he could, to destroy her confidence in her own powers, to lessen her self-respect, and to make her willing to lead a dependent and abject life.

Not until 1964, when the Civil Rights Act added "sex" to the prohibition of discrimination because of "race, color, religion or national origin," did job discrimination against women become illegal. But enforcement of a law is, as almost everyone knows, more difficult than its passage. In 1965, 40% of the most serious appeals to the Equal Employment Opportunity Commission involved discrimination because of sex. The great numbers of complaints to the EEOC in succeeding years show that working women continue to protest job discrimination. Of late, there is evidence of women uniting against it. As an example, Women,

Inc., a women's caucus of Western Pulp and Paper Workers in California, is opposing attempts to nullify California laws protecting women workers; whereas the employer argues that equal employment laws prohibit special working conditions for women, the women argue that laws protecting women workers should be extended to men workers as well. In March 1970, 100 women took over the editor's office of *Ladies' Home Journal,* demanding a female staff for the magazine, while female employees of *Newsweek* filed federal suit for job discrimination. At the 1969 convention of the American Sociological Association, as a result of demands by the women's caucus, the Association resolved to give priority to women's hiring and promotion and to provide for an undergraduate and graduate education more favorable to women. The Welfare Mothers of Wisconsin marched in January 1970 demanding adequate housing and clothing allowances; when they were offered a "clothing drive" instead of more money, the women conducted their own "clothing drive" by trashing a reputable downtown store. Though many of the women involved in these actions would deny any affiliation with the Women's Liberation movement, they are nevertheless a part of American woman's increasing demand for equality in a man's world— one of the primary demands of Women's Liberation.

For the next few years, these demands will no doubt be met with tokenism. And nothing more will happen unless what is now a large but disparate movement becomes unified. Fortunately, there are signs that unification is realizable: meetings in early May 1970 brought about a coalition of Women's Liberation groups in Boston, Minnesota, and Wisconsin; Chicago groups are uniting under the Women's Liberation Union with a citywide steering committee; in Los Angeles, a Conference to Unite Women met in May 1970; and a Congress to Unite Women met in New York in December 1969 and May 1970, articulating and summarizing demands held in common by most Women's Liberation groups: *re-education* of women through the institution of Women Studies; a rewriting of history with a view to woman's role in it; the admission of women to vocational courses; *economic equality* through an end to job discrimination and the admission of women to trade schools and unions; *physical equality* through birth control and abortion rights; and *equal representation* in their government.

The Women's Liberation movement potentially bridges class and race barriers; indeed, if the movement is to succeed, it must make attempts to reach all women. At present, it is predominantly white, middle-class, and university-centered. If it remains thus, it is destined to have little permanent effect on the society. What must be done is for women within the movement to recognize their sisterhood with all women, something Dana Densmore eloquently expresses in her essay *On Sisterhood:*

We are all sisters. We all work within the same constraints. If some of us are more successful or less oppressed it is because we are less crippled, not because we are superior, not because we are different.

Although their oppression is greatest, Black women have not yet joined Women's Liberation in great numbers since they must fight both racial and sexual discrimination. Leaders of the Black movement are, however, beginning to incorporate Women's Liberation into the wider movement. In August 1969, Eldridge Cleaver called for an end to male chauvinism and all manifestations of it, saying that:

Women are our other half, they're not our weaker half, they're not our stronger half, but they are our other half and . . . we sell ourselves out, we sell our children out and we sell our women out when we treat them in any other manner.

Notably, the December 1969 New Haven demonstrations against the imprisonment of fourteen members of the Connecticut Black Panther Party (seven of them women—"equality" with a vengeance!) were called by both the Black Panther Party and New Haven Women's Liberation. This is a far cry from Stokely Carmichael's infamous declaration that "The only position for women in S.N.C.C. is prone" or from the resolution of women delegates at a Black Power Conference in July 1966 to relinquish their dominant positions in the home, the community, and the movement. American Indian women have also begun demanding freedom from exploitation by the White Man.

As long as any women remain in servitude, no one can be liberated. "Women's Liberation" is today not a reality but a goal. At present we are all—women and men—a part of Mrs. Warren's profession, prostituting our bodies and minds in a culture which allows rich to exploit poor, white to exploit colored, men to exploit women. In demanding an end to the exploitation, women are rejecting a system which allows one group power over another group's destiny. We are not, as many men fear, out to destroy men. The Society for Cutting Up Men has, to our knowledge, very few members, and possibly only one, the author of the *S.C.U.M. Manifesto.* Men are the enemy only in the sense that they cling to an archaic system which endorses a master/slave relationship. Male fear of women's dominance is prompted by uneasiness about the demand that men give up their privileged status and by the fact that the demand is being made vehemently and impatiently. But, hopefully, that demand will be granted peacefully, and achieved through education. At this point in history women are only metaphorically echoing the dénouement of a Black Panther Party film: "Up against the wall, motherfucker. This is a stick-up. We've come for what's ours."

NOTE: Since this book went to press, there have been several significant developments in the Women's Liberation movement. In June, President Nixon signed an Executive Order barring discrimination against women in all federally contracted jobs. On August 10, the House of Representatives approved an equal rights amendment to the Constitution, sponsored by Representative Martha Griffiths (D. Mich.) and supported by all the women members of Congress. This amendment, which has been stalled in committee for the last 47 years, provides that "Equality of rights under the law shall not be denied or abridged by the United States or by any State on account of sex."

On August 26, a nation-wide women's strike observed the fiftieth anniversary of women's suffrage and dramatized the principal demands of Women's Liberation: free 24-hour day care for children, free abortions on demand, and complete equality in education and employment. Betty Friedan, who called the strike, asked that all women "visibly protest the discrimination against women." Strike action included parades, speeches, guerilla theater, and many unreported personal demonstrations of protest against the traditional oppression of women.

These and other (almost daily) indications of an increased awareness of the need for female equality with the male attest to the potential influence and strength of the movement toward Women's Liberation.

Elsie Adams & Mary Louise Briscoe
Whitewater, Wisconsin

Up
Against
The Wall,
Mother...

Part One:

The Traditional View of Women

The Second Sex

In the early 1940's Simone de Beauvoir asked the question, "Why is woman the *other*, the second sex?" She found that the answer did not lie in biology, as so many people have thought. Cultural anthropology reveals that sex roles vary according to social mores, not biological function:

> A single male can fecundate a number of females each year; but it requires a male for every female to assure the survival of the offspring after they are born, to defend them against enemies, to wrest from nature the wherewithal to satisfy their needs. In human history the equilibrium between the forces of production and of reproduction is brought about by different means under different economic conditions, and these conditions govern the relations of male and female to off-spring and in consequence to each other.[1]

In the eye of the storm called Women's Liberation is the simple truth that the working time of woman is no longer culturally confined to or dictated by her biological function of reproduction. Nor does she need to depend solely on her mate to protect and provide for her. Modern society offers the possibility of equal human rights, but the source of woman's role continues to be her reproductive function. When technology offers her time and leisure to develop her self instead of only attending to the needs of her family, the traditional role becomes a source of frustration which denies her the freedom to become anything else. Man continues to demand an identity for woman which no longer can be completely satisfying, and, as Simone de Beauvoir comments, "When she behaves as a human being she is said to imitate the male."

The selections in this section show how the literature of Western tradition—in religion, psychology and the mass media—continues to perpetrate the role of woman as the second sex.

---

[1] *The Second Sex*, trans. H. M. Parshley, New York, 1961, p. 32.

The Creation and the Fall

from Genesis

Following are two accounts from the book of Genesis of the creation of man and woman. In the first account (Genesis I:24-31), male and female are created in the image of God and are given dominion over the earth; there is no suggestion of woman as the second sex but rather the implication that she was created at the same time as man and given equal powers.

In the second account (Genesis II:4-III:24), woman is created after man—even after all the creatures of the earth—as "an help meet" for Adam. In this account, Eve, the mother of us all, derives her very physical being from man (Adam's rib). When she succumbs to the serpent's temptation, she brings down the curse of God on mankind.

Chapter 1: 24-31

24 ℐ And God said, Let the earth bring forth the living creature after his kind, cattle, and creeping thing, and beast of the earth after his kind: and it was so.

25 And God made the beast of the earth after his kind, and cattle after their kind, and every thing that creepeth upon the earth after his kind: and God saw that it was good.

26 ℐ And God said, Let us make man in our image, after our likeness: and let them have dominion over the fish of the sea, and over the fowl of the air, and over the cattle, and over all the earth, and over every creeping thing that creepeth upon the earth.

27 So God created man in his own image, in the image of God created he him; male and female created he them.

28 And God blessed them, and God said unto them, Be fruitful, and multiply, and replenish the earth, and subdue it: and have dominion over the fish of the sea, and over the fowl of the air, and over every living thing that moveth upon the earth.

29 ℐ And God said, Behold, I have given you every herb bearing seed, which is upon the face of all the earth, and every tree, in which is the fruit of a tree yielding seed; to you it shall be for meat.

30 And to every beast of the earth, and to every fowl of the air, and to every thing that creepeth upon the earth, wherein there is life, I have given every green herb for meat: and it was so.

31 And God saw every thing that he had made, and, behold, it was very good. And the evening and the morning were the sixth day.

Chapter II:4- Chapter III:24

4 ¶ These are the generations of the heavens and of the earth when they were created, in the day that the LORD God made the earth and the heavens,

5 And every plant of the field before it was in the earth, and every herb of the field before it grew: for the LORD God had not caused it to rain upon the earth, and there was not a man to till the ground.

6 But there went up a mist from the earth, and watered the whole face of the ground.

7 And the LORD God formed man of the dust of the ground, and breathed into his nostrils the breath of life; and man became a living soul.

8 ¶ And the LORD God planted a garden eastward in Eden; and there he put the man whom he had formed.

9 And out of the ground made the LORD God to grow every tree that is pleasant to the sight, and good for food; the tree of life also in the midst of the garden, and the tree of knowledge of good and evil.

10 And a river went out of Eden to water the garden; and from thence it was parted, and became into four heads.

11 The name of the first is Pison: that is it which compasseth the whole land of Hăv′-ĭ-läh, where there is gold;

12 And the gold of that land is good: there is bdellium and the onyx stone.

13 And the name of the second river is Gī-hon: the same is it that compasseth the whole land of Ethiopia.

14 And the name of the third river is Hĭd′-de-kel: that is it which goeth toward the east of Assyria. And the fourth river is Eû-phrā′-tēs.

15 And the LORD God took the man, and put him into the garden of Eden to dress it and to keep it.

16 And the LORD God commanded the man, saying, Of every tree of the garden thou mayest freely eat:

17 But of the tree of the knowledge of good and evil, thou shalt not eat of it: for in the day that thou eatest thereof thou shalt surely die.

18 ¶ And the LORD God said, It is not good that the man should be alone; I will make him an help meet for him.

19 And out of the ground the LORD God formed every beast of the field, and every fowl of the air; and brought them unto Adam to see what he would call them: and whatsoever Adam called every living creature, that was the name thereof.

20 And Adam gave names to all cattle, and to the fowl of the air, and to every beast of the field; but for Adam there was not found an help meet for him.

21 And the LORD God caused a deep sleep to fall upon Adam, and he slept: and he took one of his ribs, and closed up the flesh instead thereof;

22 And the rib, which the LORD God had taken from man, made he a woman, and brought her unto the man.

23 And Adam said, This is now bone of my bones, and flesh of my flesh: she shall be called Woman, because she was taken out of Man.

24 Therefore shall a man leave his father and his mother, and shall cleave unto his wife: and they shall be one flesh.

25 And they were both naked, the man and his wife, and were not ashamed.

Now the serpent was more subtil than any beast of the field which the LORD God had made. And he said unto the woman, Yea, hath God said, Ye shall not eat of every tree of the garden?

2 And the woman said unto the serpent, We may eat of the fruit of the trees of the garden:

3 But of the fruit of the tree which is in the midst of the garden, God hath said, Ye shall not eat of it, neither shall ye touch it, lest ye die.

4 And the serpent said unto the woman, Ye shall not surely die:

5 For God doth know that in the day ye eat thereof, then your eyes shall be opened, and ye shall be as gods, knowing good and evil.

6 And when the woman saw that the tree was good for food, and that it was pleasant to the eyes, and a tree to be desired to make one wise, she took of the fruit thereof, and did eat, and gave also unto her husband with her; and he did eat.

7 And the eyes of them both were opened, and they knew that they were naked; and they sewed fig leaves together, and made themselves aprons.

8 And they heard the voice of the LORD God walking in the garden in the cool of the day: and Adam and his wife hid themselves from the presence of the LORD God amongst the trees of the garden.

9 And the LORD God called unto Adam, and said unto him, Where art thou?

10 And he said, I heard thy voice in the garden, and I was afraid, because I was naked; and I hid myself.

11 And he said, Who told thee that thou wast naked? Hast thou eaten of the tree, whereof I commanded thee that thou shouldest not eat?

12 And the man said, The woman whom thou gavest to be with me, she gave me of the tree, and I did eat.

13 And the LORD God said unto the woman, What is this that thou hast done? And the woman said, The serpent beguiled me, and I did eat.

14 And the LORD God said unto the serpent, Because thou hast done this, thou art cursed above all cattle, and above every beast of the field; upon thy belly shalt thou go, and dust shalt thou eat all the days of thy life:

15 And I will put enmity between thee and the woman, and between thy seed and her seed; it shall bruise thy head, and thou shalt bruise his heel.

16 Unto the woman he said, I will greatly multiply thy sorrow and thy conception; in sorrow thou shalt bring forth children; and thy desire shall be to thy husband, and he shall rule over thee.

17 And unto Adam he said, Because thou hast hearkened unto the voice of thy wife, and hast eaten of the tree, of which I commanded thee, saying, Thou shalt not eat of it: cursed is the ground for thy sake; in sorrow shalt thou eat of it all the days of thy life;

18 Thorns also and thistles shall it bring forth to thee; and thou shalt eat the herb of the field;

19 In the sweat of thy face shalt thou eat bread, till thou return unto the ground; for out of it wast thou taken: for dust thou art, and unto dust shalt thou return.

20 And Adam called his wife's name Eve; because she was the mother of all living.

21 Unto Adam also and to his wife did the LORD God make coats of skins, and clothed them.

22 ¶ And the LORD God said, Behold, the man is become as one of us, to know good and evil: and now, lest he put forth his hand, and take also of the tree of life, and eat, and live for ever:

23 Therefore the LORD God sent him forth from the garden of Eden, to till the ground from whence he was taken.

24 So he drove out the man; and he placed at the east of the garden of Eden Cher-u-bims, and a flaming sword which turned every way, to keep the way of the tree of life.

A Jewish Prayer

translated by Elsie Adams

The following portion of a Jewish prayer makes a distinction between the sexes. A rabbinical interpretation has it that the man is giving thanks to God for not creating him a woman because he recognizes the woman's hard lot. Whatever the motivation that is supposed to prompt the prayer, it is significant that here, woman is included in a series which includes the "heathen" and the "slave"—the unchosen and the servile.

My Lord, the life you breathed in me is pure. You formed it, fashioned it, breathed it into me. And you guarded over it in my inner being. And you will take that life from me and give it once again in the time to come. The while I hold that life within me, I will sing psalms before your countenance, Lord, My God and God of my fathers, Master of all works, Lord of all life. Blessed are you, Lord, who gives life anew to the lifeless.

Blessed are you, Lord our God, King of eternity, who gave the cock understanding to discern between day and between night.

Blessed are you, Lord our God, King of eternity, who has not created me a heathen.

Blessed are you, Lord our God, King of eternity, who has not created me a slave.

MEN SAY: Blessed are you, Lord our God, King of eternity, who has not created me a woman.

WOMEN SAY: Blessed are you, Lord our God, King of eternity, who has created me in accord with His will.[1]

---

[1]Another possible translation of this line is, "Blessed are you . . . who has created me the object of His approbation."

The Unclean Woman

from Leviticus XV: 19-30

*The fifteenth chapter of Leviticus deals with physical secre-
tions which, in the code of Jewish law, make a person "unclean." The following passage refers to the menstruating
woman, who, during her period, is considered "menstrually
unclean." During this period and for seven days after it, a man
is forbidden to come in contact with her, lest he too become
unclean.*

19 ¶ And if a woman have an issue, and her issue in her flesh be
blood, she shall be put apart seven days: and whosoever toucheth her
shall be unclean until the even.

20 And every thing that she lieth upon in her separation shall be
unclean: every thing also that she sitteth upon shall be unclean.

21 And whosoever toucheth her bed shall wash his clothes, and bathe
himself in water, and be unclean until the even.

22 And whosoever toucheth any thing that she sat upon shall wash
his clothes, and bathe himself in water, and be unclean until the even.

23 And if it be on her bed, or on any thing whereon she sitteth, when
he toucheth it, he shall be unclean until the even.

24 And if any man lie with her at all, and her flowers be upon him,
he shall be unclean seven days; and all the bed whereon he lieth shall
be unclean.

25 And if a woman have an issue of her blood many days out of the
time of her separation, or if it run beyond the time of her separation; all
the days of the issue of her uncleanness shall be as the days of her
separation: she shall be unclean.

26 Every bed whereon she lieth all the days of her issue shall be unto
her as the bed of her separation: and whatsoever she sitteth upon shall
be unclean, as the uncleanness of her separation.

27 And whosoever toucheth those things shall be unclean, and shall
wash his clothes, and bathe himself in water, and be unclean until the
even.

28 But if she be cleansed of her issue, then she shall number to herself seven days, and after that she shall be clean.

29 And on the eighth day she shall take unto her two turtles, or two young pigeons, and bring them unto the priest, to the door of the tabernacle of the congregation.

30 And the priest shall offer the one for a sin offering, and the other for a burnt offering; and the priest shall make an atonement for her before the LORD for the issue of her uncleanness.

Catholic Teaching on Women

W. B. Faherty

The Roman Catholic Church has had extensive influence on the position of women in Western culture. The Church claims to have made great progress in liberating women from their status as chattel in Greek and Hebrew traditions, although the widespread anti-feminism of the Middle Ages which condemned women for all men's problems and labelled them the "evil daughters of Eve" was strictly a Christian campaign. The following essay from the New Catholic Encyclopedia studies the Catholic attitudes toward women codified during the pontificate of Pius XII. It is especially interesting in view of the personal and political implications of the current controversy over a woman's right to govern her body and soul via birth control and abortion. While it states that male and female are complementary images of God, it stresses the well-known fact that the Church places women in charge of rearing and educating children, a position that not only limits their experience but provides a moral rationale for men to "keep women in their place."

From *New Catholic Encyclopedia*, pp. 998–1000, Volume 14. Copyright © 1967 by the Catholic University of America, Washington, D.C. Used by permission of The McGraw-Hill Book Company.

Until the pontificate of Pius XII (1939–58), the Catholic teaching on woman remained a disorganized mass of ideas, the elements of which are found here and there in texts of Scripture, writings of the Fathers, the Code of Canon Law, decrees of Roman Congregations, and encyclicals of recent popes on such subjects as marriage and education. During his long pontificate, Pius XII gave a series of major addresses that covered wide aspects of the Catholic teaching on the position of woman. On this subject, he is pre-eminent.

Status in Transition. The role of woman is at the same time a most crucial and controverted issue in modern society. This is not to suggest that the role of man is clear-cut and noncontroversial. But there is extensive contemporary debate on woman's role, and this debate stems from two factors: the more drastic transformation in the external life of woman; and woman's greater concern in facing issues and seeking solutions.

In the middle of the 19th century, woman in the Christian world could not vote or hold public office, attend universities, or enter the professions; she was restricted in business activities, and had an uncertain legal status. Much of her life was circumscribed by the limits of the home.

Woman generally had status and prestige in the home. Since she looked forward to life there, what education she received was appropriate to that goal. Society praised her fruitfulness and her skill in housekeeping. She had an integral part in a family-based enterprise, either in the rural or small town environment.

Modern industrial developments in the late 19th and early 20th centuries took away some of the traditional economic functions of the home. A woman's education began to prepare her for a career. Yet this career would necessarily be discontinuous because she wanted, and would probably attain, the marriage state. Thus while society gave prestige to her for becoming a wife, it accorded no recognition for skillful homemaking. Conversely, while society gave no prestige to the unmarried state, it praised achievements external to the home which were more readily possible for the single woman.

All the while new opportunities in education, employment, and public life opened before her, and her status before the laws improved. By the mid-20th century a complete reversal in the external life of woman had taken place.

Papal Analysis. Pius XII analyzed this transformation and distinguished the good from the evil in the changes. He did not view the issues confronting women in the rapidly changing context of modern society as mere matters of politics, education, legal status, or even environment. To him they revolved around the basic consequences of woman's nature, her dignity, and her destiny.

Equality. Pius XII recognized woman's equality with man, as well as her distinctly feminine qualities, and kept them both in focus. "As children of God, man and woman have a dignity in which they are absolutely equal; and they are equal, too, in regard to the supreme end of human life, which is everlasting union with God in the happiness of heaven" [ActApS 37 (1945) 285]. Thus it is not valid to take one sex as the standard of value for the other. Unlike so many of his contemporaries, Pius XII overemphasized neither woman's common humanity with man nor her distinct femininity.

Man is not superior to woman, nor woman to man. They are distinct images of God, with complementary features, and, therefore, not strictly comparable. When the Second Person of the Blessed Trinity took a human nature, He became a man. But He chose to become a man by being born of a woman. Because of the manner of His birth, He ennobled both sexes.

Proper Spheres and Characteristics. In creating man and woman with equal dignity and similar destiny, God did not make them identical. He gave each distinctive attributes fitting them for their specific functions. They are not to be competitors, but counterparts as the right hand is to the left. Each has a definite function in life that the other cannot fulfill. The sphere of man is fatherhood; that of woman motherhood. "Every woman," Pius XII stated, "is called to be a mother, mother in the physical sense, or mother in a sense more spiritual and exalted, yet real, nonetheless" (*ibid.* 287). This is her specific function and sublime mission. It dominates her life internally and externally. Not only her physical but also her psychological qualities fit her for motherhood. She has a more refined sensitivity and a more delicate tenderness of heart.

While a man displays the religious side of his nature by following Christ as a leader, or by showing loyalty to the external organization of the Church, woman feels a warm personal love for Jesus Christ. Many of the world's mystics have been women. Pius XII went so far as to call woman "the crown of creation and in a certain sense its masterpiece ... that gentle creature to whose delicate hands God seems to have entrusted the future of the world ... the expression of all that is best, kindest, most lovable here below" [ActApS 48 (1956) 780].

This encomium must, of course, be modified by the fact that Pius XII recognized the occasional proneness of some women—as of some men— to act as a result of "thoughtless enthusiasms," "spurts of passion," "fateful imprudences," and "unfounded impressions" (*ibid.*). Although woman is seldom guilty of the more violent crimes, she too can commit personal sins and influence men in evil ways.

Woman's interest in people and her capacity for giving combine to develop her gift for companionship. As a result of the changing structure of the family and woman's longevity, the relative portion of her lifetime spent in rearing children has lessened. Her role of companionship in marriage has grown. To build this complementarity is a great challenge.

Vocations to Religious Life, Secular Institutes. In spite of the high dignity of the married state, and Pius XII's call to woman to work for the improvement of family life, the Pope still upheld the traditional Catholic teaching on the dignity of the religious life. Virginity combined with consecration of life to God has always held first place among the states in life. Dedicated religious have a part to play, even in the great work of strengthening family life. Further, the religious life, lived communally, under a rule approved by the Church, constitutes a public affirmation of the transcendency of God and the primacy of the supernatural.

From Apostolic times, the Church has held in honor the individual who dedicated her life to God in the lay state. Pope Pius XII went a step further in support of these women, by approving a new estate in the Church, for both men and women, the secular institutes. In his apostolic constitution *Provida Mater Ecclesia,* Feb. 2, 1947 [ActApS 39 (1947) 114], he gave formal approbation to a new way of life that had grown up in various parts of the world. The secular institute allowed a lay-woman, even a widow with children, to dedicate her life to God, and follow a rule of perfection while still remaining in her own home and continuing to follow the secular occupation of her choice.

Vocation of the Single. Pius XII advanced the Catholic teaching on woman's role quite profoundly in one instance. Even though most women wish to marry, some remain unmarried for various sound reasons. Such single women have a distinct contribution to make to society, one that is impossible both for their married sisters, involved with domestic duties, and for religious, restricted by the requirements of their rule. Behind all human happenings moves the hand of a provident, fatherly God who guides all His human children. Thus, Pius XII concluded logically, the unchosen single state was also a true "vocation" [ActApS 37 (1945) 287].

Opportunities. Recognizing the dramatic social and economic changes in the 20th century, Pius XII stated: "...there is no field of human activity which must remain closed to woman; her horizons reach out to the regions of science, politics, labor, the arts, sports; but always in subordination to the primary functions which have been fixed for her by nature itself" [ActApS 48 (1956) 782].

Whenever possible, a woman—just as a man—should seek education to develop her highest human potential. She should give special attention to those studies, technical and psychological, that will give her preparation for the rearing and educating of children.

Freedom, Careers. Woman has a free choice of a state in life, and should she choose marriage, the free choice of a marriage partner. The unmarried woman possesses the same human independence as man. While those professions that are personal rather than technical will ordinarily have greater appeal to the majority of womankind, still individual gifts and inclinations may lead woman into a variety of activities, even into political life. Just as man and woman have complementary roles in family life, so they have reciprocal contributions to the wider family which is the nation. "This direct action," Pius XII stated, "this effective cooperation in social and political life, in no way alters the distinctive character of woman's activity. Associated with the work of man in the sphere of civil institutions, she will apply herself especially to matters calling for tact, delicacy, the maternal instinct, rather than administrative rigidity. In such questions as those of woman's dignity, a girl's honor and integrity, the protection and education of the child, who better than a woman can understand what is needed? And what a number of problems there are of this kind which require the attention of government and legislature!" [ActApS 37 (1945) 293.]

Even to the technical professions, a woman will bring a distinctly feminine touch. She will seek facets of the work that allow an outlet for her personal interest and talent. For equal work at an identical level of output, she deserves pay equal to that of a male employee.

The married woman should recognize the home as the center and stage of her principal activity. If she wishes to engage in activities beyond the home, she should look first to those that will strengthen the family, and should never neglect her primary duties in pursuit of these public objectives. If she sees the need of working outside the household, she should analyze the situation carefully, lest the salary she earns be eaten up by expenses incurred because of her absence. Especially while her children are young, she should be most hesitant in assuming any time-demanding activities beyond the family circle. Her core-function in the home, as well as that of her husband, must again receive the recognition of society.

In conclusion, the proper role of woman in society cannot be developed in isolation from other factors of modern life. Only in the wider framework of a total Christian structure of sound social life will woman's true position be realized.

Some Psychical Consequences of the Anatomical Distinction between the Sexes

Sigmund Freud

In post-Freudian psychology, "penis envy" in women and the "castration complex" in men have become familiar and, to neo-Freudians, almost sacred concepts. In Some Psychical Consequences of the Anatomical Distinction between the Sexes (1925) Freud analyzes pre-Oedipal feelings in girls to account for the girl's shift from the mother as love-object to the father as love-object. This analysis depends heavily on the female sense of deficiency and humiliation—instantaneous, Freud says—when she first perceives that she is without a penis.

Freud's anti-feminist bias is evident throughout, especially in his assumptions that woman is a castrated (and therefore incomplete) being, that the penis is a source of pride, and that femininity is partially a result of sexual repression.

The essay is framed by Freud's admission that his theory is tentative; it concludes with a passing and hostile reference to "the feminists, who are anxious to force us to regard the two sexes as completely equal in position and worth."

In my own writings and in those of my followers more and more stress is laid on the necessity that the analyses of neurotics shall deal thoroughly with the remotest period of their childhood, the time of the early efflorescence of sexual life. It is only by examining the first manifesta-

---

From Chapter XVII of Volume 5 of *The Collected Papers of Sigmund Freud*, pp. 186–197 edited by Ernest Jones, M.D., Basic Books, Inc., Publishers, New York, 1959. And reprinted by courtesy of Sigmund Freud Copyrights, Ltd., The Institute of Psycho-Analysis and The Hogarth Press, printers of *The Standard Edition of The Complete Psychological Works of Sigmund Freud*, revised and edited by James Strachey. This excerpt occurs in Volume XIX of the Hogarth Press Edition.

tions of the patient's innate instinctual constitution and the effects of his earliest experiences that we can accurately gauge the motive forces that have led to his neurosis and can be secure against the errors into which we might be tempted by the degree to which things have become remodelled and overlaid in adult life. This requirement is not only of theoretical but also of practical importance, for it distinguishes our efforts from the work of those physicians whose interests are focused exclusively on therapeutic results and who employ analytic methods, but only up to a certain point. An analysis of early childhood such as we are considering is tedious and laborious and makes demands both upon the physician and upon the patient which cannot always be met. Moreover, it leads us into dark regions where there are as yet no signposts. Indeed, analysts may feel reassured, I think, that there is no risk of their work becoming mechanical, and so of losing its interest, during the next few decades.

In the following pages I bring forward some findings of analytic research which would be of great importance if they could be proved to apply universally. Why do I not postpone publication of them until further experience has given me the necessary proof, if such proof is obtainable? Because the conditions under which I work have undergone a change, with implications which I cannot disguise. Formerly, I was not one of those who are unable to hold back what seems to be a new discovery until it has been either confirmed or corrected. My *Interpretation of Dreams* (1900*a*) and my 'Fragment of an Analysis of a Case of Hysteria' (1905*e*) (the case of Dora) were suppressed by me—if not for the nine years enjoined by Horace—at all events for four or five years before I allowed them to be published. But in those days I had unlimited time before me—'oceans of time'[1] as an amiable author puts it—and material poured in upon me in such quantities that fresh experiences were hardly to be escaped. Moreover, I was the only worker in a new field, so that my reticence involved no danger to myself and no loss to others.

But now everything has changed. The time before me is limited. The whole of it is no longer spent in working, so that my opportunities for making fresh observations are not so numerous. If I think I see something new, I am uncertain whether I can wait for it to be confirmed. And further, everything that is to be seen upon the surface has already been exhausted; what remains has to be slowly and laboriously dragged up from the depths. Finally, I am no longer alone. An eager crowd of fellow-workers is ready to make use of what is unfinished or doubtful, and I can leave to them that part of the work which I should otherwise have done myself. On this occasion, therefore, I feel justified in publishing something which stands in urgent need of confirmation before its value or lack of value can be decided.

In examining the earliest mental shapes assumed by the sexual life of children we have been in the habit of taking as the subject of our investigations the male child, the little boy. With little girls, so we have supposed, things must be similar, though in some way or other they must nevertheless be different. The point in development at which this difference lay could not be clearly determined.

In boys the situation of the Oedipus complex is the first stage that can be recognized with certainty. It is easy to understand, because at that stage a child retains the same object which he previously cathected with his libido—not as yet a genital one—during the preceding period while he was being suckled and nursed. The fact, too, that in this situation he regards his father as a disturbing rival and would like to get rid of him and take his place is a straightforward consequence of the actual state of affairs. I have shown elsewhere[2] how the Oedipus attitude in little boys belongs to the phallic phase, and how its destruction is brought about by the fear of castration—that is, by narcissistic interest in their genitals. The matter is made more difficult to grasp by the complicating circumstance that even in boys the Oedipus complex has a double orientation, active and passive, in accordance with their bisexual constitution; a boy also wants to take his *mother's* place as the love-object of his *father*—a fact which we describe as the feminine attitude.[3]

As regards the prehistory of the Oedipus complex in boys we are far from complete clarity. We know that that period includes an identification of an affectionate sort with the boy's father, an identification which is still free from any sense of rivalry in regard to his mother. Another element of that stage is invariably, I believe, a masturbatory activity in connection with the genitals, the masturbation of early childhood, the more or less violent suppression of which by those in charge of the child sets the castration complex in action. It is to be assumed that this masturbation is attached to the Oedipus complex and serves as a discharge for the sexual excitation belonging to it. It is, however, uncertain whether the masturbation has this character from the first, or whether on the contrary it makes its first appearance spontaneously as an activity of a bodily organ and is only brought into relation with the Oedipus complex at some later date; this second possibility is by far the more probable. Another doubtful question is the part played by the bed-wetting and by the breaking of that habit through the intervention of training measures. We are inclined to make the simple connection that continued bed-wetting is a result of masturbation and that its suppression is regarded by boys as an inhibition of their genital activity—that is, as having the meaning of a threat of castration;[4] but whether we are always right in supposing this remains to be seen. Finally, analysis shows us in a shadowy way how the fact of a child at a very early age listening to his parents copulating may set up his first sexual excitation, and how that event may, owing to its after-effects, act as a starting-point for the child's whole sexual development. Masturbation, as well as the two attitudes in the Oedipus complex, later on become attached to this early experience, the child having subsequently interpreted its meaning. It is impossible, however, to suppose that these observations of coitus are of universal occurrence, so that at this point we are faced with the problem of 'primal phantasies'.[5] Thus the prehistory of the Oedipus complex, even in boys, raises all of these questions for sifting and explanation; and there is the further problem of whether we are to suppose that the process invariably follows the same course, or whether a great variety of different preliminary stages may not converge upon the same terminal situation.

In little girls the Oedipus complex raises one problem more than in boys. In both cases the mother is the original object; and there is no cause for surprise that boys retain that object in the Oedipus complex. But how does it happen that girls abandon it and instead take their father as an object? In pursuing this question I have been able to reach some conclusions which may throw light precisely on the prehistory of the Oedipus relation in girls.

Every analyst has come across certain women who cling with especial intensity and tenacity to the bond with their father and to the wish in which it culminates of having a child by him. We have good reason to suppose that the same wishful phantasy was also the motive force of their infantile masturbation, and it is easy to form an impression that at this point we have been brought up against an elementary and unanalysable fact of infantile sexual life. But a thorough analysis of these very cases brings something different to light—namely, that here the Oedipus complex has a long prehistory and is in some respects a secondary formation.

The old paediatrician Lindner [1879] once remarked that a child discovers the genital zones (the penis or the clitoris) as a source of pleasure while indulging in sensual sucking (thumb-sucking).[6] I shall leave it an open question whether it is really true that the child takes the newly found source of pleasure in exchange for the recent loss of the mother's nipple—a possibility to which later phantasies (fellatio) seem to point. Be that as it may, the genital zone is discovered at some time or other, and there seems no justification for attributing any psychical content to the first activities in connection with it. But the first step in the phallic phase which begins in this way is not the linking-up of the masturbation with the object-cathexes of the Oedipus complex, but a momentous discovery which little girls are destined to make. They notice the penis of a brother or playmate, strikingly visible and of large proportions, at once recognize it as the superior counterpart of their own small and inconspicuous organ, and from that time forward fall a victim to envy for the penis.

There is an interesting contrast between the behaviour of the two sexes. In the analogous situation, when a little boy first catches sight of a girl's genital region, he begins by showing irresolution and lack of interest; he sees nothing or disavows[7] what he has seen, he softens it down or looks about for expedients for bringing it into line with his expectations. It is not until later, when some threat of castration has obtained a hold upon him, that the observation becomes important to him: if he then recollects or repeats it, it arouses a terrible storm of emotion in him and forces him to believe in the reality of the threat which he has hitherto laughed at. This combination of circumstances leads to two reactions, which may become fixed and will in that case, whether separately or together or in conjunction with other factors, permanently determine the boy's relations to women: horror of the mutilated creature or triumphant contempt for her. These developments, however, belong to the future, though not to a very remote one.

A little girl behaves differently. She makes her judgement and her decision in a flash. She has seen it and knows that she is without it and wants to have it.[8]

Here what has been named the masculinity complex of women branches off.[9] It may put great difficulties in the way of their regular development towards femininity, if it cannot be got over soon enough. The hope of some day obtaining a penis in spite of everything and so of becoming like a man may persist to an incredibly late age and may become a motive for strange and otherwise unaccountable actions. Or again, a process may set in which I should like to call a 'disavowal',[10] a process which in the mental life of children seems neither uncommon nor very dangerous but which in an adult would mean the beginning of a psychosis. Thus a girl may refuse to accept the fact of being castrated, may harden herself in the conviction that she *does* possess a penis, and may subsequently be compelled to behave as though she were a man.

The psychical consequences of envy for the penis, in so far as it does not become absorbed in the reaction-formation of the masculinity complex, are various and far-reaching. After a woman has become aware of the wound to her narcissism, she develops, like a scar, a sense of inferiority.[11] When she has passed beyond her first attempt at explaining her lack of a penis as being a punishment personal to herself and has realized that that sexual character is a universal one, she begins to share the contempt felt by men for a sex which is the lesser in so important a respect, and, at least in holding that opinion, insists on being like a man.[12]

Even after penis-envy has abandoned its true object, it continues to exist: by an easy displacement it persists in the character-trait of *jealousy*. Of course, jealousy is not limited to one sex and has a wider foundation than this, but I am of opinion that it plays a far larger part in the mental life of women than of men and that that is because it is enormously reinforced from the direction of displaced penis-envy. While I was still unaware of this source of jealousy and was considering the phantasy 'a child is being beaten', which occurs so commonly in girls, I constructed a first phase for it in which its meaning was that another child, a rival of whom the subject was jealous, was to be beaten.[13] This phantasy seems to be a relic of the phallic period in girls. The peculiar rigidity which struck me so much in the monotonous formula 'a child is being beaten' can probably be interpreted in a special way. The child which is being beaten (or caressed) may ultimately be nothing more or less than the clitoris itself, so that at its very lowest level the state-ment will contain a confession of masturbation, which has remained attached to the content of the formula from its beginning in the phallic phase till later life.

A third consequence of penis-envy seems to be a loosening of the girl's relation with her mother as a love-object. The situation as a whole is not very clear, but it can be seen that in the end the girl's mother, who sent her into the world so insufficiently equipped, is almost always held responsible for her lack of a penis. The way in which this comes about historically is often that soon after the girl has discovered that her genitals are unsatisfactory she begins to show jealousy of another child on the ground that her mother is fonder of it than of her, which serves as a reason for her giving up her affectionate relation to her mother. It will fit in with this if the child which has been preferred by her mother is made into the first object of the beating-phantasy which ends in masturbation.

There is yet another surprising effect of penis-envy, or of the dis-covery of the inferiority of the clitoris, which is undoubtedly the most important of all. In the past I had often formed an impression that in general women tolerate masturbation worse than men, that they more frequently fight against it and that they are unable to make use of it in circumstances in which a man would seize upon it as a way of escape without any hesitation. Experience would no doubt elicit innumerable exceptions to this statement, if we attempted to turn it into a rule. The reactions of human individuals of both sexes are of course made up of masculine and feminine traits. But it appeared to me nevertheless as though masturbation were further removed from the nature of women than of men, and the solution of the problem could be assisted by the reflection that masturbation, at all events of the clitoris, is a masculine activity and that the elimination of clitorial sexuality is a necessary

precondition for the development of femininity.[14] Analyses of the remote phallic period have now taught me that in girls, soon after the first
signs of penis-envy, an intense current of feeling against masturbation
makes its appearance, which cannot be attributed exclusively to the
educational influence of those in charge of the child. This impulse is
clearly a forerunner of the wave of repression which at puberty will do
away with a large amount of the girl's masculine sexuality in order to
make room for the development of her femininity. It may happen that
this first opposition to auto-erotic activity fails to attain its end. And
this was in fact the case in the instances which I analysed. The conflict
continued, and both then and later the girl did everything she could to
free herself from the compulsion to masturbate. Many of the later manifestations of sexual life in women remain unintelligible unless this
powerful motive is recognized.

I cannot explain the opposition which is raised in this way by little
girls to phallic masturbation except by supposing that there is some
concurrent factor which turns her violently against that pleasurable
activity. Such a factor lies close at hand. It cannot be anything else than
her narcissistic sense of humiliation which is bound up with penis-envy,
the reminder that after all this is a point on which she cannot compete
with boys and that it would therefore be best for her to give up the idea
of doing so. Thus the little girl's recognition of the anatomical distinction
between the sexes forces her away from masculinity and masculine masturbation on to new lines which lead to the development of femininity.

So far there has been no question of the Oedipus complex, nor has it
up to this point played any part. But now the girl's libido slips into a
new position along the line—there is no other way of putting it—of the
equation 'penis = child'. She gives up her wish for a penis and puts in
place of it a wish for a child: and *with that purpose in view* she takes
her father as a love-object.[15] Her mother becomes the object of her
jealousy. The girl has turned into a little woman. If I am to credit a
single analytic instance, this new situation can give rise to physical
sensations which would have to be regarded as a premature awakening
of the female genital apparatus. When the girl's attachment to her
father comes to grief later on and has to be abandoned, it may give place
to an identification with him and the girl may thus return to her masculinity complex and perhaps remain fixated in it.

I have now said the essence of what I had to say: I will stop, therefore,
and cast an eye over our findings. We have gained some insight into
the prehistory of the Oedipus complex in girls. The corresponding period
in boys is more or less unknown. In girls the Oedipus complex is a secondary formation. The operations of the castration complex precede it and
prepare for it. As regards the relation between the Oedipus and castra-

tion complexes there is a fundamental contrast between the two sexes. *Whereas in boys the Oedipus complex is destroyed by the castration complex*[16] *in girls it is made possible and led up to by the castration complex.* This contradiction is cleared up if we reflect that the castration complex always operates in the sense implied in its subject-matter: it inhibits and limits masculinity and encourages femininity. The difference between the sexual development of males and females at the stage we have been considering is an intelligible consequence of the anatomical distinction between their genitals and of the physical situation involved in it; it corresponds to the difference between a castration that has been carried out and one that has merely been theatened. In their essentials, therefore, our findings are self-evident and it should have been possible to foresee them.

The Oedipus complex, however, is such an important thing that the manner in which one enters and leaves it cannot be without its effects. In boys (as I have shown at length in the paper to which I have just referred [1924d] and to which all of my present remarks are closely related) the complex is not simply repressed, it is literally smashed to pieces by the shock of threatened castration. Its libidinal cathexes are abandoned, desexualized and in part sublimated; its objects are incorporated into the ego, where they form the nucleus of the super-ego and give that new structure its characteristic qualities. In normal, or, it is better to say, in ideal cases, the Oedipus complex exists no longer, even in the unconscious; the super-ego has become its heir. Since the penis (to follow Ferenczi [1924]) owes its extraordinarily high narcissistic cathexis to its organic significance for the propagation of the species, the catastrophe to the Oedipus complex (the abandonment of incest and the institution of conscience and morality) may be regarded as a victory of the race over the individual. This is an interesting point of view when one considers that neurosis is based upon a struggle of the ego against the demands of the sexual function. But to leave the standpoint of individual psychology is not of any immediate help in clarifying this complicated situation.

In girls the motive for the demolition of the Oedipus complex is lacking. Castration has already had its effect, which was to force the child into the situation of the Oedipus complex. Thus the Oedipus complex escapes the fate which it meets with in boys: it may be slowly abandoned or dealt with by repression, or its effects may persist far into women's normal mental life. I cannot evade the notion (though I hesitate to give it expression) that for women the level of what is ethically normal is different from what it is in men. Their super-ego is never so inexorable, so impersonal, so independent of its emotional origins as we require it to be in men. Character-traits which critics of every epoch have brought up against women—that they show less sense of justice than men, that they are less ready to submit to the great exigencies of life, that they are more often influenced in their judgements by feelings of affection or hostility—all these would be amply accounted for by the modification in the formation of their super-ego which we have inferred above. We must not allow ourselves to be deflected from such conclusions by the denials of the feminists, who are anxious to force us to regard the two sexes as completely equal in position and worth; but we shall, of course, willingly agree that the majority of men are also far behind the masculine ideal and that all human individuals, as a result of their bisexual disposition and of cross-inheritance, combine in themselves both masculine and feminine characteristics, so that pure masculinity and femininity remain theoretical constructions of uncertain content.

I am inclined to set some value on the considerations I have brought forward upon the physical consequences of the anatomical distinction between the sexes. I am aware, however, that this opinion can only be maintained if my findings, which are based on a handful of cases, turn out to have general validity and to be typical. If not, they would remain no more than a contribution to our knowledge of the different paths along which sexual life develops.

In the valuable and comprehensive studies on the masculinity and castration complexes in women by Abraham (1921), Horney (1923) and Helene Deutsch (1925) there is much that touches closely on what I have written but nothing that coincides with it completely, so that here again I feel justified in publishing this paper.

NOTES

1. [In English in the original. It is not clear what author Freud had in mind.—The reference to Horace is to his *Ars Poetica*, 388.]
2. 'The Dissolution of the Oedipus Complex' (1924*d*), *Standard Ed.*, 19, 173. Much of what follows is an elaboration of that paper.]
3. [Cf. ibid., p. 176.]
4. [Cf. ibid., p. 175.]
5. [Cf. the discussions in the 'Wolf Man' analysis (1918*b*), *Standard Ed.*, 17, especially 48–60 and 95–7, and Lecture XXIII of the *Introductory Lectures* (1916–17).]
6. Cf. *Three Essays on the Theory of Sexuality* (1905*d*) [*Standard Ed.*, 7, 179].
7. [See Editor's footnote to 'The Infantile Genital Organization', *Standard Ed.*, 19, 143.]
8. This is an opportunity for correcting a statement which I made many years ago. I believed that the sexual interest of children, unlike that of pubescents, was aroused, not by the difference between the sexes, but

by the problem of where babies come from. We now see that, at all events with girls, this is certainly not the case. With boys it may no doubt happen sometimes one way and sometimes the other; or with both sexes chance experiences may determine the event.—[The statement mentioned at the beginning of this footnote appears in more than one place: e.g. in the paper on 'The Sexual Theories of Children' (1908c), *Standard Ed.*, 9, 212, in the case history of 'Little Hans' (1909b), ibid., 10, 133, and in a passage added in 1915 to the *Three Essays* (1905d), ibid., 7, 195. In a passage earlier than any of these, however, in a paper on 'The Sexual Enlightenment of Children' (1907c), ibid., 9, 135, Freud in fact takes the opposite view—the one advocated here.]

9. [This term seems to have been introduced by Van Ophuijsen (1917). Freud adopted it in ' "A Child is Being Beaten" ' (1919e), *Standard Ed.*, 17, 191. Cf. also *Standard Ed.*, 19, 178.]

10. [For the parallel process in boys, see 'The Infantile Genital Organization' (1923e), *Standard Ed.*, 19, 143–4.]

11. [Cf. *Beyond the Pleasure Principle* (1920g), *Standard Ed.*, 18, 20–1.]

12. In my first critical account of the 'History of the Psycho-Analytic Movement' (1914d) [*Standard Ed.*, 14, 54–5], I recognized that this fact represents the core of truth contained in Adler's theory. That theory has no hesitation in explaining the whole world by this single point ('organ-inferiority', the 'masculine protest', 'breaking away from the feminine line') and prides itself upon having in this way robbed sexuality of its importance and put the desire for power in its place! Thus the only organ which could claim to be called 'inferior' without any ambiguity would be the clitoris. On the other hand, one hears of analysts who boast that, though they have worked for dozens of years, they have never found a sign of the existence of a castration complex. We must bow our heads in recognition of the greatness of this achievement, even though it is only a negative one, a piece of virtuosity in the art of overlooking and mistaking. The two theories form an interesting pair of opposites: in the latter not a trace of a castration complex, in the former nothing else than its consequences.

13. ' "A Child is Being Beaten" ' (1919e) [*Standard Ed.*, 17, 184–5].

14. [A reference to clitorial masturbation in girls appeared in the first edition of the *Three Essays* (1905d), *Standard Ed.*, 7, 220. In the course of his 'Contributions to a Discussion on Masturbation' (1912f), Freud expressed regret at the lack of knowledge about female masturbation (*Standard Ed.*, 12, 247).]

15. [Cf. 'The Dissolution of the Oedipus Complex,' *Standard Ed.*, 19, 179.]

16. [Ibid., p. 177.]

The Womanly Image:
Character Assassination
through the Ages

Paula Stern

Paula Stern, an independent journalist and Ph.D. candidate in international relations, has published articles on Women's Liberation and day care in The New Republic *and* The Atlantic Monthly. *She holds an M.A. from Harvard and an M.A.L.D. from The Fletcher School of Law and Diplomacy.*

I had a job interview several weeks ago. Friends warned me not to be too aggressive. During the interview, I tried to present myself as a competent candidate, able to "think like a man" and yet not to be a "masculine" female. After fielding several questions relevant to the job, I suddenly heard, "Miss Stern, are you in love?"

Do you think they asked my competition—seven men—the same question? No, for a cultureful of reasons. Jacqueline Kennedy Onassis was quoted once as saying, "There are two kinds of women: those who want power in the world and those who want power in bed." And the majority seem to agree with Jackie that the latter is socially more acceptable. That's how many women in America have been taught to think. And that's how many men think women ought to think.

Children are taught sexual stereotypes early, as well as the appropriate behavior for a sex-determined role in life. Asking a little boy, "What do you want to be when you grow up?" implies to him unlimited possibilities in his future. But most often we ask a little girl, "Where did you get that pretty dress?" suggesting she has only one real option open to her. If we do ask her what she wants to be, she's likely to give the conditioned female response—"A mother." Why? So she can replace her dolls with real babies.

The inspiration for teaching girls to expect less than boys comes from a range of cultural sources, religious, literary, psychiatric, and pop. Even in the Bible, exceptional, independent women like Rebecca, Sarah, Deborah, or Ruth are practically "unknowns" compared with infamous Eve or Delilah.

Eve was made from one of Adam's spare parts, almost as an afterthought, to help him out on earth: "And the Lord God said: 'It is not good that the man should be alone; I will make him a helpmeet for him.'"

There is a contrary legend of the first female, Lilith, who was created equal to man.

When the Lord created the world and the first man, he saw that man was alone, and quickly created a woman for him, made like him from the earth, and her name was Lilith. Right away, they began to quarrel. He would say "You sleep on the bottom," and she would say "No, you sleep on the bottom, since we are equals and both formed from the earth. . . ." When Lilith saw what the situation was, she pronounced the Ineffable Name and disappeared into thin air.

But Eve, not Lilith, is the prototypal woman—man's little helper, and his temptress.

Today the heirs to the Bible in America—Jews and Christians—have formalized biblical biases in laws and ceremonies and thereby elevated folklore to religious truths. Among the Orthodox Jews, for example, discrimination against women is so blatant that they are forced to sit segregated behind a curtain or in a balcony. The rationale is that women will distract men from their prayers. It is no wonder that men thank God every morning in their ritual prayer "that Thou has not made me a woman."

The majority of Jews have modified most traditional formalities, but independent female expression is still discouraged if outside the confines of the home or not channeled through husband and children.

A Jewish wife is less subservient to her husband than a gentile wife; so say comparative studies on the subject. That's somewhat understandable since Christianity owes much to a prominent classical heritage, that held the second sex in even lower esteem. Utopia for the male chauvinist is Demosthenes' description of Hellenic male-female arrangements: "We have hetairae for the pleasure of the spirit, concubines for sensual pleasure, and wives to bear our sons."

Aristotle's definition of femininity was "a certain lack of qualities; we should regard the female nature as afflicted with a natural defectiveness." And his disciple Saint Thomas Aquinas echoed him religiously: ". . . a female is something deficient and by chance."

Contempt for women helps explain why they can't become Catholic priests, and why theologians, religious education courses, and Catholic marriage manuals highlight the supposedly inferior and passive qualities of women, who "naturally" subordinate themselves to men.

Traditional Protestant marriage services also perpetuate the attitude that the female is a second-class human being. Like a piece of property, the bride is "given" by her father to the groom, whom she promises to "obey." (Although formally removed from the liturgy, this vow still persists in the popular image of the wedding ceremony.) The clergyman reminds her of her proper place when he says, "I pronounce that they are man and wife." Not husband and wife. Not man and woman. The man keeps his status, while she takes on a new one. Her identity vanishes when she sheds her maiden name for his identification. (Blackstone's *Commentaries* on the law strips a married woman of her rights altogether as she legally dies on her wedding day and becomes "incorporated and consolidate with her husband." Accordingly, "A man cannot grant anything to his wife for the grant would be to suppose her separate existence.")

Although reputedly "progressing" beyond the attitudes of antiquity and the Middle Ages, our enlightened European ancestors continued furnishing us some not too enlightened guidelines on a woman's place— or lack of it—in the world.

High school English students learn from Shakespeare that "Frailty, thy name is woman." Rousseau's contribution to the ideas of man's equality and natural goodness makes one exception: "Woman was made to yield to man and put up with his injustice."

Samuel Johnson's word to the wise woman is that "a man is in general better pleased when he has a good dinner upon his table, than when his wife talks Greek." Honoré de Balzac adds, "A woman who is guided by the head and not the heart is a social pestilence: she has all the defects of a passionate and affectionate woman with none of her compensations: she is without pity, without love, without virtue, without sex."

When in 1776 in America, Abigail Adams asked her husband John Adams, to "be more generous and favorable to them [women] than your ancestors" and to see to it that the new government not "put such unlimited power into the hands of the husbands," John reportedly chuckled. The Continental Congress ignored her. Two hundred years later Spiro Agnew said: "Three things have been difficult to tame—the ocean, fools, and women. We may soon be able to tame the ocean; fools and women will take a little longer."

America's twentieth-century gospel is the work of Freud. Although Freud supposedly has altered the entire course of Western intellectual history, many of his ideas about women are simply male chauvinism. Letters he worte his fiancée reveal that he, too, wanted his woman kept relatively docile and ignorant so she couldn't compete with him.

His theories have given scientific status to prejudice. The Freudians— psychiatrists, clinical psychologists, psychiatric social workers, marriage counselors, pastoral counselors, educators, writers, literary critics, historians, anthropologists, sociologists, criminologists, and just plain subway psychiatrists in the newspapers, magazines, and on TV—all subscribe to the belief that "anatomy is destiny." In other words, biological differences between the sexes determine personality differences; standards of mental health depend on the sex of the sick.

How? Dr. Judd Marmor, clinical professor of psychiatry at UCLA, has summarized Freud's views on feminine psychology:

> The most significant of the biological factors . . . is the lack of the penis, which inevitably leads to "penis envy" in the woman. Freud considered penis envy to be a dominant theme in all feminine life, and one that inevitably causes women to feel inferior to men. These deep seated feelings of inadequacy can be compensated for only partially by giving birth to a male child. . . .
>
> Masochism and passivity . . . are natural aspects of normal femininity and whenever a woman behaves in non-passive or aggressive ways or competes with men, she is being neurotically unfeminine. . . .
>
> The most complicated sequence of personality development that women are subject to . . . leads inevitably . . . to less adequate superego formation than in men. This presumably is reflected in women having a poorer sense of justice and weaker social interests than men have.

The myths of marriage counselor G. C. Payetter (from his book *How To Get and Hold a Woman*) have been praised by a number of psychiatrists, and he is consulted in earnest by troubled people. Payetter counsels:

> Feelings, moods, and attitude . . . rule a woman, not facts, reason, nor logic.
>
> By herself woman is all mixed-up but superb as an auxiliary (Genesis: helper).
>
> Woman is inanimate or on the defensive until you create a feeling such as a praise. Then she goes all out.
>
> Never scold or explain when she is angry, remember she is feeling not thinking. . . .
>
> Stop bossing; just manipulate her in her feelings. . . .
>
> The acquisition of knowledge or responsibilities does not lessen women's need for support, guidance, and control. Quite the contrary.

Why ask women when they only need to be told? Why ask women when they hope to be taken?

Any resemblance between women and pet dogs or mute concubines is purely coincidental. No doubt, Payetter's model woman is the runner-up to this year's [1970, Ed.] Miss America, who said women shouldn't try to run things "because they are more emotional and men can over-come their emotions with logic."

Even more objectionable are psychiatrist-authors who pronounce final judgment on the mental health of thousands of women reading books like *The Power of Sexual Surrender*. Featured in the book, which has had at least ten paperback printings and been excerpted in *Pageant* magazine, is "The Masculine Woman." (Doctor, how can a woman be a female and be masculine simultaneously?) She's "frigid"—"a driving, competitive woman who was very successful in the business world, hav-ing graduated from a leading woman's college." "Clear thinking and logical mind, her emotionless almost masculine forthrightness in expres-sing herself belied her softly feminine appearance." Surrendering to her "real nature," the doctor's cure, is the only way she can be mentally healthy. Then miraculously

> . . . those details of life that once seemed so difficult become simple. And because they are feminine tasks, household work, planning and getting dinners, keeping the children busy or in line—whatever life demands— soon lose their irksome and irritating quality and become easy, even joyful. . . . At this juncture, or closely following on it, a woman begins to feel her full power, the power that comes to her for her surrender to her destiny.

The spuriously Freudian vision of a truly "feminine" female serves the purposes of admen who woo women to spend millions on clothes and cosmetics in vain pursuit of their "real nature." To sell a new product, industry need only simultaneously make the product and manufacture anxiety in gals, pressing them to consume or be consumed in a female identity crisis. For example, featured in every women's magazine, includ-ing those for teen-agers, are the latest advertising campaigns for vaginal deodorants, a "female necessity." One called Cupid's Quiver comes in four flavors—Orange Blossom, Raspberry, Champagne, or Jasmine. Madison Avenue courts the female, even seducing minors. Teenform, Inc., manufacturers of bras for teen-agers, estimates that nine-year-olds spend $2 million on bras annually.

Ingenue magazine pushes teen-agers into adult posturing. The format is peppered with advertisements for engagement rings, pictures of desirable adolescent boys, and occasionally a plan of attack such as dinners for two. The ads for cosmetics and clothes are practically identical to those in magazines designed for their mothers. Typical of women's magazines, *Ingenue* includes at least one psychologically centered article. Recently, it explained in "The Hardest Thing About Growing Up" that "inevitably, relationships with boys affect relationships with girls." It condoned the statement, "I don't trust other girls in the same way anymore. They become rivals." This is how girls learn the platitudes: women can't work with other women when men are around, and never work for a woman.

If a girl manages to survive *Ingenue* without succumbing to marriage, *Glamour* picks her up. ("How Five Groovy Men Would Make You Over Into Their Dream Girls") Where the boys are is where it's at for the reader who is shunted from high school to college to career to marriage to motherhood—"Find Your New Look. College Into Career Make-over. Job Into Mother Make-over."

The lucky gal who's made the grade by landing a man is promoted to *Modern Bride*, which induces her to buy "utterly feminine" wedding gowns, bride-and-groom matching wedding rings, silver, china, furniture, ad nauseam. The wedding itself is big business; Wediquette International, Inc., offers total planning—the place, time, invitations, gown, caterers, florist, photographer. . .

Ah, then conjugal bliss—and of course, a magazine for mothers. *Redbook* boasts its biggest year because it knows "Young Mamas Spend More Than Big Daddies" and so talks "to that 18-34 year old the way she wants to be talked to," which means in baby talk or kitchen chatter.

McCall's claims 16 million matrons who "buy more than the readers of any other woman's service magazine." Its reader "buys more cosmetics and toiletries, more prepared foods, owns more life insurance, more automobiles. . ."

Although *Cosmopolitan* says its reader is the career woman who desires success in her own right, it is pitched to the gal who missed the marriage boat the first time around. Female passivity is still the accepted mode of behavior. She can be assertive in the office, but when man-hunting after five, she must be seductively submissive. Who knows? She might hook a divorced man or married man looking for an affair.

Cosmo repeats an old tip from Jackie and Delilah—sex is a woman's hidden arsenal. Under a pseudonym, "a well-known American gynecologist" instructs readers "How to Love Like A Real Woman." "If your man bawls at you and you know you are in the right, what should you do?" You should take your clothes off. Sex is a woman's strongest weapon. It is her proper weapon."

Taking a cue from *The Power of Sexual Surrender,* the expert explains, "Women must give and give and give again because it is their one and only way to obtain happiness for themselves." Further, "To argue is a male activity. To fight is a male activity. I say to women: 'Don't become a man in skirts. Don't fight. Don't argue. . . .' " Any female who would practice this advice must be masochistic—typical of a "normal" female, according to Freudian thought.

A popular misconception is that in time education will erase all the ill effects of thinking in stereotypes. But the educational system takes over where cultural myths, Freudian folklore, and the media leave off in depressing a girl's aspirations and motivations. All along, she's taught to accept a double standard for success and self-esteem: It's marriage and motherhood for girls, while it's education and career for boys. She's pushed to be popular, date, and marry young (more than half of all American women are married before the age of twenty-one). Success in school only inhibits her social life. Intellectual striving, a necessity for academic success, is considered competitively aggressive; that is unnatural and unladylike behavior, since the essence of femininity, she has learned, is repressing aggressiveness. Telling her she thinks like a man is a backhanded compliment, which is discouraging if she has tried to be a woman using her brains, not sex, in the classroom and office.

While girls outperform boys intellectually in prepuberty, attrition in IQ sets in during adolescence when they learn from new, extracurricular lessons that looks, not brains, are what counts. After high school, achievement in terms of productivity and accomplishment drops off even more. More than 75 percent (some say as high as 95 percent) of all qualified high-schoolers not entering college are girls. Those who go attend more for husband-hunting than for educational self-advancement; one study at a Midwestern university revealed 70 percent of the freshmen women were there for an MRS. Women BA's are less than half as likely to try for a graduate degree as equally qualified men.

Women should not be given an even break in education and careers, says a clichéd argument, because they will get married and quit anyway. But that's because they are given an arbitrary, unfair option which men aren't forced to accept—either career or marriage. Career opportunities and salary levels for women are so poor that a calculating female would figure marriage is a better bargain. Once married, she can stop fighting the stereotypes and start teaching them to her children.

Woman-as-Object

"Sometimes I'm invited to places to brighten up the dinner table—like a musician who'll play the piano after dinner and I know you're not really invited for yourself. You're just an ornament." So said Marilyn Monroe (Norma Jean Baker) on August 3, 1962, seventeen days before she died from an overdose of barbiturates. The ornamental function of woman is a time-honored tradition and it has been turned into big business as the American woman is told to pamper her skin, make up her face, tint her hair, and aim for the magic figure of 36-24-36. Consequently, American women spend millions of dollars each year in their attempts to live up to the Miss America ideal, pouring money into a system which will then regard them, if they should approximate the ideal, as sex objects, not human beings—a loss of humanity symbolized by slang terms such as "dolls," "chicks," or, even less elegantly, "punches."

The evidence of the dehumanization of women is all around us: in poems praising the golden locks, fair complexion, and rosy lips of "my mistress"; in full-color foldouts of the Playgirl of the Month; in copious articles and books advising women "How to Be Sexy"; and, of course, in advertisements ("Be Some Body"; "Clothes Make the Woman"; "Makeup Discoveries to Make You Look Like You Just Happened!"). Women's Liberation protests the intellectual and economic waste involved in spending time, money, anxiety, and effort in an attempt to become a beautiful Object. As a Women's Liberation poster proclaims (in It Ain't Me Babe, April 28, 1970), "The inhuman mythology which murdered Marilyn Monroe is the same one which maims and kills the spirit of all women daily."

Woman in the Elizabethan Sonnet

The image of women in all Western lyric poetry, not just English, has been significantly influenced by what is called the Petrarchan tradition. Developing the themes of Provençal and Tuscan poetry, Petrarch (1304–1374) wrote the sonnets which reinforced the image of woman as object—heavenly and hellish, spiritual and sensual, submissive or antagonistic—but always mysterious and remote, a thing which both fascinated and frightened him. Many of the Petrarchan ideas and images became a part of what is called the courtly love tradition. Both have had an extensive influence on man's view of woman in the world, especially in the vestiges of chivalry remaining in our courtship rituals.

To emulate the ideal of beauty adored by poets, women used borax, ceruse (white lead), a mixture of lead and vinegar, and other bleaches to whiten their skin. The skin often withered prematurely from continual use of these agents. Many dyes and paints were used for the red coloration. More shocking was the common use of alum stone as an astringent and abrasive. The skin was rubbed with the stone to make it smooth and to cause inflammation. Bleaches were also used with skin-peelers to make the skin smooth; peeling insured the penetration of red color into the skin. Victorian women achieved a similar but more moderate end by pinching the cheeks or rubbing them vigorously with a rough cloth. They also ate chalk and drank vinegar to induce the pallor fashionable in the 1830's.

Edmund Spenser, from Amoretti

3

The souverayne beauty which I doo admyre,
    witnesse the world how worthy to be prayzed:
    the light wherof hath kindled heauenly fyre,
    in my fraile spirit by her from basenesse raysed.

From AMORETTI in *The Poetical Works of Edmund Spenser*, edited by J. C. Smith and E. De Selincourt, Oxford University Press, 1912.

That being now with her huge brightnesse dazed,
    base thing I can no more endure to view:
    but looking still on her I stand amazed,
    at wondrous sight of so celestiall hew.
So when my toung would speake her praises dew,
    it stopped is with thoughts astonishment:
    and when my pen would write her titles true,
    it rauisht is with fancies wonderment:
Yet in my hart I then both speake and write
    the wonder that my wit cannot endite.

37

What guyle is this, that those her golden tresses,
    She doth attyre vnder a net of gold:
    and with sly skill so cunningly them dresses,
    that which is gold or heare, may scarse be told?
Is it that mens frayle eyes, which gaze too bold,
    she may entangle in that golden snare:
    and being caught may craftily enfold,
    theyr weaker harts, which are not wel aware?
Take heed therefore, myne eyes, how ye doe stare
    henceforth too rashly on that guilefull net,
    in which if euer ye entrapped are,
    out of her bands ye by no meanes shall get.
Fondnesse it were for any being free,
    to couet fetters, though they golden bee.

56

Fayre ye be sure, but cruell and vnkind,
    As is a Tygre that with greedinesse
    hunts after bloud, when he by chance doth find
    a feeble beast, doth felly him oppresse.
Fayre be ye sure, but proud and pittilesse,
    as is a storme, that all things doth prostrate:
    finding a tree alone all comfortlesse,
    beats on it strongly it to ruinate.
Fayre be ye sure, but hard and obstinate,
    as is a rocke amidst the raging floods:
    gaynst which a ship of succour desolate,
    doth suffer wreck both of her selfe and goods.
That ship, that tree, and that same beast am I,
    whom ye doe wreck, doe ruine, and destroy.

William Shakespeare

18

Shall I compare thee to a summer's day?
Thou art more lovely and more temperate:
Rough winds do shake the darling buds of May,
And summer's lease hath all too short a date:
Sometime too hot the eye of heaven shines,
And often is his gold complexion dimm'd;
And every fair from fair sometime declines,
By chance or nature's changing course untrimm'd:
But thy eternal summer shall not fade
Nor lose possession of that fair thou ow'st,
Nor shall Death brag thou wand'rest in his shade,
When in eternal lines to time thou grow'st;
   So long as men can breathe or eyes can see,
   So long lives this and this gives life to thee.

130

My mistress' eyes are nothing like the sun;
Coral is far more red than her lips' red;
If snow be white, why then her breasts are dun;
If hairs be wires, black wires grow on her head.
I have seen roses damask'd, red and white,
But no such roses see I in her cheeks;
And in some perfumes is there more delight
Than in the breath that from my mistress reeks.
I love to hear her speak, yet well I know
That music hath a far more pleasing sound;
I grant I never saw a goddess go;
My mistress, when she walks, treads on the ground:
   And yet, by heaven, I think my love as rare
   As any she belied with false compare.

143

Lo! as a careful housewife runs to catch
One of her feathered creatures broke away,
Sets down her babe, and makes all swift dispatch
In pursuit of the thing she would have stay;

From *The Sonnets of William Shakespeare*, Charles Scribner's Sons.

Whilst her neglected child holds her in chase,
Cries to catch her whose busy care is bent
To follow that which flies before her face,
Not prizing her poor infant's discontent:
So runn'st thou after that which flies from thee,
Whilst I, thy babe, chase thee afar behind;
But if thou catch thy hope, turn back to me,
And play the mother's part, kiss me, be kind:
 So will I pray that thou mayst have thy *Will*,
 If thou turn back and my loud crying still.

The Victorian Woman

Anonymous

The following description of the young Victorian woman, written by a woman in 1843, is a perfect example of woman trained to be a beautiful, innocent (i.e., ignorant), useless object. It is no wonder that women began to rebel against the constraints imposed on them by a code of dress and behavior that left them physically deformed (from tight-lacing), mentally retarded (from an inadequate education), and socially crippled (from trivial occupations).

Young Ladies wear their hair in two long ringlets hanging half out of curl, and a small flat curl fastened in a most miraculous fashion on either cheek. At parties whole bands of them sit together attired in white muslin with spotless kid gloves and exquisite bouquets. If addressed, the Young Lady replies in monosyllables with great demureness, languidly agreeing with her partner that it is almost too hot to dance,

From *Feminine Attitudes in the Nineteenth Century* by C. Willet Cunnington. The Macmillan Company, New York, 1936, and by permission of William Heinemann, Ltd.

and seems relieved when at the conclusion of the set she can seek Mamma; at supper she takes nothing but a water-ice or the smallest of ratafia cakes. Mark the little start or scream which accompanies the explosion of crackers; and the bashfulness with which she positively refuses to show her motto. These young ladies are great novel readers, absolutely dote on Bulwer, think Mrs. Trollope very clever, only sometimes a little coarse. Byron they pronounce inimitable, and keep a duodecimo edition in their workboxes. They enjoy a play providing it is not too affecting, which makes one look such a fright afterwards; and can sit through an Italian Opera (without understanding a word) but are a little shocked at the ballet.

The Young Lady is the most innocent being in existence, and will put on a look of the prettiest bewilderment when anyone ventures to converse with her on any subject beyond the usual routine. A young lady, asked whether she was a Whig or a Tory, replied she did not know but supposed she was the same as Papa.

She does a great deal of needlework, such as embroidery on velvet, working slippers and bead purses and card-racks and pen-wipers, but is never guilty of mending her own stockings.

At watering-places she always wears dust-coloured shoes and purple veil, and carries a parasol to save her complexion. In the country she usually dresses in white and carefully avoids walking on the grass in case it should be in the slightest degree damp. Then how she shrieks if a grasshopper skips across the path or a cow stops to gaze at her! When she comes to a stile what laughing and confusion and vowing to turn back for she is sure she can never manage to get over it—ending by doing so with the momentary display of a slender ankle.

They never go into a passion, have no will of their own, never laugh out loud, or go anywhere without a gentleman, or take cheese at dinner —an odious vulgarism!

On Playboys and Bunnies

H. M. Hefner

Playboy is understandably nervous about Women's Liberation. In a momentarily famous office memo (see Newsweek, *May 18, 1970, 74–76), Hugh Hefner referred to Women's Lib-*

Hugh M. Hefner, "The Playboy Philosophy" (December 1964); copyright © 1964 by HMH Publishing Co., Inc.

eration as "our natural enemy" that is "unalterably opposed
to the romantic boy-girl society that Playboy promotes." The
brief statement below is taken from The Playboy Philosophy
(Playboy, December 1964) which reports a broadcast over
radio station WINS in New York. Hefner participated in Tri-
alogue, along with a Roman Catholic priest, a Protestant minister, and a Conservative rabbi, to discuss the sexual revolution
in America.

PLAYBOY's over-all point of view on the male-female relationship in
society certainly doesn't limit women to the role of Bunnies in The
Playboy Club. Essentially, what we are saying, editorially in the magazine, is that men and women should each have *separate* identities—that
they are both happiest when their roles complement rather than compete with each other.

Since the turn of the century, there has been a considerable breakdown in the cultural patterns that distinguish the sexes—especially here
in America—causing us to drift toward an asexual society, in which it
becomes increasingly difficult for either sex to find true satisfaction or
fulfillment in its interpersonal relationships with the other. This is one
of the two primary causes, I believe—the other being the increasing
complexity and automation of our civilization—for the erosion of individual identity that was mentioned earlier.

Since PLAYBOY is a magazine for men, it is natural for us to place
most of our emphasis on the problem of male identity. PLAYBOY stresses
a strongly heterosexual concept of society—in which the separate roles
of men and women are clearly defined and compatible. Though we are
sometimes accused of having a dehumanized view of women, our concept actually offers the female a far more human identity than she has
had historically in the Western world.

It is our religious tradition that has tended to look upon woman as
a depersonalized object, or possession, by continually associating her
with its antagonism toward sex. Sometimes the emphasis has been placed
upon the temptation to sin in womankind and sometimes the emphasis
has been placed upon feminine purity and chastity; but whether they
were considered creatures of the Devil, or placed upon a pedestal, their
status in our antisexual society has always been that of an *object*, rather
than a *human being*.

In Memoriam:
Sex and the Single Girl

Here we had planned to reprint a section from Helen Gurley Brown's Sex and the Single Girl, a book published in 1962 which had an important impact on the sexual revolution in that it admitted and advocated that single girls have sex. The book carries the idea of Woman-as-Object to its logical end: since society defines you as an object, read the book and learn how to be a "good" one. It is a detailed analysis of the art of attracting men, including everything from advice about where to find "the men in your life" to instructions about where to live, what to wear, how to diet and make up, or what to cook. Chapter 4, "How To Be Sexy," discusses techniques of appearance and behavior that are recommended to work in the sex-game. Unfortunately, Mrs. Brown refused to give us permission to reprint any section of her remarkable book.

Princess Grace Turns Forty

William B. Arthur

Before the American public enshrined Jacqueline Kennedy as its symbol of modern royalty, it leaned heavily on Grace Kelly, the poor little rich girl from Philadelphia who provided a living example of the Cinderella myth. The following interview suggests that Princess Grace has spent a good portion of her life worrying about her age and decay, trying every cream on the market. In short, she is the grand example of the modern woman who spends her time creating herself in the image of man's object.

In another interview (with Roderick Mann of the Ladies
Home Journal, *May, 1970) Her Most Serene Highness said
that:* "One of my few regrets is that I wasn't able to develop
more fully as an actress . . . I just hope I've developed as a person instead. That's what's important to me—to fulfill my role
as a wife and mother and princess."

There it is, on the record:

"Grimaldi, Princess Grace of Monaco (Grace Patricia Kelly); born
Philadelphia, Pennsylvania, November 12, 1929 . . ."

Now it has happened. One of the most glamorous women of our
time, the movie queen who became a real-life princess, has reached
the age most women dread: 40.

She does too. I asked her about it in the comfortable living room of
her home, "Rocagel," on a mountaintop in France, overlooking the
storybook Principality on the French Riviera.

"Oh, do I mind!" she said. "I'm an absolute basket case. I can't stand
it. It comes as a great jolt. It really does. It hits one right between the
eyes. So here I am, and you sort of stop and think, my God, I'm there
already.

"It's something you know is going to happen, but you think, why so
soon? All I can think of is Shakespeare's: *'When forty winters shall
besiege thy brow, / And dig deep trenches in thy beauty's field, / Thy
youth's proud livery, so gazed on now, / Will be a tatter'd weed, of
small worth held . . .'*"

She's still beautiful, with skin, well, peaches-and-cream *is* the best
way to describe it, still trim. I found myself thinking of the Grace Kelly
of *High Society* and *Rear Window.* Changed? Certainly. In 14 years,
anyone changes. But she's not that far removed from "the lovely April
of her prime."

"You haven't got much sympathy here," I said. "I'm past 50."

"No," she said, "I have no sympathy for men at all, because 40 is a
marvelous age for a man, but for a woman it is torture, the end.

"I think turning 40 is miserable. As a matter of fact, I am giving a
party for Scorpions, to help ease the pain. Then I'm going to forget
about age."

"How about the problem everybody faces: How do you control your
weight?"

"I'm still trying to figure that out. I haven't learned how yet. I should
worry more about it, and now that I am 40, I will start to worry more.
I try to watch my calories once in a while. September is my month to
get healthy, and I did go on a diet, but then I caught this dreadful cold
which knocked me out, so the diet went out too."

"Do you do any special exercises?"

"No, I don't, but I'm going to get into that now that I'm at this advanced age. In the past, I have taken ballet lessons and gym classes, but during this last year, I didn't have time for any of that. It's a question of taking time to exercise regularly. If it isn't done regularly, it doesn't do much good."

"That skin of yours, how do you keep it the way it is?"

"I just use every cream that comes on the market. I try them all."

"And do you tint your hair?"

"When the gray appears—and I do have telltale signs—you can say, yes."

"Do you ever wear false eyelashes?"

"On occasion. Not often, but for big occasions when I'm all done up."

"And wigs or falls or a postiche?"

"Full wigs, no, but often a fall or a postiche, or a little bit here and there."

"Now how about mini-skirts?"

"Ah, no, I'm not too keen on mini-skirts. I must say my skirts have been shortened in the last couple of years, but I've never really gone in for mini-skirts, and now I think they're going to be on the way out. I think they're fun on young girls, but I have never thought I was the mini-skirt type."

"What about pantsuits, particularly in such places as restaurants?"

"I'm in complete agreement with restaurants and hotels that don't want women to wear trousers in their places. They'll get maybe a half-dozen women who will be really chic and look elegant in trouser suits, but the rest won't, and I think they should keep to their rules. I have some trouser suits I wear on occasion, and I enjoy them."

"What is it like, in your position, to be the mother of a girl [Caroline] who is almost 13 years old?"

"Oh, I think it's absolutely marvelous. I love it. I've loved every age of the children. Each one has been fascinating, stimulating and exciting. Caroline is wonderful. She's very open, honest and forthright. She's still at the age where she discusses her problems, her anxieties with me. She is going through so many changes and has so many questions. I love her age, and I'm delighted to help her through it."

"Do you feel a generation gap?"

"I really don't understand what generation gap means. You know, it's not a question of generations, it's a question of personalities. Some people of my own age I can never talk to, never be close to. Some of Caroline's age, or Albert's or Stephanie's, I feel very close to. Then I have some friends who are 80 years old that I feel very close to. Maybe my attitude comes from having been in the theatre and having been with people of all ages when you're doing a play or a television program or a picture; you're living with people every day, and age doesn't much enter into it.

"I hope there won't be a generation gap with our children. For the moment, they love being with us and doing things with us. I'm sure that when they're older, they'll prefer being with their friends, but that's how it should be."

"What do you hope for them?"

"Well, I hope for them the same thing that my parents hoped for us: that we would have character. I think that's the most important thing you can give a child, trying to bring them up to be good sports, to learn to play the game according to the rules and to be prepared for almost anything in life."

"Princess, what do you think of the current trend in the movie world toward nudity and violence?"

"The violence, it's too much. The nudity, the sex, well, I don't like anything too obvious—sex or makeup or a way of dressing. I prefer something that's understated; that leaves a little to the imagination. I don't like it when you have to see the sex act on the stage or screen. I mean, I'm interested in my own sex life, not anyone else's. This trend, if it goes on, will probably lead us back into a terrible kind of Victorian prudish period. This is the trouble: When it goes too far one way, the pendulum will swing too far the other way. I think the people who make pictures should be more aware of their responsibilities. Movies are a mass medium, and you can't control them for selective audiences. Books, well, that's different. Theirs is more of a selective audience."

"It's been a number of years now since Hollywood. Do you miss it?"

"Oh, certainly I do. I miss acting, whether it's in Hollywood or in the theater. I loved acting. I loved my job as an actress. But if you want to do it well, acting is something that takes a great deal of time and concentration, and there's a great deal of competition. When you're married and have children, that alone makes acting complicated because when you're acting you have to think of yourself first, and when you're a mother you just can't do that. My situation is even more complicated, being Princess of Monaco and married to a head of state."

"Rumors continue to pop up that you're going to make a film. Currently, there's a rumor that Sam Spiegel has asked you to make a movie. True?"

"It is very nice, when one approaches my advanced age, to think they still would like to have me."

"But did Sam Spiegel ask you, and are you going to do it?"

"Aren't you nosy! Why don't you just wait and see?"

"If one person has asked me in the States, I'll bet 20 have. Is Princess Grace going to do the book Sam Spiegel bought? What is it?"

"*Nicholas and Alexandra.*"

"Quite a book."

"It's a wonderful book. A great book . . ."

She just smiled.

Achieving Womanhood

William H. Grier and Price M. Cobbs

The pin-up girl ideal, symbolized by the Miss America contest, has frustrated millions of white women. Those who do not fulfill the ideal strive futilely to do so; those who are beautiful are the objects of sexual and economic exploitation. How this frustration is compounded for the black woman is the subject of the following chapter from William H. Grier's and Price M. Cobbs' Black Rage.

Because "femininity in this society is defined in such terms [i.e., white and lovable] that it is out of reach" for the black woman, she has suffered both physically and psychically in striving to live up to the white male supremacist's ideal. This essay offers abundant proof that black women must, as they are today, reject this white ideal and develop a sense of personal and racial pride, in which "black is beautiful."

It should be noted that Grier and Cobbs base their analysis on the traditional Freudian view that woman is a mutilated man who "compensates," if she is "healthy," with narcissism and hyper-active motherhood.

In the world of women an abundance of feminine narcissism is not only a cheerful attribute but a vital necessity to emotional well-being. For a woman to invite and accept the love of a man whom she respects,

Chapter III of *Black Rage* by William H. Grier and Price M. Cobbs, © 1968 by William H. Grier and Price M. Cobbs, Basic Books, Inc., Publishers, New York.

she must feel herself to be eminently worthy of his interest and, in a deep and abiding sense, a lovable person. Such a conviction carries with it a compelling confidence grown out of the loving engagement of a mother with her precious child, of a family with a delightful little girl, and of a larger community likewise charmed by her. With these benevolent auspices, augmented by real physical attractiveness, the stage is set for the growth and development of a self-confident woman who can enter wholeheartedly into love relationships, bringing a richness and a warmth to her mate and to the children who issue from their union. The first measure of a child's worth is made by her mother, and if, as is the case with so many black people in America, that mother feels that she herself is a creature of little worth, this daughter, however valued and desired, represents her scorned self. Thus the girl can be loved and valued only within a limited sphere, and can never be the flawless child, because she is who she is—black and inevitably linked to her black, depreciated mother—always seen to be lacking, deficient, and faulty in some way. Nor can the family or the community at large undo this attitude, since children, however wonderful they may be to adults, are always seen in terms of the future, and in this country the future of a dark girl is dark indeed. While under other circumstances a golden future might be imagined for her, at the very beginning of her life she is comforted and commiserated with and urged to overcome her handicaps—the handicap of being born black.

A certain amount of feminine narcissism must rest ultimately on real physical attractiveness and such attractiveness is determined by the artificial standard each community selects. In this country, the standard is the blond, blue-eyed, white-skinned girl with regular features. Since communication media spread this ideal to every inhabitant of the land via television, newspapers, magazines, and motion pictures, there is not much room for deviation. Women expend great effort in bringing themselves to an approximation of the ideal. The girl who is black has no option in the matter of how much she will change herself. Her blackness is the antithesis of a creamy white skin, her lips are thick, her hair is kinky and short. She is, in fact, the antithesis of American beauty. However beautiful she might be in a different setting with different standards, in this country she is ugly. However loved and prized she may be by her mother, family, and community, she has no real basis of feminine attractiveness on which to build a sound feminine narcissism. When to her physical unattractiveness is added a discouraging, depreciating mother-family-community environment into which she is born, there can be no doubt that she will develop a damaged self-concept and an impairment of her feminine narcissism which will have profound consequences for her character development.

In addition, she takes her place within a historical context, in which women like her have never been valued, have been viewed only as depreciated sexual objects who serve as the recipients of certain debased passions of men who are ashamed to act them out with their own women. Historically she has had some value as a "breeder" of slaves and workmen. But most of all she has been viewed, as all black people have been viewed, as a source of labor: and she has been valued for the amount of work she can perform.

Born thus, depreciated by her own kind, judged grotesque by her society, and valued only as a sexually convenient laboring animal, the black girl has the disheartening prospect of a life in which the cards are stacked against her and the achievement of a healthy, mature womanhood seems a very long shot indeed. The miracle is that, in spite of such odds, the exceptional love of parents and the exceptional strength of many girls produce so many healthy, capable black women.

One aspect of the black woman's life which attracts little attention from outsiders has to do with her hair. From the time of her birth, the little girl must submit to efforts aimed at changing the appearance of her hair. When she is a babe in arms her hair is brushed and stroked, but in short order the gentle brushing gives way to more vigorous brushing and ultimately combing. Her hair is kinky and combing is painful, but her mother must hold her and force her to submit to it. As far back as her memory will take her, the black woman recalls the painful daily ritual of having her hair combed. It is not insignificant that this painful process is administered in a dispassionate way by the mother. Surely the deadly logic of children would try to explain this phenomenon in some such fashion: "If such pain is administered with such regularity by one who purports to love me, then the end result must be extremely important." And yet, however she might search, the child will never find a reason weighty enough to justify the pain to which she must submit.

For, in fact, the combing and plaiting of the hair, in whatever stylish manner the mother may adopt, results only in the child's being rendered "acceptable." The combing does not produce a stunningly beautiful child from an ugly one, but simply an acceptably groomed child. For the pain she goes through, she might well expect to be stopped on the street by strangers stunned by the beauty and the transformation wrought by the combing and the stylized plaits. Not so. She is simply considered to be of an acceptable appearance.

Again, the logic of children would raise the question: "If Mother has to inflict such pain on me to bring me to the level of acceptability, then I must have been ugly indeed before the combing." For the implications and regularity and torture involved suggest that it is of vital importance that the child not be seen in her "natural state."

Now there is nothing unique about grooming being painful for children. In fact, most people of the soap-and-water cultures may recall the agonies experienced as children when soap got in their eyes. But for most people the discomforts associated with soap, toothbrushes, combs, and slippery bathtubs are transient, experienced mainly by the child who has not quite mastered the technique. It takes only a few years to take most of the pain out of the use of soap and most of the danger out of slippery bathtubs. But for the black girl the combing continues as a daily ritual up to the magic day when she is introduced to the hairdresser.

At the time of this writing, the overwhelming majority of Negro women have their hair "fixed" by some method, including the use of a hot comb. The hair is oiled and the heated comb is applied. Usually there is some incidental burning of the scalp. The ordeal itself is long and tiresome, involving hours spent waiting while the overworked beautician moves from customer to customer. To look "presentable" the woman must have her hair pressed every week, or at least every two weeks. Thus the black woman is never free of the painful reminder that she must be transformed from her natural state to some other state in order to appear presentable to her fellow men.

One might ask how this process differs from the ritual to which her Caucasian sister submits for the purpose of similar cosmetic effect. The difference may be a fine one, but it is crucial. The Caucasian woman can brush her hair with a minimum of discomfort and look quite acceptable for any public appearance. If she submits to the pain and discomfort of the hairdresser's, it is for the purpose of *beautification*—it is to enhance her natural appearance which in itself is considered acceptable by her peers. For black women, the pressing comb is like the curse of Eve, a painful, humiliating experience to which she is bound to submit— which, moreover, seems like a wretched legacy grafted into her flesh by her mother.

Almost without exception black women in treatment recall that awful day when they first faced the swimming pool. The black woman's white companions with or without swimming caps plunged into the pool while she stood trembling on the edge, sure that her swimming cap would not fit tightly enough and that afterward she would remove her cap to find disaster.

Women recall the first few weeks at boarding school or college when the issue of having their hair pressed loomed so large. These recollections take on a humorous quality, but the humor is bitter. And not all of it is humor.

A black woman in treatment, who was a borderline schizophrenic, dreaded going to the beauty parlor. She got upset whenever she went and on occasion a visit would be the precipitating incident of her illness. She became delusional and hallucinated. She was terrified in the beauty parlor and thought that the beauticians were whispering behind her back, plotting to do dreadful things to her, and at the very least engaging in malicious gossip. She was terrified of submitting herself to their care. Her associations were to the painful hair combing administered by her devoted grandmother. In her mind the question was never resolved. Did Grandmother truly take pleasure in hurting her? This woman's weak ego may have allowed her to give voice to the silent puzzlement of her countless healthier sisters.

As if this were not sufficient, there is one final degradation associated with hair. Passionate love-making is a vigorous business and touseled hair is to be expected, but if a woman perspires too freely, her pressed hair becomes kinky and must be straightened. And thus even in the triumphant bed of Eros she is reminded that what should be her crowning glory is in fact a crown of shame.

It is against this endless circle of shame, humiliation, and the implied unacceptability of one's own person that a small but significant number of black women have turned to the "natural hairdo"; no hot irons, no pressing combs, no oils, but a soft, black, gentle cloche of cropped velvet. The effect is so engaging and feminine, and, in light of the above, so psychologically redemptive, that we can only wonder why it has taken them so long, and why even yet there are so few.

Publications designed for Negro audiences have always found a certain group of advertisers eager to purchase space. These are the merchants of bleaching creams. The buyers are promised that the cream will make them "two or three shades lighter." The advertising space and the prominent display of these items in neighborhood stores provide objective evidence of what every ghetto dweller knows. Black women have spent fortunes trying to be white.

Long, straight hair and a fair skin have seemed to be the requirements for escaping the misery of being a black woman. One can only guess at the agony of the countless black women who spent their hard-earned money for a bottled, emulsified escape from being the way they are. And it is difficult to imagine their frustration and hopelessness when they finally realized that they could not change their hair or their color.

There surely is nothing more cruelly contained than the feminine narcissism in American black women. To paraphrase Countee Cullen:

> And yet I wonder at this thing
> To make a woman black and bid her sing.

There have been lesser sources of misery too, as if these were not enough. Black women felt ashamed if their feet were big. They hid their feet and bought shoes that were too small and often earned a lifetime of foot problems.

Most cultures associate big feet with lower-class origins and thus the women (and men) value small feet. For the American Negro, "lower class" does not adequately state the condition he wants to rise above. For him, "lower class" has overtones of slavery and the lash, and the black woman's shame when her feet are large is therefore a deeper wound and a more lasting hurt.

They have also felt a special misery over skinny legs and small breasts. In fact, there was a heightened concern over all the criteria of femininity —all the criteria of physical beauty thrust upon them by a society which held beauty to be the opposite of what they were.

The softly seductive, essentially feminine quality of women is at its height during adolescence. In this country great efforts are expended in extending the period, both backward and forward: Backward, to the preadolescence of eleven- and twelve-year-olds, and forward, past the sixties and seventies to the end of a woman's life. Whatever the chronological boundaries, the effort clearly is to extend them and make it possible for a woman to appear more feminine for a longer period of her life.

For a great many black women, however, the process is reversed. Black women seem unconsciously to shorten this period more drastically than their poor circumstances might necessitate. In their thirties and forties they seem to give up competition for male interest. They neglect their figures, allow themselves to become obese, concern themselves more with the utility of their clothing and less with style, and resign themselves to a relatively asexual maternal role in which work and a hovering concern for the family occupies them entirely. They give the impression that they have no interest in men in a sexual way. The total effect such women give can be startling.

A group of relatively poor black mothers who were seen in therapy appeared at first glance to be in their forties or fifties. They were, however, all in their late twenties. Their shapeless garments, unattractive shoes, dental neglect, and general disinterest in their appearance made them seem twenty to thirty years older than they actually were.

A similar disinterest in physical appearance may be noticed in their white counterparts, but the careful observer will see a sharper, chronologically earlier, and a much more widespread relinquishment of youth on the part of black women.

The abandonment of youthful narcissism and the associated competition for male attention can occur at even earlier ages, and in fact may begin at such an early age as to subvert even the high-spirited period of adolescence.

Those who deal with the problems of adolescence are concerned about the high frequency of obesity in Negro girls. The authors are well aware that obesity is a problem of adolescence for young girls of every ethnic origin in the United States. But statistics seem to show that obesity is very much more frequent among black girls. It is also well known that women and mothers who find themselves heavily burdened with problems of day-to-day management and survival find it difficult to expend much energy on feminine frills and finery. But the incidence of abandonment of feminine adornment and narcissistic interest is much greater among black women and is not a direct function of their poverty or disadvantaged circumstances. In fact, however slow has been the movement of black people as a group toward greater advantages, a small rise in income lifts the burden of black women to a very significant degree.

Only a short time ago her task as a home maker was prodigious; home appliances are relatively recent luxuries. One would think, therefore, that she would now have more time and more energy to devote to her own person and to the pleasures of femininity. But the whole issue of work and responsibility has no place in any attempt to explain the obesity and the associated abandonment of sexual competition by adolescent black girls.

If this surrender cuts across all age groups, one must look for other reasons. The most satisfactory explanation would be that femininity is only imperfectly grasped by most black women in any event, since femininity in this society is defined in such terms that it is out of reach for her. If the society says that to be attractive is to be white, she finds herself unwittingly striving to be something she cannot possibly be; and if femininity is rooted in feeling oneself eminently lovable, then a society which views her as unattractive and repellent has also denied her this fundamental wellspring of femininity.

So it may be that after a brief struggle a black woman feels that femininity, as it is defined in these times, is something she cannot achieve. Rather than having her heart broken every day, she relinquishes the struggle and diverts her interest elsewhere. She has derived none of the intensely personal satisfaction she might have received as an honored and desirable sexual object.

There is another factor in her ready rejection of youth and it has deep historical roots. It has been said that beauty is a curse to a subject woman. From the time black people arrived in this country up to the very recent years black women have been sexually available to any white man who felt so inclined. They were not protected by the laws and their men stood in jeopardy of life if a hand was raised in their defense. For the slave or subject woman, youth and beauty meant arousing the interest of the oppressor and exposure to sexual exploitation.

The black girl found herself in a peculiar vise. If her dreams were realized and she grew into a beauty, her problems were far from solved and had in fact only begun. She now attracted the attention of the oppressor, who turned her femininity to the service of his own sexual appetite.

Thus youth and beauty, though desired, were also dreaded as the certain bearer of trouble and strife.

Even now, the pressures on the pretty girl of the ghetto are great and it requires a special heroism for her to avoid the identity of an anonymous sexual object.

Small wonder that black women flee the beauty of youth.

Much of our discussion has dealt with feminine narcissism from a genetic, dynamic, and adaptive point of view. But the perception of oneself in a favorable light includes the identification of oneself in a historical, sequential sense as well. Group identity and the gathering to oneself of the joys and sufferings of one's forebears play an important part in the construction of a self-identity. The United States presents to all its citizens, but most vividly to the black woman, a negative as well as a positive ideal. The positive ideal, as mentioned above, is in many ways unobtainable for her, inasmuch as it really involves trying to become less Negro and more white. She must be clean, neat, modest, subdued, with hair straightened and, hopefully, with skin lightened. The negative ideal or paradigm is the black, slovenly, obese, dirty, promiscuous woman. But of all the words, perhaps the most important are those that designate the black woman as ugly and repellent. Of the two forces moving her, the pull and attraction of the positive ideal and the push and repulsion of the negative, the latter is by far the more powerful.

Her situation is made worse by the fact that she can by no means approximate the positive ideal and feels always in danger of finding herself too close to the negative. Moreover, the central position of feminine narcissism in the development of character presents a problem for the black woman in her evaluation of her intelligence. Intellectual achievement is closely linked to healthy narcissism. With an impairment of narcissism, a sound synthesis of intellectual accomplishment within the character structure is difficult to achieve.

The full flowering of a woman's sexual function and her capacity to enjoy it are based on her evaluation of herself. If she considers herself an especially worthwhile person, she can joyfully submit to her lover, knowing that he will likewise prize and value her. Her enjoyment of the sexual function will not be impaired by the feeling of being degraded by the man. There is, however, a more subtle interaction between narcissism and the sexual function in women. There is a natural inclination for a woman to yield herself to a powerful lover, gaining additional narcissistic supplies in her possession of him. Her own high evaluation of herself, in turn, evokes in the man a similar high evaluation of her. If her narcissism is impaired, the sexual act is a degrading submission to a man who does not value her, and she arises from it feeling a loss of self-esteem rather than a personal enhancement.

The Negro woman's black face, African features, and kinky hair are physical attributes which place her far from the American ideal of beauty, and make her, with reference to the American ideal, ugly. When the feeling of ugliness is reinforced by the rejection of family and society, the growing girl develops a feeling not only of being undesirable and unwanted but also of being mutilated—of having been fashioned by Nature in an ill-favored manner. Anatomy determines that every little girl will struggle with feelings of having been injured and mutilated when she compares her sexual organs with the male's, but under normal circumstances the compensatory blossoming of narcissism allows her to develop a feeling of satisfaction with herself. The black woman's feelings of mutilation, both psychical and physical, are strengthened by her experiences and she is guarded from self-depreciation only by an enfeebled narcissism. As a result, her personal ambitions as an adolescent and her capacity to live out her aspirations suffer. Under the sign of discouragement and rejection which governs so much of her physical operation, she is inclined to organize her personal ambitions in terms of her achievements and to find these achievements serving to compensate for other losses and hurts.

> A dark woman who had risen rapidly in her profession experienced a worsening of her chronic depression. As her achievements grew she found opportunistic men taking an interest in her. She developed intense feelings of bitterness about her job, which she felt was the only element in her attractiveness to men. She was bitter about her intellect which had brought her to her present position. She now was attractive to men who were shallow, opportunistic fortune seekers. To compound her misery, she felt an inclination to accept even these shallow men for whatever they wanted in her.

In choosing a mate, the black woman is again faced with the undesirability of her blackness and with the fact that it is the rare black man who can resist the omnipresent presentation of the white ideal. The compromises that are necessary in the establishment of any relationship between a man and a woman can easily be felt by her to be profound compromises with her own aspirations for a love relationship. She may feel that the compromises are based, not on the difficulties faced by two quite different individuals in adjusting to an intimate union, but on the fact that her "unattractiveness" makes it impossible for her to obtain the "ideal" man.

Thus, the contemporary implications of her Negro-ness and the historical identity it imposes on her make her progress to healthy womanhood much more difficult. The problems we have spelled out here represent barriers which are high but not insurmountable. Because we also see evidence of the remarkable capacity of black people in America to survive, we see one of the adaptive modes chosen by black women to make their way in a hostile world. With youthful narcissism crushed and sexual life perverted, they drew back from these modes as primary means of life expression. Letting youth go, beauty go, and sex go, they narrowed their vision to the most essential feminine function—mothering, nurturing, and protecting their children. In such a role the black woman has been the salvation of many a family. To call such a family matriarchal, as many have done, is to obscure the essential maternal function and to suggest an authoritarian for authority's sake.

We suggest that the black woman has been beset by cruelty on all sides and as a result centered her concern on the most essential quality of womanhood. In so doing she stood by her mate or in his stead when he was crippled or crushed by the oppressor.

The mother in the play *Raisin in the Sun*—who stands as a bulwark of reason between her family and an irrational world—reflects the perception by black women of that essential female function of mothering and its triumph in a world which robs her of other joys.

So much of black women's suffering has grown out of the same feeling of helplessness that has pilloried the male. With the new black movements under way, all that we have just said may assume merely historical significance. The contorted efforts to be white, the shame of the black body, the rejection of youth—may all vanish quickly. Negro women need only see that, truly, "black is beautiful."

The Bride of Frankenstein

Edward Field

*The life story of Marilyn Monroe shows all too clearly the
despair that can result from a woman's exploitation as a sex
object. Edward Field's The Bride of Frankenstein expresses
the same despair, as "the prettiest monster-woman you ever
saw" destroys herself in the face of male rapacity. The monster,
who has been sexually repressed and then incited to rape by
"his pinching leering keeper," reacts violently and destruc-
tively when his desire is thwarted.*

The Baron has decided to mate the monster,
to breed him perhaps,
in the interests of pure science, his only god.

So he goes up into his laboratory
which he has built in the tower of the castle
to be as near the interplanetary forces as possible,
and puts together the prettiest monster-woman you ever saw
with a body like a pin-up girl
and hardly any stitching at all
where he sewed on the head of a raped and murdered beauty queen.

He sets his liquids burping, and coils blinking and buzzing,
and waits for an electric storm to send through the equipment
the spark vital for life.
The storm breaks over the castle
and the equipment really goes crazy
like a kitchen full of modern appliances
as the lightning juice starts oozing right into that pretty corpse.

He goes to get the monster
so he will be right there when she opens her eyes,
for she might fall in love with the first thing she sees
as ducklings do.

That monster is already straining at his chains and slurping
ready to go right to it:
He has been well prepared for coupling
by his pinching leering keeper who's been saying for weeks,
"You gonna get a little nookie, kid."
or "How do you go for some poontang, baby."

All the evil in him is focused on this one thing now
as he is led into her very presence.

She awakens slowly,
she bats her eyes,
she gets up out of the equipment,
and finally she stands in all her seamed glory,
a monster princess with a hairdo like a fright-wig,
lightning flashing in the background
like a halo and a wedding veil,
like a photographer snapping pictures of great moments.

She stands and stares with her electric eyes,
beginning to understand that in this life too
she was just another body to be raped.

The monster is ready to go:
He roars with joy at the sight of her,
so they let him loose and he goes right for those knockers.
And she starts screaming to break your heart
and you realize that she was just born:
In spite of her big tits she was just a baby.

But her instincts are right—
rather death than that green slobber:
She jumps off the parapet.
And then the monster's sex drive goes wild.
Thwarted, it turns to violence, demonstrating sublimation crudely,
and he wrecks the lab, those burping acids and buzzing coils,
overturning the control panel so the equipment goes off like a bomb,
the stone castle crumbling and crashing in the storm
destroying them all . . . perhaps.

Perhaps somehow the Baron got out of that wreckage of his dreams
with his evil intact if not his good looks
and more wicked than ever went on with his thrilling career.

And perhaps even the monster lived
to roam the earth, his desire still ungratified,
and lovers out walking in shadowy and deserted places
will see his shape loom up over them, their doom—
and children sleeping in their beds
will wake up in the dark night screaming
as his hideous body grabs them.

Woman-as-Enemy

Literature is filled with examples of woman as a destroyer of man. She is seen as manipulator and trouble-maker. Sometimes she controls man by sex appeal, sometimes by artfulness ("womanly wiles"), sometimes by sheer strength of will. Men respond to her with terror, repugnance, and perverse fascination. But this view of Woman-as-Enemy is a male creation. Sometimes woman has been forced to strike back by the frustrations attending her role in a male-dominated society; but, more often than not, she is hurt more than the men she afflicts.

Most male fears of Woman-as-Enemy are sheer fantasy. When women begin asking for equality, many men react hysterically, accusing women of desiring to dominate, indeed, to destroy them. In such situations, "castrating bitches" is one of the more polite terms applied. Admittedly, some of the rhetoric of the Women's Liberation movement sounds ominous, such as the slogan "Watch out. You may meet a real castrating female," or Valerie Solanas' *S.C.U.M. Manifesto*, which advocates a program for the elimination of all men. But the Women's Liberation movement is not, contrary to male fears, threatening to phase out men. Equality and supremacy are two different things—one desirable, the other not.

Tickets, Please

D. H. Lawrence

*The fury of the woman scorned is the theme of D. H. Law-
rence's Tickets, Please, a horrifying account of man-woman
relations gone awry because of conflict between the man's insistence on his sexual freedom and the woman's possessive impulse. Annie, the other women, and John Thomas are warped
by a society that makes the man a manipulator of women who
then in frustration and anger take a brutal revenge.*

*A contemporary treatment of this archetypal story of woman
as castrator of man is the film "Three in the Attic," where three
women capture, lock up, and sexually exhaust a man who has
been exploiting them.*

There is in the Midlands a single-line tramway system which boldly
leaves the county town and plunges off into the black, industrial countryside, up hill and down dale, through the long ugly villages of workmen's
houses, over canals and railways, past churches perched high and
nobly over the smoke and shadows, through stark, grimy cold little
market-places, tilting away in a rush past cinemas and shops down to
the hollow where the collieries are, then up again, past a little rural
church, under the ash trees, on in a rush to the terminus, the last little
ugly place of industry, the cold little town that shivers on the edge of
the wild, gloomy country beyond. There the green and creamy coloured
tram-cars seem to pause and purr with curious satisfaction. But in a
few minutes—the clock on the turret of the Co-operative Wholesale
Society's shops gives the time—away it starts once more on the adventure. Again there are the reckless swoops downhill, bouncing the loops:
again the chilly wait in the hill-top market-place: again the breathless

From *The Complete Short Stories of D. H. Lawrence,* Volume II. Copyright 1922 by Thomas B. Seltzer, Inc., renewed 1950 by Frieda Lawrence.
Reprinted by permission of The Viking Press, Inc.

slithering round the precipitous drop under the church: again the patient halts at the loops, waiting for the outcoming car: so on and on, for two long hours, till at last the city looms beyond: the fat gas-works, the narrow factories draw near, we are in the sordid streets of the great town, once more we sidle to a standstill at our terminus, abashed by the great crimson and cream-coloured city cars, but still perky, jaunty, somewhat dare-devil, green as a jaunty sprig of parsley out of a black colliery garden.

To ride on these cars is always an adventure. Since we are in war-time, the drivers are men unfit for active service: cripples and hunch-backs. So they have the spirit of the devil in them. The ride becomes a steeplechase. Hurray! we have leapt in a clear jump over the canal bridge —now for the four-lane corner. With a shriek and a trail of sparks we are clear again. To be sure, a tram often leaps the rails—but what matter! It sits in a ditch till other trams come to haul it out. It is quite common for a car, packed with one solid mass of living people, to come to a dead halt in the midst of unbroken blackness, the heart of nowhere on a dark night, and for the driver and the girl conductor to call: "All get off— car's on fire!" Instead, however, of rushing out in a panic, the passengers stolidly reply: "Get on—get on! We're not coming out. We're stopping where we are. Push on, George." So till flames actually appear.

The reason for this reluctance to dismount is that the nights are howl-ingly cold, black, and windswept, and a car is a haven of refuge. From village to village the miners travel, for a change of cinema, of girl, of pub. The trams are desperately packed. Who is going to risk himself in the black gulf outside, to wait perhaps an hour for another tram, then to see the forlorn notice 'Depot Only', because there is something wrong! Or to greet a unit of three bright cars all so tight with people that they sail past with a howl of derision. Trams that pass in the night.

This, the most dangerous tram-service in England, as the authorities themselves declare, with pride, is entirely conducted by girls, and driven by rash young men, a little crippled, or by delicate young men, who creep forward in terror. The girls are fearless young hussies. In their ugly blue uniform, skirts up to their knees, shapeless old peaked caps on their heads, they have all the *sang-froid* of an old non-commissioned officer. With a tram packed with howling colliers, roaring hymns down-stairs and a sort of antiphony of obscenities upstairs, the lasses are per-fectly at their ease. They pounce on the youths who try to evade their ticket-machine. They push off the men at the end of their distance. They are not going to be done in the eye—not they. They fear nobody—and everybody fears them.

"Hello, Annie!"

"Hello, Ted!"

"Oh, mind my corn, Miss Stone. It's my belief you've got a heart of stone, for you've trod on it again."

"You should keep it in your pocket," replies Miss Stone, and she goes sturdily upstairs in her high boots.

"Tickets, please."

She is peremptory, suspicious, and ready to hit first. She can hold her own against ten thousand. The step of that tram-car is her Thermopylae.

Therefore, there is a certain wild romance aboard these cars—and in the sturdy bosom of Annie herself. The time for soft romance is in the morning, between ten o'clock and one, when things are rather slack: that is, except market-day and Saturday. Thus Annie has time to look about her. Then she often hops off her car and into a shop where she has spied something, while the driver chats in the main road. There is very good feeling between the girls and the drivers. Are they not companions in peril, shipments aboard this careering vessel of a tram-car, for ever rocking on the waves of a stormy land?

Then, also, during the easy hours, the inspectors are most in evidence. For some reason, everybody employed in this tram-service is young: there are no grey heads. It would not do. Therefore the inspectors are of the right age, and one, the chief, is also good-looking. See him stand on a wet, gloomy morning, in his long oilskin, his peaked cap well down over his eyes, waiting to board a car. His face ruddy, his small brown moustache is weathered, he has a faint impudent smile. Fairly tall and agile, even in his waterproof, he springs aboard a car and greets Annie.

"Hello, Annie! Keeping the wet out?"

"Trying to."

There are only two people in the car. Inspecting is soon over. Then for a long and impudent chat on the foot-board, a good, easy, twelve-mile chat.

The inspector's name is John Thomas Raynor—always called John Thomas, except sometimes, in malice, Coddy. His face sets in fury when he is addressed, from a distance, with this abbreviation. There is considerable scandal about John Thomas in half a dozen villages. He flirts with the girl conductors in the morning, and walks out with them in the dark night, when they leave their tram-car at the depôt. Of course, the girls quit the service frequently. Then he flirts and walks out with the newcomer: always providing she is sufficiently attractive, and that she will consent to walk. It is remarkable, however, that most of the girls are quite comely, they are all young, and this roving life aboard the car gives them a sailor's dash and recklessness. What matter how they behave when the ship is in port? To-morrow they will be aboard again.

Annie, however, was something of a Tartar, and her sharp tongue had kept John Thomas at arm's length for many months. Perhaps, therefore, she liked him all the more: for he always came up smiling, with impudence. She watched him vanquish one girl, then another. She could tell by the movement of his mouth and eyes, when he flirted with her in the morning, that he had been walking out with this lass, or the other, the night before. A fine cock-of-the-walk he was. She could sum him up pretty well.

In this subtle antagonism they knew each other like old friends, they were as shrewd with one another almost as man and wife. But Annie had always kept him sufficiently at arm's length. Besides, she had a boy of her own.

The Statutes fair, however, came in November, at Bestwood. It happened that Annie had the Monday night off. It was a drizzling ugly night, yet she dressed herself up and went to the fair-ground. She was alone, but she expected soon to find a pal of some sort.

The roundabouts were veering round and grinding out their music, the side-shows were making as much commotion as possible. In the coconut shies there were no coconuts, but artificial war-time substitutes, which the lads declared were fastened into the irons. There was a sad decline in brilliance and luxury. None the less, the ground was muddy as ever, there was the same crush, the press of facts lighted up by the flares and the electric lights, the same smell of naphtha and a few potatoes, and of electricity.

Who should be the first to greet Miss Annie on the showground but John Thomas. He had a black overcoat buttoned up to his chin, and a tweed cap pulled down over his brows, his face between was ruddy and smiling and handy as ever. She knew so well the way his mouth moved.

She was very glad to have a 'boy.' To be at the Statutes without a fellow was no fun. Instantly, like the gallant he was, he took her on the Dragons, grim-toothed, roundabout switchbacks. It was not nearly so exciting as a tram-car actually. But, then, to be seated in a shaking, green dragon, uplifted above the sea of bubble faces, careering in a rickety fashion in the lower heavens, whilst John Thomas leaned over her, his cigarette in his mouth, was after all the right style. She was a plump, quick, alive little creature. So she was quite excited and happy.

John Thomas made her stay on for the next round. And therefore she could hardly for shame repulse him when he put his arm round her and drew her a little nearer to him, in a very warm and cuddly manner. Besides, he was fairly discreet, he kept his movement as hidden as possible. She looked down, and saw that his red, clean hand was out of sight of the crowd. And they knew each other so well. So they warmed up to the fair.

After the dragons they went on the horses. John Thomas paid each time, so she could but be complaisant. He, of course, sat astride on the outer horse—named 'Black Bess'—and she sat sideways, towards him, on the inner horse—named 'Wildfire'. But of course John Thomas was not going to sit discreetly on 'Black Bess', holding the brass bar. Round they spun and heaved, in the light. And round he swung on his wooden steed, flinging one leg across her mount, and perilously tipping up and down, across the space, half lying back, laughing at her. He was perfectly happy; she was afraid her hat was on one side, but she was excited.

He threw quoits on a table, and won for her two large, pale blue hatpins. And then, hearing the noise of the cinemas, announcing another performance, they climbed the boards and went in.

Of course, during these performances pitch darkness falls from time to time, when the machine goes wrong. Then there is a wild whooping, and a loud smacking of simulated kisses. In these moments John Thomas drew Anne towards him. After all, he had a wonderfully warm, cosy way of holding a girl with his arm, he seemed to make such a nice fit. And, after all, it was pleasant to be so held: so very comforting and cosy and nice. He leaned over her and she felt his breath on her hair; she knew he wanted to kiss her on the lips. And, after all, he was so warm and she fitted in to him so softly. After all, she wanted him to touch her lips.

But the light sprang up; she also started electrically, and put her hat straight. He left his arm lying nonchalantly behind her. Well, it was fun, it was exciting to be at the Statutes with John Thomas.

When the cinema was over they went for a walk across the dark, damp fields. He had all the arts of love-making. He was especially good at holding a girl, when he sat with her on a stile in the black, drizzling darkness. He seemed to be holding her in space, against his own warmth and gratification. And his kisses were soft and slow and searching.

So Annie walked out with John Thomas, though she kept her own boy dangling in the distance. Some of the tram-girls chose to be huffy. But there, you must take things as you find them, in this life.

There was no mistake about it, Annie liked John Thomas a good deal. She felt so rich and warm in herself whenever he was near. And John Thomas really liked Annie, more than usual. The soft, melting way in which she could flow into a fellow, as if she melted into his very bones, was something rare and good. He fully appreciated this.

But with a developing acquaintance there began a developing intimacy. Annie wanted to consider him a person, a man: she wanted to take an intelligent interest in him, and to have an intelligent response. She did not want a mere nocturnal presence, which was what he was so far. And she prided herself that he could not leave her.

Here she made a mistake. John Thomas intended to remain a nocturnal presence; he had no idea of becoming an all-round individual to her. When she started to take an intelligent interest in him and his life and his character, he sheered off. He hated intelligent interest. And he knew that the only way to stop it was to avoid it. The possessive female was aroused in Annie. So he left her.

It is no use saying she was not surprised. She was at first startled, thrown out of her count. For she had been so *very* sure of holding him. For a while she was staggered, and everything became uncertain to her. Then she wept with fury, indignation, desolation, and misery. Then she had a spasm of despair. And then, when he came, still impudently, on to her car, still familiar, but letting her see by the movement of his head that he had gone away to somebody else for the time being, and was enjoying pastures new, then she determined to have her own back.

She had a very shrewd idea what girls John Thomas had taken out. She went to Nora Purdy. Nora was a tall, rather pale, but well-built girl, with beautiful yellow hair. She was rather secretive.

"Hey!" said Annie, accosting her; then softly: "Who's John Thomas on with now?"

"I don't know," said Nora.

"Why, tha does," said Annie, ironically lapsing into dialect. "Tha knows as well as I do."

"Well, I do, then," said Nora. "It isn't me, so don't bother."

"It's Cissy Meakin, isn't it?"

"It is, for all I know."

"Hasn't he got a face on him!" said Annie. "I don't half like his cheek. I could knock him off the foot-board when he comes round at me."

"He'll get dropped on one of these days," said Nora.

"Ay, he will, when somebody makes up their mind to drop it on him. I should like to see him taken down a peg or two, shouldn't you?"

"I shouldn't mind," said Nora.

"You've got quite as much cause to as I have," said Annie. "But we'll drop on him one of these days, my girl. What? Don't you want to?"

"I don't mind," said Nora.

But as a matter of fact, Nora was much more vindictive than Annie.

One by one Annie went the round of the old flames. It so happened that Cissy Meakin left the tramway service in quite a short time. Her mother made her leave. Then John Thomas was on the *qui vive*. He cast his eyes over his old flock. And his eyes lighted on Annie. He thought she would be safe now. Besides, he liked her.

She arranged to walk home with him on Sunday night. It so happened that her car would be in the depôt at half-past nine: the last car would come in at 10.15. So John Thomas was to wait for her there.

At the depôt the girls had a little waiting-room of their own. It was quite rough, but cosy, with a fire and an oven and a mirror, and table and wooden chairs. The half-dozen girls who knew John Thomas only too well had arranged to take service this Sunday afternoon. So, as the cars began to come in, early, the girls dropped into the waiting-room. And instead of hurrying off home, they sat around the fire and had a cup of tea. Outside was the darkness and lawlessness of war-time.

John Thomas came on the car after Annie, at about a quarter to ten. He poked his head easily into the girls' waiting-room.

"Prayer-meeting?" he asked.

"Ay," said Laura Sharp. "Ladies only."

"That's me!" said John Thomas. It was one of his favourite exclamations.

"Shut the door, boy," said Muriel Baggaley.

"Oh, which side of me?" said John Thomas.

"Which tha likes," said Polly Birkin.

He had come in and closed the door behind him. The girls moved in their circle, to make a place for him near the fire. He took off his greatcoat and pushed back his hat.

"Who handles the teapot?" he said.

Nora Purdy silently poured him out a cup of tea.

"Want a bit o' my bread and drippin'?" said Muriel Baggaley to him.

"Ay, give us a bit."

And he began to eat his piece of bread.

"There's no place like home, girls," he said.

They all looked at him as he uttered this piece of impudence. He seemed to be sunning himself in the presence of so many damsels.

"Especially if you're not afraid to go home in the dark," said Laura Sharp.

"Me! By myself I am."

They sat till they heard the last tram come in. In a few minutes Emma Houselay entered.

"Come on, my old duck!" cried Polly Birkin.

"It *is* perishing," said Emma, holding her fingers to the fire.

"But—I'm afraid to, go home in, the dark," sang Laura Sharp, the tune having got into her mind.

"Who're you going with to-night, John Thomas?" asked Muriel Baggaley coolly.

"To-night?" said John Thomas. "Oh, I'm going home by myself to-night —all on my lonely-o."

"That's me!" said Nora Purdy, using his own ejaculation.

The girls laughed shrilly.

"Me as well, Nora," said John Thomas.

"Don't know what you mean," said Laura.

"Yes, I'm toddling," said he, rising and reaching for his overcoat.

"Nay," said Polly. "We're all here waiting for you."

"We've got to be up in good time in the morning," he said, in the benevolent official manner.

They all laughed.

"Nay," said Muriel. "Don't leave us all lonely, John Thomas. Take one!"

"I'll take the lot, if you like," he responded gallantly.

"That you won't, either," said Muriel. "Two's company; seven's too much of a good thing."

"Nay—take one," said Laura. "Fair and square, all above board and say which."

"Ay," cried Annie, speaking for the first time. "Pick, John Thomas; let's hear thee."

"Nay," he said. "I'm going home quiet to-night. Feeling good, for once."

"Whereabouts?" said Annie. "Take a good 'un, then. But tha's got to take one of us!"

"Nay, how can I take one," he said, laughing uneasily. "I don't want to make enemies."

"You'd only make *one*," said Annie.

"The chosen *one*," added Laura.

"Oh, my! Who said girls!" exclaimed John Thomas, again turning, as if to escape. "Well—good-night."

"Nay, you've got to make your pick," said Muriel. "Turn your face to the wall, and say which one touches you. Go on—we shall only just touch your back—one of us. Go on—turn your face to the wall, and don't look, and say which one touches you."

He was uneasy, mistrusting them. Yet he had not the courage to break away. They pushed him to a wall and stood him there with his face to it. Behind his back they all grimaced, tittering. He looked so comical. He looked around uneasily.

"Go on!" he cried.

"You're looking—you're looking!" they shouted.

He turned his head away. And suddenly, with a movement like a swift cat, Annie went forward and fetched him a box on the side of the head that sent his cap flying and himself staggering. He started round.

But at Annie's signal they all flew at him, slapping him, pinching him, pulling his hair, though more in fun than in spite or anger. He, however, saw red. His blue eyes flamed with strange fear as well as fury, and he butted through the girls to the door. It was locked. He wrenched at it. Roused, alert, the girls stood round and looked at him. He faced them, at bay. At that moment they were rather horrifying to him, as they stood in their short uniforms. He was distinctly afraid.

"Come on, John Thomas! Come on! Choose!" said Annie.

"What are you after? Open the door," he said.

"We shan't—not till you've chosen!" said Muriel.

"Chosen what?" he said.

"Chosen the one you're going to marry," she replied.

He hesitated a moment.

"Open the blasted door," he said, "and get back to your senses." He spoke with official authority.

"You've got to choose!" cried the girls.

"Come on!" cried Annie, looking him in the eye. "Come on! Come on!"

He went forward, rather vaguely. She had taken off her belt, and swinging it, she fetched him a sharp blow over the head with the buckle end. He sprang and seized her. But immediately the other girls rushed upon him, pulling and tearing and beating him. Their blood was now thoroughly up. He was their sport now. They were going to have their own back, out of him. Strange, wild creatures, they hung on him and rushed at him to bear him down. His tunic was torn right up the back, Nora had hold at the back of his collar, and was actually strangling him. Luckily the button burst. He struggled in a wild frenzy of fury and terror, almost mad terror. His tunic was simply torn off his back, his shirt-sleeves were torn away, his arms were naked. The girls rushed at him, clenched their hands on him and pulled at him: or they rushed at him and pushed him, butted him with all their might: or they struck him wild blows. He ducked and cringed and struck sideways. They became more intense.

At last he was down. They rushed on him, kneeling on him. He had neither breath nor strength to move. His face was bleeding with a long scratch, his brow was bruised.

Annie knelt on him, the other girls knelt and hung on to him. Their faces were flushed, their hair wild, their eyes were all glittering strangely. He lay at last quite still, with face averted, as an animal lies when it is defeated and at the mercy of the captor. Sometimes his eye glanced back at the wild faces of the girls. His breast rose heavily, his wrists were torn.

"Now, then, my fellow!" gasped Annie at length. "Now then—now——"

At the sound of her terrifying, cold triumph, he suddenly started to struggle as an animal might, but the girls threw themselves upon him with unnatural strength and power, forcing him down.

"Yes—now, then!" gasped Annie at length.

And there was a dead silence, in which the thud of heart-beating was to be heard. It was a suspense of pure silence in every soul.

"Now you know where you are," said Annie.

The sight of his white, bare arm maddened the girls. He lay in a kind of trance of fear and antagonism. They felt themselves filled with supernatural strength.

Suddenly Polly started to laugh—to giggle wildly—helplessly—and Emma and Muriel joined in. But Annie and Nora and Laura remained the same, tense, watchful, with gleaming eyes. He winced away from these eyes.

"Yes," said Annie, in a curious low tone, secret and deadly. "Yes! You've got it now. You know what you've done, don't you? You know what you've done."

He made no sound nor sign, but lay with bright, averted eyes, and averted, bleeding face.

"You ought to be *killed*, that's what you ought," said Annie, tensely. "You ought to be *killed*." And there was a terrifying lust in her voice.

Polly was ceasing to laugh, and giving long-drawn Oh-h-hs and sighs as she came to herself.

"He's got to choose," she said vaguely.

"Oh, yes, he has," said Laura, with vindictive decision.

"Do you hear—do you hear?" said Annie. And with a sharp movement, that made him wince, she turned his face to her.

"Do you hear?" she repeated, shaking him.

But he was quite dumb. She fetched him a sharp slap on the face. He started, and his eyes widened. Then his face darkened with defiance, after all.

"Do you hear?" she repeated.

He only looked at her with hostile eyes.

"Speak!" she said, putting her face devilishly near his.

"What?" he said, almost overcome.

"You've got to *choose*!" she cried, as if it were some terrible menace, and as if it hurt her that she could not exact more.

"What?" he said, in fear.

"Choose your girl, Coddy. You've got to choose her now. And you'll get your neck broken if you play any more of your tricks, my boy. You're settled now."

There was a pause. Again he averted his face. He was cunning in his overthrow. He did not give in to them really—no, not if they tore him to bits.

"All right, then," he said, "I choose Annie." His voice was strange and full of malice. Annie let go of him as if he had been a hot coal.

"He's chosen Annie!" said the girls in chorus.

"Me!" cried Annie. She was still kneeling, but away from him. He was still lying prostrate, with averted face. The girls grouped uneasily around.

"Me!" repeated Annie, with a terrible bitter accent. Then she got up, drawing away from him with strange disgust and bitterness.

"I wouldn't touch him," she said.

But her face quivered with a kind of agony, she seemed as if she would fall. The other girls turned aside. He remained lying on the floor, with his torn clothes and bleeding, averted face.

"Oh, if he's chosen—" said Polly.

"I don't want him—he can choose again," said Annie, with the same rather bitter hopelessness.

"Get up," said Polly, lifting his shoulder. "Get up."

He rose slowly, a strange, ragged, dazed creature. The girls eyed him from a distance, curiously, furtively, dangerously.

"Who wants him?" cried Laura, roughly.

"Nobody," they answered, with contempt. Yet each one of them waited for him to look at her, hoped he would look at her. All except Annie, and something was broken in her.

He, however, kept his face closed and averted from them all. There was a silence of the end. He picked up the torn pieces of his tunic, without knowing what to do with them. The girls stood about uneasily, flushed, panting, tidying their hair and their dress unconsciously, and watching him. He looked at none of them. He espied his cap in a corner, and went and picked it up. He put it on his head, and one of the girls burst into a shrill, hysteric laugh at the sight he presented. He, however, took no heed, but went straight to where his overcoat hung on a peg. The girls moved away from contact with him as if he had been an electric wire. He put on his coat and buttoned it down. Then he rolled his tunic-rags into a bundle, and stood before the locked door, dumbly.

"Open the door, somebody," said Laura.

"Annie's got the key," said one.

Annie silently offered the key to the girls. Nora unlocked the door.

"Tit for tat, old man," she said. "Show yourself a man, and don't bear a grudge."

But without a word or sign he had opened the door and gone, his face closed, his head dropped.

"That'll learn him," said Laura.

"Coddy!" said Nora.

"Shut up, for God's sake!" cried Annie fiercely, as if in torture.

"Well, I'm about ready to go, Polly. Look sharp!" said Muriel.

The girls were all anxious to be off. They were tidying themselves hurriedly, with mute, stupefied faces.

Faustine

Algernon Charles Swinburne

Swinburne's Faustine, portrays the femme fatale, using a notoriously licentious empress of decadent Rome to represent a universal type of woman. The poem begins with a portrait of Woman-as-Object, and then attributes to her unspeakable sins, associating her with "poison," "blood," and a "shameless, nameless love." She belongs to Satan, and is so far beyond salvation that even Christ could not redeem her. Her gods are Bacchus, the god of wine, and Priapus ("The Lampsacene" alluded to in the poem), the god of lasciviousness. According to the poem, Faustine derives pleasure from the destruction of men and, as a type of evil beauty personified—a succubus— threatens men throughout the ages.

Ave Faustina Imperatrix morituri te salutant
Lean back, and get some minutes' peace;
   Let your head lean
Back to the shoulder with its fleece
   Of locks, Faustine.

The shapely silver shoulder stoops,
   Weighted over clean
With state of splendid hair that droops
   Each side, Faustine.

Let me go over your good gifts
   That crown you queen,
A queen whose kingdom ebbs and shifts
   Each week, Faustine:

Bright heavy brows well gathered up—
   White gloss and sheen;
Carved lips that make my lips a cup
   To drink, Faustine,

Wine and rank poison, milk and blood,
   Being mixed therein

Since first the devil threw dice with God
    For you, Faustine.

Your naked new-born soul, their stake,
    Stood blind between;
God said, "Let him that wins her take
    And keep Faustine."

But this time Satan throve, no doubt;
    Long since, I ween,
God's part in you was battered out—
    Long since, Faustine.

The die rang sideways as it fell,
    Rang cracked and thin,
Like a man's laughter heard in hell
    Far down, Faustine.

A shadow of laughter like a sigh,
    Dead sorrow's kin;
So rang, thrown down, the devil's die
    That won Faustine.

A suckling of his breed you were,
    One hard to wean;
But God, who lost you, left you fair,
    We see, Faustine.

You have the face that suits a woman
    For her soul's screen—
The sort of beauty that's called human
    In hell, Faustine.

You could do all things but be good
    Or chaste of mien;
And that you would not if you could,
    We know, Faustine.

Even He who cast seven devils out
    Of Magdalene
Could hardly do as much, I doubt,
    For you, Faustine.

Did Satan make you to spite God?
　Or did God mean
To scourge with scorpions for a rod
　Our sins, Faustine?

I know what queen at first you were,
　As though I had seen
Red gold and black imperious hair
　Twice crown Faustine.

As if your fed sarcophagus
　Spared flesh and skin,
You come back face to face with us,
　The same Faustine.

She loved the games men played with death,
　Where death must win;
As though the slain man's blood and breath
　Revived Faustine.

Nets caught the pike, pikes tore the net;
　Lithe limbs and lean
From drained-out pores dripped thick red
　　sweat
　To soothe Faustine.

She drank the steaming drift and dust
　Blown off the scene;
Blood could not ease the bitter lust
　That galled Faustine.

All round the foul fat furrows reeked,
　Where blood sank in;
The circus splashed and seethed and shrieked
　All round Faustine.

But these are gone now; years entomb
　The dust and din;
Yea, even the bath's fierce reek and fume
　That slew Faustine.

Was life worth living then? and now
　Is life worth sin?

Where are the imperial years? and how
    Are you Faustine?

Your soul forgot her joys, forgot
    Her times of teen;
Yea, this life likewise will you not
    Forget, Faustine?

For in the time we know not of
    Did fate begin
Weaving the web of days that wove
    Your doom, Faustine.

The threads were wet with wine, and all
    Were smooth to spin;
They wove you like a Bacchanal,
    The first Faustine.

And Bacchus cast your mates and you
    Wild grapes to glean;
Your flower-like lips were dashed with dew
    From his, Faustine.

Your drenched loose hands were stretched to
      hold
    The vine's wet green,
Long ere they coined in Roman gold
    Your face, Faustine.

Then after change of soaring feather
    And winnowing fin,
You woke in weeks of feverish weather,
    A new Faustine.

A star upon your birthday burned,
    Whose fierce serene
Red pulseless planet never yearned
    In heaven, Faustine.

Stray breaths of Sapphic song that blew
    Through Mitylene
Shook the fierce quivering blood in you
    By night, Faustine.

The shameless nameless love that makes
   Hell's iron gin
Shut on you like a trap that breaks
   The soul, Faustine.

And when your veins were void and dead,
   What ghosts unclean
Swarmed round the straitened barren bed
   That hid Faustine?

What sterile growths of sexless root
   Or epicene?
What flower of kisses without fruit
   Of love, Faustine?

What adders came to shed their coats?
   What coiled obscene
Small serpents with soft stretching throats
   Caressed Faustine?

But the time came of famished hours,
   Maimed loves and mean,
This ghastly thin-faced time of ours,
   To spoil Faustine.

You seem a thing that hinges hold,
   A love-machine
With clockwork joints of supple gold—
   No more, Faustine.

Not godless, for you serve one god,
   The Lampsacene,
Who metes the gardens with his rod;
   Your lord, Faustine.

If one should love you with real love
   (Such things have been,
Things your fair face knows nothing of,
   It seems, Faustine);

That clear hair heavily bound back,
   The lights wherein

Shift from dead blue to burnt-up black;
   Your throat, Faustine,

Strong, heavy, throwing out the face
   And hard bright chin
And shameful scornful lips that grace
   Their shame, Faustine,

Curled lips, long since half kissed away,
   Still sweet and keen;
You'd give him—poison shall we say?
   Or what, Faustine?

from *The Mill on the Floss*

George Eliot

The Mill on the Floss, *by the nineteenth-century British novel-ist George Eliot (Mary Ann Evans), tells of a quick-witted and rebellious girl who, thwarted in her desire for education and reduced to poverty in her teens, becomes a woman who finds her fulfillment only in self-renunciation. Ironically, Maggie Tulliver's adult refusal to yield to her desires (she elopes with a man she loves but at the last moment will not marry him be-cause of obligations to others) leads to her personal disgrace, her friends' unhappiness, and her brother's strong disapproval. It is a story of a woman wrecked by a society that denies to her the possibility of independent development.*

As a child, Maggie is a misfit: she desires freedom from the "feminine" role. For example, tired of hearing comments about her unruly hair, she cuts it off short "with a sense of clearness and freedom"; or, on another occasion, she runs away to join the gypsies. The following passage shows Maggie's hostility at constantly being told that she is not behaving in a "ladylike" way. Here the doll suffers as a result of Maggie's frustration; Maggie has become Little-Girl-as-Enemy. What motivates her destructive and cruel impulses?

This attic was Maggie's favourite retreat on a wet day when the weather was not too cold; here she fretted out all her ill humours and talked aloud to the worm-eaten floors and the worm-eaten shelves and the dark rafters festooned with cobwebs; and here she kept a fetish, which she punished for all her misfortunes. This was the trunk of a large wooden doll, which once stared with the roundest of eyes above the reddest of cheeks, but was now entirely defaced by a long career of victorious suffering. Three nails driven into the head commemorated as many crises in Maggie's nine years of earthly struggle, that luxury of vengeance having been suggested to her by the picture of Jael destroying Sisera in the old Bible. The last nail had been driven in with a fiercer stroke than usual, for the fetish on that occasion represented aunt Glegg. But immediately afterwards Maggie had reflected that if she drove many nails in, she would not be so well able to fancy that the head was hurt when she knocked it against the wall, nor to comfort it and make believe to poultice it when her fury was abated, for even aunt Glegg would be pitiable when she had been hurt very much and thoroughly humiliated so as to beg her niece's pardon. Since then she had driven no more nails in, but had soothed herself by alternately grinding and beating the wooden head against the rough brick of the great chimneys that made two square pillars supporting the roof. That was what she did this morning on reaching the attic, sobbing all the while with a passion that expelled every other form of consciousness—even the memory of the grievance that had caused it.

from S.C.U.M. Manifesto

Valerie Solanas

At long last, the male fear of destruction at the hands of females has been realized. Valerie Solanas is not a part of the myth of Woman-as-Enemy; she is for real—a woman who has given up hope for men and the culture they have created. Her Society for Cutting Up Men presents the most extreme of Women's Liberation positions: In order for women to be free, they must rid themselves of men. The first sentence of the S. C. U. M. Manifesto says it all.

Reprinted by permission of The Olympia Press, Inc., N.Y.

Life in this society being, at best, an utter bore and no aspect of
society being at all relevant to women, there remains to civic-minded,
responsible, thrill-seeking females only to overthrow the government,
eliminate the money system, institute complete automation and destroy
the male sex.

It is now technically possible to reproduce without the aid of males
(or, for that matter, females) and to produce only females. We must
begin immediately to do so. The male is a biological accident: the y
(male) gene is an incomplete x (female) gene, that is, has an incomplete
set of chromosomes. In other words, the male is an incomplete female,
a walking abortion, aborted at the gene stage. To be male is to be
deficient, emotionally limited; maleness is a deficiency disease and males
are emotional cripples.

The male is completely egocentric, trapped inside himself, incapable
of empathizing or identifying with others, of love, friendship, affection
or tenderness. He is a completely isolated unit, incapable of rapport
with anyone. His responses are entirely visceral, not cerebral; his intelligence is a mere tool in the service of his drives and needs; he is incapable of mental passion, mental interaction; he can't relate to anything
other than his own physical sensations. He is a half dead, unresponsive
lump, incapable of giving or receiving pleasure or happiness; consequently, he is at best an utter bore, an inoffensive blob, since only those
capable of absorption in others can be charming. He is trapped in a
twilight zone halfway between humans and apes, and is far worse off
than the apes, because unlike the apes he is capable of a large array of
negative feelings— hate, jealously, contempt, disgust, guilt, shame, doubt
—and, moreover he is *aware* of what he is and isn't.

Although completely physical, the male is unfit even for stud service.
Even assuming mechanical proficiency, which few men have, he is, first
of all, incapable of zestfully, lustfully, tearing off a piece, but is instead
eaten up with guilt, shame, fear and insecurity, feelings rooted in male
nature, which the most enlightened training can only minimize; second,
the physical feeling he attains is next to nothing; and, third, he is not
empathizing with his partner, but is obsessed with how he's doing,
turning in an A performance, doing a good plumbing job. To call a man
an animal is to flatter him; he's a machine, a walking dildo. It's often
said that men use women. Use them for what? Surely not pleasure.

Eaten up with guilt, shame, fears and insecurities and obtaining, if
he's lucky, a barely perceptible physical feeling, the male is, nonetheless,
obsessed with screwing; he'll swim a river of snot, wade nostril-deep
through a mile of vomit, if he thinks there'll be a friendly pussy awaiting
him. He'll screw a woman he despises, any snaggle-toothed hag, and,

furthermore, pay for the opportunity. Why? Relieving physical tension isn't the answer, as masturbation suffices for that. It's not ego satisfaction; that doesn't explain screwing corpses and babies.

Completely egocentric, unable to relate, empathize or identify, and filled with a vast, pervasive, diffuse sexuality, the male is psychically passive. He hates his passivity, so he projects it onto women, defines the male as active, then sets out to prove that he is ("prove he's a Man"). His main means of attempting to prove it is screwing (Big Man with a Big Dick tearing off a Big Piece). Since he's attempting to prove an error, he must "prove" it again and again. Screwing, then, is a desperate, compulsive attempt to prove he's not passive, not a woman; but he *is* passive and *does* want to be a woman.

Being an incomplete female, the male spends his life attempting to complete himself, to become female. He attempts to do this by constantly seeking out, fraternizing with and trying to live through and fuse with the female, and by claiming as his own all female characteristics— emotional strength and independence, forcefulness, dynamism, decisiveness, coolness, objectivity, assertiveness, courage, integrity, vitality, intensity, depth of character, grooviness, etc.—and projecting onto women all male traits—vanity, frivolity, triviality, weakness, etc. It should be said, though, that the male has one glaring area of superiority over the female—public relations. (He has done a brilliant job of convincing millions of women that men are women and women are men.) The male claim that females find fulfillment through motherhood and sexuality reflects what males think they'd find fulfilling if they were female.

Women, in other words, don't have penis envy; men have pussy envy. When the male accepts his passivity, defines himself as a woman (Males as well as females think men are women and women are men), and becomes a transvestite he loses his desire to screw (or to do anything else, for that matter; he fulfills himself as a drag queen) and gets his cock chopped off. He then achieves a continuous diffuse sexual feeling from "being a woman." Screwing is, for a man, a defense against his desire to be female. Sex is itself a sublimation.

The male, because of his obsession to compensate for not being female combined with his inability to relate and to feel compassion, has made of the world a shitpile. . . .

[Following this excerpt is a long catalog of the social evils that man has caused. Solanas finally outlines a program for S.C.U.M., including destruction of the male-dominated society by sabotage, loot, and murder. Men as well as women will find reading the entire Manifesto a mind-blowing experience.]

Common Women

Philip Wylie

Philip Wylie uses Mom as a symbol of the corruption of Ameri-can society in his famous essay from Generation of Vipers. *He sees Mom and mom-worship as indicative of the collapse of social and religious values which have been replaced, under the influence of "the destroying mother," by materialism, competition, and sentimentality. In his Prefatory Note, written in 1955, a dozen years after* Common Women, *he blames not only Mom but also the culture that created her. By viewing woman as an inferior being, degrading her as sex object, and then perversely idealizing her as goddess, we are all responsi-ble for Mom—an un-beautiful femme fatale.*

Prefatory Note

You are now about to read (or re-read) one of the most renowned (or notorious) passages in modern English Letters.

This chapter has put the word "momism" indelibly in our language; it has broken a path through sacred preserves into which all manner of amateur critics (along with the stateliest psychiatrists and the United States Armed Services) have since proceeded, pouring out articles, monographs, bulletins, research reports and shelves of books showing how right I was to speak as I did of a certain, prevalent sub-species of middle-class American woman; and the chapter has typed me apparently forever as a woman hater—indeed, as the all-out, all-time, high-scoring world champion misogynist.

It is this last I regret. The fact that legions of individuals, and finally the Army, followed me in condemnation of that special type of American mother I called "mom" merely affirms my work: the Oedipus complex had become a social fiat and a dominant neurosis in our land. It was past time somebody said so. As a way of life, it is shameful in grownups of both sexes; as a national cult, it is a catastrophe.

From *Generation of Vipers* by Philip Wylie. Copyright 1942; © 1970 by Philip Wylie. Reprinted by permission of Holt, Rinehart and Winston, Inc.

But, since I love women more than most men, I believe I love them more deeply and knowingly, and since I respect motherhood whenever and wherever it is worthy of respect, I find it somewhat distressing to be forever tagged as Woman's Nemesis. The fact is that only moms— or incipient moms—could imagine, after a close reading of this very chapter, that I had any other sensation for *real* women than love. Quite a few thousand ladies perceived that fact and so wrote to me. But millions, who thought they read otherwise—or who never read the text but took rumor of my diatribe as Gospel (in mom's fashion)—have given me a false name.

To such females, womanhood is more sacrosanct by a thousand times than the Virgin Mary to popes—and motherhood, that degree raised to astronomic power. They have eaten the legend about themselves and believe it; they live it; they require fealty of us all.

From them, I received dozens of scurrilous, savage, illiterate, vulgar and obscene epistles, letters which but made my point that much clearer —to me. But I have had hundreds of *times* as many communications from moms who confessed, from the sons and daughters of moms who suddenly saw whence their sickly dependencies came, and from multitudes of the learned, the celebrated, the world's leaders, who said in effect: *Thanks.*

So, for individuals, the message has often been of value. But insofar as its effect on this great nation is concerned (about which possibility people sometimes enquire), my risky effort to sever the psychic umbilicus by which millions of moms hold millions of grown American men and women is diseased serfdom, *achieved nothing.*

Mom still commands. Mom's more than ever in charge. Hardly five Americans in a hundred know today that mom and her bogus authority have ever been questioned—by me, or by anybody else. The nation can no longer say it contains many great, free, dreaming men. We are deep in the predicted nightmare now and mom sits on its decaying throne—who bore us, who will soon, most likely, wrap civilization in mom's final, tender garment: a shroud.

Today, as the news photos abundantly make plain, mom composes the majority of Senator McCarthy's shock troops—paying blind tribute to a blind authoritarianism like her own. Mom reaches out from her shrieking hordes, cries, "I touched him!" and faints away. The tragic Senator stalks smiling to the podium and leads the litany of panic, the rituals of logic perverted, the induced madness of those the gods have marked for destruction. "McCarthyism," the rule of unreason, is one with momism: a noble end aborted by sick-minded means, a righteous intent—in terrorism fouled and tyranny foundered.

Today, too, there is mom and her mass affaire with Liberace. . . .

Tomorrow, she will shriek around and dote upon some other Hero, as sick, or as fatuous.

Today, while decent men struggle for seats in government with the hope of saving our Republic, mom makes a condition of their election the legalizing of Bingo. What will she want tomorrow when the world needs saving even more urgently?

We must understand mom before we lose touch with understanding itself.

I showed her as she is—ridiculous, vain, vicious, a little mad. She is her own fault first of all and she is dangerous. But she is also everybody's fault. When we and our culture and our religions agreed to hold woman the inferior sex, cursed, unclean and sinful—we made her mom. And when we agreed upon the American Ideal Woman. the Dream Girl of National Adolescence, the Queen of Bedpan Week, the Pin-up, the Glamour Puss—we insulted women and disenfranchised millions from love. We thus made mom. The hen-harpy is but the Cinderella chick come home to roost: the taloned, cackling residue of burnt-out puberty in a land that has no use for mature men or women.

Mom is a human calamity. She is also, like every calamity, a cause for sorrow, a reproach, a warning siren and a terrible appeal for amends.

While she exists, she will exploit the little "sacredness" we have given motherhood as a cheap-holy compensation for our degradation of woman: she will remain irresponsible and unreasoning—for what we have believed of her is reckless and untrue. She will act the tyrant—because she is a slave. God pity her—and us all!

Common Women (from *Generation of Vipers*)

She is Cinderella . . . the shining haired, the starry-eyed, the ruby-lipped virgo aeternis, of which there is presumably one, and only one, or a one-and-only for each male, whose dream is fixed upon her deflowerment and subsequent perpetual possession. This act is a sacrament in all churches and a civil affair in our society. The collective aspects of marriage are thus largely compressed into the rituals and social perquisites of one day. Unless some element of mayhem or intention of divorce subsequently obtrudes, a sort of privacy engulfs the union and all further developments are deemed to be the business of each separate pair, including the transition of Cinderella into mom, which, if it occasions any shock, only adds to the huge, invisible burthen every man carries with him into eternity. It is the weight of this bundle which, incidentally, squeezes out of him the wish for death, his last positive biological resource.

Mom is an American creation. Her elaboration was necessary because she was launched as Cinderella. Past generations of men have accorded to their mothers, as a rule, only such honors as they earned by meritorious action in their individual daily lives Filial *duty* was recognized by many sorts of civilizations and loyalty to it has been highly regarded among most peoples. But I cannot think, offhand, of any civilization except ours in which an entire division of living men has been used, during wartime, or at any time, to spell out the word "mom" on a drill field, or to perform any equivalent act.

The adoration of motherhood has even been made the basis of a religious cult, but the mother so worshiped achieved maternity without change in her virgin status—a distinction worthy of contemplation in itself—and she thus in one way resembled mom.

Hitherto, in fact, man has shown a considerable qui vive to the dangers which arise from momism and freely perceived that his "old wives" were often vixens, dragons, and Xanthippes. Classical literature makes a constant point of it. Shakespeare dwelt on it. Man has also kept before his mind an awareness that, even in the most lambent mother love, there is always a chance some extraneous current will blow up a change, and the thing will become a consuming furnace. The spectacle of the female devouring her young in the firm belief that it is for their own good is too old in man's legends to be overlooked by any but the most flimsily constructed society.

Freud has made a fierce and wondrous catalogue of examples of mother-love-in-action which traces its origin to an incestuous perversion of a normal instinct. That description is, of course, sound. Unfortunately, Americans, who are the most prissy people on earth, have been unable to benefit from Freud's wisdom because they can *prove* that they do not, by and large, sleep with their mothers. That is their interpretation of Freud. Moreover, no matter how many times they repeat the Scriptures, they cannot get the true sense of the passage about lusting in one's heart—especially when they are mothers thinking about their sons, or vice versa.

Meanwhile, megaloid momworship has got completely out of hand. Our land, subjectively mapped, would have more silver cords and apron strings crisscrossing it than railroads and telephone wires. Mom is everywhere and everything and damned near everybody, and from her depends all the rest of the U. S. Disguised as good old mom, dear old mom, sweet old mom, your loving mom, and so on, she is the bride at every funeral and the corpse at every wedding. Men live for her and die for her, dote upon her and whisper her name as they pass away, and I believe she has now achieved, in the hierarchy of miscellaneous articles, a spot next to the Bible and the Flag, being reckoned part of both in a way. She may therefore soon be granted by the House of Representatives the especial supreme and extraordinary right of sitting on top of both when she chooses, which, God knows, she does. At any rate, if no such bill is under consideration, the presentation of one would cause little debate among the solons. These sages take cracks at their native land and make jokes about Holy Writ, but nobody among them—no great man or brave—from the first day of the first congressional meeting to the present ever stood in our halls of state and pronounced the one indubitably most-needed American verity: "Gentlemen, mom is a jerk."

Mom is something new in the world of men. Hitherto, mom has been so busy raising a large family, keeping house, doing the chores, and fabricating everything in every home except the floor and the walls that she was rarely a problem to her family or to her equally busy friends, and never one to herself. Usually, until very recently, mom folded up and died of hard work somewhere in the middle of her life. Old ladies were scarce and those who managed to get old did so by making remarkable inner adjustments and by virtue of a fabulous horniness of body, so that they lent to old age not only dignity but metal.

Nowadays, with nothing to do, and all the tens of thousands of men to maintain her, every clattering prickamette in the republic survives for an incredible number of years, to stamp and jibber in the midst of man, a noisy neuter by natural default or a scientific gelding sustained by science, all tongue and teat and razzmatazz. The machine has deprived her of social usefulness; time has stripped away her biological possibilities and poured her hide full of liquid soap; and man has sealed his own soul beneath the clamorous cordillera by handing her the checkbook and going to work in the service of her caprices.

These caprices are of a menopausal nature at best—hot flashes, rage, infantilism, weeping, sentimentality, peculiar appetite, and all the ragged reticule of tricks, wooings, wiles, suborned fornications, slobby onanisms, indulgences, crotchets, superstitions, phlegms, debilities, vapors, butterflies-in-the-belly, plaints, connivings, cries, malingerings, deceptions, visions, hallucinations, needlings and wheedlings, which pop out of every personality in the act of abandoning itself and humanity. At worst—*i.e.*, the finis—this salaginous mess tapers off into senility, which is man's caricature of himself by reversed ontogeny. But behind this vast aurora of pitiable weakness is mom, the brass-breasted Baal, or mom, the thin and enfeebled martyr whose very urine, nevertheless, will etch glass.

Satan, we are told, finds work for idle hands to do. There is no mistaking the accuracy of this proverb. Millions of men have heaped up riches and made a conquest of idleness so as to discover what it is that

Satan puts them up to. Not one has failed to find out. But never before has a great nation of brave and dreaming men absent-mindedly
created a huge class of idle, middle-aged women. Satan himself has
been taxed to dig up enterprises enough for them. But the field is so
rich, so profligate, so perfectly to his taste, that his first effort, obviously, has been to make it self-enlarging and self-perpetuating. This
he has done by whispering into the ears of girls that the only way
they can cushion the shock destined to follow the rude disillusionment
over the fact that they are not really Cinderella is to institute mom-
worship. Since he had already infested both male and female with the
love of worldly goods, a single step accomplished the entire triumph:
he taught the gals to teach their men that dowry went the other way,
that it was a weekly contribution, and that any male worthy of a Cinderella would have to work like a piston after getting one, so as to be
worthy, also, of all the moms in the world.

The road to hell is spiral, a mere bend in the strait and narrow, but
a persistent one. This was the given torque, and most men are up to
their necks in it now. The devil whispered. The pretty girl then blind-
folded her man so he would not see that she was turning from a but-
terfly into a caterpillar. She told him, too, that although caterpillars
ate every damned leaf in sight, they were moms, hence sacred. Finally,
having him sightless and whirling, she snitched his checkbook. Man
was a party to the deception because he wanted to be fooled about
Cinderella, because he was glad to have a convenient explanation of
mom, and also because there burned within him a dim ideal which
had to do with proper behavior, getting along, and, especially, making
his mark. Mom had already shaken him out of that notion of being a
surveyor in the Andes which had bloomed in him when he was nine
years old, so there was nothing left to do, anyway, but to take a stock-
room job in the hairpin factory and try to work up to the vice presidency.
Thus the women of America raped the men, not sexually, unfortunately,
but morally, since neuters come hard by morals.

I pass over the obvious reference to the deadliness of the female of
the species, excepting only to note that perhaps, having a creative
physical part in the universe, she falls more easily than man into the
contraposite role of spiritual saboteur.

Mom got herself out of the nursery and the kitchen. She then got out
of the house. She did not get out of the church, but, instead, got the
stern stuff out of *it*, padded the guild room, and moved in more solidly
than ever before. No longer either hesitant or reverent, because there
was no cause for either attitude after her purge, she swung the church
by the tail as she swung everything else. In a preliminary test of strength,
she also got herself the vote and, although politics never interested her

(unless she was exceptionally naive, a hairy foghorn, or a size forty scorpion), the damage she forthwith did to society was so enormous and so rapid that even the best men lost track of things. Mom's first gracious presence at the ballot-box was roughly concomitant with the start toward a new all-time low in political scurviness, hoodlumism, gangsterism, labor strife, monopolistic thuggery, moral degeneration, civic corruption, smuggling, bribery, theft, murder, homosexuality, drunkenness, financial depression, chaos and war. Note that.

The degenerating era, however, marked new highs in the production of junk. Note that, also.

Mom, however, is a great little guy. Pulling pants onto her by these words, let us look at mom.

She is a middle-aged puffin with an eye like a hawk that has just seen a rabbit twitch far below. She is about twenty-five pounds overweight, with no sprint, but sharp heels and hard backhand which she does not regard as a foul but a womanly defense. In a thousand of her there is not sex appeal enough to budge a hermit ten paces off a rock ledge. She none the less spends several hundred dollars a year on permanents and transformations, pomades, cleansers, rouges, lipsticks, and the like—and fools nobody except herself. If a man kisses her with any earnestness, it is time for mom to feel for her pocketbook, and this occasionally does happen.

She smokes thirty cigarettes a day, chews gum, and consumes tons of bonbons and petits fours. The shortening in the latter, stripped from pigs, sheep and cattle, shortens mom. She plays bridge with the stupid voracity of a hammerhead shark, which cannot see what it is trying to gobble but never stops snapping its jaws and roiling the waves with its tail. She drinks moderately, which is to say, two or three cocktails before dinner every night and a brandy and a couple of highballs afterward. She doesn't count the two cocktails she takes before lunch when she lunches out, which is every day she can. On Saturday nights, at the club or in the juke joint, she loses count of her drinks and is liable to get a little tiddly, which is to say, shot or blind. But it is her man who worries about where to acquire the money while she worries only about how to spend it, so he has the ulcers and colitis and she has the guts of a bear; she can get pretty stiff before she topples.

Her sports are all spectator sports.

She was graduated from high school or a "finishing" school or even a college in her distant past and made up for the unhappiness of compulsory education by sloughing all that she learned so completely that she could not pass the final examinations of a fifth grader. She reads the fiction in three women's magazines each month and occasionally skims through an article, which usually angers her so that she gets other moms to skim through it, and then they have a session on the subject over a canister of spiked coffee in order to damn the magazine, the editors, the author, and the silly girls who run about these days. She reads two or three motion-picture fan magazines also, and goes to the movies about two nights a week. If a picture does not coincide precisely with her attitude of the moment, she converses through all of it and so whiles away the time. She does not appear to be lecherous toward the moving photographs as men do, but that is because she is a realist and a little shy on imagination. However, if she gets to Hollywood and encounters the flesh-and-blood article known as a male star, she and her sister moms will run forward in a mob, wearing a joint expression that must make God rue his invention of bisexuality, and tear the man's clothes from his body, yea, verily, down to his B.V.D.'s.

Mom is organization-minded. Organizations, she has happily discovered, are intimidating to all men, not just to mere men. They frighten politicians to sniveling servility and they terrify pastors; they bother bank presidents and they pulverize school boards. Mom has many such organizations, the real purpose of which is to compel an abject compliance of her environs to her personal desires. With these associations and committees she has double parking ignored, for example. With them she drives out of the town and the state, if possible, all young harlots and all proprietors of places where "questionable" young women (though why they are called that—being of all women the least in question) could possibly foregather, not because she competes with such creatures but because she contrasts so unfavorably with them. With her clubs (a solid term!) she causes bus lines to run where they are convenient for her rather than for workers, plants flowers in sordid spots that would do better with sanitation, snaps independent men out of office and replaces them with clammy castrates, throws prodigious fairs and parties for charity and gives the proceeds, usually about eight dollars, to the janitor to buy the committee some beer for its headache in the morning after, and builds clubhouses for the entertainment of soldiers where she succeeds in persuading thousands of them that they are momsick and would rather talk to her than take Betty into the shrubs. All this, of course, is considered social service, charity, care of the poor, civic reform, patriotism, and self-sacrifice.

As an interesting sidelight, clubs afford mom an infinite opportunity for nosing into other people's business. Nosing is not a mere psychological ornament of her; it is a basic necessity. Only by nosing can she uncover all incipient revolutions against her dominion and so warn and assemble her co-cannibals.

Knowing nothing about medicine, art, science, religion, law, sanitation, civics, hygiene, psychology, morals, history, geography, poetry,

literature, or any other topic except the all-consuming one of momism, she seldom has any especial interest in *what*, exactly, she is doing
as a member of any of these endless organizations, so long as it is
something.

I, who grew up as a "motherless" minister's son and hence was
smothered in multimomism for a decade and a half, had an unusual
opportunity to observe the phenomenon at zero range. Also, as a man
stirring about in the cesspool of my society, I have been foolhardy
enough to try, on occasion, to steer moms into useful work. For example, owing to the fact that there was no pasteurization law in Miami
and hundreds of people were flecking the pavement with tubercular
sputum, while scores, including my own wife, lay sick and miserable
with undulant fever, I got a gaggle of these creatures behind a move
toward a pasteurization law, only to find, within a few weeks, that there
was a large, alarmed, and earnest committee at work in my wake to
prevent the passage of any such law. This falange, fanned by the milk
dealers, who would not even deliver the stuff if they could get their
money without, had undone even that one small crusade because it had
uncovered a quack doctor, unknown and unheard-of, who had printed
the incandescent notion that cancer, the big boogie of the moms, was
caused by the pasteurization of milk!

In the paragraph above I have given, I know, the golden tip for which
any moms able to read this volume have been searching all the long way.
I had no mother: therefore, all my bitterness and—especially—this cruel
and wanton attack of moms for which, they will doubtless think, I should
be shot or locked up. Well, let them make the most of that. All mothers
are not such a ravening purulence as they, and mine was not. Mine, I
can show, felt much as I do about the thundering third sex, as do all
good women, of whom there are still a few. But I have researched the
moms, to the beady brains behind their beady eyes and to the stones
in the center of their fat hearts. I am immune to their devotion because
I have already had enough. Learning the hard way. I have found out
that it is that same devotion which at the altar, splits the lamb from his
nave to his chaps. And none of the moms, at least, will believe that I am
a lamb. Let them mark time on that.

In churches, the true purpose of organized momhood is to unseat
bishops, snatch the frocks off prelates, change rectors just for variety,
cross-jet community gossip, take the customary organizational kudos
out of the pot each for each, bestow and receive titles, and short-circuit
one another.

Mom also has patriotism. If a war comes, this may even turn into a
genuine feeling and the departure of her son may be her means to
grace in old age. Often, however, the going of her son is only an occasion for more show. She has, in that case, no deep respect for him.

What he has permitted her to do to him has rendered him unworthy of consideration—and she has shown him none since puberty. She does not miss him—only his varletry—but over that she can weep interminably. I have seen the unmistakable evidence in a blue star mom of envy of gold star mom: and I have a firsthand account by a woman of unimpeachable integrity, of the doings of a shipload of these super-moms-of-the-gold-star, en route at government expense to France to visit the graves of their sons, which I forbear to set down here, because it is a document of such naked awfulness that, by publishing it, I would be inciting to riot, and the printed thing might even rouse the dead soldiers and set them tramping like Dunsany's idol all the way from Flanders to hunt and haunt their archenemy progenitrices—who loved them—to death.

But, peace or war, the moms have another kind of patriotism that, in the department of the human spirit, is identical to commercialized vice, because it captures a good thing and doles it out for the coin of unctuous pride—at the expense of deceased ancestors rather than young female offspring. By becoming a Daughter of this historic war or that, a woman makes herself into a sort of madam who fills the coffers of her ego with the prestige that has accrued to the doings of others. A frantic emptiness of those coffers provides the impulse for the act. There are, of course, other means of filling them, but they are difficult, and mom never does anything that is difficult—either the moving of a piano or the breaking of a nasty habit.

Some legionnaires accept, in a similar way, accolade due their associates only. But legionnaires learned a little wisdom, since they still can function in ways that have some resemblance to normality. Furthermore, competition with the legions from the new war will probably make veritable sages out of thousands.

But mom never meets competition. Like Hitler, she betrays the people who would give her a battle before she brings up her troops. Her whole personal life, so far as outward expression is concerned, is, in consequence, a mopping-up action. Traitors are shot, yellow stars are slapped on those beneath notice, the good-looking men and boys are rounded up and beaten or sucked into pliability, a new slave population continually goes to work at making more munitions for momism, and mom herself sticks up her head, or maybe the periscope of the woman next door, to find some new region that needs taking over. This technique pervades all she does.

In the matter of her affiliation of herself with the Daughters of some war the Hitler analogue especially holds, because these sororities of the sword often constitute her Party—her shirtism. Ancestor worship, like all other forms of religion, contained an instinctual reason and developed rituals thought to be germane to the reason. People sedulously followed those rituals, which were basically intended to remind them that they, too, were going to be ancestors someday and would have to labor for personal merit in order to be worthy of veneration. But mom's reverence for her bold forebears lacks even a ritualistic significance, and so instructs her in nothing. She is peremptory about historical truth, mandates, custom, fact, and point. She brushes aside the ideals and concepts for which her forebears perished fighting, as if they were the crumbs of melba toast. Instead, she attributes to the noble dead her own immediate and selfish attitudes. She "knows full well what they would have thought and done," and in that whole-cloth trumpery she goes busting on her way.

Thus the long-vanished warriors who liberated this land from one George in order to make another its first president guide mom divinely as she barges along the badgering boulevard of her life, relaying fiats from the grave on birth control, rayon, vitamins, the power trust, and a hundred other items of which the dead had no knowledge. To some degree most people, these days, are guilty of this absurd procedure. There has been more nonsense printed lately detailing what Jefferson would say about matters he never dreamed of than a sensible man can endure. (I do not have any idea, for instance, and I am sure nobody has any idea, what Jefferson would think about the giddy bungle of interstate truck commerce; but people, columnists especially, will tell you.)

Mom, however, does not merely quote Thomas Jefferson on modern topics: she *is* Thomas Jefferson. This removes her twice from sanity. Mom wraps herself in the mantle of every canny man and coward who has drilled with a musket on this continent and reproduced a line that zigzagged down to mom. In that cloak, together with the other miters, rings, scepters, and power symbols which she has swiped, she has become the American pope.

People are feebly aware of this situation and it has been pointed out at one time or another that the phrase "Mother knows best" has practically worn out the staircase to private hell. Most decriers of matriarchy, however, are men of middle age, like me.

Young men whose natures are attuned to a female image with more feelings than mom possesses and different purposes from those of our synthetic archetype of Cinderella-the-go-getter bounce anxiously away from their first few brutal contacts with modern young women, frightened to find their shining hair is vulcanized, their agate eyes are embedded in cement, and their ruby lips casehardened into pliers for the bending males like wire. These young men, fresh-startled by learning that She is a chrome-plated afreet, but not able to discern that the condition is mom's unconscious preparation of somebody's sister for a place in the gynecocracy—are, again, presented with a soft and shimmering resting place, the bosom of mom.

Perseus was carefully *not* told that the Gorgons had blonde back hair and faces on the other side, like Janus, which, instead of turning him to stone, would have produced orgasms in him. Thus informed he would have failed to slay Medusa and bring back her head. He might have been congealed—but he might not. Our young men are screened from a knowledge of this duality also, but they are told only about the blonde side. When they glimpse the other, and find their blood running cold and their limbs becoming like concrete, they carom off, instanter, to mom. Consequently, no Gorgons are ever clearly seen, let alone slain, in our society. Mom dishes out her sweetness to all fugitives, and it turns them not to stone, but to slime.

"Her boy," having been "protected" by her love, and carefully, even shudderingly, shielded from his logical development through his barbaric period, or childhood (so that he has either to become a barbarian as a man or else to spend most of his energy denying the barbarism that howls in his brain—an autonomous remnant of the youth he was forbidden), is cushioned against any major step in his progress toward maturity. Mom steals from the generation of women behind her (which she has, as a still further defense, also sterilized of integrity and courage) that part of her boy's personality which should have become the love of a female contemporary. Mom transmutes it into sentimentality for herself.

The process has given rise to the mother-problem, and the mother-in-law problem, and mom has occasionally been caught tipping the bat, but she has contrived even then to make the thing an American joke in order to hide what it really is—as invidious a spiritual parasitism as any in the book. With her captive son or sons in a state of automatic adoration of herself (and just enough dubiety of their wives to keep them limp or querulous at home), mom has ushered in the new form of American marriage: eternal ricochet. The oppositeness of the sexes provides enough of that without mom's doubling of the dose and loading of the dice, but mom does it—for mom. Her policy of protection, from the beginning, was not love of her boy but of herself, and as she found returns coming in from the disoriented young boy in smiles, pats, presents, praise, kisses, and all manner of childish representations of the real business, she moved on to possession.

Possession of the physical person of a man is slavery; possession of the spirit of a man is slavery also, because his body obeys his spirit and his spirit obeys its possessor. Mom's boy will be allowed to have his psychobiological struggle with dad: to reach the day when he stands, emotionally, toe-to-toe with his father and wins the slugging-out. That contest is as unavoidable as the ripening of an apple. It may last only a second—in which a young man says, "I will," and an older man says, "You will not," and the younger man does. And it is a struggle no youth can engage in, but only a youth who has reached full manhood. But if it occurs prematurely, as under mom's ruinous aegis it usually does, it leads to more serfdom for the boy. He is too young for independence. Thus the sixteen-year-old who tells his indignant dad that he, not dad, is going to have the car that night and takes it—while mom looks on, dewy-eyed and anxious—has sold his soul to mom and made himself into a lifelong sucking-egg. His father, already well up the creek, loses in this process the stick with which he had been trying to paddle. It is here that mom has thrust her oar into the very guts of man—and while she has made him think she is operating a gondola through the tunnels of love, and even believes it herself, she is actually taking tickets for the one-way ferry ride across the Styx.

As men grow older, they tend to become more like women, and vice versa. Even physically, their characteristics swap; men's voices rise, their breasts grow, and their chins recede; women develop bass voices and mustaches. This is another complementary, or opposite, turn of nature. It is meant to reconcile sexuality and provide a fountainhead of wisdom uncompromised by it, in the persons of those individuals who are hardy enough and lucky enough to survive to old age in a natural environment. But survival, as I have said, no longer depends on any sort of natural selection, excepting a great basic one which our brains are intended to deal with, and which, if allowed to go brainlessly on, will have to reduce our species to savagery in order to get back to a level on which instinct itself can rule effectively.

The mealy look of men today is the result of momism and so is the pinched and baffled fury in the eyes of womankind. I said a while ago that I had been a motherless minister's son and implied that I had been mauled by every type of mom produced in this nation. I pointed out that the situation was one on which the moms would try to fix their pincers. I did not bother to prod at any misgivings they might feel about what the rude minister's boy, trained in snoopery by the example of the moms, might have found out about the matriarchy and its motivations through hanging around sewing clubrooms, hiding in heavy draperies, and holing up in choir lofts. Rather, I let any moms and adherents of momism who may be reading this slug along in the happy belief that, whether or not *I* knew it, they had got me off base.

Now, really.

Some of the doting ones, ready to write off all I have said if I will only make up and shove myself back into the groove for them, are now about to be clipped—but good. For, by a second contumelious revelation, I have caught onto all of middle-aged, middle-class, earth-owning Mrs. America that I happened to miss in the portieres. Hold your seats, ladies. I have been a *clerk* in a *department store*. Not merely that, but I have been a clerk behind the dress goods remnant counter. And not only that, but I have served and observed the matriarchy from the vantage point during *sales*. If there is a woman still on her feet and not laughing, nab her, because that will mark her as a ringleader in this horrid business.

Much of the psychological material which got me studying this matter of moms came into my possession as I watched the flowerhatted goddesses battle over fabric. I have seen the rich and the poor, the well-dressed and the shabby, the educated and the unlettered, tear into the stacked remnants day after day, shoving and harassing, trampling each other's feet, knocking hats, coiffures and glasses awry, cackling, screaming, bellowing, and giving the elbow, without any differential of behavior no matter how you sliced them. I have watched them deliberately drive quiet clerks out of their heads and their jobs and heard them whoop over the success of the stratagem. I have seen them cheat and steal and lie and rage and whip and harry and stampede—not just a few times but week after week, and not just a few women but thousands and thousands and thousands, from everywhere. I know the magnitude of their rationalizing ability down to the last pale tint and I know the blackguard rapacity of them down to the last pennyworth.

I have, as a matter of confidential fact, twice beheld the extraordinary spectacle occasioned by two different pairs of rich and world-famous women who managed, in the morass the moms make of the remnant counter by ten o'clock each morning, to get hold of opposite ends of the same three and a half yards of Liberty crepe or dotted swiss and who found out that the object under scrutiny was also being considered by another. This I hold to be the Supreme Evidence.

In both cases both women were "merely looking," but immediately they sensed possible antagonism for what *might* be a purchase (though the statistics ran about five thousand to one against *that*) they began to struggle with the state most insufferable to momism: competition.

First, perhaps, a lifting of a lorgnette; then a cold stare; next, a reproachful glance at the clerk, and a refined but snappy little jerk designed to yank free the far end of the goods. Riposte: a fierce clutch and a facial response in kind. Next, the buttery attempt—the so-called "social" smile—like a valentine laced around an ice pick, and a few words, "I *beg* your pardon—but I—er—am *looking* at—this remnant." The wise clerk will now begin to search for the floorwalker and, in general, canvass his resources. (I would say, of course, that while I have seen only four renowned women engaged in this contretemps I have seen dozens of less distinguished moms hit the same jackpot.) The upper-class rejoinder to the foregoing gambit is, of course, "I'm quite sorry, but *I* happened to notice that *I* selected *this* piece quite some time before *you* picked up the *end* of it." At this point a hard yank is, of course, optional. But usually there come two simultaneous jerks which loosen hair, knock both hats askew, and set the costume jewelry clattering. The women now start toward each other, down the remnant, hand over hand. Bystanders are buffeted. All dress goods that cover the rope of cloth are flung about. The dialogue takes a turn to "I'll have to ask you to be good enough to let go of *my* material!" It rises in register to a near-scream. Upper lips begin to sweat. Chests heave. Elbows swing up to the ready.

Both women are now yelling at once and the tonal quality is like the sound of fingernails drawn along slates. They punctuate their words with loud cries of "Manager!" and begin to jostle each other. Peripheral moms, punched by accident in the aggression, now take up with each other a contagion of brawls and bickerings. The principles, meanwhile, have met knuckle to knuckle in the middle of the fabric and are yowling in each other's faces. Toward this the floorwalker or section manager moves cautiously. The thing has an almost invariable denouement. One woman stalks out of the store and closes her account by mail, only to open it within a matter of days. The other triumphantly purchases the draggled cloth, charges it, signs for it, bears it away, and has the truck pick it up the following afternoon.

I have been a clerk. Clerks are wallpaper to mom, and it has never occurred to her that she needs to hide her spurting soul from them. Clerks see moms in the raw—with their husbands, sons, daughters, nieces, nephews, gigolos, and companion viragoes. That anybody such as I, an articulate man with a memory like a tombstone, should be standing behind a counter conducting an inadvertent espionage on the moms has never entered their brawling brains. But there I was— and I was there, too, in the church, and at the manse. And I have hung around hospitals a lot—and insane asylums.

It can be pointed out—and has, indeed, been pointed out before, though not, so far as I know, by any chap who has had such diverse and intimate contacts with the moms as I—that they are taking over the male functions and interpreting those functions in female terms. When the mothers built up their pyramid of perquisite and required reverence in order to get at the checkbook, and so took over the schools (into which they have put gelding moms), churches, stores, and mass production (which included, of course, the railroads, boats, and airplanes and, through advertising, the radio and the magazines), they donned the breeches of Uncle Sam. To this inversion I shall refer again. Note it.

I have explained how the moms turned Cinderellaism to their advantage and I have explained that women possess some eighty per cent of the nation's money (the crystal form of its energy) and I need only allude, I think, to the statistical reviews which show that the women are the spenders, wherefore the controlling consumers of nearly all we make with our machines. The steel puddler in Pittsburgh may not think of himself as a feminine tool, but he is really only getting a Chevrolet ready for mom to drive through a garden wall. I should round out this picture of America existing for mom with one or two more details, such as annual increase in the depth of padding in vehicles over the past thirty years due to the fact that a fat rump is more easily irritated than a lean one, and the final essential detail of mom's main subjective pre-occupation, which is listening to the radio. The radio is mom's soul; a detail, indeed.[1]

It is also a book in itself, and one I would prefer to have my reader write after he has learned a little of the art of catching overtones as a trained ear, such as mine, catches them. But there must be a note on it.

The radio has made sentimentality the twentieth century Plymouth Rock. As a discipline, I have forced myself to sit a whole morning listening to the soap operas, along with twenty million moms who were busy sweeping dust under carpets while planning to drown their progeny in honey or bash in their heads. This filthy and indecent abomination, this trash with which, until lately, only moron servant girls could dull their credulous minds in the tawdry privacy of their cubicles, is now the national saga. Team after team of feeble-minded Annies and Davids crawl from the loudspeaker into the front rooms of America. The characters are impossible, their adventures would make a saint spew, their morals are lower than those of ghouls, their habits are uncleanly, their humor is the substance that starts whole races grinding bayonets, they have no manners, no sense, no goals, no worthy ambitions, no hope, no faith, no information, no values related to reality, and no estimate of truth. They merely sob and snicker—as they cheat each other.

Babies die every hour on the hour to jerk so many hundred gallons

---

1. In place of, "radio," of course, the alert reader will now automatically substitute "TV." He (or she) may do this, currently, with some such question as, "Is TV truly as dreadful as was radio?" Time will erase the optimistic doubt.

For a few years, and until mom's commerce saturated it entirely, radio made a feeble effort to undo some of our prodigious self-subversion. TV, being a new medium, still does as much—with furtive attempts to expose mom or Cinderella in a soap opera, with big exhibits of big men doing big things at the nation's Capitol, with courtroom trials, educational movie shorts, and such.

But give mom time.

She will not rest until every electronic moment has been bought to sell suds and every bought program censored to the last decibel and syllable according to her self-adulation—along with that (to the degree the mom-indoctrinated pops are permitted access to the dials) of her de-sexed, de-souled, de-cerebrated mate.

of tears. Cinderella kidnaps the Prince and then mortgages the palace
to hire herself a gigolo. The most oafish cluck the radio executives can
find, with a voice like a damp pillow—a mother-lover of the most degraded sort—is given to America as the ideal young husband. His wife,
with a tin voice and a heart of corrosive sublimate, alternately stands at
his side to abet some spiritual swindle or leaves him with a rival for as
much time as is needed to titillate mom without scaring her.

The radio is mom's final tool, for it stamps everybody who listens with
the matriarchal brand—its superstitions, prejudices, devotional rules,
taboos, musts, and all other qualifications needful to its maintenance.
Just as Goebbels has revealed what can be done with such a mass-
stamping of the public psyche in his nation, so our land is a living
representation of the same fact worked out in matriarchal sentimentality, goo, slop, hidden cruelty, and the foreshadow of national death.

That alone is sinister enough, but the process is still more vicious,
because it fills in every crack and cranny of mom's time and mind—
and pop's also, since he has long ago yielded the dial-privilege to his
female; so that a whole nation of people lives in eternal fugue and never
has to deal for one second with itself or its own problems. Any interior
sign of worry, wonder, speculation, anxiety, apprehension—or even a
stirring of an enfeebled will to plan sanely—can be annihilated by an
electric click whereby the populace puts itself in the place, the untenable place—of somebody called Myrt, for Christ's sake—and never has
even to try to *be* itself alone in the presence of this real world.

This is Nirvana at last. It is also entropy. For here the spirit of man,
absorbed, disoriented, confused, identified with ten thousand spurious
personalities and motives, has utterly lost itself. By this means is man
altogether lost. The radio, in very truth, sells soap. We could confine it
to music, intelligent discourse, and news—all other uses being dangerous
—but mom will not let us. Rather than study herself and her environment
with the necessary honesty, she will fight for this poisoned syrup to the
last. Rather than take up her democratic responsibility in this mighty
and tottering republic, she will bring it crashing down simply to maintain to the final rumble of ruin her personal feudalism. Once, sentimen-
talism was piecework, or cost the price of a movie or a book; now it is
mass produced and not merely free, but almost compulsory.

I give you mom. I give you the destroying mother. I give you her
justice—from which we have never removed the eye bandage. I give
you the angel—and point to the sword in her hand. I give you death—
the hundred million deaths that are muttered under Yggdrasill's ash. I
give you Medusa and Stheno and Euryale. I give you the harpies and
the witches, and the Fates. I give you the woman in pants, and the new
religion: she-popery. I give you Pandora. I give you Proserpine, the
Queen of Hell. The five-and-ten-cent-store Lilith, the mother of Cain,

the black widow who is poisonous and eats her mate, and I designate at
the bottom of your program the grand finale of all the soap operas: the
mother of America's Cinderella.

We must face the dynasty of the dames at once, deprive them of our
pocketbooks when they waste the substance in them, and take back our
dreams which, without the perfidious materialism of mom, were shaping
up a new and braver world. We must drive roads to Rio and to Moscow
and stop spending all our strength in the manufacture of girdles: it is
time that mom's sag became known to the desperate public; we must
plunge into our psyches and find out there, each for each, scientifically,
about immortality and miracles. To do such deeds, we will first have to
make the conquest of momism, which grew up from male default.

Our society is too much an institution built to appease the rapacity
of loving mothers. If that condition is an ineluctable experiment of
nature, then we are the victims of a failure. But I do not think it is. Even
while the regiments spell out "mom" on the parade grounds, I think
mom's grip can be broken by private integrity. Even though, indeed,
it is the moms who have made this war.

For, when the young men come back from the war, what then will
they feel concerning mom and her works?[2]

---

2. The young men never did come back from the war.
   They came back—but the war went on.
   This, mom decided was intolerable, and millions supported that repugnance. When some of the boys went forth anew to fight, the moms
and the mom-pinioned pops soon tore the government apart to get a truce
that brought not one day of peace.
   So the young men and the moms and pops decided that they had not
been fighting for freedom, after all, or against tyrants, after all.
   They decided they had been fighting, all that while, for security. They
had fought, not to save liberty, but for hot dogs, the corner drugstore, the
right to throw pop bottles at the umpire—and the girl next door, mom
briefly disguised as Cinderella.
   They have it all, now.
   Except Security.
   For that, too, they accepted a counterfeit: secrecy. But not one secret
remained undiscovered by the enemy. (The measures of security are—so
predictably!—specious.)
   Years passed. The young men and the moms and the pops grow ever
more fervent in their trust of security-through-secrecy. The ship of state
settles slowly and they bail with sieves, saying, "See? We float still."
   The enemy explodes uranium, plutonium, hydrogen; still they absurdly
cry, "Keep these things forever an American secret—for security's sweet
sake. Peace, peace, peace!"
   A great victory—for momish "thinking." For "love." The boys are
indeed—home.
   But where's man's freedom?

from *Lysistrata*

—Aristophanes

translated by Blanche Yurka

Aristophanes' comedy Lysistrata, written in the 5th century B. C., has as its central idea a sex strike by all the women of the warring Greek states. The women vow total abstinence from sex until the war stops; they also seize the state treasury. By these two moves, they deprive the men of what they value most: sex and money. The women, led by the outspoken and dynamic Lysistrata, eventually triumph; the play ends with a peace treaty followed by feasting, love-making, and dancing, all symbolizing the new harmony between men and women and between nation and nation. In this classic "Make love, not war" play, the procreative urge proves stronger than the destructive one.

Modern parallels to the Lysistrata situation may be seen in the women's groups organized in opposition to the Vietnam war. One such group is significantly named Women Strike for Peace; one of its founders echoed Lysistrata when she explained the purpose of WSP after a 1967 demonstration which began in front of Selective Service headquarters and moved to the White House: "We women have to mobilize our political strength.... We intend to use it in the coming elections, in which we will only vote for candidates who advocate peace. Politicians will now have to address themselves to women as a visible group." Another woman justified the demonstration in this way: "There wasn't a woman there whose husband or son or some man in her family hadn't been affected by this war and we have just had enough of it!" (National Guardian, September 30, 1967, pp. 1, 12). In the following excerpt, Lysistrata says essentially the same things to the Magistrate.

From *Three Classic Greek Plays*, Blanche Yurka, ed. Copyright © 1964 by Blanche Yurka. Reprinted by permission of Simon & Schuster, Inc.

Enter a MAGISTRATE

MAGISTRATE. What is going on here? What's happening in this town? The streets are swarming with crazy women, all coming in this direction! What's going on here, I say!

LEADER. It's the women—

ALL THE MEN. Those women! A whole mob of them, assembled in the citadel.

MAGISTRATE. How dare any group assemble without first notifying me? Why didn't you tell me?

LEADER. We came up first, to quell the incipient riot, your Honor. Then we were going to tell you about it. But you see what they've done to us.

DRACES. They've drenched us to the skin!

FIRST OLD WOMAN. We thought we'd water you so your beards could grow a bit!

MAGISTRATE. Silence, hag! Rioting? How dare anyone riot without my permission? What are those women doing up there anyway?

VERY OLD MAN. That's the riot, your Honor!

LEADER. The women have captured the citadel.

MAGISTRATE. Captured the citadel? Have you all gone mad? They can't invade the citadel!

LEADER. No, of course not!—But they have!

MAGISTRATE. By Castor! It's our own fault! We've pampered and spoiled them! Only yesterday I was saying to Aristophanes—or was it to Euripides?—"It's hell to live with them, and without them it's worse hell." They'll be using that in one of their plays, I'll wager! However, I have business to get on with here. I'm commissioned to draw on the war-fund—an order for new oar blades.

(He is stopped by two Spartan Women.)

Officers, drive those women out. Clear the citadel.

(Two Men ascend.)

WOMEN. Scat!

(The two Men retreat.)

LEADER. You see? There's nothing to be done with them!

MAGISTRATE. Nothing to be done? By all the Gods, man, you'd best think of something to be done! Officers, up with that battering ram! Forward, now, all together!

LYSISTRATA. *(entering).* Stand aside, you futile fools! You'll accomplish nothing with force. Try a little common sense!

MAGISTRATE. Seize that shameless vixen! Tie up her hands and her mouth! Above all, tie up her mouth! She's one of the chatty kind. Grab her, I say! Turn her upside down! Have at her!

LYSISTRATA. By Phosphor! If he so much as touches me, he'll get something he'll remember to the last day of his life!

MAGISTRATE. Silence, you! I've had enough of your insolence! Officers, didn't you hear me? Clear those women out!

LYSISTRATA. When it suits our good purpose to leave, we'll leave! Until then, call off your gaping fools.

MAGISTRATE. Your tongue wags too freely. Where is that officer? Don't you hear me? Seize her. Trip her up! Grab her waist, and tie her arms behind.

ALL OLD WOMEN. Lay a hand on her, and we'll comb your guts!

MAGISTRATE. Really! Such language! Officer, arrest those women, too. Their choice of words offends me!

SECOND OLD WOMAN. Have you surgeons somewhere handy? You'll be needing them!

MAGISTRATE. Now, all together, men—at 'em! We've had enough of their chatter!

LYSISTRATA. You don't know what you're asking for! Companies, 'tenshun! Vendors of grain and garlic, forward! Battalion of pulse and egg sellers, forward!

(Small groups advance.)

Cooks and keepers of bakeries, forward! Warriors—Attack!

(A battle ensues.)

DRACES. Holy Zeus! There are whole regiments of them!

MAGISTRATE. By Apollo and Poseidon, the Furies are let loose upon the world! Close up your ranks! Forward, men!

LEADER. Oh, what's the use of arguing with a lot of wild beasts! Why don't you find out what they want? As an officer of the law, it's certainly your duty to get to the bottom of this!

MAGISTRATE. Well, perhaps you're right! You, there! Come down, then, and parley. What's this silly disturbance about? Why have you dared occupy the Acropolis, shutting an authorized officer out? I want to know what is back of all this!

LYSISTRATA. There's much that you are going to learn, my friend. This is only the first step we're taking toward a new order of affairs. First, we're keeping the war-fund securely in custody. Henceforth, it's going to be handled by us.

MAGISTRATE. By you? Why?

LYSISTRATA. To keep the money safe, and shut off the supplies for war.

MAGISTRATE. And what's that for?

LYSISTRATA. That's to put an end to the war.

MAGISTRATE. Money, you think, then, is the cause of war?

LYSISTRATA. Of course. Without money, there could be no war-fund. No war-fund, no pickings for those in authority. But all that is over! The women will safeguard the treasury now!

MAGISTRATE. You? You'll be the treasurers?

LYSISTRATA. Yes. Why not? Statekeeping, like housekeeping, is a matter of domestic economy, isn't it?

MAGISTRATE. I don't see the resemblance. State funds are needed to carry on war.

LYSISTRATA. But since we've decided there is to be no more war—

MAGISTRATE. You've decided! You! You impudent hussies!

LYSISTRATA. My friend, heretofore the waging of war has always been considered to be the business of men. Now we've decided that the ending of war is the business of women!

CHORUS. The ending of war is the business of women!

MAGISTRATE. Delightful! And how, if it is not asking too much, are you proposing to do it? It's simple, I'm sure.

LYSISTRATA. Simple as truth—or as Barter and Sale, and that at least you should be able to understand! Stop fuming and fussing. Sit down and I'll tell you.

MAGISTRATE. I'll not sit down!

(Two Women push him down.)

LYSISTRATA. For one thing, we'll put a stop to all this parading around in uniforms, this stamping about the market place in shield and spurs and helmet, all to buy a bowl of pea soup, or a dish of steaming eels! Then—do you happen to know how we women card the wool?

MAGISTRATE. Wool—! What has wool to do with the running of the State?

LYSISTRATA. More than you think. You see, first we cleanse the wool, washing away all the dirt and the dust. Just so, must your worthless citizens be eliminated from the State: political parasites, grafters, leeches, and thieves—they must be sorted out and discarded, like the clots of the wool. Then, when the clean wool is ready for weaving, we gather in all the loose threads: the worthy citizens of the various cities, colonies. . . . Attach all these threads to the center— that's Athens . . . twine them together in strands of good fellowship, and thus weave a garment of strength and endurance, to be worn by the people with comfort and dignity.

MAGISTRATE. *(contemptuously).* And so, with your wool and your weaving, you'd reform the State and you'd end the war! You witless women, who know nothing of its hardships, its horrors!

LYSISTRATA. *We* know nothing of war? We, who silently suffer its most heartbreaking woes; whose wombs bear the burden of giving you sons? We, who face death gladly each time we bring forth life, only to have you again dedicate it to death?

MAGISTRATE. *(rising).* Silence! Those are necessary evils. The waging of war is a citizen's sacred duty!

LYSISTRATA. And *why* is war so sacred, so necessary? Do you even re-

member what you first began fighting for? For twenty years Greece
has been a vast armed battlefield. Which of you can even tell me
what started the war? And no matter how it started, can you not see
that there can be no real victory at the price we are all paying?
Even the maddest war-worshipper must now count the cost! I tell
you, a little more of this madness, and we face annihilation!

MAGISTRATE. Subversive propaganda! You're a radical—you could be
hanged for such talk!

LYSISTRATA. Is it not time, my friend, that someone risked that? Your
soldiers take the risks of war, someone must take the risk for peace!
You've fed us on false hope, on the thrill of martial music and the
glitter and glamour of soldiers' armour. Is it not our duty as women
to face the facts?

MAGISTRATE. Your first duty, as women, is to propagate the race!

LYSISTRATA. Yes, and what of the waste of glorious womanhood passing,
lonely, loveless, into barren futility—the May morning of life, fading
into its Autumn with never a Summer of blooming at all? The wine
of life, souring—the sap running dry—even that can be borne when
we've had our fulfillment. But what of the maidens whose girlhood
must vanish, never, perhaps, having flowered into womanhood?

FOURTH OLD MAN. Men, one would think, have their youth everlastingly?

LYSISTRATA. No. But it isn't the same with a man. Grizzled he may be—
and scarred—maimed, yes, war torn; still, if he wishes to marry,
he can. But girlhood is brief: the Spring is soon over; once it slips
by, it comes never again.

MAGISTRATE. These are all matters that cannot be helped. After all, war
is war!

LYSISTRATA. And how long will war be war, if we give you no more
soldiers?

MAGISTRATE. By all the Gods, that's treason! Arrant treason!

LYSISTRATA. So that is treason? But what of the treason of you and your
kind, who fatten and grow rich by fertilizing our land with human
flesh and blood and tears? Flesh of our flesh, blood of our blood,
and tears of our shedding! You stand in the Senate and vote for
more soldiers, but the young men you send out to die are the children we bore, to whom we gave our strength and our youth. And
when their bodies lie buried in strange lands, a part of us lies buried
there! You and your kind have bled the nation white—until now
there's scarce a man left in Athens fit to carry a sword. But still
your cry is "War! War!" You know no language other than the
clanking of the saber and the slaughter of the spear. But a new voice
has been raised in the land, and it speaks the language of all
womankind. Hear ye, masters of this war-sick world. We'll breed
no more sons until this senseless, iniquitous slaughter has stopped!

MAGISTRATE. You'll breed no more sons! And you expect me to take seriously threats like that, from frivolous creatures like you and these? Just wait until the next truce, when the young men come home!

DRACES. Besides, even old men are often hearty enough to—er—

SPARTAN WOMAN. Silence, old reprobate!

DRACES. Silence for you? For an impudent female?

MAGISTRATE. We're to take orders from a wench draped in veils?

LYSISTRATA. Here, then, take it and wear it, and bury your nose in it.

> *(She throws one of her veils about his head and whirls him until he staggers.)*

VARIOUS WOMEN. We'll get you a spindle!

A basket as well!

Cook the stew!

Card the wool!

Sweep the hearth!

Do the marketing!

LYSISTRATA. We'll handle the State in our own sweet way!

CHORUS. Yes, we'll run the whole State in our own sweet way!

MAGISTRATE. Harlots! She-devils!

The Eternal Feminine

All myths are a product of the interchange between man's mind and his environment. The concept of "The Eternal Feminine" evolved from the agrarian myths of the Great Mother. It has always involved feelings of ambivalence towards the female and often includes some of the same characteristics as the Woman-as-Object and -Enemy syndromes. Woman is worshipped, respected, but feared for the powers which seem to link her to the mysterious spheres unknown to man. When primitive man plowed his fields and his woman and noticed that they both bore fruit, he saw woman and earth as embodying productive powers. His reaction to this observation included wonder and envy and fear.

A good source book for the myths of the eternal feminine in ancient cultures is Robert Graves' *The White Goddess* (New York: Vintage Books, 1958). Sir James George Frazer's *The Golden Bough: A Study in Magic and Religion* (New York: The Macmillan Co., 1958) provides extensive information on the vegetation myths.

The eternal feminine appears in many places throughout the history of Western thought. Among them: the intellectual form of Philosophy to Boethius; the pristine innocence of Beatrice to Dante; the political and moral force of the Faerie Queene to Spenser; the ambivalent illusion of Gretchen to Goethe's Faust; the life force to George Bernard Shaw (see *Candida, Man and Superman*); and the peasant earth mother in Willa Cather's *My Antonia* and William Faulkner's Lena of *Light in August*. Modern film versions include the earthy but sophisticated peasant form of Sophia Loren and the less subtle and decidedly more plastic model of Raquel Welch.

Whatever the changes in mythical and artistic renderings of the eternal feminine, there is one constant: Men imagine her able to endure and overcome whatever confronts her.

The Goddess

—Apuleius

translated by William Aldington (1566)

In this passage from The Golden Ass (written in the 2nd century, A.D.) Lucius invokes the invincible goddess to aid him in his time of spiritual degradation. He sees the feminine spirit as an all-pervasive life force, a deliverer and protector of man that incorporates the power of many feminine myths: Juno, queen of heaven; Ceres, giver of food; Venus, giver of love; Diana, the healer (like St. Margaret she assuages the pain of childbirth); Proserpine, power over underground spirits. She is giver of light, of nourishing growth, and of peace. She answers his plea and offers to give him a blessed life and immortality if he will be bound absolutely in her service.

About the first watch of the night, when as I had slept my first sleep, I awaked with sudden fear, and saw the moon shining bright as when she is at the full, and seeming as though she leaped out of the sea. Then I thought with myself that this was the most secret time, when that goddess had most puissance and force, considering that all human things be governed by her providence; and that not only all beasts private and tame, wild and savage, be made strong by the governance of her light and god-head, but also things inanimate and without life; and I considered that all bodies in the heavens, the earth, and the seas be by her increasing motions increased, and by her diminishing motions diminished: then as weary of all my cruel fortune and calamity, I found good hope and sovereign remedy, though it were very late, to be delivered of all my misery, by invocation and prayer to the excellent beauty of this powerful goddess. Wherefore shaking off my drowsy sleep I arose with a joyful face, and moved by a great affection to purify myself, I plunged my head seven times into the water of the sea; which number

From Apuleius, *The Golden Ass*, Book XI, pp. 539–547, translated by W. Adlington, revised by S. Gaselee, 1915. Reprinted by permission of the Harvard University Press and THE LOEB CLASSICAL LIBRARY.

of seven is convenable and agreeable to holy and divine things, as the worthy and sage philosopher Pythagoras hath declared. Then very lively and joyfuly, though with a weeping countenance, I made this oration to the puissant goddess:

"O blessed queen of heaven, whether Thou be the Dame Ceres which art the original and motherly nurse of all fruitful things in the earth, who, after the finding of Thy daughter Proserpine, through the great joy which Thou didst presently conceive, didst utterly take away and abolish the food of them of old time, the acorn, and madest the barren and unfruitful ground of Eleusis to be ploughed and sown, and now givest men a more better and milder food; or whether Thou be the celestial Venus, who, in the beginning of the world, didst couple together male and female with an engendered love, and didst so make an eternal propagation of human kind, being now worshipped within the temples of the Isle Paphos; or whether Thou be the sister of the god Phoebus, who hast saved so many people by lightening and lessening with thy medicines the pangs of travail and art now adored at the sacred places of Ephesus; or whether Thou be called terrible Proserpine, by reason of the deadly howlings which Thou yieldest, that hast power with triple face to stop and put away the invasion of hags and ghosts which appear unto men, and to keep them down in the closures of the Earth, which dost wander in sundry groves and art worshipped in divers manners; Thou, which dost luminate all the cities of the earth by Thy feminine light; Thou, which nourishest all the seeds of the world by Thy damp heat, giving Thy changing light according to the wanderings, near or far, of the sun: by whatsoever name or fashion or shape it is lawful to call upon Thee, I pray Thee to end my great travail and misery and raise up my fallen hopes, and deliver me from the wretched fortune which so long time pursued me. Grant peace and rest, if it please Thee, to my adversities, for I have endured enough labour and peril. Remove from me the hateful shape of mine ass, and render me to my kindred and to mine own self Lucius: and if I have offended in any point Thy divine majesty, let me rather die if I may not live."

When I had ended this oration, discovering my plaints to the goddess, I fortuned to fall again asleep upon that same bed; and by and by (for mine eyes were but newly closed) appeared to me from the midst of the sea a divine and venerable face, worshipped even of the gods themselves. Then, by little and little, I seemed to see the whole figure of her body, bright and mounting out of the sea and standing before me: wherefore I purpose to describe her divine semblance, if the poverty of my human speech will suffer me, or her divine power give me a power of eloquence rich enough to express it. First she had a great abundance of hair, flowing and curling, dispersed and scattered about her divine neck; on the crown of her head she bare many garlands interlaced with flowers, and in the middle of her forehead was a plain circlet in fashion of a mirror, or rather resembling the moon by the light that it gave forth; and this was borne up on either side by serpents that seemed to rise from the furrows of the earth, and above it were blades of corn set out. Her vestment was of finest linen yielding divers colours, somewhere white and shining, somewhere yellow like the crocus flower, somewhere rosy red, somewhere flaming; and (which troubled my sight and spirit sore) her cloak was utterly dark and obscure covered with shining black, and being wrapped round her from under her left arm to her right shoulder in manner of a shield, part of it fell down, pleated in most subtle fashion, to the skirts of her garment so that the welts appeared comely. Here and there upon the edge thereof and throughout its surface the stars glimpsed, and in the middle of them was placed the moon in mid-month, which shone like a flame of fire; and round about the whole length of the border of that goodly robe was a crown or garland wreathing unbroken, made with all flowers and all fruits. Things quite diverse did she bear: for in her right hand she had a timbrel of brass, a flat piece of metal curved in manner of a girdle, wherein passed not many rods through the periphery of it; and when with her arm she moved these triple chords, they gave forth a shrill and clear sound. In her left hand she bare a cup of gold like unto a boat, upon the handle whereof, in the upper part which is best seen, an asp lifted up his head with a wide-swelling throat. Her odoriferous feet were covered with shoes interlaced and wrought with victorious palm. Thus the divine shape, breathing out the pleasant spice of fertile Arabia, disdained not with her holy voice to utter these words unto me:

"Behold, Lucius, I am come; thy weeping and prayer hath moved me to succour thee. I am she that is the natural mother of all things, mistress and governess of all the elements, the intitial progeny of worlds, chief of the powers divine, queen of all that are in hell, the principal of them that dwell in heaven, manifested alone and under one form of all the gods and goddesses. At my will the planets of the sky, the wholesome winds of the seas, and the lamentable silences of hell be disposed; my name, my divinity is adored throughout all the world, in divers manners, in variable customs, and by many names. For the Phrygians that are the first of all men call me the Mother of the gods at Pessinus; the Athenians, which are sprung from their own soil, Cecropian Minerva; the Cyprians, which are girt about by the sea, Paphian Venus; the Cretans which bear arrows, Dictynnian Diana; the Sicilians, which speak three tongues, infernal Proserpine; the Eleusians their ancient goddess Ceres; some Juno, other Bellona, other Hecate, other Rhamnusia, and principally both sort of the Ethiopians which dwell in the Orient and are enlightened by the morning rays of the sun, and the Egyptians, which are excellent in all kind of ancient doctrine, and by their proper ceremonies accustom to worship me, do call me by my true name, Queen Isis. Behold I am come to take pity of thy fortune and tribulation; behold I am present to favour and aid thee; leave off thy weeping and lamentation, put away all thy sorrow, for behold the healthful day which is ordained by my providence.

True Woman—Herself

Dante Gabriel Rossetti

This poem from Rossetti's sonnet sequence, The House of Life, *views "True Woman" as both beautiful object and sacred mystery. To Rossetti, woman's sweetness and exotic beauty hide the "sacred secret" of her pure and lovely soul. Rossetti idolized beautiful woman ("stunners," he called them), using them as models and as mistresses. His wife, Elizabeth Siddal, died from an overdose of laudanum (tincture of opium), a drug used to ease pain. As a sentimental gesture, Rossetti buried his poems with "Lizzie." Several years later he decided to publish his works and exhumed both.*

To be a sweetness more desired than Spring;
A bodily beauty more acceptable
Than the wild rose-tree's arch that crowns the fell;
To be an essence more environing
Than wine's drained juice; a music ravishing
More than the passionate pulse of Philomel:
To be all this 'neath one soft bosom's swell
That is the flower of life:—how strange a thing!
How strange a thing to be what Man can know
But as a sacred secret! Heaven's own screen
Hides her soul's purest depth and loveliest glow;
Closely withheld, as all things most unseen,—
The wave-bowered pearl,—the heart-shaped seal of green
That flecks the snowdrop underneath the snow.

from *Riders to the Sea*

John Millington Synge

Riders to the Sea, *by the Irish playwright John Millington Synge, dramatizes the hard life of seafaring folk in an island fishing village. The play focuses on the suffering of the women who are left at home grieving as sons, husbands, and fathers are inevitably destroyed by the cruel sea. At the beginning of the play, the body of Maurya's son Michael has just been found in the far north, and Maurya has only one son, Bartley, left. Now Bartley has also gone to sea, and Maurya, in bidding him good-bye, has seen a vision of the dead son Michael riding on a gray pony after him. At this point, the women begin to keen.*

CATHLEEN [*begins to keen*]. It's destroyed we are from this day. It's destroyed, surely.

NORA. Didn't the young priest say the Almighty God wouldn't leave her destitute with no son living?

MAURYA [*in a low voice, but clearly*]. It's little the like of him knows of the sea. . . . Bartley will be lost now, and let you call in Eamon and make me a good coffin out of the white boards, for I won't live after them. I've had a husband, and a husband's father, and six sons in this house—six fine men, though it was a hard birth I had with every one of them and they coming to the world—and some of them were found and some of them were not found, but they're gone now the lot of them. . . . There were Stephen, and Shawn, were lost in the great wind, and found after in the Bay of Gregory of the Golden Mouth, and carried up the two of them on the one plank, and in by that door.

From *Riders to the Sea*, in *The Complete Works of John M. Synge*, Random House, Inc.

[*She pauses for a moment, the girls start as if they heard something through the door that is half open behind them.*]

NORA [*in a whisper*]. Did you hear that, Cathleen? Did you hear a noise in the north-east?

CATHLEEN. [*in a whisper*]. There's some one after crying out by the seashore.

MAURYA [*continues without hearing anything*].There was Sheamus and his father, and his own father again, were lost in a dark night, and not a stick or sign was seen of them when the sun went up. There was Patch after was drowned out of a curagh that turned over. I was sitting here with Bartley, and he a baby, lying on my two knees, and I seen two women, and three women, and four women coming in, and they crossing themselves, and not saying a word. I looked out then, and there were men coming after them, and they holding a thing in the half of a red sail, and water dripping out of it—it was a dry day, Nora—and leaving a track to the door.

[*She pauses again with her hand stretched out towards the door. It opens softly and old women begin to come in, crossing themselves on the threshold, and kneeling down in front of the stage with red petticoats over their heads.*]

MAURYA [*half in a dream, to Cathleen*]. Is it Patch, or Michael, or what is it at all?

CATHLEEN. Michael is after being found in the far north, and when he is found there how could he be here in this place?

MAURYA. There does be a power of young men floating round in the sea, and what way would they know if it was Michael they had, or another man like him, for when a man is nine days in the sea, and the wind blowing, it's hard set his own mother would be to say what man was it.

CATHLEEN. It's Michael, God spare him, for they're after sending us a bit of his clothes from the far north.

[*She reaches out and hands Maurya the clothes that belonged to Michael. Maurya stands up slowly and takes them in her hands. Nora looks out.*]

NORA. They're carrying a thing among them and there's water dripping out of it and leaving a track by the big stones.

CATHLEEN [*in a whisper to the women who have come in*]. Is it Bartley it is?

ONE OF THE WOMEN. It is surely, God rest his soul.

[*Two younger women come in and pull out the table. Then men carry in the body of Bartley, laid on a plank, with a bit of a sail over it, and lay it on the table.*]

CATHLEEN [*to the women, as they are doing so*]. What way was he drowned?

ONE OF THE WOMEN. The gray pony knocked him into the sea, and he

was washed out where there is a great surf on the white rocks.
[*Maurya has gone over and knelt down at the head of the table.
The women are keening softly and swaying themselves with a
slow movement Cathleen and Nora kneel at the other end of
the table. The men kneel near the door.*]
MAURYA [*raising her head and speaking as if she did not see the people
around her*]. They're all gone now, and there isn't anything more the
sea can do to me. . . . I'll have no call now to be up crying and praying
when the wind breaks from the south, and you can hear the surf is in
the east, and the surf is in the west, making a great stir with the two
noises, and they hitting one on the other. I'll have no call now to be
going down and getting Holy Water in the dark nights after Samhain,
and I won't care what way the sea is when the other women will be
keening. [*To Nora.*] Give me the Holy Water, Nora, there's a small sup
still on the dresser.
[*Nora gives it to her.*]
MAURYA [*drops Michael's clothes across Bartley's feet, and sprinkles
the Holy Water over him*]. It isn't that I haven't prayed for you, Bartley,
to the Almighty God. It isn't that I haven't said prayers in the dark night
till you wouldn't know what I'ld be saying; but it's a great rest I'll have
now, and great sleeping in the long nights after Samhain, if it's only a
bit of wet flour we do have to eat, and maybe a fish that would be
stinking.
[*She kneels down again, crossing herself, and saying prayers
under her breath.*]
CATHLEEN [*to an old man*]. Maybe yourself and Eamon would make a
coffin when the sun rises. We have fine white boards herself bought,
Gold help her, thinking Michael would be found, and I have a new cake
you can eat while you'll be working.
THE OLD MAN [*looking at the boards*]. Are there nails with them?
CATHLEEN. There are not, Colum; we didn't think of the nails.
ANOTHER MAN. It's a great wonder she wouldn't think of the nails, and all
the coffins she's seen made already.
CATHLEEN. It's getting old she is, and broken.
[*Maurya stands up again very slowly and spreads out the pieces
of Michael's clothes beside the body, sprinkling them with the
last of the Holy Water.*]
NORA [*in a whisper to Cathleen*]. She's quiet now and easy; but the day
Michael was drowned you could hear her crying out from this to the
spring well. It's fonder she was of Michael, and would any one have
thought that?
CATHLEEN [*slowly and clearly*]. An old woman will be soon tired with
anything she will do, and isn't it nine days herself is after crying and
keening, and making great sorrow in the house?

MAURYA [*puts the empty cup mouth downwards on the table, and lays her hands together on Bartley's feet*]. They're all together this time, and the end is come. May the Almighty God have mercy on Bartley's soul, and on Michael's soul, and on the souls of Sheamus and Patch, and Stephen and Shawn [*bending her head*]; and may He have mercy on my soul, Nora, and on the soul of every one is left living in the world. [*She pauses, and the keen rises a little more loudly from the women, then sinks away.*]

MAURYA [*continuing*]. Michael has a clean burial in the far north, by the grace of the Almighty God. Bartley will have a fine coffin out of the white boards, and a deep grave surely. What more can we want than that? No man at all can be living for ever, and we must be satisfied. [*She kneels down again and the curtain falls slowly.*]

Three Poems

Robert Graves

The poems of Robert Graves often reflect the eerie ambivalence toward women typical of his book, The White Goddess.

The Three-Faced

Who calls her two-faced? Faces, she has three:
The first inscrutable, for the outer world;
The second shrouded in self-contemplation;
The third, her face of love,
Once for an endless moment turned on me.

Between Trains

Arguing over coffee at the station,
Neither of us noticed her dark beauty,
Though she sat close by, until suddenly

Three casual words—does it matter what they were?—
Spoken without remarkable intonation
Or accent, so bewildered him and me,
As it were catching the breath of our conversation,
That each set down his coffee-cup, to stare.
'You have come for us?' my lips cautiously framed—
Her eyes were almost brighter than I could bear—
But she rose and left, unready to be named.

At Best, Poets

Woman with her forests, moons, flowers, waters,
And watchful fingers:
We claim no magic comparable to hers—
At best, poets; at worst, sorcerers.

Karintha

Jean Toomer

The first section of Jean Toomer's Cane *is a eulogy to the black beauty and perfection of Karintha, a young woman who embodies the spirit of life, color, and song. Inspiring voluptuous dreams in young and old, her innocence and youth are destroyed because "the soul of her was a growing thing ripened too soon."* Cane *contains other memorable portraits of beautiful, strong, and soul-stirring women.*

Her skin is like dusk on the eastern horizon,
O cant you see it, O cant you see it,
Her skin is like dusk on the eastern horizon
. . . When the sun goes down.

Men had always wanted her, this Karintha, even as a child, Karintha carrying beauty, perfect as dusk when the sun goes down. Old men rode her hobby-horse upon their knees. Young men danced with her at frolics when they should have been dancing with their grown-up girls. God grant us youth, secretly prayed the old men. The young fellows counted the time to pass before she would be old enough to mate with them. This interest of the male, who wishes to ripen a growing thing too soon, could mean no good to her.

Karintha, at twelve, was a wild flash that told the other folks just what it was to live. At sunset, when there was no wind, and the pine-smoke from over by the sawmill hugged the earth, and you couldnt see more than a few feet in front, her sudden darting past you was a bit of vivid color, like a black bird that flashes in light. With the other children one could hear, some distance off, their feet flopping in the two-inch dust. Karintha's running was a whir. It had the sound of the red dust that sometimes makes a spiral in the road. At dusk, during the hush just after the sawmill had closed down, and before any of the women had started their supper-getting-ready songs, her voice, high-pitched, shrill, would put one's ears to itching. But no one ever thought to make her stop because of it. She stoned the cows, and beat her dog, and fought the other children... Even the preacher, who caught her at mischief, told himself that she was as innocently lovely as a November cotton flower. Already, rumors were out about her. Homes in Georgia are most often built on the two-room plan. In one, you cook and eat, in the other you sleep, and there love goes on. Karintha had seen or heard, perhaps she had felt her parents loving. One could but imitate one's parents, for to follow them was the way of God. She played "home" with a small boy who was not afraid to do her bidding. That started the whole thing. Old men could no longer ride her hobby-horse upon their knees. But young men counted faster.

> Her skin is like dusk,
> O cant you see it,
> Her skin is like dusk,
> When the sun goes down.

Karintha is a woman. She who carries beauty, perfect as dusk when the sun goes down. She has been married many times. Old men remind her that a few years back they rode her hobby-horse upon their knees. Karintha smiles, and indulges them when she is in the mood for it. She has contempt for them. Karintha is a woman. Young men run stills to make her money. Young men go to the big cities and run on the road. Young men go away to college. They all want to bring her money.

These are the young men who thought that all they had to do was to count time. But Karintha is a woman, and she has had a child. A child fell out of her womb onto a bed of pine-needles in the forest. Pine-needles are smooth and sweet. They are elastic to the feet of rabbits. . . A sawmill was nearby. Its pyramidal sawdust pile smouldered. It is a year before one completely burns. Meanwhile, the smoke curls up and hangs in odd wraiths about the trees, curls up, and spreads itself out over the valley. . . Weeks after Karintha returned home the smoke was so heavy you tasted it in water. Some one made a song:

> Smoke is on the hills. Rise up.
> Smoke is on the hills, O rise
> And take my soul to Jesus.

Karintha is a woman. Men do not know that the soul of her was a growing thing ripened too soon. They will bring their money; they will die not having found it out. . . Karintha at twenty, carrying beauty, perfect as dusk when the sun goes down. Karintha. . .

> Her skin is like dusk on the eastern horizon,
> O cant you see it, O cant you see it,
> Her skin is like dusk on the eastern horizon
> . . . When the sun goes down.

> Goes down. . .

Rembrandt. *Bathsheba at her Toilet.* 1654.
Miró. *Nude with Looking Glass.* 1919.
In Western painting there are literally thousands of studies
of the female nude, and relatively few of the male. These
paintings by Rembrandt and Joan Miró reflect the consistent
preoccupation of male artists with the idealization of women
as languid objects of pleasure who spend their time with
mirrors, baths, and toilets.

Head of Nefertiti. (18th Dynasty—14th century B.C.)
For centuries students of art have admired the idealized beauty of Nefertiti; however, in the name of Beauty, her hair was shaved from her head and her eyebrows plucked one by one. Presumably Nefertiti found these minor inconveniences worthwhile.

Profile of a Black Women. 1970.
The elegant beauty and regal bearing of Queen Nefertiti finds a modern equivalent in this profile of a black woman.

MESSALINA.

Beardsley. *Messalina Returning from Her Bath.*
Aubrey Beardsley's drawing of Messalina, empress of decadent Rome (d. A.D. 48), emphasizes her sullen determination and aggressive evil. Many of Beardsley's works show woman as grotesque and vile.

de Kooning. *Woman I*. 1950-52.
The view of Woman-as-Enemy is frighteningly portrayed in Willem de Kooning's
Woman I.

Mother Goddess from Ur. Second millennium B.C.
(University Museum, Philadelphia)
This Babylonian statue reflects the ancient reverence for the ideal of eternal motherhood, an image which unites the fixed earth-bound status of women to eternal reproduction, i.e., to the permanence of man.

Raphael. *The Small Cowper Madonna.* c. 1505.
Christian art portrays the mother goddess in the many renderings of the Madonna and Child, as in Raphael's famous *Small Cowper Madonna.* The picture brings to mind Bernard Shaw's comment about another of Raphael's madonnas: (she is) "the ideal wet nurse, healthy, comely, and completely brainless."

Erwitt. *Birth.*
Motherhood is idealized in Elliot Erwitt's picture of a resting pregnant woman. Here the equation between the kitten and the woman is inescapable: they are cute, soft, and cuddly.

Millet. *The Gleaners.* 1857.
Jean-François Millet is noted for his muted depiction of the noble humility of peasant life. In *The Gleaners*, he represents in sculptured figures farm women at work. Their job is to go through the fields after the harvest to pick up the leftover grain.

Rossetti. *Beata Beatrix.* 1863.
Dante Gabriel Rossetti's vision of the divine Beatrice reflects a worship of womankind as spiritual as well as physical beauty. The model was Elizabeth Siddal, Rossetti's wife; the picture was painted soon after her death. For a poetic rendering of the same attitude, see Rossetti's poem, "True Woman—Herself."

Egg. *Past and Present:I*. 1858.
  Past and Present: III. 1858.
The faithless wife is the subject of Augustus Leopold Egg's series of three paintings entitled *Past and Present*. In the first picture, the man sits grim and morally
superior after confronting his wife, who lies degraded and distraught on the floor.
The last picture shows her horrible fate: she has been driven from her home,
severed from her husband and children, and is a homeless mother of an illegitimate child.

Part Two:

The Nature of Woman

Who Is She?

Little is known about the nature of woman. Though millions of books exist anatomizing her body, her mind, and her soul, most of these books iterate and reiterate traditional views. Virginia Woolf tells of a trip to the British Museum to research the subject of women in preparation for *A Room of One's Own*; there she discovered that men have written copiously about women, but that their writings reflect the values of a male-dominated society in which women are used to enlarge male egos. She detected in their works a sense of anger mixed "with all kinds of other emotions." The selections in this section are innovative in that they try to break through the emotional and culturally conditioned male hypotheses about woman's intellectual, political, economic, biological, and psychological nature.

from *The Subjection*
of Women

John Stuart Mill

An important document in the history of Women's Liberation is John Stuart Mill's The Subjection of Women *(1869). Mill pleads for an end to the legal subordination of women to men, arguing on grounds of both expediency and justice. In his opening chapters, Mill develops an analogy between the status of women and the institution of slavery, pointing out that, under existing laws, a woman lives with her master, "with no means of combining against him, no power of even locally overmastering him, and, on the other hand, with the strongest motives for seeking his favour and avoiding to give him offence." She lives, Mill says, "in a chronic state of bribery and intimidation combined," with her real character "distorted and disguised." Unlike the black slave, she cannot escape to her own life when she is off duty. Furthermore, society educates her to her submissive role, thus enslaving her mind as well as her body.*

The following excerpt from Chapter III argues that women be given the vote and equal employment opportunities. Mill finds that intellectual differences between men and women derive from social, not natural, causes and that, until women are provided with equal education, their intellectual and creative capacity will remain unknown and society will continue to suffer the waste of one-half of its brain power. He concludes his historic work with the observation that "The moral regeneration of mankind will only really commence, when the most fundamental of the social relations is placed under the rule of equal justice."

From *The Subjection of Women*—John Stuart Mill. Everyman's Library. Published by E. P. Dutton & Co., Inc. and reprinted with their permission. And reprinted by permisson of J. M. Dent & Sons Ltd.

On the other point which is involved in the just equality of women, their admissibility to all the functions and occupations hitherto retained as the monopoly of the stronger sex, I should anticipate no difficulty in convincing anyone who has gone with me on the subject of the equality of women in the family. I believe that their (women's) disabilities elsewhere are only clung to in order to maintain their subordination in domestic life; because the generality of the male sex cannot yet tolerate the idea of living with an equal. Were it not for that, I think that almost everyone, in the existing state of opinion in politics and political economy, would admit the injustice of excluding half the human race from the greater number of lucrative occupations, and from almost all high social functions; ordaining from their birth either that they are not, and cannot by any possibility become, fit for employments which are legally open to the stupidest and basest of the other sex, or else that however fit they may be, those employments shall be interdicted to them, in order to be preserved for the exclusive benefit of males. In the last two centuries, when (which was seldom the case) any reason beyond the mere existence of the fact was thought to be required to justify the disabilities of women, people seldom assigned as a reason their inferior mental capacity; which, in times when there was a real trial of personal faculties (from which all women were not excluded) in the struggles of public life, no one really believed in. The reason given in those days was not women's unfitness, but the interest of society, by which was meant the interest of men: just as the *raison d'état*, meaning the convenience of the government, and the support of existing authority, was deemed a sufficient explanation and excuse for the most flagitious crimes. In the present day, power holds a smoother language, and whomsoever it oppresses, always pretends to do so for their own good: accordingly, when anything is forbidden to women, it is thought necessary to say, and desirable to believe, that they are incapable of doing it, and that they depart from their real path of success and happiness when they aspire to it. But to make this reason plausible (I do not say valid), those by whom it is urged must be prepared to carry it to a much gerater length than anyone ventures to do in the face of present experience. It is not sufficient to maintain that women on the average are less gifted then men on the average, with certain of the higher mental faculties, or that a smaller number of women than of men are fit for occupations and functions of the highest intellectual character. It is necessary to maintain that no women at all are fit for them, and that the most eminent women are inferior in mental faculties to the most mediocre of the men on whom those functions at present devolve. For if the performance of the function is decided either by competition, or by any mode of choice which secures regard to the public interest, there needs be no apprehension that any important employments will fall into the hands of women inferior to average men, or to the average of their male competitors. The only result would be that there would be fewer women than men in such employments; a result certain to happen in any case, if only from the preference always likely to be felt by the majority of women for the one vocation in which there is nobody to compete with them. Now, the most determined depreciator of women will not venture to deny, that when we add the experience of recent times to that of ages past, women, and not a few merely, but many women, have proved themselves capable of everything, perhaps without a single exception, which is done by men, and of doing it successfully and creditably. The utmost that can be said is, that there are many things which none of them have succeeded in doing as well as they have been done by some men—many in which they have not reached the very highest rank. But there are extremely few, dependent only on mental faculties, in which they have not attained the rank next to the highest. Is not this enough, and much more than enough, to make it a tyranny to them, and a detriment to society, that they should not be allowed to compete with men for the exercise of these functions? Is it not a mere truism to say, that such functions are often filled by men far less fit for them than numbers of women, and who would be beaten by women in any fair field of competition? What difference does it make that there may be men somewhere, fully employed about other things, who may be still better qualified for the things in question than these women? Does not this take place in all competitions? Is there so great a superfluity of men fit for high duties, that society can afford to reject the service of any competent person? Are we so certain of always finding a man made to our hands for any duty or function of social importance which falls vacant, that we lose nothing by putting a ban upon one half of mankind, and refusing beforehand to make their faculties available, however distinguished they may be? And even if we could do without them, would it be consistent with justice to refuse to them their fair share of honour and distinction, or to deny to them the equal moral right of all human beings to choose their occupation (short of injury to others) according to their own preferences, at their own risk? Nor is the injustice confined to them: it is shared by those who are in a position to benefit by their services. To ordain that any kind of persons shall not be physicians, or shall not be advocates, or shall not be Members of Parliament, is to injure not them only, but all who employ physicians or advocates, or elect Members of Parliament, and who are deprived of the stimulating effect of greater competition on the exertions of the competitors, as well as restricted to a narrower range of individual choice.

It will perhaps be sufficient if I confine myself, in the details of my argument, to functions of a public nature: since, if I am successful as to those, it probably will be readily granted that women should be admissible to all other occupations to which it is at all material whether they are admitted or not. And here let me begin by marking out one function, broadly distinguished from all others, their right to which is entirely independent of any question which can be raised concerning their faculties. I mean the suffrage, both parliamentary and municipal. The right to share in the choice of those who are to exercise a public trust, is altogether a distinct thing from that of competing for the trust itself. If no one could vote for a Member of Parliament who was not fit to be a candidate, the government would be a narrow oligarchy indeed. To have a voice in choosing those by whom one is to be governed, is a means of self-protection due to everyone, though he were to remain for ever excluded from the function of governing: and that women are considered fit to have such a choice, may be presumed from the fact, that the law already gives it to women in the most important of all cases to themselves: for the choice of the man who is to govern a woman to the end of life, is always supposed to be voluntarily made by herself. In the case of election to public trusts, it is the business of constitutional law to surround the right of suffrage with all needful securities and limitations; but whatever securities are sufficient in the case of the male sex, no others need be required in the case of women. Under whatever conditions, and within whatever limits, men are admitted to the suffrage, there is not a shadow of justification for not admitting women under the same. The majority of the women of any class are not likely to differ in political opinion from the majority of the men of the same class, unless the question be one in which the interests of women, as such, are in some way involved; and if they are so, women require the suffrage, as their guarantee of just and equal consideration. This ought to be obvious even to those who coincide in no other of the doctrines for which I contend. Even if every woman were a wife, and if every wife ought to be a slave, all the more would these slaves stand in need of legal protection: and we know what legal protection the slaves have, where the laws are made by their masters.

With regard to the fitness of women, not only to participate in elections, but themselves to hold offices or practise professions involving important public responsibilities; I have already observed that this consideration is not essential to the practical question in dispute: since any woman, who succeeds in an open profession, proves by that very fact that she is qualified for it. And in the case of public offices, if the political system of the country is such as to exclude unfit men, it will equally exclude unfit women: while if it is not, there is no additional evil in the fact that the unfit persons whom it admits may be either women or men. As long therefore as it is acknowledged that even a few women may be fit for these duties, the laws which shut the door on those exceptions cannot be justified by any opinion which can be held respecting the capacities of women in general. But, though this last consideration is not essential, it is far from being irrelevant. An unprejudiced view of it gives additional strength to the arguments against the disabilities of women, and reinforces them by high considerations of practical utility.

Let us first make entire abstraction of all psychological considerations tending to show, that any of the mental differences supposed to exist between women and men are but the natural effect of the differences in their education and circumstances, and indicate no radical difference, far less radical inferiority, of nature. Let us consider women only as they already are, or as they are known to have been; and the capacities which they have already practically shown. What they have done, that at least, if nothing else, it is proved that they can do. When we consider how sedulously they are all trained away from, instead of being trained towards, any of the occupations or objects reserved for men, it is evident that I am taking a very humble ground for them, when I rest their case on what they have actually achieved. For, in this case, negative evidence is worth little, while any positive evidence is conclusive. It cannot be inferred to be impossible that a woman should be a Homer, or an Aristotle, or a Michael Angelo, or a Beethoven, because no woman has yet actually produced works comparable to theirs in any of those lines of excellence. This negative fact at most leaves the question uncertain, and open to psychological discussion. But it is quite certain that a woman can be a Queen Elizabeth, or a Deborah, or a Joan of Arc, since this is not inference, but fact. Now it is a curious consideration, that the only things which the existing law excludes women from doing, are the things which they have proved that they are able to do. There is no law to prevent a woman from having written all the plays of Shakespeare, or composed all the operas of Mozart. But Queen Elizabeth or Queen Victoria, had they not inherited the throne, could not have been entrusted with the smallest of the political duties, of which the former showed herself equal to the greatest.

If anything conclusive could be inferred from experience, without psychological analysis, it would be that the things which women are not allowed to do are the very ones for which they are peculiarly qualified; since their vocation for government has made its way, and become conspicuous, through the very few opportunities which have been given; while in the lines of distinction which apparently were freely open to them, they have by no means so eminently distinguished themselves ...

Is it reasonable to think that those who are fit for the greater functions of politics, are incapable of qualifying themselves for the less? Is there any reason in the nature of things, that the wives and sisters of princes should, whenever called on, be found as competent as the princes themselves to *their* business, but that the wives and sisters of statesmen, and administrators, and directors of companies, and managers of public institutions, should be unable to do what is done by their brothers and husbands? The real reason is plain enough; it is that princesses, being more raised above the generality of men by their rank than placed below them by their sex, have never been taught that it was improper for them to concern themselves with politics; but have been allowed to feel the liberal interest natural to any cultivated human being, in the great transactions which took place around them, and in which they might be called on to take a part. The ladies of reigning families are the only women who are allowed the same range of interests and freedom of development as men; and it is precisely in their case that there is not found to be any inferiority. Exactly where and in proportion as women's capacities for government have been tried, in that proportion have they been found adequate.

This fact is in accordance with the best general conclusions which the world's imperfect experience seems as yet to suggest, concerning the peculiar tendencies and aptitudes characteristic of women, as women have hitherto been. I do not say, as they will continue to be; for, as I have already said more than once, I consider it presumption in anyone to pretend to decide what women are or are not, can or cannot be, by natural constitution. They have always hitherto been kept, as far as regards spontaneous development, in so unnatural a state, that their nature cannot but have been greatly distorted and disguised; and no one can safely pronounce that if women's nature were left to choose its direction as freely as men's, and if no artificial bent were attempted to be given to it except that required by the conditions of human society, and given to both sexes alike, there would be any material difference, or perhaps any difference at all, in the character and capacities which would unfold themselves. I shall presently show, that even the least contestable of the differences which now exist, are such as may very well have been produced merely by circumstances, without any difference of natural capacity. But, looking at women as they are known in experience, it may be said of them, with more truth than belongs to most other generalisations on the subject, that the general bent of their talents is towards the practical. This statement is conformable to all the public history of women, in the present and the past. It is no less borne out by common and daily experience. Let us consider the special nature of the mental capacities most character- istic of a woman of talent. They are all of a kind which fits them for practice, and makes them tend towards it. What is meant by a woman's capacity of intuitive perception? It means, a rapid and correct insight into present fact. It has nothing to do with general principles. Nobody ever perceived a scientific law of nature by intuition, nor arrived at a general rule of duty or prudence by it. These are results of slow and careful collection and comparison of experience; and neither the men nor the women of intuition usually shine in this department, unless, indeed, the experience necessary is such as they can acquire by them- selves. For what is called their intuitive sagacity makes them peculiarly apt in gathering such general truths as can be collected from their indi- vidual means of observation. When, consequently, they chance to be as well provided as men are with the results of other people's experience, by reading and education (I use the word chance advisedly, for, in respect to the knowledge that tends to fit them for the greater concerns of life, the only educated women are the self-educated) they are better furnished than men in general with the essential requisites of skilful and successful practice. Men who have been much taught, are apt to be deficient in the sense of present fact; they do not see, in the facts which they are called upon to deal with, what is really there, but what they have been taught to expect. This is seldom the case with women of any ability. Their capacity of "intuition" preserves them from it. With equality of experience and of general faculties, a woman usually sees much more than a man of what is immediately before her. Now this sensibility to the present, is the main quality on which the capacity for practice, as distinguished from theory, depends. To discover general principles, belongs to the speculative faculty: to discern and discrim- inate the particular cases in which they are and are not applicable, constitutes practical talent: and for this, women as they now are have a peculiar aptitude. I admit that there can be no good practice without principles, and that the predominant place which quickness of observa- tion holds among a woman's faculties, makes her particularly apt to build overhasty generalisations upon her own observation; though at the same time no less ready in rectifying those generalisations, as her observation takes a wider range. But the corrective to this defect, is access to the experience of the human race; general knowledge—exactly the thing which education can best supply. A woman's mistakes are specifically those of a clever self-educated man, who often sees what men trained in routine do not see, but falls into errors for want of knowing things which have long been known. Of course he has acquired much of the pre-existing knowledge, or he could not have got on at all; but what he knows of it he has picked up in fragments and at random, as women do.

But this gravitation of women's minds to the present, to the real, to actual fact, while in its exclusiveness it is a source of errors, is also a most useful counteractive of the contrary error. The principal and most characteristic aberration of speculative minds as such, consists precisely in the deficiency of this lively perception and ever-present sense of objective fact. For want of this, they often not only overlook the contradiction which outward facts oppose to their theories, but lose sight of the legitimate purpose of speculation altogether, and let their speculative faculties go astray into regions not peopled with real beings, animate or inanimate, even idealised, but with personified shadows created by the illusions of metaphysics or by the mere entanglement of words, and think these shadows the proper objects of the highest, the most transcendant, philosophy. Hardly anything can be of greater value to a man of theory and speculation who employs himself not in collecting materials of knowledge by observation, but in working them up by processes of thought into comprehensive truths of science and laws of conduct, than to carry on his speculations in the companionship, and under the criticism, of a really superior woman. There is nothing comparable to it for keeping his thoughts within the limits of real things, and the actual facts of nature. A woman seldom runs wild after an abstraction. The habitual direction of her mind to dealing with things as individuals rather than in groups, and (what is closely connected with it) her more lively interest in the present feelings of persons, which makes her consider first of all, in anything which claims to be applied to practice, in what manner persons will be affected by it—these two things make her extremely unlikely to put faith in any speculation which loses sight of individuals, and deals with things as if they existed for the benefit of some imaginary entity, some mere creation of the mind, not resolvable into the feelings of living beings. Women's thoughts are thus as useful in giving reality to those of thinking men, as men's thoughts in giving width and largeness to those of women. In depth, as distinguished from breadth, I greatly doubt if even now, women, compared with men, are at any disadvantage.

If the existing mental characteristics of women are thus valuable even in aid of speculation, they are still more important, when speculation has done its work, for carrying out the results of speculation into practice. For the reasons already given, women are comparatively unlikely to fall into the common error of men, that of sticking to their rules in a case whose specialties either take it out of the class to which the rules are applicable, or require a special adaptation of them. Let us now consider another of the admitted superiorities of clever women, greater quickness of apprehension. Is not this preeminently a quality which fits a person for practice? In action, everything continually depends upon deciding promptly. In speculation, nothing does. A mere thinker can wait, can take time to consider, can collect additional evidence; he is not obliged to complete his philosophy at once, lest the opportunity should go by. The power of drawing the best conclusion possible from insufficient data is not indeed useless in philosophy; the construction of a provisional hypothesis consistent with all known facts is often the needful basis for further inquiry. But this faculty is rather serviceable in philosophy, than the main qualification for it: and, for the auxiliary as well as for the main operation, the philosopher can allow himself any time he pleases. He is in no need of the capacity of doing rapidly what he does; what he rather needs is patience, to work on slowly until imperfect lights have become perfect, and a conjecture has ripened into a theorem. For those, on the contrary, whose business is with the fugitive and perishable— with individual facts, not kinds of facts—rapidity of thought is a qualification next only in importance to the power of thought itself. He who has not his faculties under immediate command, in the contingencies of action, might as well not have them at all. He may be fit to criticise, but he is not fit to act. Now it is in this that women, and the men who are most like women, confessedly excel. The other sort of man, however pre-eminent may be his faculties, arrives slowly at complete command of them: rapidity of judgment and promptitude of judicious action, even in the things he knows best, are the gradual and late result of strenuous effort grown into habit.

It will be said, perhaps, that the greater nervous susceptibility of women is a disqualification for practice, in anything but domestic life, by rendering them mobile, changeable, too vehemently under the influence of the moment, incapable of dogged perseverance, unequal and uncertain in the power of using their faculties. I think that these phrases sum up the greater part of the objections commonly made to the fitness of women for the higher class of serious business. Much of all this is the mere overflow of nervous energy run to waste, and would cease when the energy was directed to a definite end. Much is also the result of conscious or unconscious cultivation; as we see by the almost total disappearance of "hysterics" and fainting-fits, since they have gone out of fashion. Moreover, when people are brought up, like many women of the higher classes (though less so in our own country than in any other), a kind of hot-house plants, shielded from the wholesome vicissitudes of air and temperature, and untrained in any of the occupations and exercises which give stimulus and development to the circulatory and muscular system, while their nervous system, especially in its emotional department, is kept in unnaturally active play; it is no wonder if those of them who do not die of consumption, grow up with constitutions liable to derangement from slight causes, both internal and external, and without stamina to support any task, physical or mental, requiring continuity of effort. But women brought up to work for their livelihood show none of these morbid characteristics, unless indeed they are chained to an excess of sedentary work in confined and unhealthy rooms. Women who in their early years have shared in the healthful physical education and bodily freedom of their brothers, and who obtain a sufficiency of pure air and exercise in after-life, very rarely have any excessive susceptibility of nerves which can disqualify them for active pursuits. There is indeed a certain proportion of persons, in both sexes, in whom an unusual degree of nervous sensibility is constitutional, and of so marked a character as to be the feature of their organisation which exercises the greatest influence over the whole character of the vital phenomena. This constitution, like other physical conformations, is hereditary, and is transmitted to sons as well as daughters; but it is possible, and probable, that the nervous temperament (as it is called) is inherited by a greater number of women than of men. We will assume this as a fact: and let me then ask, are men of nervous temperament found to be unfit for the duties and pursuits usually followed by men? If not, why should women of the same temperament be unfit for them? The peculiarities of the temperament are, no doubt, within certain limits, an obstacle to success in some employments, though an aid to it in others. But when the occupation is suitable to the temperament, and sometimes even when it is unsuitable, the most brilliant examples of success are continually given by the men of high nervous sensibility. They are distinguished in their practical manifestations chiefly by this, that being susceptible of a higher degree of excitement than those of another physical constitution, their powers when excited differ more than in the case of other people, from those shown in their ordinary state: they are raised, as it were, above themselves, and do things with ease which they are wholly incapable of at other times. But this lofty excitement is not, except in weak bodily constitutions, a mere flash, which passes away immediately, leaving no permanent traces, and incompatible with persistent and steady pursuit of an object. It is the character of the nervous temperament to be capable of *sustained* excitement, holding out through long-continued efforts. It is what is meant by *spirit*. It is what makes the high-bred racehorse run without slackening speed till he drops down dead. It is what has enabled so many delicate women to maintain the most sublime constancy not only at the stake, but through a long preliminary succession of mental and bodily tortures. It is evident that people of this temperament are particularly apt for what may be called the executive department of the leadership of mankind. They are the material of great orators, great preachers, impressive diffusers of moral influences. Their constitution might be deemed less favourable to the qualities required from a states- man in the cabinet, or from a judge. It would be so, if the consequence necessarily followed that because people are excitable they must always be in a state of excitement. But this is wholly a question of training. Strong feeling is the instrument and element of strong self-control: but it requires to be cultivated in that direction. When it is, it forms not the heroes of impulse only, but those also of self-conquest. History and experience prove that the most passionate characters are the most fanatically rigid in their feelings of duty, when their passion has been trained to act in that direction. The judge who gives a just decision in a case where his feelings are intensely interested on the other side, derives from that same strength of feeling the determined sense of the obligation of justice, which enables him to achieve this victory over himself. The capability of that lofty enthusiasm which takes the human being out of his every-day character, reacts upon the daily character itself. His aspirations and powers when he is in this exceptional state, become the type with which he compares, and by which he estimates, his sentiments and proceedings at other times: and his habitual pur- poses assume a character moulded by and assimilated to the moments of lofty excitement, although those, from the physical nature of a human being, can only be transient . . .

Supposing it, however, to be true that women's minds are by nature more mobile than those of men, less capable of persisting long in the same continuous effort, more fitted for dividing their faculties among many things than for travelling in any one path to the highest point which can be reached by it: this may be true of women as they now are (though not without great and numerous exceptions), and may account for their having remained behind the highest order of men in precisely the things in which this absorption of the whole mind in one set of ideas and occupations may seem to be most requisite. Still, this difference is one which can only affect the kind of excellence, not the excellence itself, or its practical worth: and it remains to be shown whether this exclusive working of a part of the mind, this absorption of the whole thinking faculty in a single subject, and concentration of it on a single work, is the normal and healthful condition of the human faculties, even for speculative uses. I believe that what is gained in special de- velopment by this concentration, is lost in the capacity of the mind for the other purposes of life; and even in abstract thought, it is my decided opinion that the mind does more by frequently returning to a difficult problem, than by sticking to it without interruption. For the purposes, at all events, of practice, from its highest to its humblest departments, the capacity of passing promptly from one subject of consideration to another, without letting the active spring of the intellect run down between the two, is a power far more valuable; and this power women pre-eminently possess, by virtue of the very mobility of which they are accused. They perhaps have it from nature, but they certainly have it by training and education; for nearly the whole of the occupations of women consist in the management of small but multitudinous details, on each of which the mind cannot dwell even for a minute, but must pass on to other things, and if anything requires longer thought, must steal time at odd moments for thinking of it. The capacity indeed which women show for doing their thinking in circumstances and at times which almost any man would make an excuse to himself for not attempting it, has often been noticed: and a woman's mind, though it may be occupied only with small things, can hardly ever permit itself to be vacant, as a man's so often is when not engaged in what he chooses to consider the business of his life. The business of a woman's ordinary life is things in general, and can as little cease to go on as the world to go round.

But (it is said) there is anatomical evidence of the superior mental capacity of men compared with women: they have a larger brain. I reply, that in the first place the fact itself is doubtful. It is by no means established that the brain of a woman is smaller than that of a man. If it is inferred merely because a woman's bodily frame generally is of less dimensions than a man's, this criterion would lead to strange consequences. A tall and large-boned man must on this showing be wonderfully superior in intelligence to a small man, and an elephant or a whale must prodigiously excel mankind. The size of the brain in human beings, anatomists say, varies much less than the size of the body, or even of the head, and the one cannot be at all inferred from the other. It is certain that some women have as large a brain as any man. It is within my knowledge that a man who had weighed many human brains, said that the heaviest he knew of, heavier even than Cuvier's (the heaviest previously recorded), was that of a woman. Next, I must observe that the precise relation which exists between the brain and the intellectual powers is not yet well understood, but is a subject of great dispute. That there is a very close relation we cannot doubt. The brain is certainly the material organ of thought and feeling: and (making abstraction of the great unsettled controversy respecting the appropriation of different parts of the brain to different mental faculties) I admit that it would be an anomaly, and an exception to all we know of the general laws of life and organisation, if the size of the organ were wholly indifferent to the function; if not accession of power were derived from the great magnitude of the instrument. But the exception and the anomaly would be fully as great if the organ exercised influence by its magnitude *only*. In all the more delicate operations of nature—of which those of the animated creation are the most delicate, and those of the nervous system by far the most delicate of these— differences in the effect depend as much on differences of quality in the physical agents, as on their quantity: and if the quality of an instrument is to be tested by the nicety and delicacy of the work it can do, the indications point to a greater average fineness of quality in the brain and nervous system of women than of men. Dismissing abstract difference of quality, a thing difficult to verify, the efficiency of an organ is known to depend not solely on its size but on its activity: and of this we have an approximate measure in the energy with which the blood circulates through it, both the stimulus and the reparative force being mainly dependent on the circulation. It would not be surprising—it is indeed an hypothesis which accords well with the differences actually observed between the mental operations of the two sexes—if men on the average should have the advantage in the size of the brain, and women in activity of cerebral circulation. The results which conjecture, founded on analogy, would lead us to expect from this difference of organisation, would correspond to some of those which we most commonly see. In the first place, the mental operations of men might be expected to be slower. They would neither be so prompt as women in thinking, nor so quick to feel. Large bodies take more time to get into full action. On the other hand, when once got thoroughly into play, men's brain would bear more work. It would be more persistent in the line first taken; it would have more difficulty in changing from one mode of action to another, but, in the one thing it was doing, it could go on longer without loss of power or sense of fatigue. And do we not find that the things in which men most excel women are those which require most plodding and long hammering at a single thought, while women do best what must be done rapidly? A woman's brain is sooner fatigued, sooner exhausted; but given the degree of exhaustion, we should expect to find that it would recover itself sooner. I repeat that this speculation is entirely hypothetical; it pretends to no more than to suggest a line of inquiry. I have before repudiated the notion of its being yet certainly known that there is any natural difference at all in the average strength or direction of the mental capacities of the two sexes, much less what that difference is. Nor is it possible that this should be known, so long as the psychological laws of the formation of character have been so little studied, even in a general way, and in the particular case never scientifically applied at all; so long as the most obvious external causes of difference of character are habitually disregarded—left unnoticed by the observer, and looked down upon with a kind of supercilious contempt by the prevalent schools both of natural history and of mental philosophy: who, whether they look for the source of what mainly distinguishes human beings from one another, in the world of matter or in that of spirit, agree in running down those who prefer to explain these differences by the different relations of human beings to society and life...

As for moral differences, considered as distinguished from intellectual, the distinction commonly drawn is to the advantage of women. They are declared to be better than men; an empty compliment, which must provoke a bitter smile from every woman of spirit, since there is no other situation in life in which it is the established order, and considered quite natural and suitable, that the better should obey the worse. If this piece of idle talk is good for anything, it is only as an admission by men, of the corrupting influence of power; for that is certainly the only truth which the fact, if it be a fact, either proves or illustrates. And it *is* true that servitude, except when it actually brutalises, though corrupting to both, is less so to the slaves than to the slave-masters. It is wholesomer for the moral nature to be restrained, even by arbitrary power, than to be allowed to exercise arbitrary power without restraint. Women, it is said, seldomer fall under the penal law—contribute a much smaller number of offenders to the criminal calendar, than men. I doubt not that the same thing may be said, with the same truth, of negro slaves. Those who are under the control of others cannot often commit crimes, unless at the command and for the purposes of their masters. I do not know a more signal instance of the blindness with which the world, including the herd of studious men, ignore and pass over all the influences of social circumstances, than their silly depreciation of the intellectual, and silly panegyrics on the moral, nature of women.

The complimentary dictum about women's superior moral goodness may be allowed to pair off with the disparaging one respecting their greater liability to moral bias. Women, we are told, are not capable of resisting their personal partialities: their judgment in grave affairs is warped by their sympathies and antipathies. Assuming it to be so, it is still to be proved that women are oftener misled by their personal feelings than men by their personal interests. The chief difference would seem in that case to be, that men are led from the course of duty and the public interest by their regard for themselves, women (not being allowed to have private interests of their own) by their regard for somebody else. It is also to be considered, that all the education which women receive from society inculcates on them the feeling that the individuals connected with them are the only ones to whom they owe any duty—the only ones whose interest they are called upon to care for; while, as far as education is concerned, they are left strangers even to the elementary ideas which are presupposed in any intelligent regard for larger interests or higher moral objects. The complaint against them resolves itself merely into this, that they fulfil only too faithfully the sole duty which they are taught, and almost the only one which they are permitted to practise.

The concessions of the privileged to the unprivileged are so seldom brought about by any better motive than the power of the unprivileged to extort them, that any arguments against the prerogative of sex are likely to be little attended to by the generality, as long as they are able to say to themselves that women do not complain of it. That fact certainly enables men to retain the unjust privilege some time longer; but does not render it less unjust. Exactly the same thing may be said of the women in the harem of an Oriental: they do not complain of not being allowed the freedom of European women. They think our women insufferably bold and unfeminine. How rarely it is that even men complain of the general order of society; and how much rarer still would such complaint be, if they did not know of any different order existing anywhere else. Women do not complain of the general lot of women; or rather they do, for plaintive elegies on it are very common in the writings of women, and were still more so as long as the lamentations could not be suspected of having any practical object. Their complaints are like the complaints which men make of the general unsatisfactoriness of human life, they are not meant to imply blame, or to plead for any change. But though women do not complain of the power of husbands, each complains of her own husband, or of the husbands of her friends. It is the same in all other cases of servitude, at least in the commencement of the emancipatory movement. The serfs did not at first complain of the power of their lords, but only of their tyranny. The commons began by claiming a few municipal privileges; they next asked an exemption for themselves from being taxed without their own consent; but they would at that time have thought it a great presumption to claim any share in the king's sovereign authority. The case of women is now the only case in which to rebel against established rules is still looked upon with the same eyes as was formerly a subject's claim to the right of rebelling against his king. A woman who joins in any movement which her husband disapproves, makes herself a martyr, without even being able to be an apostle, for the husband can legally put a stop to her apostleship. Women cannot be expected to devote themselves to the emancipation of women, until men in considerable number are prepared to join with them in the undertaking.

Political and Civil Status
of Woman as of January 1, 1969

The following chapter from the U. S. Government's Handbook
on Women Workers *shows that the legal status of women,
though improved since the Seneca Falls Women's Rights Convention in 1848, is still that of a second-class citizen. For example, a married woman's rights to a room of her own (see
"Domicile"), money of her own (see "Ownership, Control, and
Use of Property"), a life of her own (see "Contracts") are in
many instances uncertain.*

New Trends

Progress continues to be made in the direction of revising outmoded
laws and practices which differentiate between men and women unfairly
and unrealistically. The philosophy favoring the dominance of the husband in the marital relation has generally been replaced by the idea
that both parties have rights and responsibilities in marriage, and that
while the wife is entitled to a measure of legal protection she does have
responsibilities.

The status of women has enjoyed a continuous improvement since
the 19th century, when the first Married Women's Property Acts were
passed. These first legal steps toward releasing a married woman's property and property rights from her husband's control started a trend,
which has continued over the years, to equalize married women's rights
with those of married men in the enjoyment and disposition of property.
A married woman's citizenship no longer automatically follows that of
her husband—she neither gains U.S. citizenship by marriage to a citizen
of the United States, nor loses her U.S. citizenship by marriage to an
alien. The adoption of the 19th amendment to the Constitution, which
gave both married and single women the right to vote, marked the beginning of the political emancipation of women and established the basis
for them to participate fully in the political life of the country.

Reprinted by permission of The United States Government Printing Office,
Division of Public Documents, Washington, D.C.

More recently, attention has been given to eliminating the other artificial barriers which kept many Americans, especially Negro men and women, from the polls. Women slowly have been catching up with men in terms of equal eligibility for jury service—an important privilege and responsibility of all citizens—by the enactment of laws which base qualifications for, and disqualifications and exemptions from, jury service on factors other than sex.

Commissions on the status of women have been active in recommending and supporting programs to improve the civil and political status of women. As of January 1, 1969, almost all of the commissions had made interim or final reports on a wide range of subjects, including property rights, marriage and divorce law, consortium, homestead law, and domicile law.

Political Status

Citizenship

Citizenship in the United States is acquired in the same way by men and women; that is, by birth within the domain, by birth abroad of a parent who is a citizen, or by naturalization. Mothers as well as fathers confer citizenship on their minor children.

A married woman's citizenship does not automatically follow that of her husband. An alien wife may become a citizen whether or not her alien husband desires or qualifies for that privilege. When a woman citizen marries an alien, she retains her citizenship until she renounces it by declaring allegiance to another government.

Voting and Public Office

Federal elections.—Women and men have equal rights of suffrage in the election of Federal Government officials and on pro-postals for change in the Federal Constitution.

Qualifications for election or appointment to posts in the executive and legislative branches of the Federal Government or for appointment to the judiciary are the same for women and men.

State elections.—Women and men have equal rights of suffrage in the election of State and local officials ond in the determination of public issues within the State.

Qualifications for election to State and local government positions are the same for women and men.

Civil service positions.—Positions in both Federal and State civil service are generally open to women who qualify. Through fair employment practices laws or executive policy statements, some States prohibit sex discrimination in hiring, promotion, and training in public employ-ment.

In Federal employment a policy developed as a result of the hiring statute of 1870, which resulted in sex discrimination in hiring and pro-motion, was reversed on June 4, 1962, when the Attorney General de-clared this practice unjustified and invalid. Subsequently a Presidential directive of July 23, 1962, required Federal agency heads to fill positions without reference to sex where experience and physical requirements were met, and the Civil· Service Commission issued appropriate rules and regulations to implement this directive. In order to preclude any possibility of reversion to the previous policy, in 1965 Congress repealed the 1870 law.

In 1967 the President signed Executive Order 11375, which spe-cifically prohibts discrimination on the basis of sex in Federal and Federal contract employment. This order was a direct outgrowth of the recommendations of the Federal Woman's Award Study Group created by the President in 1966 to examine and make suggestions with respect to careers for women in the executive branch. The Study Group is composed of outstanding women in Federal service who have received special recognition for their contributions. The group recommended that in order to increase the number of women in professional, adminis-trative, and technical positions in the Federal Government, the Civil Service Commission develop a reporting system to provide necessary data for an appraisal of the position of women in the Federal Govern-ment; review examination and qualification requirements with a view toward providing more flexibility in examinations and insuring appro-priate credit for participation in community, cultural, social service, and professional association activities; and develop a program to recruit women for part-time employment.

Courts—jury service.—Since the enactment of the Civil Rights Act of 1957 removing the disqualification of women for service on Federal juries in all States, many States have equalized laws affecting service on State grand and petit juries. The Federal Jury Selection and Service Act of 1968, which provides for selection of Federal juries at random from a fair cross section of the community and specifically prohibits exclusion because of race, color, religion, sex, national origin, or eco-nomic status, implements the 1957 Civil Rights Act.

Women are now eligible by law to serve on State juries in all 50 States and on juries in the District of Columbia and Puerto Rico. The last 3 States amended their laws since 1966 to permit women to serve. In *White* v. *Crook* (251 F. Supp. 401 (1966)), the Alabama law excluding women from State juries was declared unconstitutional by a Federal court on the ground that the State law denied equal protection to women in violation of the 14th amendment. Thereafter the legislature enacted a law permitting women to serve on State juries.

In 1966 South Carolina voters approved a constitutional amendment to permit women to serve on State juries. The amendment was ratified by the General Assembly in 1957. In 1968 the Mississippi legislature amended the law which barred women from serving on State juries, so that women may now serve on the same basis as men.

In 28 States[1] women serve under the same terms and conditions as men, with the same qualifications, disqualifications, and exemptions. In 22 States and the District of Columbia, women may be excused on grounds not available to men. Of these, 11 States[2] permit a woman to be excused solely on the basis of her sex. An additional 10 States,[3] the District of Columbia, and Puerto Rico permit women to claim an exemption because of child care or family responsibilities. Rhode Island further provides that women shall be included for jury service only when courthouse facilities permit. In 1967 Florida and New Hampshire removed their requirement that women register before they may be considered for jury service. Louisiana is now the only State with this requirement.

Domicile

A person's domicile is determined by the coexistence of physical presence and intent to reside permanently in a particular place. Residence is mere physical presence. The concept of domicile is important since many legal rights and duties attach to it, e.g., the right to vote and run for public office and the duty to pay taxes. As a general rule, the domicile of a married woman is deemed, by operation of law, to be that of her husband. If the husband changes his domicile, and makes reasonable provision for his wife at the new domicile, she is under a duty to follow him, unless to do so would be a recognized hardship. However, a married woman may establish a separate domicile when the interests of husband and wife are hostile and result in a separation of the parties. In addition, an increasing number of jurisdictions are permitting a wife to establish a separate domicile when the marital unity has been breached and the parties are living separately by mutual consent or acquiescence. In such cases separate existence, interest, and rights are recognized.

[1]Alaska, Arizona, California, Colorado, Delaware, Hawaii, Idaho, Illinois, Indiana, Iowa, Kentucky, Maine, Maryland, Mississippi, Montana, Nebraska, New Jersey, New Mexico, North Dakota, Ohio, Oregon, Pennsylvania, South Dakota, Vermont, Washington, West Virginia, Wisconsin.

[2]Alabama, Arkansas, Georgia, Kansas, Minnesota, Missouri, Nevada, New York, Rhode Island, Tennessee, Virginia.

[3]Connecticut, Florida, Massachusetts, New Hampshire, North Carolina, Oklahoma, South Carolina, Texas, Utah, Wyoming.

However, problems may arise in this area of the law for the married woman whose marriage is intact but who for some good and valid reason has a residence separate from that of her husband. In recognition of the inequities that may result from the rigid application of the general rule, an increasing number of States are permitting a married woman to have a separate domicile, either for all purposes or for specified purposes. At present, 5 States—Alaska, Arkansas, Delaware, Hawaii, and Wisconsin—permit a married woman to establish a separate domicile for all purposes. In addition, 3 States[4] permit a separate domicile for eligibility to public office; 2 States[5] permit a separate domicile for jury service; 3 States[6] recognize a separate domicile for probate; and 13 States[7] permit a separate domicile for voting.

Civil Status—Family Relations

Marriage

State laws establishing marriage requirements generally do not make distinctions based on sex except in setting minimum ages—usually lower for women than for men. When parental consent is not required, the minimum age for women is 18 years in 35 States[8] and the District of Columbia; it is 19, 20, or 21 in the remaining jurisdictions. Girls may marry with parental consent at the age of 16 years in 38 States[9] and the District of Columbia, at age 15 in 5 States,[10] and at age 14 in 4 States.[11] The minimum age in Washington is 17 years; in Kansas, 18 years. In New Hampshire a girl who marries below the age of 18 must have both the consent of her parents and that of the court. All but 4 States [12] require

---

[4]Maine, New Jersey, New York.

[5]Maine, New Jersey.

[6]California, Florida, New Jersey.

[7]California, Connecticut, Florida, Illinois, Indiana, Iowa, Maine, Massachusetts, Michigan, New Jersey, New York, North Dakota, Wyoming.

[8]Alabama, Alaska, Arizona, Arkansas, California, Colorado, Delaware, Idaho, Illinois, Indiana, Iowa, Kansas, Maine, Maryland, Massachusetts, Michigan, Minnesota, Missouri, Montana, Nevada, New Hampshire, New Jersey, New Mexico, New York, North Carolina, North Dakota, Oklahoma, Oregon, South Carolina, South Dakota, Texas, Utah, Vermont, Washington, Wisconsin.

[9]Alaska, Arizona, Arkansas, California, Colorado, Connecticut, Delaware, Florida, Georgia, Hawaii, Idaho, Illinois, Indiana, Iowa, Kentucky, Louisiana, Maine, Maryland, Massachusetts, Michigan, Minnesota, Montana, Nebraska, Nevada, New Jersey, New Mexico, New York, North Carolina, Ohio, Pennsylvania, Rhode Island, South Dakota, Tennessee, Vermont, Virginia, West Virginia, Wisconsin, Wyoming.

[10]Mississippi, Missouri, North Dakota, Oklahoma, Oregon.

[11]Alabama, South Carolina, Texas, Utah.

[12]Maryland, Minnesota, Nevada, South Carolina.

a premarital health examination for both applicants for a marriage license. In these 4 jurisdictions the health examination is not required for either applicant.

The landmark decision of the U.S. Supreme Court in *Loving* v. *Virginia* (338 U.S. 1 (1967)) held Virginia's miscegenation law unconstitutional as a denial of equal protection of the laws and a deprivation of due process of law, in violation of the 14th amendment to the Constitution. This decision appears to have invalidated laws in 15 other States[13] which prohibit marriage between persons of different races.

Divorce

All States and the District of Columbia permit divorce on more than one ground. For the most part grounds for divorce are the same for husband and wife, although more than half the States recognize nonsupport by the husband as a ground for granting a divorce to the wife, and at least 13 States[14] permit a man to seek divorce on the basis of his wife's pregnancy by another man at the time of their marriage.

Adultery is recognized as a ground for divorce in all States and the District of Columbia. The most common other grounds for divorce are desertion, separation for a specified period, cruelty, alcoholism, impotency, felony conviction, and insanity. Some jurisdictions permit divorce on the grounds of drug addiction or commission of an infamous crime.

Forty-eight States and the District of Columbia have laws which permit the award of permanent alimony to the wife in the discretion of the court when divorce is granted. In North Carolina alimony is limited to specified circumstances. Pennsylvania and Texas make no general provisions for alimony on final decree, although in Pennsylvania the court is empowered to decree alimony for the support of either an insane wife or an insane husband. In addition to Pennsylvania, in at least 6 States[15] with no general provision for alimony to the husband, the wife may be held liable for the support of the husband in case of divorce on the basis of his mental illness.

---

[13]Alabama, Arkansas, Delaware, Florida, Georgia, Kentucky, Louisiana, Mississippi, Missouri, North Carolina, Oklahoma, South Carolina, Tennessee, Texas, West Virginia. (Maryland repealed its miscegenation law in early 1967 prior to the Supreme Court's decision.)

[14]Alabama, Arizona, Georgia, Iowa, Kentucky, Mississippi, Missouri, New Mexico, North Carolina, Oklahoma, Tennessee, Virginia, Wyoming.

[15]Connecticut, Delaware, Kansas, Mississippi, Nebraska, Wyoming.

Twelve States[16] may allow alimony to either spouse; in addition, Massachusetts and New Hampshire allow the husband a portion of the wife's estate in the nature of alimony. The statutes of Colorado and Virginia are broad enough to apply to either spouse, but in actual practice alimony may be limited to the wife since in neither State does there appear to be a judicial determination permitting alimony to the husband.

Parent and Child

Under the common law, the father was the preferred natural guardian of the person of a minor child and as such had the care, custody, control, and responsibility for the education of the child. This rule has been abrogated by statute in the majority of States to provide that the natural guardianship of a minor child is vested jointly in both parents. Seven States[17] presently provide by statute that the father is the preferred natural guardian of a minor child.

State laws usually provide that when a minor becomes the owner of a specified amount of property a guardian of the minor's estate must be appointed to manage and conserve the estate. Six States[18] and the District of Columbia specify by statute that the father is preferred when it is necessary to appoint a guardian of the estate of a minor.

If a marriage is broken by divorce or legal separation, generally neither parent has any legal advantage over the other as to custody of a minor child; the best interests of the child guide the court's disposition of custody. If there is a contest between the parents regarding custody or guardianship of a minor child, at least 8 States[19] provide by statute that, all other things being equal, the mother has a preferred right if the child is of an age to require education or preparation for labor or business.

Unmarried parents.—An unmarried mother is considered the natural guardian and entitled to the custody of her child. The father becomes the natural guardian only if he legally acknowledges his relationship to the child or marries the mother.

Inheritance by parents from children.—No distinction exists between the rights of the father and those of the mother to inherit from legitimate

---

[16]Alaska, California, Hawaii, Illinois, Iowa, North Carolina, North Dakota, Ohio, Oklahoma, Oregon, Utah, West Virginia.

[17]Alaska, Georgia, Louisiana, New Mexico, North Carolina, Oklahoma, Texas.

[18]Alabama, Georgia, Louisiana, Montana, New Mexico, North Dakota.

[19]Arizona, California, Michigan, Montana, North Dakota, Oklahoma, South Dakota, Utah.

children. Most States allow an unmarried mother to inherit from her child.

Family Support

Notwithstanding the legal emancipation of women and their increased participation in the labor force, in all States a husband is liable for the support of his wife. In most States a wife is responsible for the support of her husband when he is unable to support himself. Nearly all States make both the mother and father liable for the support of their legitimate minor child; however, the liability of the mother is frequently secondary. In the 8 States[20] with community property laws of ownership between husband and wife, the common estate of husband and wife is liable for debts for family support. In addition, most States specify that children are liable for the support of needy parents under specified circumstances. A money judgment stemming from duties of support may be enforced against either the person or his property.

Unmarried parents.—The mother is primarily liable for support of her child born out of wedlock. Most States have legal procedures for establishing paternity. Until paternity is established or voluntarily assumed, the father has no legal obligation to support the child, or to contribute to the expense of the mother at childbirth.

Uniform Reciprocal Enforcement of Support Act.—Uniform Reciprocal Enforcement of Support Acts are now in effect in all jurisdictions of the United States, following the 1957 law enacted by Congress for the District of Columbia. This legislation does not create new duties of support, but provides by reciprocal legislation for enforcement across State lines of support duties already existing. Each State applies its own law, but the act makes binding the support duty regardless of the presence or residence of the obligee. New judgments may be obtained, or existing judgments enforced from State to State under this legislation.

Enforcement of these laws by courts throughout the country has lightened the burden of welfare agencies to a large extent; and the civil rather than criminal emphasis has contributed to the preservation of the family, since it is thus easier for the parties to become reconciled.

One problem, however, has persisted to hamper the effective administration of these acts: that of finding the deserting party responsible for the support of his dependents. A New York law directs the State Department of Social Welfare to establish a central registry of records

---

[20]Arizona, California, Idaho, Louisiana, Nevada, New Mexico, Texas, Washington.

for locating deserting parents of children who are receiving or likely to need public assistance. The department is authorized to obtain information from other State agencies (e.g., motor vehicle and tax records) concerning the identity and whereabouts of deserting parents. Many other States permit responsible State agencies to request and receive information from the records of all other State agencies to assist in locating parents who have deserted their children or any other persons liable for support of dependents. Various Federal agencies are authorized to attempt to locate the parent responsible for support in certain circumstances where the children are eligible for assistance under the aid to families with dependent children program.

Civil Status—Property and Contract Law

Property

Property is broadly divided into two categories—personal and real (real estate and things permanently attached thereto). In property management and control, inheritance, and freedom of enjoyment of earnings, no distinction is made between the rights of unmarried women and unmarried men. However, there may be distinctions between rights of married and single women.

There are two different property systems within the United States— the community property system, which grew out of French and Spanish law, and the common law system, which developed from the English common law.

Ownership, Control, and Use of Property

Personal earnings.—Personal earnings of married women are made their separate property by specific statute in most of the States not having a community property law. Earnings are considered part of the community in the community property States. In 4 of these States— Arizona, Louisiana, Nevada, and New Mexico—the community property is managed and controlled by the husband, but the remaining 4—California, Idaho, Texas, and Washington—provide that the wife may control her earnings. In Texas a provision giving married women such right by vesting control over community property in the spouse who would have control had the property not become part of the community became effective January 1, 1968.

Real property owned separately.—Although a married woman has the power to contract with reference to her separate real property, a number of States—either directly or indirectly—restrict a married person's right to convey or encumber his or her separate real property. In 22 States[21] and the District of Columbia, where both the husband and wife have either curtesy, dower, or a statutory interest in the nature of dower in the spouse's property, it is necessary that either spouse join in the conveyance of the real estate belonging to the other spouse in order to bar this interest. This requirement may be of benefit to a married woman in that it can help prevent the dissipation of the assets of her spouse.

Six States[22] provide dower or a statutory interest in the nature of dower for a wife without giving her husband a similar interest in her property, thereby making it necessary for the wife to join in her husband's conveyance of his realty without subjecting her real estate to similar restrictions. Two States—Alabama and Florida—while not giving a husband a curtesy or statutory dower interest in the wife's property, specifically require him to join in the conveyance of his wife's property.

Recent enactments in this area include a 1967 amendment to Indiana law to remove a provision that a married woman could not convey her separate real property without the signature of her husband. And in the Texas amendments referred to earlier, the marital property law was changed to provide, among other things, for elimination of any inequality caused through use of the terms "husband" and "wife" by referring to "spouses," so that provisions for the husband and wife are identical. Texas amendments also provided for joint management of community property by husband and wife.

Real and personal property acquired by joint efforts after marriage. —Under the community property system, all property acquired after marriage is classified as either separate or community property. Separate property is under the control and management of the individual owning it, and in 7 of the 8 community property States the husband generally has control of the community property. In Texas each spouse now has control of that community property which he or she would have owned if a single person.

Under the common law system, all property is owned separately or jointly in accordance with the title to it, and control of the property

---

[21]Delaware, Hawaii, Illinois, Iowa, Kansas, Kentucky, Maine, Maryland, Minnesota, Nebraska, New Hampshire, New Jersey, North Carolina, Ohio, Oregon, Pennsylvania, Rhode Island, Tennessee, Vermont, Virginia, West Virginia, Wisconsin. (Also Missouri for all estates vested as of 1955, when the statutory dower law of 1939 was repealed.)

[22]Arkansas, Indiana, Michigan, Montana, South Carolina, Utah. (In Utah joinder of a wife to bar dower is necessary only if the wife is a resident of Utah.)

depends upon the type of ownership under which it is held. Separate property belongs to one of the spouses and is under the exclusive control of that spouse. Joint property is that in which both spouses have an interest, and the control is generally shared.

Control of real estate depends upon the type of ownership under which it is held. Under the old common law, real estate conveyed or devised to a husband and wife created an estate by the entireties held by them as one person, with the husband entitled to all the rents, profits, and enjoyment thereof. Today, while the common law estate by the entireties may still be created in the District of Columbia and the majority of the 42 common law States, it is also generally possible for married persons to own real estate by some other form of ownership, under which each spouse is entitled to one-half of the rents, profits, and enjoyment of the property.

Personal property accumulated during marriage by the cooperative efforts of husband and wife is generally under the control of the husband, subject to certain restrictions; for example, in many States the husband cannot mortgage the family furniture without the wife's consent. The effect of this common law rule may be overcome by private agreement between the parties, or by a title or record (such as a bill of sale) establishing otherwise. It may be necessary for a court of equity to decide the ownership.

Disposition of property after death.—Married women may dispose of their separate property by will as freely as married men. The majority of States provide that, in the absence of a will, a widow or widower inherits from the deceased spouse in a similar manner. The surviving spouse's share of the estate generally depends on whether there are surviving issue, parents, or other next of kin.

In both common law and community property States, a surviving husband or wife generally receives all of the property separately owned by the deceased spouse if there are no descendants; one-half or one-third if there are descendants. In all the community property States, a wife receives her half of the community property. In 4 of these States—California, Idaho, Nevada, and New Mexico—she receives her husband's half; in 2—Arizona and Texas—she receives her husband's half if there are no descendants; and in the remaining 2—Louisiana and Washington —she receives his half if there are no descendants or parents. In the common law States, jointly owned property is divided according to the title.

Contracts

All States with a common law background recognize a married woman's legal capacity to contract her personal services in employment outside her home and her entitlement to earnings from such work without the formal consent of her husband. In the 8 community property States a married woman may contract with respect to her employment and earnings from such employment, but the earnings are considered part of the community property. (See the preceding section for discussion of earnings.)

In most States a married woman may contract with respect to her separate property. However, in at least 3 States—Georgia, Idaho, and Kentucky—a married woman does not have the legal capacity to become a surety or a guarantor.

In 4 States—California, Florida, Nevada, and Pennsylvania—court sanction and, in some cases, the husband's consent, is required for a wife's legal venture into an independent business. In addition, Massachusetts requires a married woman or her husband to file a certificate with the city or town clerk's office in order to prevent the personal property of her business from being liable for her husband's debts.

Although married women in general may contract freely with third parties, transactions between husband and wife are still subject to legal limitations in many States. In some States such contracts are restricted by the general rule that controls the actions of persons occupying confidential relations with each other. In some States such contracts may be executed by a formal written document, and in others no authority exists to make such contracts.

The Matriarchal Myth

Eve Merriam

In her book, After Nora Slammed the Door, *Eve Merriam examines the progress toward human rights made by women since Nora, the heroine of Ibsen's* A Doll's House *(1879), told off her husband and walked out. Examining woman as mother, as career woman, and as "In Limbo" (the unmarried female), she finds that woman still faces a fight "to be permitted to be human instead of non-male." As a partial solution to woman's plight, she recommends a restructuring of family life into communities, instead of isolated units, and government-financed child care and housework; in short, she asks for radical social change.*

The Matriarchal Myth *answers the notion that the American woman is dominant over the male. Though Merriam admits that American men "are pretty passive specimens," she places the blame for their emasculation on corporate capitalism rather than on Big Momma.*

As a footnote to Merriam's comments on the myth of the American woman's economic power, consider the following information from Handbook on Women Workers, *published by the U. S. Department of Labor in 1969: "Women constituted 33 percent of the total stockholders of record reported by public corporations. The number of shares owned individually by women stockholders equaled 18 percent of the total as compared with 24 percent owned individually by men. The remaining 58 percent were held or owned by institutions, brokers and dealers, persons with joint accounts, nominees (who hold shares for others), and foreign owners. The estimated market value of the stock registered in women's names was 18 percent of the total compared with 20 percent of stock registered in men's names."*

The myth of Nora, the independent woman, as a matriarchal menace is on the upswing. When Philip Wylie crusaded some years ago for misogyny, a fair-sized opposition protested. Today, almost everybody is in his corner; you couldn't get up a skirmish if you wanted to. It would seem that Wylie's rantings weren't wrong: he was simply a bit prematurely anti-Mom. Nowadays no one would be caught dead saying a kind word for anybody's mother. The image of Big Bad Bold Momma is becoming part of the American way of life.

Farewell to the little woman puttering in her petunia garden. In her stead strides the All-American Female: she doesn't raise flowers, she eats them. Ordering our tastes, conditioning our entire culture, with money and mores in her grip, she indoctrinates us all from prenatal to unhappy ever after. We may free ourselves from the dictatorship of Big Brother, but not from Sister Sue.

Correspondents returning from global tours report that American wives are considered the most dominating in the world. "From Thailand to Timbuctoo, the American housewife is acknowledged queen above the droners. She makes and breaks the social engagements; she arranges the children's education and upbringing; she chooses the furnishings, the food, even her husband's clothes; the entire decor of their married way of life is all to suit *her* taste. She is the manager, the superintendent, the principal, the arbiter, the riding boss."

There's no escape-hatch open; the *New York Times* takes note of women as bartenders, women in board rooms, women, women everywhere. The Amazonian flood rolls on, and we are all inundated by this monstrous matriarchal force. *Après Ma, le deluge.*

As Big Momma thus brazenly ascends in the scale of things, so Big Daddy has come down in the world. Belittled, bothered and bewildered, it is now his turn to play Button, button, where's my emotional status? Harvard historian Arthur Schlesinger, Jr., is merely one of many pundits who have come to ponder "The Crisis In American Masculinity." (The editors of *Esquire*, where his article first appeared, were not content with such an equivocal title, and headlined it on the front cover as "The Decay Of American Manhood.") And as the women's magazines month after month feature new ways to lasso your man and new ways to cook him, such general magazines as *Look* re-echo rhetorical questions: "Why does the American male let women dominate him? Does he like petticoat rule or has it been forced on him by the stronger sex?"

All around us Big Momma swings high on the rope-pull while the bells toll for the passing of our national manhood. Russell Lynes moans that the once-authoritative father has been reduced to "part man, part-time mother and part-time maid. He is the chief cook and bottle washer; the chauffeur, the gardener and the houseboy; the maid and the laundress and the char-woman."

Can we keep the last lusty Tarzan of the tree-tops from turning into Stuart the servile suburban hedge-trimmer? Or has the ultimate saltpeter been slipped into Mr. Murphy's chowder? We can well understand why an army of publications has sprouted with healthy Anglo-Saxon titles such as *Male* and *Stag*. They are desperately needed to bolster Hemingwaysmanship. Save our whooping cranes and daddies.

Too little, however, and too late, since that other sex has definitely done us in. No wonder Dwight Eisenhower, when queried by a woman reporter about the Equal Rights Amendment, could only smile ruefully and remark: "As a mere man, how can I presume to offer an opinion?" And the late President Kennedy, at a state dinner in Paris, introduced himself by remarking, "I am here as the husband of Jacqueline Kennedy."

A whole battery of anthropologists, sociologists, and fact-finders assures us that the myth of Big Momma is honest-to-gospel, and they've got the appropriate inter-personal quotations to prove that women have

taken us over economically, socially, culturally, relatively, and absolutely. French expert Ameury de Riencourt lectures to large audiences
who listen attentively while he tells them: "Man has become a member
of an oppressed minority. Preconditioned to female dominance by his
own mother, he is a volunteer for slavery." De Reincourt sees one glim-
mer of hope on the distant horizon, for although it is clearly too late for
American woman to save her mate from matriarchal dominance, perhaps she can save her sons by helping them to "see womanhood in its
right perspective." British observer Eric Dingwall sees no such hope
at all—and thereby gets his book reissued in a large paperback edition. At
the annual conference of the Child Study Association, educators and
psychiatrists feared that men may become at last no more than "mother's
little helpers."

The worst is happening, yet the worst is yet in store as geneticist Her-
man Muller predicts a future civilization with sperm banks in the deep
freeze. It won't be necessary to have a man around the atom-bomb
shelter for anything.

Backed by such authorities, the myth gathers momentum. Big
Momma becomes packageable, swift-selling merchandise. No longer
confined to the sophisticated magazines are Thurberlike cartoons showing the female as a slovenly behemoth. Such drawings are reproduced
on ceramic ashtrays, pen-and-pencil sets, trays, bowls, tiles, paper nap-
kins, plaques to hang on the wall. What was once a somewhat cynical
and dry Martini view is now a cheery-beery middle-class household
maxim.

Is there any fire to all this smoke about Big Momma, or is it just
plain smog?

The myth-makers contend that there is no power like womanpower
in American life today.

Now it is true that women have been continuing their advance in
many fields. The tempo, however, is less than the speed of lightning.
Recently, one woman was appointed New York State supreme court
justice; there are two U.N. delegates; a score of bank managers; thousands of technicians. More than one-third of all married women are
going outside the home to work—a good many of them at part-time or
seasonal jobs where they do not earn very much; still and all, the trend
away from total housewifery appears irreversible. Women *are* less dependent than they used to be. The number of positive gains is definitely
on the increase. Nevertheless, taken all together, they do not confer a
legitimate status, let alone a dominant one. To claim that women are a
major force is as foolish as supposing that a series of victorious "sit-ins"
at lunch counters in the South meant that the Negro has achieved first-
class citizenship.

The myth-makers, nonetheless, would have it that our entire national economy is at women's mercy. Buttressed by statistics, they point out to us that solid property and portable assets are concentrated in her hands to an alarming degree. Higher and higher balloon the statistics of what women own. Latest reports show that sixty per cent of our national wealth is in feminine hands.

Now why should this automatically be worse than having it in the hands of the opposite sex? But the bulk of the money in this country is not controlled by women, of course; it is merely held by them. Some widows inherit fortunes, and much property is nominally owned by wives to beat that old devil income-tax. But does anyone truly feel that Helena Rubinstein's or Lily Daché's empires are a threat to the houses of Rockefeller, Morgan, Du Pont and the other tried-and-true blue chip boys?

The case of Big Momma flouts reality full in the face, as a good myth should, and her matriarchal image—a sort of combination giant slicing machine, loud speaker, and wringer—keeps coming at us. So pervasive is it that even an historian like Schlesinger states in all seriousness that the American woman "takes over more and more of the big decisions, controlling them indirectly when she cannot do so directly."

The truth is that far from being dictating tycoons or the power behind the arras most females continue to take it all down on their shorthand pads with a snappy, "Yes, sir!" It is obvious that where American woman-power still earns only sixty-three per cent as much as manpower; where their human skills are expended for the most part in clerical, minor assembly-line and domestic work; and where sex prejudice is still one of the cornerstones of our social structure (you have only to compare the status of any extra woman at a party with that of any extra man)— Big Momma is not a factor, she's a fraud. Furthermore, no amount of full-fledged Moms would be capable of mopping up the thousand years and more of patriarchal rule. But it makes for a pleasantly haunting specter: the kind you can afford to fear, because it's only make-believe— unlike the uncertainty of living in a real world where fall-out is not a made-up plot gimmick.

So the fairy tale of Big Momma as the menace that's the most proceeds: as the wicked witch, she get cloaked with all kinds of marvelous powers. Not only does she have Moneypower and Jobpower at her command, but an even more magical power is hers: Buyingpower. Ultimately everything comes to the consumer, and bullseye!—she is the highest consumer of us all. For lo, does she rule over our patterns of buying in everything from which thickness of steak for Rover to which dog-biscuit for Daddy? Mrs. America is the queen in this land of brands; hail to the queen not just for a day but for ever and ever and foreverness just as sure as little olives are put into jars and labeled Colossal.

Is she not the one who decides to which company's product America will give the nod or the nix? Detergent or soap powder? Ammoniated toothpaste or plain? Roll-on deodorant or spray? The sample surveys wait breathlessly for her decisions which don't matter in the slightest, since the same Proctor and Gamble makes them all. If proof were required of the powerlessness of woman's influence as a consumer, consider the results of a McCall's Conference for Better Living held in Washington. Unanimously, the women asked designers for ovens at stand-up levels so they wouldn't have to go on stooping down to the floor every time they had to baste a roast. A sensible request, but apparently it was more profitable for the stove manufacturers to go on making the same old style instead of retooling, so thank you very much ladies and do send us more suggestions.

The myth-makers remain undaunted. There's always another layer to peel on this womanpower onion. Big Mamma is not merely the nation's number one public force, she's our private powerhouse as well. The family is the pivot of society, is it not? The myth perks up to consider Big Momma's influence in every aspect of daily living. She decides which house to buy in which neighborhood; then she chooses everything that goes into the house; even the male's choice of what tie, socks, suit, and shirt to wear on any particular day have to be from the wardrobe that she has pre-selected.

Now this last-named supposed female prerogative is strictly a wily appeal to manufacturers of menswear to place more advertising in the segregated women's magazines. More men purchase their clothing than not; the manufacturers know it and stay in their own bailiwick. By and large, however, the family finances are hers to apportion; she is in a position to carve up the weekly budget as she sees fit. The joker is that Big Momma's free choices are completely circumscribed by the family income and the mortgage payments. She might like them to spend their vacation on the Riviera; Papa's paycheck says a public camp-site.

This does not cause the builders of Big Momma to worry that they have a defective rocket. They simply address themselves to another part of the dream forest. A myth is many womanpowers, and we move on to Presencepower. By just being there, she rules the children, the home, and the school system. He empire is monolithic and unchallengeable as she reigns supreme over the impressionable years.

The force of her presence is such that when Junior grows up he will never but never be able to unravel the knots in the silver cord. We can see for ourselves that this is the case every time we pick up a magazine, go to the movies, or watch a television program. Father and/or son are constantly being victimized by mother's praying mantis tactics. Hideously grasping, gloating, she reduces whatever is male to the most miniscule level.

Science-fiction sagas are on the wane. Anybody's mother can inspire the same feelings of nervous fright and approaching purple doom. Playwrights and novelists, less hampered than the mass media in their choice of language and situation, not only describe how American women crush the spirit out of the male's vital juices, but drive them to homosexuality and other Kinsey categories.

The anti-mamma drama is a surefire hit, and the harridan heroines come in two sizes: over- and under-sexed. Over-, however, is simply a crude disguise for the total iceberg below. The cold war in international politics has a close second in the cold war currently being staged between the sexes.

Has anyone considered that along with the Loch Ness monster and Piltdown man, the deep-freeze female may be something of a hoax? Quite possibly, the case of the frigid wife could be an ingenious alibi for the middle-aged husband. It would be more natural if he were delinquent in this department rather than she, and in fact this may be so. For by all that is known about physiology, the middle-aged husband is no match for his wife. The woman of thirty-five or forty is at the height of her sexual powers; the male of the same age is looking back a good fifteen years to when he was at his most potent. It may be that his wife requires some sort of masculine Lolita as a supplement to her diet: a male counterpart of the youthful vigor displayed by Nabokov's nymphet.

If the middle-aging husband is not up to it, what better face to put on for the world to see than that his wife is not willing? If this is indeed the case, it may help account for some of the popularity of pornography today. This titillating playboy type of literature presents a dream fulfillment picture of the hyper-active male, a picture that bears little resemblance to reality.

One hero of recent times was the handsome, intelligent, wealthy Republican who was revealed during a political campaign as a bigamist. Wife number one and children in one city; wife the second and children in another. He made almost no effort to dissemble, since in both marriages he used his real name, merely switching his first and second initials for different checking accounts. Women admired him for his gallantry, men for his prowess.

For over and above not wanting a run-in with the law, most men are incapable of fulfilling the sexual demands made upon the bigamist. They are more likely to be keeping up two jobs rather than two women. It is interesting that the term "moonlighting," which somehow suggests tomcat gallivanting, applies to the sober condition of holding down two jobs: one in the daytime and another in the evening, in order to make ends meet on the mortgage, the insurance policy, and the children's college fund.

Our affluent society does not encompass an affluent sex life for husbands and fathers.

Of all the rights claimed by emancipated females today, perhaps the hardest for men to accede to is the sexual one. For how can a man make money in these times and make love too? Their wives, newer in the job world, come home stimulated; the husbands come home exhausted. The retreat after dinner to the newspaper curtain, television screen, or basement workshop is often not so much a reflection of masculine interest as a reluctance to meet the challenge that awaits in the bedroom.

To Nora's husband, sex is an old story; to her it is new and exulting. Like Molière's character who was delighted to discover that he'd been speaking prose all his life, hers is a talent for enjoyment she never knew she possessed.

In the old days, a man married; his wife took his name and his commands, bore his children and kept on bearing. In return, he supported her with money and muscles. He was the stronger and taller and therefore required more sustenance. His appetite was conceded to be the larger, both at table and in bed. It was understood that fidelity applied to women only. All that, of course, was changed by the coming of the Noras who no longer accepted the old-fashioned male supremacy flattery that the female was "superior" by nature, that she required "spiritual" values in sex while his needs were strictly biological. Nora recognizes that such compliments to her artistic, highflown character are merely a façade for the double standard of the not so good old days.

As for today, her needs are sometimes greater than his. If she does not get satisfaction, she learns to ask for it. (Her training in brand names has not been in vain.) The husband who does not deliver may be called to account. And living by the numbers, working his way up to the two-car garage and the four-window office, he may be asked to deliver in bed in geometric procession. For one of the marks of our salesmanship times is to label quantity as quality in all things, including the measure of a man. He who would copulate contentedly had best hie his companion to a lodging remote from billboards, television commercials and women's "service" magazines.

Yet the image of Iceberg Bertha as the prototype of American women continues to loom large on our social horizon. Big Bad Momma has to be the most in everything.

Of course, women exert an influence, but it is scarcely a monopolistic one. And it would have to be a Big Momma indeed who could hold her own against some of the forces shaping our youth today. Mothers can try forbidding comic books, the singing of cigarette commercials, and the viewing of too-wild Westerns and war programs on television. And they can keep on trying.

But Big Momma, we are told, is not only the dominant influence on the child's home life; womanpower also runs the schools. To be sure, Parent-Teacher Associations list heavily to the distaff side. Unfortunately, their controlling influence does not necessarily extend to where the appropriations for education are voted.

Still the myth continues to be expounded. Womanpower has not only taken us over in every other way—Big Momma's even got us over a barrel physically. Don't statistics prove that women live ten per cent longer and are healthier than men?

If the finger on the push-button bomb should get trigger-happy, the question of living longer becomes academic. As for her health, the arguments are always trotted out that only one-fifth as many women commit suicide as compared to men; there are fewer women alcoholics; they are less subject to heart attacks, ulcers, and other ailments. If it's any consolation in the battle to stem the feminine tide, alcoholism among women is on the rise, and for the first time liquor advertising is being accepted in the women's magazines. Ulcers too are increasing; so are nervous breakdowns; and if the cigarette-to-cancer link is proven conclusively, that may open up new democratic vistas, since women are smoking more than ever. Perhaps we could even get up a special Freedom Fighter Fund to encourage mothers to become despondent and abandon their families.

But surely we should be able to find *something* to confirm the existence of a matriarchal state? Finally, by coming back to the men, we seem to have it. Today's men do tend to be meeker than they once were. On the whole, they are pretty passive specimens.

The responsibility must be placed somewhere for this loss of self-respect and down-priding—and there's no more convenient doorstep to leave it on than Big Momma's.

As Dr. Pangloss understood so well that noses were made for the purpose of holding spectacles, the matriarchal myth can be made a convenient catch-all for most of the ills that Organization Man is prone to. *She's* dominated him so that he's lost his natural gumption and guts. Why, he could very well be vice-president of the company right this minute, but what with having to help dry the dishes and carry out the garbage for her, he's surrendered his manliness.

Is it so? Has this mutation of the male really taken place because lady lion-tamers have been standing over them with high heels digging into their groins? I think not. I think that this pretended relationship between the sexes is merely a sideshow of the main bout. And the main bout shapes up in this form: Man Meets Job. Man Wants To Hold Onto Job. How Can He?

I think that is the heart of the matter, heartless as it may be. Within the framework of our contemporary capitalist culture, most men can hold onto their jobs best by surrendering the qualities customarily considered male. At a certain level, the old openly aggressive, so-called masculine drive has been superseded. The robber barons, the Big Jim Bradys are no more. Gone the flashing knives and brass knuckles. Today we have the silent wire-tap and the subliminal sapping of the nerve centers. The fight is fixed so that nobody refers to it as fighting. It's in-groupness. The art of getting ahead is to look as if you are standing still. Play it contained, smooth as flannel, cool as a circle signifying cipher. It is no accident that gray is the favored shade for menswear; it blends so readily into the neuter atmosphere.

Everything positive is accomplished in terms of negatives. You can become branch manager by not sticking your neck out. You can make it to the vice-presidency of the corporation by not contradicting and by not being too egghead grammatical. The man who knows says nothing controversial. The man who is serious about getting ahead cultivates a well-blended personality: colorless, tasteless, smell-less, feelingless. Since he dare not say what he thinks, he might as well give up the practice of any mental exercise whatever.

In short, the formula for the male today is to learn to be a good old-fashioned wife. And if you lose your male pride in the process, well, was it so essential to retain? After all, it's not like losing a wallet.

For if you accept the standards of the society, you have to behave as a law-abiding citizen. You daren't live in sin; you've got to marry that corporation. Promise to love, honor, and obey and then follow through. Say yes, dear. . . coming, sweetheart . . . exactly my opinion in the matter, J.B., you've expressed it far better than I ever could myself . . . Isn't it cozy, the corporation and I always think alike; we never quarrel; we like the same people, the same four-color ads. Whither thou goest, I go, to the branch office in Des Moines or Delaware, whatever you say, dear, it's all the same to me.

One out of five American families pulls up stakes and moves every year—not because of the whim of Big Momma who got bored with the old neighborhood, but because the Company says go man go.

So many men have become acquiescent, compliant, as the job with the most security and the safest income tax bracket beckons. The job demands all the qualities traditionally associated with women: subservience, unquestioning loyalty, a dependence based on fear, the subduing of one's own personality to another's. The good old-fashioned woman does not stand out in a crowd or make herself conspicuous by dissenting; when she takes on her husband's name, she literally becomes Mrs. John Dough. As why should she not? If she wants to or needs to be supported by him, she must remain subordinate and cater to his master position.

Hence the goodman married to the corporation, to the science foundation, to the university, to whatever organization punches out his paycheck. The emasculation of man has not been caused by women. It is a social not a sexual affair. The winning mystery word is not Momism but capitalism.

However, it is far too unsettling to criticize the real power structure that exists. Besides, everybody knows that there is no form of society possible other than the private profit system, so what's a man to do? When he's got the beat, baffled, rundown and maybe-I'll-be-out-of-a-job-next-month blues, he's got to blame somebody for the spot he's in and there is nothing like a dame. For it can't be free enterprise that's made the failure. Well, we can stop looking so glum; we don't have to face reality yet. Here's the matriarchal myth come along to turn all our solid worries into bubbles. And who in his heart of hearts does not bear some sensible grudge against Mother? Mac if you dont hate your old lady you're a square; you're not with it. Let's get with it; let's get this handy form of Miltown that can tranquilize both the sexes and keep them contented in their properly down-under places.

Mrs. Mister like to read all those pieces telling her how big and bad and powerful she is. Wouldn't you like to feel more important than you are?

And Mr. Mister likes the picture, too; it gives him something safe to sound off about. Practically every other topic of conversation is still on the Attorney General's subversive list anyway.

So the myth goes on making money, which is the proper function for any art form in our society. Onward and upward with the matriarchal menace that's the most, in a serene world where there are no bosses to be mad at, where there are no classes anymore, but only Big Mommies and little daddies.

"X" Doesn't Equal "Y"

Ashley Montagu

The thesis of Ashley Montagu's The Natural Superiority of Women *is that women are biologically, psychologically, and emotionally superior to men. For support of his theories he*

*leans heavily on the jealousy of man for woman the child-
bearer. The book is interesting and informative, but must be
read with caution. For example, his chapter on "Women and
Creativity" argues that women have not excelled in the creative arts because they "create naturally," hence are not competitive, being "more interested in human relationships, in
which they can creatively love and be loved." In this chapter,
Montagu stereotypes women as casually as the most ardent
male chauvinist. Eve Merriam has astutely said of Montagu's
analysis: "This is the natural superiority of the minnow that can
exist on less food than the whale. . . . In his estimation, woman
is biologically so superior and altogether so marvelous in her
own inner nature that actually she doesn't require much from
the exterior world" (After Nora Slammed the Door, pp. 132–
133).*

The following chapter from The Natural Superiority of
Women, *describing the chromosome structure of male and
female, develops the idea that "to commence life as a male is
to start off with a disadvantage." It is interesting to compare
Montagu's view of man as "an incomplete female" with Valerie
Solanas' view in* S.C.U.M. Manifesto *as well as with Freud's
view of woman as an incomplete man.*

We have already seen that there is very good reason to believe that
the female enjoys, on the whole, a very definite biological advantage over
the male. Does there exist some biological differentiating factor which
may serve to explain or possibly throw some light upon the origin and
meaning of these differences? The answer is "Yes." And I should like
this "Yes" to resound all over the world, for I do not know that anyone
has made anything of a key fact which lies at the base of practically all
the differences between the sexes and the biological superiority of the
female to the male. I refer to the chromosomal structure of the sexes,
the chromosomes being the small cellular bodies which contain the
hereditary particles, or genes, which so substantially influence one's
fate as an organism.

In the sex cells there are twenty-four chromosomes, but only one of
these is a sex chromosome. There are two kinds of sex chromosomes,
X and Y. Half the sperm cells carry X- and half carry Y-chromosomes.
All the female ova in the female ovaries contain only X-chromosomes.
When an X-bearing sperm fertilizes an ovum, the offspring is always
female. When a Y-bearing chromosome fertilizes an ovum, the offspring
is always male. It is the initial difference in chromosome composition
which determines the differences between the sexes in a constitutionally

decisive manner. This is not to say that the chromosomes are eventually entirely responsible for the development of all the differences in sex characteristics; it *is* to say that the chromosomes are decisive in determining whether an organism shall develop as a male or a female. The sex chromosomes regulate the transformation of the fertilized ovum into an embryo which, during the first few weeks of development, is sexually neutral; except for its chromosomal composition, it is neither of one sex nor of the other. Shortly the rudiments of the sex organs begin to appear, but these are still neutral, for under the proper hormonal influences they can be converted into the sex organs of the male or the female sex in spite of the chromosomal composition of the embryo. However, under normal conditions the sex rudiments are differentially affected toward maleness or femaleness depending upon whether the chromosomal composition (the genotype) is XY or XX. The genotype or chromosomal composition, therefore, is decisive in initiating the direction of sexual development; thereafter it is largely under the influence of the developing hormones secreted by the endocrine glands. The development of all bodily structures and their functions, in relation to the environment in which they develop, is set by the sex chromosomes at the time the sex rudiments and the gonads (the sexually indifferent organs which may develop either as ovaries or testes) are sexually differentiated.

What is the difference between an XX and an XY cell? Well, if you look at the XX cell under the microscope (all the body cells of a female are XX), and you get a nice clear view (which is the exception rather than the rule), you will not recognize the XX sex-chromosomes as two distinctive chromosomes among the other forty-six because they look exactly like the other chromosomes; nevertheless the X-chromosomes are there. Now, if you look at the body cell of a male and you are lucky enough, say at a magnification of 2,000 diameters, to see the chromosomes, then you will be able to find one that is much smaller than the forty-seven other chromosomes, and this will almost certainly be the Y-chromosome. It may have the shape of a comma, the merest remnant, a sad-looking affair compared to the well upholstered other chromosomes! As we shall soon see, the Y-chromosome really is a sad affair; in fact, it isn't really sex chromosome at all—and there lies part of the answer to the question: How do the sexes get that way?

The chromosomes which are neither X nor Y are called "autosomes." There are twenty-three pairs of them in the body cells, and only twenty-three single ones in the sex cells. Each of the autosomes contains genes which tend toward the production of maleness. Each of the X-chromosomes contains genes which tend toward the production of femaleness. The Y-chromosome doesn't contain any sex-producing genes at all. Hence, when a Y-carrying sperm fertilizes an ovum, the XY chromosomes, in the presence of the twenty-three pairs of autosomes carrying genes so strongly directed toward maleness, are insufficiently powerful to reduce their influence, and the result is the development of a male. On the other hand, the combination of two X-chromosomes is sufficient to overcome the influence of the maleness genes in the autosomes, and the result is a female. The X-chromosomes together have quite a pull to them; and the explanation of the biological superiority of the female lies in the fact that the male has only one X-chromosome and the female has two. It is largely to the original X-chromosomal deficiency of the male that almost all the troubles to which the male falls heir may be traced, and to the presence of two well appointed, well furnished X-chromosomes that the female owes her biological superiority.

In birds and some insects two X-chromosomes produce a male and an XY combination produces a female, but otherwise the conditions are precisely the same as in man, except that the autosomes contain the sex genes which are strongly organized toward femaleness, whereas the X-chromosomes are strongly, and in double dose, more powerfully organized toward maleness. That it is the X-chromosome which counts is borne out by the fact that embryo deaths are much higher among the female birds than among the males.

What the origin of the X- and Y-chromosomes may have been no one knows, but I find it amusing and helpful to think of the Y-chromosome as an undeveloped X-chromosome, or perhaps as a remnant of an X-chromosome. It is as if the evolution of sex a fragment at one time broke away from an X-chromosome, carrying with it some rather unfortunate genes, and thereafter in relation to the other chromosomes was helpless to prevent them from expressing themselves in the form of an incomplete female, the creature we call the male! This "just-so" story makes the male a sort of crippled female, a creature who by virtue of the fact that he has only one X-chromosome is not so well equipped biologically as the female.

But that is not the whole story. The fact that the male is endowed with a Y-chromosome seems to put him at a greater disadvantage than if he had no Y-chromosome at all; for while the Y-chromosome may have quite a number of genes which may be of some value, it also has several that are, to say the least, unfortunate. Thus far at least four conditions have been traced to genes which occur only in the Y-chromosome, and hence can be transmitted only by fathers to their sons. These are bark-like skin (ichthyosis hystrix gravior), dense hairy growth on the ears (hypertrichosis), non-painful hard lesions of the hands and feet (keratoma dissipatum), and a form of webbing of the toes in which there is fusion of the skin between the second and third toes.

It is probable that the biological disadvantages accruing to the male are not so much due to what is in the Y-chromosome as to what is not in it. This is well exemplified by the manner in which the male inherits

such a serious disorder as hemophilia (bleeder's disease). This disease
is due to a mutant gene which is carried in the X-chromosome. A mutant
gene is one in which a physico-chemical change of a heritable kind occurs. It has been calculated that the normal gene for blood clotting
mutates to the defective hemophilia gene in one out of every hundred
thousand persons of European origin in each generation. Since most
hemophiliacs die before they can leave any offspring, the number of
such unfortunate persons alive at any time is relatively small. Hemophilia is inherited as a single sex-linked recessive gene, that is, a gene
which is linked to the X-chromosome and which will not express itself
in the presence of a normal gene on the opposite X-chromosome. When,
then, an X-chromosome which carries the hemophilia gene is transmitted
to a female, it is highly improbable that it will encounter another
X-chromosome carrying such a gene; it is for this reason that hemophilia
is of the very greatest rarity in a female. Since the survival rate to reproductive age is very low, it is obvious why females are the most usual
transmitters of the hemophilia gene, and it should also be clear why
females practically never exhibit the condition. The males are affected
because they don't have any properties in their Y-chromosome which
are capable of suppressing the action of the hemophilia gene. Women
could only exhibit the condition if they inherited a hemophilia gene
from their mother and another hemophilia gene from their father, and
this is extremely unlikely to occur. The usual pattern of inheritance is
that the female inherits a hemophilia X-chromosome from her father
and a normal X-chromosome from her mother. Because the normal
X-chromosome suppresses or inhibits the action of the hemophilia
X-chromosome, she does not suffer from hemophilia; but if she marries
a normal man and has a number of children she will pass on the hemo-
philia-bearing X-chromosome to some of them. The girls who inherit it
will show no ill effects, but the males who have received the gene may
show the effects even before they are born and die of hemophilia *in
utero*, or they may fall victim to the disease at any time from birth to
adult life; but exhibit the condition they will, and in the greater number
of instances they will die of its effects.

The mechanism of color blindness (red-green, mostly) and its explanation are precisely the same as for hemophilia. About 4 per cent of
American men are completely red-green color blind, while another 4
per cent are color blind in varying degrees to red-green or other colors,
whereas only half of 1 per cent of American women are so affected.

More than thirty serious disorders occurring in the male are known
to be due to genes present in the X-chromosomes; these conditions can
occur in a woman only if her father was affected and her mother carried
the gene. Below are listed some of the conditions occurring more frequently in males because of sex-linked genes.

CONDITIONS LARGELY DUE TO
SEX-LINKED GENES MOSTLY FOUND IN MALES

Albinism of the eyes (depigmentation of the eyes)
Alopecia congenita (congenital baldness)
Anhidrotic ectodermal dysplasia (maldevelopment of the sweat glands)
Coloboma iridis (congenital cleft of the iris)
Color blindness of the red-green type
Day blindness
Defective hair follicles
Defective iris
Defective tooth enamel
Distichiasis (double eyelashes)
Epidermal cysts (skin cysts)
Glaucoma of the juvenile type (increase in fluids of eyeball)
Hemophilia (bleeder's disease)
Ichthyosis (scale-like skin)
Megalocornea (enlargement of the cornea of the eyeball)
Microcornea (diminution of the cornea of the eyeball)
Mitral stenosis (stricture of the bicuspid valve of the heart)
Myopia (short-sightedness)
Night blindness
Nystagmus (rhythmical oscillation of the eyeballs)
Optic atrophy (wasting of the eye)
Peroneal atrophy (wasting of the muscles of the legs)
Pseudo-hypertrophic muscular dystrophy (weakening of the muscles
    with growth of connective tissue in them)
Retinal detachment
Thromboasthenia (a defect in the thrombin, fibrin, and blood platelet
    formation of the blood)
White occipital lock of hair

So much, then, for the conditions which are directly traceable to genetic factors. It should by this time be quite clear that to commence life as a male is to start off with a disadvantage—a disadvantage which operates at every stage of life, from fertilization on.

Even though male-producing sperms are produced in the same numbers as female-producing sperms, between 120 and 150 males are conceived as compared with 100 females. Why this should be so we do not know, but it is a fact. The ratio at birth for American whites is 106 males to 100 females. (The ratios vary for different human groups, depending largely upon their socio-economic or nutritional status.) In India the sex ratio of boys is 98.7 to 100 girls. In other words the poorer the nutritional conditions, the greater the lethality of the males; even fetal females are stronger than fetal males. The records uniformly show that from fertilization on, the mortality rates before birth are higher for the male than for the female fetus, and that males after birth continue to have a higher mortality rate than females for every year of age. Within every age range, more males die than females. For example, in 1946–1948 three boy babies in the first year of life died for every two girl babies. At about the age of twenty-one, for every girl who dies almost two boys die. Thereafter, at the age of thirty-five, 1,400 men die for every 1,000 women; at fifty-five 1,800 men die for every 1,000 women; after that the difference in death rate diminishes, though it always remains in favor of the female.

Life expectancy at birth is higher for women than for men all over the world (except certain parts of India), and this fact holds true for females as compared with males for the greater part of the animal kingdom. In the United States life expectancy at birth for a white female is 71.0 years, and for a while male 65.5 years; for a non-white female 62.5 years, and for a non-white male 58.1 years. These facts constitute further evidence that the female is constitutionally stronger than the male. There have been some who have argued that women live longer than men because they don't usually work so hard. Most men, it is argued, work harder, work longer hours, and usually under greater strain and tension than most women. I think these statements are open to question. I am under the impression that most housewives work at least as hard as their husbands, and under at least as great a strain. If we compare the longevity rates of bachelors with jobs with those of spinsters with jobs, we find that the advantage is again with the females. Spinsters with jobs live longer than bachelors with jobs. In 1940 the age-adjusted death rate for single men was one and one-half times that for married men, whereas among single women the death rate was only 10 per cent higher than that for the married. It is an interesting fact that both among men and among women, the married have lower death rates than the single, widowed, or divorced.

Women are healthier than men—if by health one means the capacity to deal with germs and illness. Statistics from the public health services of various countries, and especially the United States, show that while after the age of fifteen the sickness rate is higher among females than among males, females recover from illnesses much more frequently than males do. Death from almost all causes are more frequent in males at all ages. Almost the only disorders from which women die more frequently than men are those subserving the functional systems of reproduction; namely, the reproductive tract and the endocrine glandular system.

Epilepsy has about the same incidence in both sexes, but according to the vital statistics of the Bureau of the Census the death rate from epilepsy is about 30 per cent higher for men than for women.

For every female stutterer there are five male stutterers. The "stutter-type personality," who is characterized by a certain jerkiness or "stutter" of movements, as well as of speech, occurs in the ratio of eight males to one female. Word deafness, the inherited inability to understand the meaning of sounds, occurs very much more frequently in the male than in the female, and so do baldness, gout, and ulcers of the stomach. Need one go on?

The evidence is clear: From the constitutional standpoint woman is the stronger sex. The explanation of the greater constitutional strength of the female lies largely, if not entirely, in the fact that she possesses two complete X-chromosomes and the male possesses only one. This may not be the whole explanation of the physical constitutional superiority of the female, but it is certainly scientifically the most acceptable explanation and the one least open to question.

To the unbiased student of the facts there can no longer remain any doubt of the constitutional superiority of the female.

At the present time the insurance companies charge the same insurance rates for women as for men. This hardly seems fair to women. But then when has anyone ever been fair to women? The occasions have been the exceptions. Man has projected his own weaknesses upon her, and as the "muscle man" has maintained the myth of feminine weakness until the present time. But it is not woman who is weak; it is man, and in more senses than one. But the last thing on earth we want to do is to give the male a feeling of inferiority. On the other hand, we consider it a wise thing for a man to know both his limitations and his weaknesses, for in knowing them he may learn how to make himself strong. The truth about the sexes will not only serve to set women free; it will also serve to set men free; for if women have been the slaves of men, men have been the slaves of their own prejudices about women, and this has worked no good to anyone.

Three Sexual Myths Exploded

Ruth and Edward Brecher

A woman brought up on the standard marriage manuals may end up on the psychiatrist's couch trying to understand why she has "failed as a woman" in her husband's bed. The idea of

From *An Analysis of Human Sexual Response* edited by Ruth and Edward Brecher. Copyright © 1966 by Ruth and Edward Brecher. Reprinted by arrangement with The New American Library, Inc., N.Y.

the "frigid" woman is a commonplace in our society; and the
woman who has not experienced orgasm often begins to question her own sexuality. The fact is that most women know very
little about the functioning of their bodies—it is not considered
"ladylike" to inquire too closely; and it is considered even less
ladylike to make sexual demands of one's lover. Recent studies,
notably those of Alfred C. Kinsey (Sexual Behavior in the
Human Male, 1948; Sexual Behavior in the Human Female,
1953) and of William H. Masters and Virginia E. Johnson
(Human Sexual Response, 1966), have shed new light on
woman's sexual capacity. The following excerpt from Ruth
and Edward Brecher's An Analysis of Human Sexual Response
negates three sexual myths that have contributed to woman's
ignorance about her sexuality.

Through the generations, men—and some women—have speculated
on the nature of sexual response, basing their speculations on their personal experience and on the accounts of others who, in turn, have had
to rely on personal experience. Out of this vast sexual literature, several
myths have arisen, which the detailed Masters-Johnson observations
disprove. Among them are:

(1) The myth that a man's sexual performance is related to the size of
     his penis.
(2) The myth that women can have two kinds of orgasm—one clitoral
     and the other vaginal.
(3) The myth that a woman, like a man, is limited to one climactic
     orgasm that produces satiety.

Size of Penis

Many men and boys are worried by the small size of their penis. A
man generally reaches the conclusion that his own is small by observing
and comparing the unerected penises of other men in showers, swimming
pools, or other places. He assumes that the larger organs he has observed
will increase in size during sexual stimulation proportionately more than
his own smaller penis. Psychiatrists report that the resulting feeling of
inferiority is a serious problem for substantial numbers of men.

In reply, Masters and Johnson point out first that a penis that is large
in its unstimulated state does *not* increase in length proportionately during erection. On the contrary, short penises as a general rule increase in
length more impressively than do long ones. A striking comparison illus-

trates this point. One man in the Masters-Johnson study group with an organ less than three inches long in the flaccid state experienced a 120-percent increase in penile length during erection, so that his erect penis measured nearly seven inches. Another man in the group with a penis half again as long when flaccid (nearly four and one-half inches) experienced an increase in length during erection of only 50 percent. As a result, his fully erect penis was also a little less than seven inches long. In general, there is significantly less variation in length among erect than among flaccid penises. Penile size, moreover, turned out to have little relationship to a marital partner's satisfaction in sexual intercourse, for the vagina accommodates itself to the size of the male organ.

This accommodation reaction was repeatedly demonstrated during artificial coition with a plastic artificial penis whose length and diameter a woman could select to suit herself and could change from time to time. "Full accommodation usually is accomplished," Dr. Masters and Mrs. Johnson report, "with the first few thrusts of the penis, regardless of penile size."

The size of the vagina also has little effect on mutual satisfaction in most cases; and accommodation can be helped by suitable timing of the entry of the penis. If the husband has a relatively small penis and the wife a relatively large vagina, for example, he can introduce his penis into the vagina earlier in the excitement phase. When this is done, Dr. Masters and Mrs. Johnson report, "the fully erect smaller penis can and does function as a dilating agent as effectively as a larger penis." Conversely, a husband with a relatively large penis can help his wife with a small vagina by delaying entry until a more advanced stage of sexual excitation. "It becomes obvious," Dr. Masters and Mrs. Johnson conclude, "that penile size usually is a minor factor in sexual stimulation of the female partner."

Clitoral vs. Vaginal Orgasm

More than sixty years ago, Sigmund Freud presented, in *Three Essays on the Theory of Sexuality,* a theory that women can experience two kinds of orgasm—one clitoral, the other vaginal.

Little girls, he explained, discover that they can achieve orgasm by stimulating the clitoris. Later, in marriage, they must transfer their sexual responses from the clitoris to the vagina. Some women fail to make this transfer. As a result, even though they may continue to have orgasm following stimulation of the clitoris, they are "vaginally frigid."

Since Freud wrote, this doctrine of the vaginal orgasm as distinct from the clitoral orgasm has permeated sexual literature and has troubled many women. The Masters-Johnson research should put these worries to rest.

During ordinary vaginal intercourse, their studies show, a remarkable feature of female anatomy comes into play. The thrusting of the penis causes motion of the inner lips, or minor labia, at the entrance of the vagina. These lips come together above the vaginal opening to form the "hood" or prepuce of the clitoris. The rhythmic motion of the inner lips produced by rhythmic coital thrusting slides the hood rhythmically back and forth against the exquisitely sensitive glans of the clitoris, stimulating it lightly but most effectively. Thus the clitoris participates fully in ordinary vaginal intercourse, even though neither husband nor wife makes special efforts to stimulate it directly.

There are undoubtedly great psychological differences between masturbation and sexual intercourse—but these differences cannot be traced back to two different kinds of orgasm. To quote directly from the paper by Masters and Johnson in the *Western Journal of Surgery, Gynecology, and Obstetrics* for September–October 1962:

> From an *anatomic* point of view, there is absolutely no difference in the response of the pelvic viscera to effective sexual stimulation, regardless of whether stimulation occurs as a result of clitoral area manipulation, natural or artificial coition, or, for that matter, from breast stimulation alone. . . . The human female's physiologic responses to effective sexual stimulation develop with consistency regardless of the source of the psychic or physical sexual stimulation.

Women concerned by their failure to reach "vaginal orgasm" can thus be reassured. There is neither a purely clitoral orgasm nor a purely vaginal organism. There is only one kind of orgasm from the physiological point of view—a *sexual* orgasm.

Multiple Orgasms in Women

Most men, as noted above, experience a "refractory period" following orgasm and ejaculation. They cannot experience a second erection and orgasm for many minutes or even hours. This is not true of women.

If a woman who is capable of regular orgasms is properly stimulated within a short period after her first climax [Dr. Masters and Mrs. Johnson report], she will in most instances be capable of having a second, third, fourth, and even fifth and sixth orgasm before she is fully satiated. As contrasted with the male's usual inability to have more than one orgasm in a short period, many females, especially when clitorally stimulated, can regularly have five or six full orgasms within a matter of minutes.

The possibility of multiple orgasms in women was not a Masters-Johnson discovery, of course; 14 percent of the women interviewed by Kinsey and his associates reported that they sometimes had multiple orgasms, and the same was true of 13 percent of the women interviewed by Terman. But these findings were often dismissed as unreliable by male writers who referred to multiple orgasms as "minor," and who even called multiorgasmic women "frigid" and incapable of experiencing true orgasm.

This kind of nonsense has now been laid to rest by the Masters-Johnson laboratory observations. Multiple orgasms do not differ physiologically in any significant respect from single orgasms, they report, except in their multiplicity. And they are not "minor" experiences:

> When female study subjects were interrogated in the laboratory after multiorgasmic experiences, the second or third orgasmic episode usually was identified subjectively as more satisfying or more sensually pleasurable than the first orgasmic episode.

The physiology of multiple orgasm in women can be simply explained. Three events in the genital region occur rapidly after a woman's first orgasm: her clitoris descends to its resting position overhanging the pubic bone, the orgasmic platform relaxes and loses its engorgement with excess blood, and her outer and inner lips (major and minor labia) also lose their engorgement. All three of these events, however, are reversible. With renewal of erotic stimulation—or with continuing stimulation—the clitoris again elevates, the veins refill with blood, the muscles again contract, and another orgasm is initiated.

Some women prefer continuous stimulation, going from one orgasm to another with practically no time lapse; others prefer to fall back to the plateau or excitement phase before stimulation is renewed.

Masters and Johnson report that multiple orgasms are more apt to occur with autostimulation (masturbation) than with intravaginal coition. The reason should be obvious: few men can maintain an erection long enough to produce multiple orgasms in their partners. The limit is not the woman's responsivity, but the male's erectile endurance.

In sexual cycles produced by direct stimulation of the woman's mons area, in contrast, her responsivity is the sole limit and she can match her self-stimulation to her responsive needs. Under such circumstances, Masters and Johnson report, a woman may "experience five to 20 recurrent orgasmic experiences with the sexual tension never allowed to drop below a plateau phase maintenance level until physical exhaustion terminates the session."

The belief that masculine endurance rather than feminine responsivity limits a woman's coital responses is confirmed by another remarkable set of Masters-Johnson findings. Five of the men seen in their clinic for infertile couples, they report, were fully potent sexually in all other ways, but were unable to ejaculate into a vagina. As a result, these five men "can and do maintain coital connection for 30 to 60 minutes at any given opportunity." In three of the five cases, the wives reap the full benefit. They "are multiorgasmic as a result of the constant opportunity for long-maintained coition." As in the cases of other women in self-stimulatory episodes, these women have one orgasm after another until "coition is terminated by the female partner's admission of sexual satiation." Multiple orgasm, in short, is not a characteristic of self-stimulation; it is a characteristic of any effective stimulation sufficiently prolonged to trigger multiple responses.

Dr. Masters and Mrs. Johnson have indicated just how far this process can go:

> The average female with optimal arousal will usually be satisfied with 3–5 manually induced orgasms; whereas mechanical stimulation, as with the electric vibrator is less tiring and induces her to go on to long stimulative sessions of an hour or more during which she may have 20 to 50 consecutive orgasms. She will stop only when totally exhausted. Such sessions, occurring as often as 2–3 times a week, create a chronic passive congestion of the pelvis and work hypertrophy of the clitoral shaft.

A practicing psychiatrist, Dr. Mary Jane Sherfey, has confirmed a portion of this finding, which she reported in the *Journal of the American Psychoanalytic Association* for January 1966:

> In clinical practice a number of married and single women using the electric vibrator to achieve up to fifty orgasms in a single session have come to my attention in the past few years. To have the comfort of a label, I had considered them to be cases of nymphomania without promiscuity. From the standpoint of our cultural norm, this may be an accurate enough phrase. From the standpoint of normal physiological functioning, these women exhibit a healthy, uninhibited sexuality—and the number of orgasms attained, a measure of the human female's orgasmic potentiality.

In the past it was reasonable to believe, on the basis of the Kinsey and Terman studies, that the capacity for multiple orgasm was limited to a minority of women—thirteen or fourteen out of every one hundred. The Masters-Johnson work indicates that this is not true. In addition to their research with erotically responsive subjects, Masters and Johnson since 1959 have also been treating married couples for sexual inadequacy. Some of the wives in this treatment group were "frigid" by even the strictest standards. They were incapable of achieving orgasm by any means whatever, and had never achieved orgasm throughout their lives, including five years or more of marriage. All of them had received prior medical or psychiatric treatment without results. These women, in short, were as far removed from the rapidly multiorgasmic women as could possibly be imagined. Yet following successful short-term therapy, they began within ten days to three weeks to experience not only orgasm but, in many cases, intense multiple orgasms; and once this capacity was achieved they were able to respond with increasing ease and rapidity. Details are not yet available; but in the light of what is already known concerning the Masters-Johnson therapeutic program, it would be dogmatic indeed to assert that even the seemingly most "frigid" women are not in fact capable, under suitable conditions, of experiencing intense multiple orgasms.

The Myth of the Vaginal Orgasm

Anne Koedt

In his 1931 essay on Female Sexuality, *Sigmund Freud declared that a woman's normal sexual development demands that she change from the mother to the father as love-object and that she move from a "masculine" (clitoral) phase to a "feminine" (vaginal) phase. This analysis has contributed to a myth about the nature of woman: The woman who does not experience vaginal orgasm has not achieved femininity; she is "frigid," and in need of psychiatric help. Anne Koedt discusses this myth, presenting biological evidence refuting it and offering reasons for the myth's survival to today.*

Whenever female orgasm and frigidity are discussed, a false distinction is made between the vaginal and the clitoral orgasm. Frigidity has generally been defined by men as the failure of women to have vaginal orgasms. Actually the vagina is not a highly sensitive area and is not constructed to achieve orgasm. It is the clitoris which is the center of sexual sensitivity and which is the female equivalent of the penis.

I think this explains a great many things: First of all, the fact that the so-called frigidity rate among women is phenomenally high. Rather than tracing female frigidity to the false assumptions about female anatomy, our "experts" have declared frigidity a psychological problem of women. Those who complained about it were recommended psychiatrists, so that they might discover their "problem"—diagnosed generally as a failure to adjust to their role as women.

The facts of female anatomy and sexual response tell a different story. There is only one area for sexual climax, although there are many area for sexual arousal; that area is the clitoris. All orgasms are extensions of sensation from this area. Since the clitoris is not necessarily stimulated sufficiently in the conventional sexual positions, we are left "frigid."

Aside from physical stimulation, which is the common cause of orgasm for most people, there is also stimulation through primarily mental processes. Some women, for example, may achieve orgasm through sexual fantasies, or through fetishes. However, while the stimulation may be psychological, the orgasm manifests itself physically. Thus, while the cause is psychological, the *effect* is still physical, and the orgasm necessarily takes place in the sexual organ equipped for sexual climax—the clitoris. The orgasm experience may also differ in degree of intensity—some more localized, and some more diffuse and sensitive. But they are all clitoral orgasms.

All this leads to some interesting questions about conventional sex and our role in it. Men have orgasms essentially by friction with the vagina, not the clitoral area, which is external and not able to cause friction the way penetration does. Women have thus been defined sexually in terms of what pleases men; our own biology has not been properly analyzed. Instead, we are fed the myth of the liberated woman and her vaginal orgasm—an orgasm which in fact does not exist.

What we must do is redefine our sexuality. We must discard the "normal" concepts of sex and create new guidelines which take into account mutual sexual enjoyment. While the idea of mutual enjoyment is liberally applauded in marriage manuals, it is not followed to its logical conclusion. We must begin to demand that if certain sexual positions now defined as "standard" are not mutually conducive to orgasm, they no longer be defined as standard. New techniques must be used or devised which transform this particular aspect of our current sexual exploitation.

Freud—A Father of the Vaginal Orgasm

Freud contended that the clitoral orgasm was adolescent, and that upon puberty, when women began having intercourse with men, women should transfer the center of orgasm to the vagina. The vagina, it was assumed, was able to produce a parallel, but more mature, orgasm than the clitoris. Much work was done to elaborate on this theory, but little was done to challenge the basic assumptions.

To fully appreciate this incredible invention, perhaps Freud's general attitude about women should first be recalled. Mary Ellman, in *Thinking About Women*, summed it up this way:

> Everything in Freud's patronizing and fearful attitude toward women follows from their lack of a penis, but it is only in his essay *The Psychology of Women* that Freud makes explicit . . . the deprecations of women which are implicit in his work. He then prescribes for them the abandonment of the life of the mind, which will interfere with their sexual function. When the psychoanalyzed patient is male, the analyst sets himself the task of developing the man's capacities; but with women patients, the job is to resign them to the limits of their sexuality. As Mr. Rieff puts it: "For Freud, Analysis cannot encourage in women new energies for success and achievement, but only teach them the lesson of rational resignation."

It was Freud's feelings about women's secondary and inferior relationship to men that formed the basis for his theories on female sexuality.

Once having laid down the law about the nature of our sexuality, Freud not so strangely discovered a tremendous problem of frigidity in women. His recommended cure for a woman who was frigid was psychiatric care. She was suffering from failure to mentally adjust to her "natural" role as a woman. Frank S. Caprio, a contemporary follower of these ideas, states:

> . . . whenever a woman is incapable of achieving an orgasm via coitus, provided her husband is an adequate partner, and prefers clitoral stimulation to any other form of sexual activity, she can be regarded as suffering from frigidity and requires psychiatric assistance. (*The Sexually Adequate Female*, p. 64.)

The explanation given was that women were envious of men—"renunciation of womanhood." Thus it was diagnosed as an anti-male phenomenon.

It is important to emphasize that Freud did not base his theory upon a study of woman's anatomy, but rather upon his assumptions of woman as an inferior appendage to man, and her consequent social and psychological role. In their attempts to deal with the ensuing problem of mass frigidity, Freudians created elaborate mental gymnastics. Marie Bonaparte, in *Female Sexuality*, goes so far as to suggest surgery to help women back on their rightful path. Having discovered a strange connection between the non-frigid woman and the location of the clitoris near the vagina,

> it then occurred to me that where, in certain women, this gap was excessive, and clitoridal fixation obdurate, a clitoral-vaginal recon-ciliation might be effected by surgical means, which would then benefit the normal erotic function. Professor Halban, of Vienna, as much a biologist as surgeon, became interested in the problem and worked out a simple operative technique. In this, the suspensory ligament of the clitoris was severed and the clitoris secured to the underlying struc-tures, thus fixing it in a lower position, with eventual reduction of the labia minora. (p. 148.)

But the severest damage was not in the area of surgery, where Freudians ran around absurdly trying to change female anatomy to fit their basic assumptions. The worst damage was done to the mental health of women, who either suffered silently with self-blame, or flocked to the psychiatrists looking desperately for the hidden and terrible repression that kept from them their vaginal destiny.

Lack of Evidence?

One may perhaps at first claim that these are unknown and un-explored areas, but upon closer examination this is certainly not true today, nor was it true even in the past. For example, men have known that women suffered from frigidity often during intercourse. So the problem was there. Also, there is much specific evidence. Men knew that the clitoris was and is the essential organ for masturbation, whether in children or adult women. So obviously women made it clear where *they* thought their sexuality was located. Men also seem suspiciously aware of the clitoral power during "foreplay," when they want to arouse women and produce the necessary lubrication for penetration. Foreplay is a concept created for male purposes, but works to the disadvantage of many women, since as soon as the woman is aroused the man changes to vaginal stimulation, leaving her both aroused and unsatisfied.

It has also been known that women need no anesthesia inside the vagina during surgery, thus pointing to the fact that the vagina is in fact not a highly sensitive area.

Today, with extensive knowledge of anatomy, with Kinsey, and Masters and Johnson, to mention just a few sources, there is no ignorance on the subject. There are, however, social reasons why this knowledge has not been popularized. We are living in a male society which has not sought change in women's role.

Anatomical Evidence

Rather than starting with what women *ought* to feel, it would seem logical to start out with the anatomical facts regarding the clitoris and vagina.

The Clitoris is a small equivalent of the penis, except for the fact that the urethra does not go through it as in the man's penis. Its erection is similar to the male erection, and the head of the clitoris has the same type of structure and function as the head of the penis. G. Lombard Kelly, in *Sexual Feeling in Married Men and Women,* says:

> The head of the clitoris is also composed of erectile tissue, and it possesses a very sensitive epithelium or surface covering, supplied with special nerve endings called genital corpuscles, which are peculiarly adapted for sensory stimulation that under proper mental conditions terminates in the sexual orgasm. No other part of the female generative tract has such corpuscles. (Pocketbooks; p. 35.)

The clitoris has no other function than that of sexual pleasure.

The Vagina—Its functions are related to the reproduction function. Principally, 1) menstruation, 2) receive penis, 3) hold semen, and 4) birth passage. The interior of the vagina, which according to the defenders of the vaginally caused orgasm is the center and producer of the orgasm, is:

> like nearly all other internal body structures, poorly supplied with end organs of touch. The internal entodermal origin of the lining of the vagina makes it similar in this respect to the rectum and other parts of the digestive tract. (Kinsey, *Sexual Behavior in the Human Female,* p. 580.)

The degree of insensitivity inside the vagina is so high that "Among the women who were tested in our gynecologic sample, less than 14% were at all conscious that they had been touched." (Kinsey, p. 580.)

Even the importance of the vagina as an *erotic* center (as opposed to an orgasmic center) has been found to be minor.

Other Areas—Labia minora and the vestibule of the vagina. These two sensitive areas may trigger off a clitoral orgasm. Because they can be effectively stimulated during "normal" coitus, though infrequent, this kind of stimulation is incorrectly thought to be vaginal orgasm. However, it is important to distinguish between areas which can stimulate the clitoris, incapable of producing the orgasm themselves, and the clitoris:

> Regardless of what means of excitation is used to bring the individual to the state of sexual climax, the sensation is perceived by the genital corpuscles and is localized where they are situated: in the head of the clitoris or penis. (Kelly, p. 49.)

Psychologically Stimulated Orgasm—Aside from the above mentioned direct and indirect stimulations of the clitoris, there is a third way an orgasm may be triggered. This is through mental (cortical) stimulation, where the imagination stimulates the brain, which in turn stimulates the genital corpuscles of the glans to set off an orgasm.

Women Who Say They Have Vaginal Orgasms

Confusion—Because of the lack of knowledge of their own anatomy, some women accept the idea that an orgasm felt during "normal" intercourse was vaginally caused. This confusion is caused by a combination of two factors. One, failing to locate the center of the orgasm, and two, by a desire to fit her experience to the male-defined idea of sexual normalcy. Considering that women know little about their anatomy, it is easy to be confused.

Deception—The vast majority of women who pretend vaginal orgasm to their men are faking it to, as Ti-Grace Atkinson says, "get the job." In a new best-selling Danish book, *I Accuse* (my own translation), Mette Ejlersen specifically deals with this common problem, which she calls the "sex comedy." This comedy has many causes. First of all, the man brings a great deal of pressure to bear on the woman, because he considers his ability as a lover at stake. So as not to offend his ego, the woman will comply with the prescribed role and go through simulated ecstasy. In some of the other Danish women mentioned, women who were left frigid were turned off to sex, and pretended vaginal orgasm to hurry up the sex act. Others admitted that they had faked vaginal orgasm to catch a man. In one case, the woman pretended vaginal orgasm to get him to leave his first wife, who admitted being vaginally frigid. Later she was forced to continue the deception, since obviously she couldn't tell him to stimulate her clitorally.

Many more women were simply afraid to establish their right to equal enjoyment, seeing the sexual act as being primarily for the man's benefit, and any pleasure that the woman got as an added extra.

Other women, with just enough ego to reject the man's idea that they needed psychiatric care, refused to admit their frigidity. They wouldn't accept self-blame, but they didn't know how to solve the problem, not knowing the physiological facts about themselves. So they were left in a peculiar limbo.

Again, perhaps one of the most infuriating and damaging results of this whole charade has been that women who were perfectly healthy sexually were taught that they were not. So in addition to being sexually deprived, these women were told to blame themselves when they deserved no blame. Looking for a cure to a problem that has none can lead a woman on an endless path of self-hatred and insecurity. For she is told by her analyst that not even in her one role allowed in a male society—the role of a woman—is she successful. She is put on the defensive, with phony data as evidence that she better try to be even more feminine, think more feminine, and reject her envy of men. That is, shuffle even harder, baby.

Why Men Maintain the Myth

1. *Sexual Penetration Is Preferred*—The best stimulant for the penis is the woman's vagina. It supplies the necessary friction and lubrication. From a strictly technical point of view this position offers the best physical conditions, even though the man may try other positions for variation.

2. *The Invisible Woman*—One of the elements of male chauvinism is the refusal or inability to see women as total, separate human beings. Rather, men have chosen to define women only in terms of how they benefited men's lives. Sexually, a woman was not seen as an individual wanting to share equally in the sexual act, any more than she was seen as a person with independent desires when she did anything else in society. Thus, it was easy to make up what was convenient about women; for on top of that, society has been a function of male interests, and women were not organized to form even a vocal opposition to the male experts.

3. *The Penis as Epitome of Masculinity* — Men define their lives greatly in terms of masculinity. It is a *universal*, as opposed to racial, ego boosting, which is localized by the geography of racial mixtures.

The essence of male chauvinism is not the practical, economic services women supply. It is the psychological superiority. This kind of negative definition of self, rather than positive definition based upon one's own achievements and development, has of course chained the victim and the oppressor both. But by far the most brutalized of the two is the victim.

An analogy is racism, where the white racist compensates his feelings of unworthiness by creating an image of the black man (it is primarily a male struggle) as biologically inferior to him. Because of his power in a white male power structure, the white man can socially enforce this mythical division.

To the extent that men try to rationalize and justify male superiority through physical differentiation, masculinity may be symbolized by being the *most* muscular, the most hairy, the deepest voice, and the biggest penis. Women, on the other hand, are approved of (i.e., called feminine) if they are weak, petite, shave their legs, have high soft voices, and no penis.

Since the clitoris is almost identical to the penis, one finds a great deal of evidence of men in various societies trying to either ignore the clitoris and emphasize the vagina (as did Freud), or, as in some places in the Mideast, actually performing clitoridectomy. Freud saw this ancient and still practiced custom as a way of further "feminizing" the female by removing this cardinal vestige of her masculinity. It should be noted also that a big clitoris is considered ugly and masculine. Some cultures engage in the practice of pouring a chemical on the clitoris to make it shrivel up into proper size.

It seems clear to me that men in fact fear the clitoris as a threat to their masculinity.

4. *Sexually Expendable Male*—Men fear that they will become sexually expendable if the clitoris is substituted for the vagina as the center of pleasure for women. Actually this has a great deal of validity if one considers *only* the anatomy. The position of the penis inside the vagina, while perfect for reproduction, does not necessarily stimulate an orgasm in women because the clitoris is located externally and higher up. Women must rely upon indirect stimulation in the "normal" position.

Lesbian sexuality could make an excellent case, based upon anatomical data, for the extinction of the male organ. Albert Ellis says something to the effect that a man without a penis can make a woman an excellent lover.

Considering that the vagina is very desirable from a man's point of view, purely on physical grounds, one begins to see the dilemma for men. And it forces us as well to discard many "physical" arguments explaining why women go to bed with men. What is left, it seems to me, are primarily psychological reasons why women select men at the exclusion of women as sexual partners.

5. *Control of Women*—One reason given to explain the Mideastern practice of clitoridectomy is that it will keep the women from straying. By removing the sexual organ capable of orgasm, it must be assumed that her sexual drive will diminish. Considering how men look upon their women as property, particularly in very backward nations, we should begin to consider a great deal more why it is not in the men's interest to have women totally free sexually. The double standard, as practiced for example in Latin America, is set up to keep the woman as total property of the husband, while he is free to have affairs as he wishes.

6. *Lesbianism and Bisexuality*—Aside from the strictly anatomical reasons why women might equally seek other women as lovers, there is a fear on men's part that women will seek the company of other women on a full, humble basis. The establishment of clitoral orgasm as fact would threaten the heterosexual *institution.* For it would indicate that sexual pleasure was obtainable from either men *or* women, thus making heterosexuality not an absolute, but an option. It would thus open up the whole question of *human* sexual relationships beyond the confines of the present male-female role system.

REFERENCES

Sexual Behavior in the Human Female, Alfred C. Kinsey, Pocketbooks
Female Sexuality, Marie Bonaparte, Grove Press
Sex Without Guilt, Albert Ellis, Grove Press
Sexual Feelings in Married Men and Women, G. Lombard Kelly, Pocketbooks
I Accuse (Jeg Anklager), Mette Ejlersen, Chr. Erichsens Forlag (Danish)
The Sexually Adequate Female, Frank S. Caprio, Fawcett Gold Medal Books
Thinking About Women, Mary Ellman; Harcourt, Brace & World
Human Sexual Response, Masters and Johnson; Little, Brown
Also see:
The ABZ of Love, Inge and Sten Hegeler, Alexicon Corp.

Psychology Constructs the Female, or the Fantasy Life of the Male Psychologist

Naomi Weisstein

The following essay by Naomi Weisstein has become a standard text for the study of Women's Liberation. It has appeared in several versions, printed by Motive XXIX (March-April 1969), Psychology Today (October 1969), and in pamphlet form by the New England Free Press. Naomi Weisstein received her Ph.D. from Harvard where she studied perceptual and cognitive psychology. At 30, she is an assistant professor of psychology at Loyola University in Chicago. She has been involved in women's action groups since 1967.

It is an implicit assumption that the area of psychology which concerns itself with personality has the onerous but necessary task of describing the limits of human possibility. Thus when we are about to consider the liberation of women, we naturally look to psychology to tell us what "true" liberation would mean: what would give women the freedom to fulfill their own intrinsic natures. Psychologists have set about describing the true natures of women with a certainty and a sense of their own infallibility rarely found in the secular world. Bruno Bettelheim, of the University of Chicago, tells us (1965) that "We must start with the realization that, as much as women want to be good scientists or engineers, they want first and foremost to be womanly companions of men and to be mothers." Erik Erikson of Harvard University (1964), upon noting that young women often ask whether they can "have an identity before they know whom they will marry, and for

---

This is a revised and expanded version of *"Kinder, Küche, Kirche as Scientific Law: Psychology Constructs the Female,"* published by the New England Free Press, 791 Tremont Street, Boston, Massachusetts (1968). Reprinted by permission of the author. Copyright Naomi Weisstein.

whom they will make a home", explains somewhat elegiacally that "Much of a young woman's identity is already defined in her kind of attractiveness and in the selectivity of her search for the man (or men) by whom she wishes to be sought..." Mature womanly fulfillment, for Erikson, rests on the fact that a woman's "... somatic design harbors an 'inner space' destined to bear the offspring of chosen men, and with it, a biological, psychological, and ethical commitment to take care of human infancy! Some psychiatrists even see the acceptance of woman's role by women as a solution to societal problems. "Woman is nurturance ...," writes Joseph Rheingold (1964), a psychiatrist at Harvard Medical School, "... anatomy decrees the life of a woman ... when women grow up without dread of their biological functions and without subversion by feminist doctrine, and therefore enter upon motherhood with a sense of fulfillment and altruistic sentiment, we shall attain the goal of a good life and a secure world in which to live it." (p. 714)

These views from men who are assumed to be experts reflect, in a surprisingly transparent way, the cultural consensus. They not only assert that a woman is defined by her ability to attract men, they see no alternative definitions. They think that the definition of a woman in terms of a man is the way it should be; and they back it up with psychosexual incantation and biological ritual curses. A woman has an identity if she is attractive enough to obtain a man, and thus, a home; for this will allow her to set about her life's task of "joyful altruism and nurturance".

Business certainly does not disagree. If views such as Bettelheim's and Erikson's do indeed have something to do with real liberation for women, then seldom in human history has so much money and effort been spent on helping a group of people realize their true potential. Clothing, cosmetics, home furnishings, are multi-million dollar businesses: if you don't like investing in firms that make weaponry and flaming gasoline, then there's a lot of cash in "inner space". Sheet and pillowcase manufacturers are concerned to fill this inner space:

> Mother, for a while this morning, I thought I wasn't cut out for married life. Hank was late for work and forgot his apricot juice and walked out without kissing me, and when I was all alone I started crying. But then the postman came with the sheets and towels you sent, that look like big bandana handkerchiefs, and you know what I thought? That those big red and blue handkerchiefs, are for girls like me to dry their tears on so they can get busy and do what a housewife has to do. Throw open the windows and start getting the house ready, and the dinner, maybe clean the silver and put new geraniums in the box. *Everything to be ready for him when he walks through that door.* (Fieldcrest 1966; emphasis added.)

Of course, it is not only the sheet and pillowcase manufacturers, the cosmetics industry, the home furnishings salesmen who profit from and make use of the cultural definitions of man and woman. The example above is blatantly and overtly pitched to a particular kind of sexist stereotype: the child nymph. But almost all aspects of the media are normative, that is, they have to do with the ways in which beautiful people, or just folks, or ordinary Americans, or extraordinary Americans should live their lives. They define the possible; and the possibilities are usually in terms of what is male and what is female. Men and women alike are waiting for Hank, the Silva Thins man, to walk back through that door.

It is interesting but limited exercise to show that psychologists and psychiatrists embrace these sexist norms of our culture, that they do not see beyond the most superficial and stultifying media conceptions of female nature, and that their ideas of female nature serve industry and commerce so well. Just because it's good for business doesn't mean it's wrong. What I will show is that it *is wrong*; that there isn't the tiniest shred of evidence that these fantasies of servitude and childish dependence have anything to do with women's true potential; that the idea of the nature of human possibility which rests on the accidents of individual development of genitalia, on what is possible today because of what happened yesterday, on the fundamentalist myth of sex organ causality, has strangled and deflected psychology so that it is relatively useless in describing, explaining or predicting humans and their behavior. It then goes without saying that present psychology is less than worthless in contributing to a vision which could truly liberate —men as well as women.

The central argument of my paper, then, is this. Psychology has nothing to say about what women are really like, what they need and what they want, essentially because psychology does not know. I want to stress that this failure is not limited to women; rather, the kind of psychology which has addressed itself to how people act and who they are has failed to understand, in the first place, why people act the way they do, and certainly failed to understand what might make them act differently.

The kind of psychology which has addressed itself to these questions divides into two professional areas: academic personality research, and clinical psychology and psychiatry. The basic reason for failure is the same in both these areas: the central assumption for most psychologists of human personality has been that human behavior rests on an individual and inner dynamic, perhaps fixed in infancy, perhaps fixed by genitalia, perhaps simply arranged in a rather immovable cognitive network. But this assumption is rapidly losing ground as personality psychol-

ogists fail again and again to get consistency in the assumed personalities of their subjects (Block, 1968). Meanwhile, the evidence is
collecting that what a person does and who he believes himself to be,
will in general be a function of what people around him expect him to
be, and what the overall situation in which he is acting implies that he
is. Compared to the influence of the social context within which a person
lives, his or her history and 'traits', as well as biological makeup, may
simply be random variations, 'noise' superimposed on the true signal
which can predict behavior.

Some academic personality psychologists are at least looking at the
counter evidence and questioning their theories; no such corrective is
occurring in clinical psychology and psychiatry. Freudians and neo-
Freudians, Adlerians and neo-Adlerians, classicists and swingers, clinicians and psychiatrists, simply refuse to look at the evidence against
their theory and practice. And they support their theory and their practice with stuff so transparently biased as to have absolutely no standing
as empirical evidence.

To summarize: the first reason for psychology's failure to understand
what people are and how they act is that psychology has looked for inner
traits when it should have been looking for social context; the second
reason for psychology's failure is that the theoreticians of personality
have generally been clinicians and psychiatrists, and they have never
considered it necessary to have evidence in support of their theories.

Theory Without Evidence

Let us turn to this latter cause of failure first: the acceptance by
psychiatrists and clinical psychologists of theory without evidence. If
we inspect the literature of personality, it is immediately obvious that
the bulk of it is written by clinicians and psychiatrists, and that the
major support for their theories is "years of intensive clinical experience". This is a tradition started by Freud. His "insights" occurred
during the course of his work with his patients. Now there is nothing
wrong with such an approach to theory *formulation*; a person is free to
make up theories with any inspiration which works: divine revelation,
intensive clinical practice, a random numbers table. But he is not free
to claim any validity for his theory until it has been tested and confirmed.
But theories are treated in no such tentative way in ordinary clinical
practice. Consider Freud. What he thought constituted evidence violated the most minimal conditions of scientific rigor. In *The Sexual
Enlightenment of Children* (1963), the classic document which is supposed to demonstrate empirically the existence of a castration complex
and its connection to a phobia, Freud based his analysis on the reports

of the father of the little boy, himself in therapy, and a devotee of Freudian theory. I really don't have to comment further on the contamination in this kind of evidence. It is remarkable that only recently has Freud's classic theory on the sexuality of women—the notion of the double orgasm—been actually tested physiologically and found just plain wrong. Now those who claim that fifty years of psychoanalytic experience constitute evidence enough of the essential truths of Freud's theory should ponder the robust health of the double orgasm. Did women, until Masters and Johnson (1966), believe they were having two different kinds of orgasm? Did their psychiatrists cow them into reporting something that was not true? If so, were there other things they reported that were also not true? Did psychiatrists ever learn anything different than their theories had led them to believe? If clinical experience means anything at all, surely we should have been done with the double orgasm myth long before the Masters and Johnson studies.

But certainly, you may object, "years of intensive clinical experience" is the only reliable measure in a discipline which rests for its findings on insight, sensitivity, and intuition. The problem with insight, sensitivity, and intuition, is that they can confirm for all time the biases that one started out with. People used to be absolutely convinced of their ability to tell which of their number were engaging in witchcraft. All it required was some sensitivity to the workings of the devil.

Years of intensive clinical experience are not the same thing as empirical evidence. The first thing an experimenter learns in any kind of experiment which involves humans is the concept of the "double blind". The term is taken from medical experiments, where one group is given a drug which is presumably supposed to change behavior in a certain way, and a control group is given a placebo. If the observers or the subjects know which group took which drug, the result invariably comes out on the positive side for the new drug. Only when it is not known which subject took which pill, is validity remotely approximated. In addition, with judgments of human behavior, it is so difficult to precisely tie down just what behavior is going on, let alone what behavior should be expected, that one must test again and again the reliability of judgments. How many judges, blind, will agree in their observations? Can they replicate their own judgments at some later time? When, in actual practice, these judgment criteria are tested for clinical judgments, then we find that the judges cannot judge reliably, nor can they judge consistently: they do no better than chance in identifying which of a certain set of stories were written by men and which by women; which of a whole battery of clinical test results are the products of homosexuals and which are the products of heterosexuals (Hooker, 1957), and which, of a battery of clinical test results *and* interviews (where questions are asked such as "Do you have delusions?"—Little & Schneidman, 1959) are products of psychotics, neurotics, psychosomatics, or normals. Lest this summary escape your notice, let me stress the implications of these findings. The ability of judges, chosen for their clinical expertise, to distinguish male heterosexuals from male homosexuals on the basis of three widely used clinical projective tests—the Rorschach, the TAT, and the MAP—was *no better than chance*. The reason this is such devastating news, of course, is that sexuality is supposed to be of fundamental importance in the deep dynamic of personality; if what is considered gross sexual deviance cannot be caught, then what are psychologists talking about when they, for example, claim that at the basis of paranoid psychosis is "latent homosexual panic"? They can't even identify what homosexual anything is, let alone 'latent homosexual panic'. More frightening, expert clinicians cannot be consistent on what diagnostic category to assign to a person, again on the basis of both tests and interviews; a number of normals in the Little & Schneidman study were described as psychotic, in such categories as 'schizophrenic with homosexual tendencies' or 'schizoid character with depressive trends'. But most disheartening, when the judges were asked to rejudge the test protocols some weeks later, their diagnoses of the same subjects on the basis of the same protocol differed markedly from their initial judgments. It is obvious that even simple descriptive conventions in clinical psychology cannot be consistently applied; that these descriptive conventions have any explanatory significance is therefore, of course, out of the question.

As a graduate student at Harvard some years ago, I was a member of a seminar which was asked to identify which of two piles of a clinical test, the TAT, had been written by males and which by females. Only four students out of twenty identified the piles correctly, and this was after one and a half months of intensively studying the differences between men and women. Since this result is below chance—that is, this result would occur by chance about four out of a thousand times—we may conclude that there is finally a consistency here; students are judging knowledgeably within the context of psychological teaching about the differences between men and women; the teachings themselves are simply erroneous.

You may argue that the theory may be scientifically 'unsound' but at least it cures people. There is no evidence that it does. In 1952, Eysenck reported the results of what is called an 'outcome of therapy' study of neurotics which showed that, of the patients who received psychoanalysis the improvement rate was 44%; of the patients who received psychotherapy the improvement rate was 64%; and of the patients who received no treatment at all the improvement rate was 72%. These findings have never been refuted; subsequently, later studies have confirmed the negative results of the Eysenck study. (Barron & Leary, 1955; Bergin, 1963; Cartwright and Vogel, 1960; Truax, 1963; Powers and Witmer, 1951) How can good clinicians and psychiatrists, then, in all good conscience, continue to practice? Largely by ignoring these results and being careful not to do outcome-of-therapy studies. The attitude is nicely summarized by Rotter (1960) (quoted in Astin, 1961): 'Research studies in psychotherapy tend to be concerned with psychotherapeutic procedure and less with outcome . . . to some extent, it reflects an interest in the psychotherapy situation as a kind of personality laboratory". Some laboratory.

The Social Context

Thus, since clinical experience and tools can be shown to be worse than useless when tested for consistency, efficacy, agreement, and reliability, we can safely conclude that theories of a clinical nature advanced about women are also worse than useless. I want to turn now to the second major point in my paper, which is that, even when psychological theory is constructed so that it may be tested, and rigorous standards of evidence are used, it has become increasingly clear that in order to understand why people do what they do, and certainly in order to change what people do, psychologists must turn away from the theory of the causal nature of the inner dynamic and look to the social context within which individuals live.

2. It should be noted that psychologists have been as quick to assert absolute truths about the nature of homosexuality as they have about the nature of women. The arguments presented in this paper apply equally to the nature of homosexuality; psychologists know nothing about it; there is no more evidence for the "naturalness" of heterosexuality than for the "naturalness" of homosexuality. Psychology has functioned as a pseudo-scientific buttress for our cultural sex-role notions, that is, as a buttress for patriarchal ideology and patriarchal social organization: women's liberation and gay liberation fight against a common victimization.

Before examining the relevance of this approach for the question of women, let me first sketch the groundwork for this assertion.

In the first place, it is clear (Block, 1968) that personality tests never yield consistent predictions; a rigid authoritarian on one measure will be an unauthoritarian on the next. But the reason for this inconsistency is only now becoming clear, and it seems overwhelmingly to have much more to do with the social situation in which the subject finds himself than with the subject himself.

In a series of brilliant experiments, Rosenthal and his co-workers (Rosenthal and Jacobson, 1968; Rosenthal, 1966) have shown that if one group of experimenters has one hypothesis about what they expect to find, and another group of experimenters has the opposite hypothesis, both groups will obtain results in accord with their hypotheses. The results obtained are not due to mishandling of data by biased experimenters; rather, somehow, the bias of the experimenter creates a changed environment in. which subjects actually act differently. For instance, in one experiment, subjects were to assign numbers to pictures of men's faces, with high numbers representing the subject's judgment that the man in the picture was a successful person, and low numbers representing the subject's judgment that the man in the picture was an unsuccessful person. The experimenters read the same set of instructions to two groups of subjects, and were required to say nothing else than what was in the instructions. One group of experimenters was told that the subjects tended to rate the faces high; another group of experimenters was told that the subjects tended to rate the faces low. Each group of experimenters was instructed to follow precisely the same procedure: they were required to read to subjects a set of instructions, and to *say nothing else.* For the 375 subjects run, the results showed clearly that those subjects who performed the task with experimenters who expected high ratings gave high ratings, and those subjects who performed the task with experimenters who expected low ratings gave low ratings. How did this happen? The experimenters all used the same words; it was something in their conduct which made one group of subjects do one thing, and another group of subjects do another thing.

The concreteness of the changed conditions produced by expectation is a fact, a reality: even with animal subjects, in two separate studies (Rosenthal & Fode, 1960; Rosenthal & Lawson, 1961), those experimenters who were told that rats learning mazes had been especially bred for brightness obtained better learning from their rats than did experimenters believing their rats to have been bred for dullness. In a very recent study, Rosenthal & Jacobson (1968) extended their analysis to the natural classroom situation. Here, they tested a group of students and reported to the teachers that some among the students tested "showed great promise". Actually, the students so named had been selected on a random basis. Some time later, the experimenters retested the group of students: those students whose teachers had been told that they were "promising" showed real and dramatic increments in their

IQ's as compared to the rest of the students. Something in the conduct of the teachers towards who the teachers believed to be the "bright" students, made those students brighter.

Thus, even in carefully controlled experiments, and with no outward or conscious difference in behavior, the hypotheses we start with will influence enormously the behavior of another organism. These studies are extremely important when assessing the validity of psychological studies of women. Since it is beyond doubt that most of us start with notions as to the nature of men and women, the validity of a number of observations of sex differences is questionable, even when these observations have been made under carefully controlled conditions. Second, and more important, the Rosenthal experiments point quite clearly to the influence of social expectation. In some extremely important ways, people are what you expect them to be or at least they behave as you expect them to behave. Thus, if women, according to Bettelheim, want first and foremost to be good wives and mothers, it is extremely likely that this is what Bruno Bettelheim, and the rest of society, want them to be.

There is another series of brilliant social psychological experiments which point to the overwhelming effect of social context. These are the obedience experiments of Stanley Milgram (1965) in which subjects are asked to obey the orders of unknown experimenters, orders which carry with them the distinct possibility that the subject is killing somebody.

In Milgram's experiments, a subject is told that he is administering a learning experiment, and that he is to deal out shocks each time the other "subject" (in reality, a confederate of the experimenter) answers incorrectly. The equipment appears to provide graduated shocks ranging upwards from 15 volts through 450 volts; for each of four consecutive voltages there are verbal descriptions such as "mild shock", "danger, severe shock", and, finally, for the 435 and 450 volt switches, a red XXX marked over the switches. Each time the stooge answers incorrectly the subject is supposed to increase the voltage. As the voltage increases, the stooge begins to cry in pain; he demands that the experiment stop; finally, he refuses to answer at all. When he stops responding, the experimenter instructs the subject to continue increasing the voltage; for each shock administered the stooge shrieks in agony. Under these conditions, about 62.5% of the subjects administered shock that they believed to be possibly lethal.

No tested individual differences between subjects predicted how many would continue to obey, and which would break off the experiment. When forty psychiatrists predicted how many of a group of 100 subjects would go on to give the lethal shock, their predictions were orders of magnitude below the actual percentages; most expected only one-tenth of one per cent of the subjects to obey to the end.

But even though *psychiatrists* have no idea how people will behave in this situation, and even though individual differences do not predict which subjects will obey and which will not, it is easy to predict when subjects will be obedient and when they will be defiant. All the experimenter has to do is change the social situation. In a variant of Milgram's experiment, two stooges were present in addition to the "victim"; these worked along with the subject in administering electric shocks. When these two stooges refused to go on with the experiment, only ten per cent of the subjects continued to the maximum voltage. This is critical for personality theory. It says that behavior is predicted from the social situation, not from the individual history.

Finally, an ingenious experiment by Schachter and Singer (1962) showed that subjects injected with adrenalin, which produces a state of physiological arousal in all but minor respects identical to that which occurs when subjects are extremely afraid, became euphoric when they were in a room with a stooge who was acting euphoric, and became extremely angry when they were placed in a room with a stooge who was acting extremely angry.

To summarize: If subjects under quite innocuous and non-coercive social conditions can be made to kill other subjects and under other types of social conditions will positively refuse to do so; if subjects can react to a state of physiological fear by becoming euphoric because there is somebody else around who is euphoric or angry because there is somebody else around who is angry; if students become intelligent because teachers expect them to be intelligent, and rats run mazes better because experimenters are told the rats are bright, then it is obvious that a study of human behavior requires, first and foremost, a study of the social contexts within which people move, the expectations as to how they will behave, and the authority which tells them who they are and what they are supposed to do.

Biologically Based Theories

Two theories of the nature of women, which come not from psychiatric and clinical tradition, but from biology, can be disposed of now with little difficulty. The first biological theory of sex differences argues that since females and males differ in their sex hormones, and sex hormones enter the brain (Hamburg & Lunde in Maccoby, 1966), there must be innate differences in "nature". But the only thing this argument tells us is that there are differences in physiological state. The problem is whether these differences are at all relevant to behavior. Recall that

Schachter and Singer (1962) have shown that a particular physiological state can itself lead to a multiplicity of felt emotional states, and outward behavior, depending on the social situation.

The second theory is a form of biological reductionism: sex-role behavior in some primate species is described, and it is concluded that this is the "natural" behavior for humans. Putting aside the not insignificant problem of observer bias (for instance, Harlow, 1962, of the University of Wisconsin, after observing differences between male and female rhesus monkeys, quotes Lawrence Sterne to the effect that women are silly and trivial, and concludes that "men and women have differed in the past and they will differ in the future"), there are a number of problems with this approach.

The most general and serious problem is that there are no grounds to assume that anything primates do is necessary, natural, or desirable in humans, for the simple reason that humans are not non-humans. For instance, it is found that male chimpanzees placed alone with infants will not "mother" them. Jumping from hard data to ideological speculation researchers conclude from this information that *human* females are necessary for the safe growth of human infants. It would be as reasonable to conclude, following this logic, that it is quite useless to teach human infants to speak, since it has been tried with chimpanzees and it does not work.

One strategy that has been used is to extrapolate from primate behavior to "innate" human preference by noticing certain trends in primate behavior as one moves phylogenetically closer to humans. But there are great difficulties with this approach. When behaviors from lower primates are directly opposite to those of higher primates, or to those one expects of humans, they can be dismissed on evolutionary grounds—higher primates and/or humans grew out of that kid stuff. On the other hand, if the behavior of higher primates is counter to the behavior considered natural for humans, while the behavior of some lower primate is considered the natural one for humans, the higher primate behavior can be dismissed also, on the grounds that it has diverged from an older, prototypical pattern. So either way, one can select those behaviors one wants to prove as innate for humans. In addition, one does not know whether the sex-role behavior exhibited is dependent on the phylogenetic rank, or on the environmental conditions (both physical and social) under which different species live.

Is there then any value at all in primate observations as they relate to human females and males? There is a value but it is limited: its function can be no more than to show some extent examples of diverse sex-role behavior. It must be stressed, however, that this is an extremely limited function. The extant behavior does not begin to suggest all the possibilities, either for non-human primates or for humans. Bearing these caveats in mind, it is nonetheless interesting that if one inspects the limited set of existing non-human primate sex-role behaviors, one finds, in fact, a much larger range of sex-role behavior than is commonly believed to exist. "Biology" appears to limit very little; the fact that a female gives birth does not mean, even in non-humans, that she necessarily cares for the infant (in marmosets, for instance, the male carries the infant at all times except when the infant is feeding [Mitchell, 1969]); "natural" female and male behavior varies all the way from females who are much more aggressive and competitive than males (e.g., Tamarins, see Mitchell, 1969) and male "mothers" (e.g., Titi monkeys, night monkeys, and marmosets, see Mitchell, 1969) to submissive and passive females and male antagonists (e.g., rhesus monkeys).

But even for the limited function that primate arguments serve, the evidence has been misused. Invariably, only those primates have been cited which exhibit exactly the kind of behavior that the proponents of the biological basis of human female behavior wish were true for humans. Thus, baboons and rhesus monkeys are generally cited: males in these groups exhibit some of the most irritable and aggressive behavior found in primates, and if one wishes to argue that females are naturally passive and submissive, these groups provide vivid examples. There are abundant counter examples, such as those mentioned above (Mitchell, 1969); in fact, in general, a counter example can be found for every sex-role behavior cited, including, as mentioned in the case of marmosets, male "mothers".

But the presence of counter examples has not stopped florid and overarching theories of the natural or biological basis of male privilege from proliferating. For instance, there have been a number of theories dealing with the innate incapacity in human males for monogamy. Here, as in most of this type of theorizing, baboons are a favorite example, probably because of their fantasy value: the family unit of the hamadryas baboon, for instance, consists of a highly constant pattern of one male and a number of females and their young. And again, the counter examples, such as the invariably monogamous gibbon, are ignored.

An extreme example of this maiming and selective truncation of the evidence in the service of a plea for the maintenance of male privilege is a recent book, *Men in Groups* (1969) by a man who calls himself Tiger. The central claim of this book is that females are incapable of honorable collective action because they are incapable of "bonding" as in "male bonding". What is "male bonding"? Its surface definition is simple: "... a particular relationship between two or more males such that they react differently to members of their bonding units as compared to individuals outside of it" (pp. 19–20). If one deletes the word male, the definition, on its face, would seem to include all organisms that have any kind of social organization. But this is not what Tiger means. For instance, Tiger asserts that females are incapable of bonding; and this alleged incapacity indicates to Tiger that females should be restricted from public life. Why is bonding an exclusively male behavior? Because, says Tiger, it is seen in male primates. All male primates? No, very few male primates. Tiger cites two examples where male bonding is seen: rhesus monkeys and baboons. Surprise, surprise. But not even all baboons; as mentioned above, the hamadryas social organization consists of one-male units; so does that of the Gelada baboon. (Mitchell, 1969). And the great apes do not go in for male bonding much either. The "male bond" is hardly a serious contribution to scholarship; one reviewer for *Science* has observed that the book "... shows basically more resemblance to a partisan political tract than to a work of objective social science", with male bonding being "... some kind of behavioral phlogiston" (Fried, 1969, p. 884).

In short, primate arguments have generally misused the evidence; primate studies themselves have, in any case, only the very limited function of describing some possible sex-role behavior; and at present, primate observations have been sufficiently limited so that even the range of possible sex-role behavior for non-human primates is not known. This range is not known since there is only minimal observation of what happens to behavior if the physical or social environment is changed. In one study (Itani, 1963), different troops of Japanese macaques were observed. Here, there appeared to be cultural difference: males in 3 out of the 18 troops observed differed in their amount of aggressiveness and infant-caring behavior. There could be no possibility of differential evolution here; the differences seemed largely transmitted by infant socialization. Thus, the very limited evidence points to some plasticity in the sex-role behavior of non-human primates; if we can figure out experiments which massively change the social organization of primate groups, it is possible that we might observe great changes in behavior. At present, however, we must conclude that, since non-human primates are too stupid to change their social conditions by themselves, the "innateness" and fixedness of their behavior is simply not known. Thus, even if there were some way, which there isn't, to settle on the behavior of a particular primate species as being the "natural" way for humans, we would not know whether or not this were simply some function of the present social organization of that species. And finally, once again it must be stressed that even if non-human primate behavior turned out to be relatively fixed, this would say little about our behavior. More immediate and relevant evidence, i.e., the evidence from social psychology, points to the enormous plasticity in human behavior, not only from one culture to the next, but from one experimental group to the next. One of the most salient features of human social organization is its variety; there are a number of cultures where there is at least a rough equality between men and women (Mead, 1949). In summary, primate arguments can tell us very little about our "innate" sex-role behavior; if they tell us anything at all, they tell us that there is no one biologically "natural" female or male behavior, and that sex-role behavior in non-human primates is much more varied than has previously been thought.

In brief, the uselessness of present psychology with regard to women is simply a special case of the general conclusion: one must understand social expectations about women if one is going to characterize the behavior of women.

How are women characterized in our culture, and in psychology? They are inconsistent, emotionally unstable, lacking in a strong conscience or superego, weaker, "nuturant" rather than productive, "intuitive" rather than intelligent, and, if they are at all "normal," suited to the home and the family. In short, the list adds up to a typical minority group stereotype of inferiority (Hacker, 1951): if they know their place, which is in the home, they are really quite lovable, happy, childlike, loving creatures. In a review of the intellectual differences between little boys and little girls, Eleanor Maccoby (1966) has shown that there are no intellectual differences until about high school, or, if there are, girls are slightly ahead of boys. At high school, girls begin to do worse on a few intellectual tasks, such as arithmetic reasoning, and beyond high school, the achievement of women now measured in terms of productivity and accomplishment drops off even more rapidly. There are a number of other, non-intellectual tests which show sex differences; I chose the intellectual differences since it is seen clearly that women start becoming inferior. It is no use to talk about women being different but equal; all of the tests I can think of have a "good" outcome and a "bad" outcome. Women usually end up at the "bad" outcome. In light of social expectations about women, what is surprising is not that women end up where society expects they will; what is surprising is that little girls don't get the message that they are supposed to be stupid until high school; and what is even more remarkable is that some women resist this message even after high school, college, and graduate school.

My paper began with remarks on the task of the discovery of the limits of human potential. Psychologists must realize that it is they who are limiting discovery of human potential. They refuse to accept evidence, if they are clinical psychologists, or, if they are rigorous, they assume that people move in a context-free ether, with only their innate dispositions and their individual traits determining what they will do.

Until psychologists begin to respect evidence, and until they begin looking at the social contexts within which people move psychology will have nothing of substance to offer in this task of discovery. I don't know what immutable differences exist between men and women apart from differences in their genitals; perhaps there are some other unchangeable differences; probably there are a number of irrelevant differences. But it is clear that until social expectations for men and women are equal, until we provide equal respect for both men and women, our answers to this question will simply reflect our prejudices.

REFERENCES

Astin, A. W., The functional autonomy of psychotherapy. *American Psychologist,* 1961, *16,* 75-78.

Barron, F. & Leary, T., Changes in psychoneurotic patients with and without psychotherapy. *Journal Consulting Psychology,* 1955, *19,* 239-245.

Bregin, A. E., The effects of psychotherapy: negative results revisited. *Journal of Consulting Psychology,* 1963, *10,* 244-250.

Bettelheim, B., The Commitment required of a woman entering a scientific profession in present day American society. *Woman and the Scientific Professions,* The MIT Symposium on American Women in Science and Engineering, 1965.

Block, J., Some reasons for the apparent inconsistency of personality. *Psychological Bulletin,* 1968, *70,* 210-212.

Cartwright, R. D. & Vogel, J. L., A comparison of changes in psychoneurotic patients during matched periods of therapy and no-therapy. *Journal of Consulting Psychology,* 1960, *24,* 121-127.

Erikson, E., Inner and outer space: reflections on womanhood. *Daedalus,* 1964, *93,* 582-606.

Eysenck, H. J., The effects of psychotherapy: an evaluation. *Journal of Consulting Psychology,* 1952, *16,* 319-324.

Fieldcrest—Advertisement in the *New Yorker,* 1965.

Fried, M. H. "Mankind excluding woman", review of Tiger's *Men in Groups. Science, 165,* 1969, pp. 883-884.

Freud, S., *The Sexual Enlightenment of Children,* Collier Books Edition, 1963.

Goldstein, A. P. & Dean, S. J., *The Investigation of Psychotherapy: Commentaries and Readings.* John Wiley & Sons, New York: 1966.

Hamburg, D. A. & Lunde, D. T., Sex hormones in the development of sex differences in human behavior. In Maccoby, ed., *The Development of Sex Differences,* pp. 1-24, Stanford University Press, 1966.

Hacker, H. M., Women as a minority group. *Social Forces*, 1951, *30*, 60-69.

Harlow, H. F., The heterosexual affectional system in monkeys. *The American Psychologist*, 1962, *17*, 1-9.

Hooker, E., Male Homosexuality in the Rorschach. *Journal of Projective Techniques*, 1957, *21*, 18-31.

Itani, J., Paternal care in the wild Japanese monkeys, *Macaca fuscata*. In C. H. Southwick (Ed.) *Primate Social Behavior*. Princeton: Van Nostrand, 1963. ·

Little, K. B. & Schneidman, E. S., Congruences among interpretations of psychological and anamestic data. *Psychological Monographs*, 1959, 73, 1-42.

Maccoby, Eleanor E., Sex differences in intellectual functioning. In Maccoby, ed., *The Development of Sex Differences*, 25-55. Stanford University Press, 1966.

Masters, W. H. & Johnson, V. E., *Human Sexual Response*, Little Brown: Boston, 1966.

Mead, M., *Male and Female: A study of the sexes in a changing world*, William Morrow, New York, 1949.

Milgram, S., Some conditions of obedience and disobedience to authority. *Human Relations*, 1965a, *18*, 57-76.

Milgram, S., Liberating effects of group pressure. *Journal of Personality and Social Psychology*, 1965b, *1*, 127-134.

Mitchell, G. D. "Paternalistic behavior in primates". *Psychological Bulletin* 1969, *71*, pp. 399-417.

Powers, E. & Witmer, H., *An Experiment in the Prevention of Delinquency*, New York: Columbia University Press, 1951.

Rheingold, J., *The Fear of Being a Woman*. Grune & Stratton, New York: 1964.

Rosenthal, R., On the social psychology of the psychological experiment: The experimenter's hypothesis as unintended determinant of experimental results. *American Scientist*, 1963, *51*, 268-283.

Rosenthal, R., *Experimenter Effects in Behavioral Research*. New York: Appleton-Century Crofts, 1966.

Rosenthal, R. & Jacobson, L., *Pygmalion in the Classroom: teacher expectation and pupil's intellectual development*. New York: Holt Rinehart & Winston, 1968.

Rosenthal, R. & Lawson, R., A longitudinal study of the effects of experimenter bias on the operant learning of laboratory rats. Unpublished Manuscript, Harvard University, 1961.

Rosenthal, R. & Fode, K. L., The effect of experimenter bias on the performance of the albino rat. Unpublished manuscript, Harvard University, 1960.

Rotter, J. B., Psychotherapy. *Annual Review of Psychology*, 1960, *11*, 381-414.

Schachter, S. & Singer, J. E., Cognitive, social and physiological determinants of emotional state. *Psychological Review*, 1962, *69*, 379-399.

Schwarz-Belkin, M. "Les Fleurs du Mal", in *Festschrift for Gordon Piltdown*, Ponzi Press, New York, 1914.

Tiger, L. *Men in Groups*, Random House, New York, 1969.

Truax, C. B., Effective ingredients in psychotherapy: an approach to unraveling the patient-therapist interaction. *Journal of Counseling Psychology*, 1963, *10*, 256-263.

Part Three:

Adjustment
For
Survival

The "Better Half"

"Tell her nothing, my dear madam, for if they knew they would not marry." This advice of a physician to a young Victorian woman's mother (quoted in C. Willett Cunnington, *Feminine Attitudes in the Nineteenth Century,* The Macmillan Company, New York, 1936, p. 214) indicates all too clearly the ignorance in which females have been kept concerning the biological, psychological, and sociological realities of marriage. Though men jokingly refer to their wives as "my better half," and popular mythology describes marriage as a partnership, the fact is that in most marriages husband and wife are not equals. The wife is expected to tend the children, clean the house, manage the household budget and, above all, keep her husband happy—usually this means hiding from him the fact that hers is a servile role which, in manic moods, she may enjoy but which, in depressed ones, she abhors. She is not paid for her services, except in the form of platitudes about the nobility of her mission and the never-ending nature of her work. And she is taught that her sole purpose in life is to marry and bear children. A woman who has not married is called "an old maid," a term of opprobrium so horrifying to most women that they will sell their bodies and souls to avoid it. Childlessness, at least until the recent overpopulation scare, has been looked on as an abnormality.

Yet when women marry they often discover that, contrary to the endings of countless Hollywood movies (the adult fairy tales), they do not live happily ever after. They discover that the role of housewife and mother is just that—a role, a part they play in a bourgeois drama which is neither comic nor tragic, certainly not melodramatic, usually just dull. The reactions of women to the housewife-mother role are shown in this section. In order to survive, the woman adjusts as best she can. Sometimes she wheedles, lies, or fusses; most often she quietly despairs, wondering what is missing in her life.

The Monogamous Family

Frederich Engels

In Chapter II of The Origins of Family, Private Property, and the
State *(1884), the Marxist theoretician Frederich Engels discusses the development of the monogamous family unit. Out
of communal group marriage grew the pairing family, where
a man had a chief wife among many wives and she regarded
him as her chief husband. In the pairing family, marriage was
easily dissolved by either party and the children belonged to
the mother. With the advent of private property and wealth,
however, came the patriarchal family and the overthrowing
of the mother's right to her children. Monogamy developed,
Engels says, as an economic—not a natural—arrangement, and
it presented from its beginnings a picture of class opposition—
male oppressor versus female oppressed.*

The monogamous family develops out of the pairing family in the
transitional period between the upper and middle stages of barbarism;
its decisive victory is one of the signs that civilization is beginning. It is
based on the supremacy of the man, the express purpose being to produce children of undisputed paternity; such paternity is demanded
because these children are later to come into their father's property
as his natural heirs. It is distinguished from pairing marriage by the
much greater strength of the marriage tie, which can no longer be dissolved at either partner's wish. As a rule, it is now only the man who
can dissolve it, and put away his wife. The right of conjugal infidelity
also remains secured to him, at any rate by custom (the *Code Napoléon*
explicitly accords it to the husband as long as he does not bring his
concubine into the house), and as social life develops he exercises his
right more and more; should the wife recall the old form of sexual life
and attempt to revive it, she is punished more severely than ever.

We meet this new form of the family in all its severity among the
Greeks. While the position of the goddesses in their mythology, as Marx
points out, brings before us an earlier period when the position of

women was freer and more respected, in the heroic age we find the woman already being humiliated by the domination of the man and by competition from girl slaves. Note how Telemachus in the *Odyssey* silences his mother.[1] In Homer young women are booty and are handed over to the pleasure of the conquerors, the handsomest being picked by the commanders in order of rank; the entire *Iliad*, it will be remembered, turns on the quarrel of Achilles and Agamemnon over one of these slaves. If a hero is of any importance, Homer also mentions the captive girl with whom he shares his tent and his bed. These girls were also taken back to Greece and brought under the same roof as the wife, as Cassandra was brought by Agamemnon in Aeschylus; the sons begotten of them received a small share of the paternal inheritance and had the full status of freemen. Teucer, for instance, is a natural son of Telamon by one of these slaves and has the right to use his father's name. The legitimate wife was expected to put up with all this, but herself to remain strictly chaste and faithful. In the heroic age a Greek woman is, indeed, more respected than in the period of civilization, but to her husband she is after all nothing but the mother of his legitimate children and heirs, his chief housekeeper and the supervisor of his female slaves, whom he can and does take as concubines if he so fancies. It is the existence of slavery side by side with monogamy, the presence of young, beautiful slaves belonging unreservedly to the *man*, that stamps monogamy from the very beginning with its specific character of monogamy *for the woman only*, but not for the man. And that is the character it still has today.

Coming to the later Greeks, we must distinguish between Dorians and Ionians. Among the former—Sparta is the classic example—marriage relations are in some ways still more archaic than even in Homer. The recognized form of marriage in Sparta was a pairing marriage, modified according to the Spartan conceptions of the state, in which there still survived vestiges of group marriages. Childless marriages were dissolved; King Anaxandridas (about 650 B.C.), whose first wife was childless, took a second and kept two households; about the same time, King Ariston, who had two unfruitful wives, took a third, but dismissed one of the other two. On the other hand, several brothers could have a wife in common; a friend who preferred his friend's wife could share her with him; and it was considered quite proper to place one's wife at the disposal of a sturdy "stallion," as Bismarck would say, even if he was not a citizen. A passage in Plutarch, where a Spartan woman refers an

---

[1]The reference is to a passage where Telemachus, son of Odysseus and Penelope, tells his mother to get on with her weaving and leave the men to mind their own business (*Odyssey*, Bk. 21, ll. 350 ff.).—*Ed.*

importunate wooer to her husband, seems to indicate, according to Schömann, even greater freedom. Real adultery, secret infidelity by the woman without the husband's knowledge, was therefore unheard of. On the other hand, domestic slavery was unknown in Sparta, at least during its best period; the unfree helots were segregated on the estates and the Spartans were therefore less tempted to take the helots' wives. Inevitably in these conditions women held a much more honored position in Sparta than anywhere else in Greece. The Spartan women and the élite of the Athenian *hetairai* are the only Greek women of whom the ancients speak with respect and whose words they thought it worth while to record.

The position is quite different among the Ionians; here Athens is typical. Girls only learned spinning, weaving, and sewing, and at most a little reading and writing. They lived more or less behind locked doors and had no company except other women. The women's apartments formed a separate part of the house, on the upper floor or at the back, where men, especially strangers, could not easily enter, and to which the women retired when men visited the house. They never went out without being accompanied by a female slave; indoors they were kept under regular guard. Aristophanes speaks of Molossian dogs kept to frighten away adulterers, and, at any rate in the Asiatic towns, eunuchs were employed to keep watch over the women—making and exporting eunuchs was an industry in Chios as early as Herodotus' time, and, according to Wachsmuth, it was not only the barbarians who bought the supply. In Euripides a woman is called an *oikourema*, a thing (the word is neuter) for looking after the house, and, apart from her business of bearing children, that was all she was for the Athenian—his chief female domestic servant. The man had his athletics and his public business, from which women were barred; in addition, he often had female slaves at his disposal and during the most flourishing days of Athens an extensive system of prostitution which the state at least favored. It was precisely through this system of prostitution that the only Greek women of personality were able to develop, and to acquire that intellectual and artistic culture by which they stand out as high above the general level of classical womanhood as the Spartan women by their qualities of character. But that a woman had to be a *hetaira* before she could be a woman is the worst condemnation of the Athenian family.

This Athenian family became in time the accepted model for domestic relations, not only among the Ionians, but to an increasing extent among all the Greeks of the mainland and colonies also. But, in spite of locks and guards, Greek women found plenty of opportunity for deceiving their husbands. The men, who would have been ashamed to show any love for their wives, amused themselves by all sorts of love affairs with *hetairai*; but this degradation of the women was avenged on the men and degraded them also, till they fell into the abominable practice of sodomy and degraded alike their gods and themselves with the myth of Ganymede.

This is the origin of monogamy as far as we can trace it back among the most civilized and highly developed people of antiquity. It was not in any way the fruit of individual sex-love, with which it had nothing whatever to do; marriages remained as before marriages of convenience. It was the first form of the family to be based, not on natural, but on economic conditions—on'the victory of private property over primitive, natural communal property. The Greeks themselves put the matter quite frankly: the sole exclusive aims of monogamous marriage were to make the man supreme in the family, and to propagate, as the future heirs to his wealth, children indisputably his own. Otherwise, marriage was a burden, a duty which had to be performed, whether one liked it or not, to gods, state, and one's ancestors. In Athens the law exacted from the man not only marriage but also the performance of a minimum of so-called conjugal duties.

Thus when monogamous marriage first makes its appearance in history, it is not as the reconciliation of man and woman, still less as the highest form of such a reconciliation. Quite the contrary. Monogamous marriage comes on the scene as the subjugation of the one sex by the other; it announces a struggle between the sexes unknown throughout the whole previous prehistoric period. In an old unpublished manuscript, written by Marx and myself in 1846,[2] I find the words: "The first division of labor is that between man and woman for the propagation of children." And today I can add: The first class opposition that appears in history coincides with the development of the antagonism between man and woman in monogamous marriage, and the first class oppression coincides with that of the female sex by the male. Monogamous marriage was a great historical step forward; nevertheless, together with slavery and private wealth, it opens the period that has lasted until today in which every step forward is also relatively a step backward, in which prosperity and development for some is won through the misery and frustration of others. It is the cellular form of civilized society, in which the nature of the oppositions and contradictions fully active in that society can be already studied.

The old comparative freedom of sexual intercourse by no means

---

[2]The reference here is to the *Deutsche Ideologie* (*German Ideology*), written by Marx and Engels in Brussels in 1845-46 and first published in 1932 by the Marx-Engels-Lenin Institute in Moscow. See *German Ideology,* New York, 1939.—*Ed.*

disappeared with the victory of pairing marriage or even of monogamous marriage:

> The old conjugal system, now reduced to narrower limits by the gradual disappearance of the punaluan groups, still environed the advancing family, which it was to follow to the verge of civilization. . . . It finally disappeared in the new form of hetaerism, which still follows mankind in civilization as a dark shadow upon the family.[3]

By "hetaerism" Morgan understands the practice, *co-existent with monogamous marriage*, of sexual intercourse between men and unmarried women outside marriage, which, as we know, flourishes in the most varied forms throughout the whole period of civilization and develops more and more into open prostitution. This hetaerism derives quite directly from group marriage, from the ceremonial surrender by which women purchased the right of chastity. Surrender for money was at first a religious act; it took place in the temple of the goddess of love, and the money originally went into the temple treasury. The temple slaves of Anaitis in Armenia and of Aphrodite in Corinth, like the sacred dancing-girls attached to the temples of India, the so-called *bayaderes* (the word is a corruption of the Portuguese word *bailadeira*, meaning female dancer), were the first prostitutes. Originally the duty of every woman, this surrender was later performed by these priestesses alone as representatives of all other women. Among other peoples, hetaerism derives from the sexual freedom allowed to girls before marriage— again, therefore, a relic of group marriage, but handed down in a different way. With the rise of the inequality of property—already at the upper stage of barbarism, therefore—wage-labor appears sporadically side by side with slave labor, and at the same time, as its necessary correlate, the professional prostitution of free women side by side with the forced surrender of the slave. Thus the heritage which group marriage has bequeathed to civilization is double-edged, just as everything civilization brings forth is double-edged, double-tongued, divided against itself, contradictory: here monogamy, there hetaerism, with its most extreme form, prostitution. For hetaerism is as much a social institution as any other; it continues the old sexual freedom—to the advantage of the men. Actually not merely tolerated, but gaily practiced, by the ruling classes particularly, it is condemned in words. But in reality this condemnation never falls on the men concerned, but only on the women;

---

[3]Lewis H. Morgan, *Ancient Society, or Researches in the Lines of Human Progress from Savagery, through Barbarism to Civilization,* Chicago c. 1907, p. 511.

they are despised and outcast, in order that the unconditional supremacy of men over the female sex may be once more proclaimed as a fundamental law of society.

But a second contradiction thus develops within monogamous marriage itself. At the side of the husband who embellishes his existence with hetaerism stands the neglected wife. And one cannot have one side of this contradiction without the other, any more than a man has a whole apple in his hand after eating half. But that seems to have been the husbands' notion, until their wives taught them better. With monogamous marriage, two constant social types, unknown hitherto, make their appearance on the scene—the wife's attendant lover and the cuckold husband. The husbands had won the victory over the wives, but the vanquished magnanimously provided the crown. Together with monogamous marriage and hetaerism, adultery became an unavoidable social institution—denounced, severely penalized, but impossible to suppress. At best, the certain paternity of the children rested on moral conviction as before, and to solve the insoluble contradiction the *Code Napoléon*, Art. 312, decreed: *"L'enfant conçu pendant le mariage a pour père le mari,"* the father of a child conceived during marriage is—the husband. Such is the final result of three thousand years of monogamous marriage.

Thus, wherever the monogamous family remains true to its historical origin and clearly reveals the antagonism between the man and the woman expressed in the man's exclusive supremacy, it exhibits in miniature the same oppositions and contradictions as those in which society has been moving, without power to resolve or overcome them, ever since it split into classes at the beginning of civilization. I am speaking here, of course, only of those cases of monogamous marriage where matrimonial life actually proceeds according to the original character of the whole institution, but where the wife rebels against the husband's supremacy. Not all marriages turn out thus, as nobody knows better than the German philistine, who can no more assert his rule in the home than he can in the state, and whose wife, with every right, wears the trousers he is unworthy of. But, to make up for it, he considers himself far above his French companion in misfortune, to whom, oftener than to him, something much worse happens.

However, monogamous marriage did not by any means appear always and everywhere in the classically harsh form it took among the Greeks. Among the Romans, who, as future world-conquerors, had a larger, if a less fine vision than the Greeks, women were freer and more respected. A Roman considered that his power of life and death over his wife sufficiently guaranteed her conjugal fidelity. Here, moreover, the wife equally with the husband could dissolve the marriage at will. But the greatest progress in the development of individual marriage cer-

tainly came with the entry of the Germans into history, and for the
reason that the Germans—on account of their poverty, very probably—
were still at a stage where monogamy seems not yet to have become
perfectly distinct from pairing marriage. We infer this from three facts
mentioned by Tacitus. First, though marriage was held in great reverence—"they content themselves with one wife, the women live hedged
round with chastity"—polygamy was the rule for the distinguished
members and the leaders of the tribe, a condition of things similar to
that among the Americans, where pairing marriage was the rule. Secondly, the transition from mother-right to father-right could only have
been made a short time previously, for the brother on the mother's side
—the nearest gentile male relation according to mother-right—was still
considered almost closer of kin than the father, corresponding again to
the standpoint of the American Indians, among whom Marx, as he often
said, found the key to the understanding of our own primitive age.
And, thirdly, women were greatly respected among the Germans, and
also influential in public affairs, which is in direct contradiction to the
supremacy of men in monogamy. In almost all these points the Germans
agree with the Spartans, among whom also, as we saw, pairing marriage
had not yet been completely overcome. Thus, here again an entirely
new influence came to power in the world with the Germans. The new
monogamy, which now developed from the mingling of peoples amid
the ruins of the Roman world, clothed the supremacy of the men in
milder forms and gave women a position which, outwardly at any rate,
was much more free and respected than it had ever been in classical
antiquity. Only now were the conditions realized in which through
monogamy—within it, parallel to it, or in opposition to it, as the case
might be—the greatest moral advance we owe to it could be achieved:
modern individual sex-love, which had hitherto been unknown to the
entire world.

   This advance, however, undoubtedly sprang from the fact that the
Germans still lived in pairing families and grafted the corresponding
position of women onto the monogamous system, so far as that was possible. It most decidedly did not spring from the legendary virtue and
wonderful moral purity of the German character, which was nothing
more than the freedom of the pairing family from the crying moral
contradictions of monogamy. On the contrary, in the course of their
migrations the Germans had morally much deteriorated, particularly
during their southeasterly wanderings among the nomads of the Black
Sea steppes, from whom they acquired, not only equestrian skill, but
also gross, unnatural vices, as Ammianus expressly states of the Tai-
falians and Procopius of the Herulians.

But if monogamy was the only one of all the known forms of the family through which modern sex-love could develop, that does not mean that within monogamy modern sexual love developed exclusively or even chiefly as the love of husband and wife for each other. That was precluded by the very nature of strictly monogamous marriage under the rule of the man. Among all historically active classes—that is, among all ruling classes—matrimony remained what it had been since the pairing marriage, a matter of convenience which was arranged by the parents. The first historical form of sexual love as passion, a passion recognized as natural to all human beings (at least if they belonged to the ruling classes), and as the highest form of the sexual impulse—and that is what constitutes its specific character—this first form of individual sexual love, the chivalrous love of the middle ages, was by no means conjugal. Quite the contrary. In its classic form among the Provençals, it heads straight for adultery, and the poets of love celebrated adultery. The flower of Provençal love poetry are the Albas (*aubades*, songs of dawn). They describe in glowing colors how the knight lies in bed beside his love—the wife of another man—while outside stands the watchman who calls to him as soon as the first gray of dawn (*alba*) appears, so that he can get away unobserved; the parting scene then forms the climax of the poem. The northern French and also the worthy Germans adopted this kind of poetry together with the corresponding fashion of chivalrous love; old Wolfram of Eschenbach has left us three wonderfully beautiful songs of dawn on this same improper subject, which I like better than his three long heroic poems.

Nowadays there are two ways of concluding a bourgeois marriage. In Catholic countries the parents, as before, procure a suitable wife for their young bourgeois son, and the consequence is, of course, the fullest development of the contradiction inherent in monogamy: the husband abandons himself to hetaerism and the wife to adultery. Probably the only reason why the Catholic Church abolished divorce was because it had convinced itself that there is no more a cure for adultery than there is for death. In Protestant countries, on the other hand, the rule is that the son of a bourgeois family is allowed to choose a wife from his own class with more or less freedom; hence there may be a certain element of love in the marriage, as, indeed, in accordance with Protestant hypocrisy, is always assumed, for decency's sake. Here the husband's hetaerism is a more sleepy kind of business, and adultery by the wife is less the rule. But since, in every kind of marriage, people remain what they were before, and since the bourgeois of Protestant countries are mostly philistines, all that this Protestant monogamy achieves, taking the average of the best cases, is a conjugal partnership of leaden boredom, known as "domestic bliss." The best mirror of these two methods of marrying is the novel—the French novel for the Catholic manner, the German for the Protestant. In both, the hero "gets" them: in the German, the young man gets the girl; in the French, the husband gets the horns. Which of them is worse off is sometimes questionable. This is why the French bourgeois is as much horrified by the dullness of the German novel as the German philistine is by the "immorality" of the French. However, now that "Berlin is a world capital," the German novel is beginning with a little less timidity to use as part of its regular stock-in-trade the hetaerism and adultery long familiar to that town.

In both cases, however, the marriage is conditioned by the class position of the parties and is to that extent always a marriage of convenience. In both cases this marriage of convenience turns often enough into crassest prostitution—sometimes of both partners, but far more commonly of the woman, who only differs from the ordinary courtesan in that she does not let out her body on piece-work as a wage-worker, but sells it once and for all into slavery. And of all marriages of convenience Fourier's words hold true: "As in grammar two negatives make an affirmative, so in matrimonial morality two prostitutions pass for a virtue."[4] Sex-love in the relationship with a woman becomes, and can only become, the real rule among the oppressed classes, which means today among the proletariat—whether this relation is officially sanctioned or not. But here all the foundations of typical monogamy are cleared away. Here there is no property, for the preservation and inheritance of which monogamy and male supremacy were established; hence there is no incentive to make this male supremacy effective. What is more, there are no means of making it so. Bourgeois law, which protects this supremacy, exists only for the possessing class and their dealings with the proletarians. The law costs money and, on account of the worker's poverty, it has no validity for his relation to his wife. Here quite other personal and social conditions decide. And now that large-scale industry has taken the wife out of the home onto the labor market and into the factory, and made her often the bread-winner of the family, no basis for any kind of male supremacy is left in the proletarian household—except, perhaps, for something of the brutality towards women that has spread since the introduction of monogamy. The proletarian family is therefore no longer monogamous in the strict sense, even where there is passionate love and firmest loyalty on both sides, and maybe all the blessings of religious and civil authority. Here, therefore, the eternal attendants of monogamy, hetaerism and adultery, play only an almost

[4]Charles Fourier, *Théorie de l'Unité Universelle*. Paris, 1841-45, Vol. III, p. 120.—*Ed.*

vanishing part. The wife has in fact regained the right to dissolve the marriage, and if two people cannot get on with one another, they prefer to separate. In short, proletarian marriage is monogamous in the etymological sense of the word, but not at all in its historical sense.

Our jurists, of course, find that progress in legislation is leaving women with no further ground of complaint. Modern civilized systems of law increasingly acknowledge, first, that for a marriage to be legal, it must be a contract freely entered into by both partners, and, secondly, that also in the married state both partners must stand on a common footing of equal rights and duties. If both these demands are consistently carried out, say the jurists, women have all they can ask.

This typically legalist method of argument is exactly the same as that which the radical republican bourgeois uses to put the proletarian in his place. The labor contract is to be freely entered into by both partners. But it is considered to have been freely entered into as soon as the law makes both parties equal on *paper*. The power conferred on the one party by the difference of class position, the pressure thereby brought to bear on the other party—the real economic position of both—that is not the law's business. Again, for the duration of the labor contract both parties are to have equal rights, in so far as one or the other does not expressly surrender them. That economic relations compel the worker to surrender even the last semblance of equal rights—here again, that is no concern of the law.

In regard to marriage, the law, even the most advanced, is fully satisfied as soon as the partners have formally recorded that they are entering into the marriage of their own free consent. What goes on in real life behind the juridical scenes, how this free consent comes about—that is not the business of the law and the jurist. And yet the most elementary comparative jurisprudence should show the jurist what this free consent really amounts to. In the countries where an obligatory share of the paternal inheritance is secured to the children by law and they cannot therefore be disinherited—in Germany, in the countries with French law and elsewhere—the children are obliged to obtain their parents' consent to their marriage. In the countries with English law, where parental consent to a marriage is not legally required, the parents on their side have full freedom in the testamentary disposal of their property and can disinherit their children at their pleasure. It is obvious that, in spite and precisely because of this fact, freedom of marriage among the classes with something to inherit is in reality not a whit greater in England and America than it is in France and Germany.

As regards the legal equality of husband and wife in marriage, the position is no better. The legal inequality of the two partners, bequeathed to us from earlier social conditions, is not the cause but the effect of the economic oppression of the woman. In the old communistic household, which comprised many couples and their children, the task entrusted to the women of managing the household was as much a public and socially necessary industry as the procuring of food by the men. With the patriarchal family, and still more with the single monogamous family, a change came. Household management lost its public character. It no longer concerned society. It became a *private service*; the wife became the head servant, excluded from all participation in social production. Not until the coming of modern large-scale industry was the road to social production opened to her again—and then only to the proletarian wife. But it was opened in such a manner that, if she carries out her duties in the private service of her family, she remains excluded from public production and unable to earn; and if she wants to take part in public production and earn independently, she cannot carry out family duties. And the wife's position in the factory is the position of women in all branches of business, right up to medicine and the law. The modern individual family is founded on the open or concealed domestic slavery of the wife, and modern society is a mass composed of these individual families as its molecules.

In the great majority of cases today, at least in the possessing classes, the husband is obliged to earn a living and support his family, and that in itself gives him a position of supremacy, without any need for special legal titles and privileges. Within the family he is the bourgeois and the wife represents the proletariat. In the industrial world, the specific character of the economic oppression burdening the proletariat is visible in all its sharpness only when all special legal privileges of the capitalist class have been abolished and complete legal equality of both classes established. The democratic republic does not do away with the opposition of the two classes; on the contrary, it provides the clear field on which the fight can be fought out. And in the same way, the peculiar character of the supremacy of the husband over the wife in the modern family, the necessity of creating real social equality between them, and the way to do it, will only be seen in the clear light of day when both possess legally complete equality of rights. Then it will be plain that the first condition for the liberation of the wife is to bring the whole female sex back into public industry, and that this in turn demands the abolition of the monogamous family as the economic unit of society.

The Problem that Has No Name

Betty Friedan

When Betty Friedan wrote The Feminine Mystique *in 1963, no one, she says, was "muttering angrily about women's rights." The fact that today women are questioning, demanding, demonstrating, as well as muttering and shouting about women's rights is in large part the result of Friedan's important and influential book. Today women are readily admitting that they get no "mysterious fulfillment" from housewifely chores but regard them as trivial work, garbage work, which nobody—female or male—likes to do.*

You will want to compare Friedan's analysis of the quiet desperation of the housewife of the 1960's with Sinclair Lewis' dramatization of the same problem in Main Street. *You may also contemplate the following findings of the National Opinion Research Center (University of Chicago) concerning those most and least happy in American society: Most happy are married men; next, single women; next, married women; least happy are unmarried men.*

The problem lay buried, unspoken, for many years in the minds of American women. It was a strange stirring, a sense of dissatisfaction, a yearning that women suffered in the middle of the twentieth century in the United States. Each suburban wife struggled with it alone. As she made the beds, shopped for groceries, matched slipcover material, ate peanut butter sandwiches with her children, chauffeured Cub Scouts and Brownies, lay beside her husband at night—she was afraid to ask even of herself the silent question—"Is this all?"

For over fifteen years there was no word of this yearning in the millions of words written about women, for women, in all the columns, books and articles by experts telling women their role was to seek fulfillment as wives and mothers. Over and over women heard in voices of tradition and of Freudian sophistication that they could desire no greater destiny than to glory in their own femininity. Experts told them how to catch a man and keep him, how to breastfeed children and handle their toilet training, how to cope with sibling rivalry and adolescent rebellion; how to buy a dishwasher, bake bread, cook gourmet snails, and build a swimming pool with their own hands; how to dress, look, and act more feminine and make marriage more exciting; how to keep their husbands from dying young and their sons from growing into delinquents. They were taught to pity the neurotic, unfeminine, unhappy women who wanted to be poets or physicists or presidents. They learned that truly feminine women do not want careers, higher education, political rights—the independence and the opportunities that the old-fashioned feminists fought for. Some women, in their forties and fifties, still remembered painfully giving up those dreams, but most of the younger women no longer even thought about them. A thousand expert voices applauded their femininity, their adjustment, their new maturity. All they had to do was devote their lives from earliest girlhood to finding a husband and bearing children.

By the end of the nineteen-fifties, the average marriage age of women in America dropped to 20, and was still dropping, into the teens. Fourteen million girls were engaged by 17. The proportion of women attending college in comparison with men dropped from 47 per cent in 1920 to 35 per cent in 1958. A century earlier, women had fought for higher education; now girls went to college to get a husband. By the mid-fifties, 60 per cent dropped out of college to marry, or because they were afraid too much education would be a marriage bar. Colleges built dormitories for "married students," but the students were almost always the husbands. A new degree was instituted for the wives—"Ph.T." (Putting Husband Through).

Then American girls began getting married in high school. And the women's magazines, deploring the unhappy statistics about these young marriages, urged that courses on marriage, and marriage counselors, be installed in the high schools. Girls started going steady at twelve and thirteen, in junior high. Manufacturers put out brassieres with false bosoms of foam rubber for little girls of ten. And on advertisement for a child's dress, sizes 3–6x, in the *New York Times* in the fall of 1960, said: "She Too Can Join the Man-Trap Set."

By the end of the fifties, the United States birthrate was overtaking India's. The birth-control movement, renamed Planned Parenthood, was asked to find a method whereby women who had been advised that a third or fourth baby would be born dead or defective might have it anyhow. Statisticians were especially astounded at the fantastic increase in the number of babies among college women. Where once they had two children, now they had four, five, six. Women who had once wanted careers were now making careers out of having babies. So rejoiced *Life* magazine in a 1956 paean to the movement of American women back to the home.

In a New York hospital, a woman had a nervous breakdown when she found she could not breastfeed her baby. In other hospitals, women dying of cancer refused a drug which research had proved might save their lives: its side effects were said to be unfeminine. "If I have only one life, let me live it as a blonde," a larger-than-life-sized picture of a pretty, vacuous woman proclaimed from newspaper, magazine, and drugstore ads. And across America, three out of every ten women dyed their hair blonde. They ate a chalk called Metrecal, instead of food, to shrink to the size of the thin young models. Department-store buyers reported that American women, since 1939, had become three and four sizes smaller. "Women are out to fit the clothes, instead of vice-versa," one buyer said.

Interior decorators were designing kitchens with mosaic murals and original paintings, for kitchens were once again the center of women's lives. Home sewing became a million-dollar industry. Many women no longer left their homes, except to shop, chauffeur their children, or attend a social engagement with their husbands. Girls were growing up in America without ever having jobs outside the home. In the late fifties, a sociological phenomenon was suddenly remarked: a third of American women now worked, but most were no longer young and very few were pursuing careers. They were married women who held part-time jobs, selling or secretarial, to put their husbands through school, their sons through college, or to help pay the mortgage. Or they were widows supporting families. Fewer and fewer women were entering professional work. The shortages in the nursing, social work, and teaching professions caused crises in almost every American city. Concerned over the Soviet Union's lead in the space race, scientists noted that America's greatest source of unused brain-power was women. But girls would not study physics: it was "unfeminine." A girl refused a science fellowship at Johns Hopkins to take a job in a real-estate office. All she wanted, she said, was what every other American girl wanted—to get married, have four children and live in a nice house in a nice suburb.

The suburban housewife—she was the dream image of the young American women and the envy, it was said, of women all over the world. The American housewife—freed by science and labor-saving appliances from the drudgery, the dangers of childbirth and the illnesses of her grandmother. She was healthy, beautiful, educated, concerned only about her husband, her children, her home. She had found true feminine fulfillment. As a housewife and mother, she was respected as a full and equal partner to man in his world. She was free to choose automobiles, clothes, appliances, supermarkets; she had everything that women ever dreamed of.

In the fifteen years after World War II, this mystique of feminine fulfillment became the cherished and self-perpetuating core of contemporary American culture. Millions of women lived their lives in the image of those pretty pictures of the American suburban housewife, kissing their husbands goodbye in front of the picture window, depositing their stationwagonsful of children at school, and smiling as they ran the new electric waxer over the spotless kitchen floor. They baked their own bread, sewed their own and their children's clothes, kept their new washing machines and dryers running all day. They changed the sheets on the beds twice a week instead of once, took the rug-hooking class in adult education, and pitied their poor frustrated mothers, who had dreamed of having a career. Their only dream was to be perfect wives and mothers; their highest ambition to have five children and a beautiful house, their only fight to get and keep their husbands. They had no thought for the unfeminine problems of the world outside the home; they wanted the men to make the major decisions. They gloried in their role as women, and wrote proudly on the census blank: "Occupation: housewife."

For over fifteen years, the words written for women, and the words women used when they talked to each other, while their husbands sat on the other side of the room and talked shop or politics or septic tanks, were about problems with their children, or how to keep their husbands happy, or improve their children's school, or cook chicken or make slipcovers. Nobody argued whether women were inferior or superior to men; they were simply different. Words like "emancipation" and "career" sounded strange and embarrassing; no one had used them for years. When a Frenchwoman named Simone de Beauvoir wrote a book called *The Second Sex*, an American critic commented that she obviously "didn't know what life was all about," and besides, she was talking about French women. The "woman problem" in America no longer existed.

If a woman had a problem in the 1950's and 1960's, she knew that something must be wrong with her marriage, or with herself. Other women were satisfied with their lives, she thought. What kind of a woman was she if she did not feel this mysterious fulfillment waxing the kitchen floor? She was so ashamed to admit her dissatisfaction that she never knew how many other women shared it. If she tried to tell her husband, he didn't understand what she was talking about. She did not really understand it herself. For over fifteen years women in America found it harder to talk about the problem than about sex. Even the psychoanalysts had no name for it. When a woman went to a psychiatrist for help, as many women did, she would say, "I'm so ashamed," or "I must be hopelessly neurotic." "I don't know what's wrong with women today," a suburban psychiatrist said uneasily. "I only know something is wrong because most of my patients happen to be women. And their problem isn't sexual." Most women with this problem did not go to see a psychoanalyst, however. "There's nothing wrong really," they kept telling themselves. "There isn't any problem."

But on an April morning in 1959, I heard a mother of four, having coffee with four other mothers in a suburban development fifteen miles from New York, say in a tone of quiet desperation, "the problem." And the others knew, without words, that she was not talking about a problem with her husband, or her children, or her home. Suddenly they realized they all shared the same problem, the problem that has no name. They began, hesitantly, to talk about it. Later, after they had picked up their children at nursery school and taken them home to nap, two of the women cried, in sheer relief, just to knew they were not alone.

Gradually I came to realize that the problem that has no name was shared by countless women in America. As a magazine writer I often interviewed women about problems with their children, or their marriages, or their houses, or their communities. But after a while I began to recognize the telltale signs of this other problem. I saw the same signs in suburban ranch houses and split-levels on Long Island and in New Jersey and Westchester County; in colonial houses in a small Massachusetts town; on patios in Memphis; in suburban and city apartments; in living rooms in the Midwest. Sometimes I sensed the problem, not as a reporter, but as a suburban housewife, for during this time I was also bringing up my own three children in Rockland County, New York. I heard echoes of the problem in college dormitories and semiprivate maternity wards, at PTA meetings and luncheons of the League of Women Voters, at suburban cocktail parties, in station wagons waiting for trains, and in snatches of conversation overheard at Schrafft's. The groping words I heard from other women, on quiet afternoons when children were at school or on quiet evenings when husbands worked late, I think I understood first as a woman long before I understood their larger social and psychological implications.

Just what was this problem that has no name? What were the words women used when they tried to express it? Sometimes a woman would say "I feel empty somehow . . . incomplete." Or she would say, "I feel as if I don't exist." Sometimes she blotted out the feeling with a tranquilizer. Sometimes she thought the problem was with her husband, or her children, or that what she really needed was to redecorate her house, or move to a better neighborhood, or have an affair, or another baby. Sometimes, she went to a doctor with symptoms she could hardly describe: "A tired feeling . . . I get so angry with the children it scares me . . . I feel like crying without any reason." (A Cleveland doctor called it "the housewife's syndrome.") A number of women told me about great bleeding blisters that break out on their hands and arms. "I call it the housewife's blight," said a family doctor in Pennsylvania. "I see it so often lately in these young women with four, five and six children who bury themselves in their dishpans. But it isn't caused by detergent and it isn't cured by cortisone."

Sometimes a woman would tell me that the feeling gets so strong she runs out of the house and walks through the streets. Or she stays inside her house and cries. Or her children tell her a joke, and she doesn't laugh because she doesn't hear it. I talked to women who had spent years on the analyst's couch, working out their "adjustment to the feminine role," their blocks to "fulfillment as a wife and mother." But the desperate tone in these women's voices, and the look in their eyes, was the same as the tone and the look of other women, who were sure they had no problem, even though they did have a strange feeling of desperation.

A mother of four who left college at nineteen to get married told me:

> I've tried everything women are supposed to do—hobbies, gardening, pickling, canning, being very social with my neighbors, joining committees, running PTA teas. I can do it all, and I like it, but it doesn't leave you anything to think about—any feeling of who you are. I never had any career ambitions. All I wanted was to get married and have four children. I love the kids and Bob and my home. There's no problem you can even put a name to. But I'm desperate. I begin to feel I have no personality. I'm a server of food and putter-on of pants and a bedmaker, somebody who can be called on when you want something. But who am I?

A twenty-three-year-old mother in blue jeans said:

> I ask myself why I'm so dissatisfied. I've got my health, fine children, a lovely new home, enough money. My husband has a real future as an electronics engineer. He doesn't have any of these feelings. He says maybe I need a vacation, let's go to New York for a weekend. But that isn't it. I always had this idea we should do everything together. I can't sit down and read a book alone. If the children are napping and I have one hour to myself I just walk through the house waiting for them to wake up. I don't make a move until I know where the rest of the crowd is going. It's as if ever since you were a little girl, there's always been somebody or something that will take care of your life: your parents, or college, or falling in love, or having a child, or moving to a new house. Then you wake up one morning and there's nothing to look forward to.

A young wife in a Long Island development said:

> I seem to sleep so much. I don't know why I should be so tired. This house isn't nearly so hard to clean as the cold-water flat we had when I was working. The children are at school all day. It's not the work. I just don't feel alive.

In 1960, the problem that has no name burst like a boil through the image of the happy American housewife. In the television commercials the pretty housewives still beamed over their foaming dishpans and *Time's* cover story on "The Suburban Wife, an American Phenomenon" protested: "Having too good a time . . . to believe that they should be unhappy." But the actual unhappiness of the American housewife was suddenly being reported—from the *New York Times* and *Newsweek* to *Good Housekeeping* and CBS Television ("The Trapped Housewife"), although almost everybody who talked about it found some superficial reason to dismiss it. It was attributed to incompetent appliance repairmen *(New York Times)*, or the distances children must be chauffeured in the suburbs *(Time)*, or too much PTA *(Redbook)*. Some said it was the old problem—education: more and more women had education, which naturally made them unhappy in their role as housewives. "The road from Freud to Frigidaire, from Sophocles to Spock, has turned out to be a bumpy one," reported the *New York Times* (June 28, 1960). "Many young women—certainly not all—whose education plunged them into a world of ideas feel stifled in their homes. They find their routine lives out of joint with their training. Like shut-ins, they feel left out. In the last year, the problem of the educated housewife has provided the meat of dozens of speeches made by troubled presidents of women's colleges who maintain, in the face of complaints, that sixteen years of academic training is realistic preparation for wifehood and motherhood."

There was much sympathy for the educated housewife. ("Like a two-headed schizophrenic . . . once she wrote a paper on the Graveyard poets; now she writes notes to the milkman. Once she determined the boiling point of sulphuric acid; now she determines her boiling point with the overdue repairman. . . . The housewife often is reduced to screams and tears. . . . No one, it seems, is appreciative, least of all herself, of the kind of person she becomes in the process of turning from poetess into shrew.")

Home economists suggested more realistic preparation for housewives, such as high-school workshops in home appliances. College educators suggested more discussion groups on home management and the family, to prepare women for the adjustment to domestic life. A spate of articles appeared in the mass magazines offering "Fifty-eight

Ways to Make Your Marriage More Exciting." No month went by
without a new book by a psychiatrist or sexologist offering technical
advice on finding greater fulfillment through sex.

A male humorist joked in *Harper's Bazaar* (July, 1960) that the
problem could be solved by taking away woman's right to vote. ("In
the pre-19th Amendment era, the American woman was placid, sheltered and sure of her role in American society. She left all the political
decisions to her husband and he, in turn, left all the family decisions
to her. Today a woman has to make both the family *and* the political
decisions, and it's too much for her.")

A number of educators suggested seriously that women no longer
be admitted to the four-year colleges and universities: in the growing
college crisis, the education which girls could not use as housewives
was more urgently needed than ever by boys to do the work of the
atomic age.

The problem was also dismissed with drastic solutions no one could
take seriously. (A woman writer proposed in *Harper's* that women be
drafted for compulsory service as nurses' aides and baby-sitters.) And
it was smoothed over with the age-old panaceas: "love is their answer,"
"the only answer is inner help," "the secret of completeness—children,"
"a private means of intellectual fulfillment," "to cure this toothache of
the spirit—the simple formula of handling one's self and one's will over
to God."[1]

The problem was dismissed by telling the housewife she doesn't
realize how lucky she is—her own boss, no time clock, no junior executive gunning for her job. What if she isn't happy—does she think men
are happy in this world? Does she really, secretly, still want to be a
man? Doesn't she know yet how lucky she is to be a woman?

The problem was also, and finally, dismissed by shrugging that there
are no solutions: this is what being a woman means, and what is wrong
with American women that they can't accept their role gracefully? As
Newsweek put it (March 7, 1960):

> She is dissatisfied with a lot that women of other lands can only
> dream of. Her discontent is deep, pervasive, and impervious to the
> superficial remedies which are offered at every hand. . . . An army
> of professional explorers have already charted the major sources of
> trouble. . . . From the beginning of time, the female cycle has defined
> and confined woman's role. As Freud was credited with saying:
> "Anatomy is destiny." Though no group of women has ever pushed
> these natural restrictions as far as the American wife, it seems that
> she still cannot accept them with good grace. . . . A young mother
> with a beautiful family, charm, talent and brains is apt to dismiss her
> role apologetically. "What do I do?" you hear her say. "Why nothing.

I'm just a housewife." A good education, it seems, has given this para-
gon among women an understanding of the value of everything except
her own worth . . .

And so she must accept the fact that "American women's unhappiness is merely the most recently won of women's rights," and adjust
and say with the happy housewife found by *Newsweek:* "We ought to
salute the wonderful freedom we all have and be proud of our lives
today. I have had college and I've worked, but being a housewife is
the most rewarding and satisfying role. . . . My mother was never included in my father's business affairs . . . she couldn't get out of the
house and away from us children. But I am an equal to my husband;
I can go along with him on business trips and to social business affairs."

The alternative offered was a choice that few women would contemplate. In the sympathetic words of the *New York Times:* "All admit
to being deeply frustrated at times by the lack of privacy, the physical
burden, the routine of family life, the confinement of it. However, none
would give up her home and family if she had the choice to make
again." *Redbook* commented: "Few women would want to thumb their
noses at husbands, children and community and go off on their own.
Those who do may be talented individuals, but they rarely are successful women."

The year American women's discontent boiled over, it was also reported *(Look)* that the more than 21,000,000 American women who
are single, widowed, or divorced do not cease even after fifty their
frenzied, desperate search for a man. And the search begins early—
for seventy per cent of all American women now marry before they
are twenty-four. A pretty twenty-five-year-old secretary took thirty-five
different jobs in six months in the futile hope of finding a husband.
Women were moving from one political club to another, taking evening
courses in accounting or sailing, learning to play golf or ski, joining a
number of churches in succession, going to bars alone, in their cease-
less search for a man.

Of the growing thousands of women currently getting private psychiatric help in the United States, the married ones were reported
dissatisfied with their marriages, the unmarried ones suffering from
anxiety and, finally, depression. Strangely, a number of psychiatrists
stated that, in their experience, unmarried women patients were happier
than married ones. So the door of all those pretty suburban houses
opened a crack to permit a glimpse of uncounted thousands of American
housewives who suffered alone from a problem that suddenly everyone was talking about, and beginning to take for granted, as one of
those unreal problems in American life that can never be solved—like

the hydrogen bomb. By 1962 the plight of the trapped American house-wife had become a national parlor game. Whole issues of magazines, newspaper columns, books learned and frivolous, educational confer-ences and television panels were devoted to the problem.

Even so, most men, and some women, still did not know that this problem was real. But those who had faced it honestly knew that all the superficial remedies, the sympathetic advice, the scolding words and the cheering words were somehow drowning the problem in un-reality. A bitter laugh was beginning to be heard from American women. They were admired, envied, pitied, theorized over until they were sick of it, offered drastic solutions or silly choices that no one could take seriously. They got all kinds of advice from the growing armies of marriage and child-guidance counselors, psychotherapists, and armchair psychologists, on how to adjust to their role as housewives. No other road to fulfillment was offered to American women in the middle of the twentieth century. Most adjusted to their role and suffered or ignored the problem that has no name. It can be less painful for a woman, not to hear the strange, dissatisfied voice stirring within her.

It is no longer possible to ignore that voice, to dismiss the despera-tion of so many American women. This is not what being a woman means, no matter what the experts say. For human suffering there is a reason; perhaps the reason has not been found because the right questions have not been asked, or pressed far enough. I do not accept the answer that there is no problem because American women have luxuries that women in other times and lands never dreamed of; part of the strange newness of the problem is that it cannot be understood in terms of the age-old material problems of man: poverty, sickness, hunger, cold. The women who suffer this problem have a hunger that food cannot fill. It persists in women whose husbands are struggling internes and law clerks, or prosperous doctors and lawyers; in wives of workers and executives who make $5,000 a year or $50,000. It is not caused by lack of material advantages; it may not even be felt by women preoccupied with desperate problems of hunger, poverty or illness. And women who think it will be solved by more money, a bigger house, a second car, moving to a better suburb, often discover it gets worse.

It is no longer possible today to blame the problem on loss of feminin-ity: to say that education and independence and equality with men have made American women unfeminine. I have heard so many women try to deny this dissatisfied voice within themselves because it does not fit the pretty picture of femininity the experts have given them. I think, in fact, that this is the first clue to the mystery; the problem cannot be understood in the generally accepted terms by which scientists have studied women, doctors have treated them, counselors have advised them, and writers have written about them. Women who suffer this problem, in whom this voice is stirring, have lived their whole lives in the pursuit of feminine fulfillment. They are not career women (although career women may have other problems); they are women whose greatest ambition has been marriage and children. For the oldest of these women, these daughters of the American middle class, no other dream was possible. The ones in their forties and fifties who once had other dreams gave them up and threw themselves joyously into life as housewives. For the youngest, the new wives and mothers, this was the only dream. They are the ones who quit high school and college to marry, or marked time in some job in which they had no real interest until they married. These women are very "feminine" in the usual sense, and yet they still suffer the problem.

Are the women who finished college, the women who once had dreams beyond housewifery, the ones who suffer the most? According to the experts they are, but listen to these four women:

> My days are all busy, and dull, too. All I ever do is mess around. I get up at eight—I make breakfast, so I do the dishes, have lunch, do some more dishes, and some laundry and cleaning in the afternoon. Then it's supper dishes and I get to sit down a few minutes, before the children have to be sent to bed. . . . That's all there is to my day. It's just like any other wife's day. Humdrum. The biggest time, I am chasing kids.

> Ye Gods, what do I do with my time? Well, I get up at six. I get my son dressed and then give him breakfast. After that I wash dishes and bathe and feed the baby. Then I get lunch and while the children nap, I sew or mend or iron and do all the other things I can't get done before noon. Then I cook supper for the family and my husband watches TV while I do the dishes. After I get the children to bed, I set my hair and then I go to bed.

> The problem is always being the children's mommy, or the minister's wife and never being myself.

> A film made of any typical morning in my house would look like an old Marx Brothers' comedy. I wash the dishes, rush the older children off to school, dash out in the yard to cultivate the chrysanthemums, run back in to make a phone call about a committee meeting, help the youngest child build a blockhouse, spend fifteen minutes skimming the newspapers so I can be well-informed, then scamper down to the washing machines where my thrice-weekly laundry includes enough clothes to keep a primitive village going for an entire year. By noon I'm ready for a padded cell. Very little of what I've

done has been really necessary or important. Outside pressures lash
me through the day. Yet I look upon myself as one of the more relaxed
housewives in the neighborhood. Many of my friends are even more
frantic. In the past sixty years we have come full circle and the American housewife is once again trapped in a squirrel cage. If the cage is
now a modern plate-glass-and-broadloom ranch house or a convenient
modern apartment, the situation is no less painful than when her
grandmother sat over an embroidery hoop in her gilt-and-plush parlor
and muttered angrily about women's rights.

The first two women never went to college. They live in developments in Levittown, New Jersey, and Tacoma, Washington, and were
interviewed by a team of sociologists studying workingmen's wives.[2]
The third, a minister's wife, wrote on the fifteenth reunion questionnaire of her college that she never had any career ambitions, but wishes
now she had.[3] The fourth, who has a Ph.D. in anthropology, is today a
Nebraska housewife with three children.[4] Their words seem to indicate
that housewifes of all educational levels suffer the same feeling of
desperation.

The fact is that no one today is muttering angrily about "women's
rights," even though more and more women have gone to college. In
a recent study of all the classes that have graduated from Barnard
College,[5] a significant minority of earlier graduates blamed their education for making them want "rights," later classes blamed their education for giving them career dreams, but recent graduates blamed the
college for making them feel it was not enough simply to be a housewife and mother; they did not want to feel guilty if they did not read
books or take part in community activities. But if education is not the
cause of the problem, the fact that education somehow festers in these
women may be a clue.

If the secret of feminine fulfillment is having children, never have
so many women, with the freedom to choose, had so many children,
in so few years, so willingly. If the answer is love, never have women
searched for love with such determination. And yet there is a growing
suspicion that the problem may not be sexual, though it must somehow
be related to sex. I have heard from many doctors evidence of new
sexual problems between man and wife—sexual hunger in wives so
great their husbands cannot satisfy it. "We have made women a sex
creature," said a psychiatrist at the Margaret Sanger marriage counseling clinic. "She has no identity except as a wife and mother. She does
not know who she is herself. She waits all day for her husband to come
home at night to make her feel alive. And now it is the husband who is
not interested. It is terrible for the women, to lie there, night after night,
waiting for her husband to make her feel alive." Why is there such a

market for books and articles offering sexual advice? The kind of sexual orgasm which Kinsey found in statistical plenitude in the recent generations of American women does not seem to make this problem go away.

On the contrary, new neuroses are being seen among women—and problems as yet unnamed as neuroses—which Freud and his followers did not predict, with physical symptoms, anxieties, and defense mechanisms equal to those caused by sexual repression. And strange new problems are being reported in the growing generations of children whose mothers were always there, driving them around, helping them with their homework—an inability to endure pain or discipline or pursue any self-sustained goal of any sort, a devastating boredom with life. Educators are increasingly uneasy about the dependence, the lack of self-reliance, of the boys and girls who are entering college today. "We fight a continual battle to make our students assume manhood," said a Columbia dean.

A White House conference was held on the physical and muscular deterioration of American children: were they being over-nurtured? Sociologists noted the astounding organization of suburban children's lives: the lessons, parties, entertainments, play and study groups organized for them. A suburban housewife in Portland, Oregon, wondered why the children "need" Brownies and Boy Scouts out here. "This is not the slums. The kids out here have the great outdoors. I think people are so bored, they organize the children, and then try to hook everyone else on it. And the poor kids have no time left just to lie on their beds and daydream."

Can the problem that has no name be somehow related to the domestic routine of the housewife? When a woman tries to put the problem into words, she often merely describes the daily life she leads. What is there in this recital of comfortable domestic detail that could possibly cause such a feeling of desperation? Is she trapped simply by the enormous demands of her role as modern housewife: wife, mistress, mother, nurse, consumer, cook, chauffeur; expert on interior decoration, child care, appliance repair, furniture refinishing, nutrition, and education? Her day is fragmented as she rushes from dishwasher to washing machine to telephone to dryer to station wagon to supermarket, and delivers Johnny to the Little League field, takes Janey to dancing class, gets the lawnmower fixed and meets the 6:45. She can never spend more than 15 minutes on any one thing; she has no time to read books, only magazines; even if she had time, she has lost the power to concentrate. At the end of the day, she is so terribly tired that sometimes her husband has to take over and put the children to bed.

Thus terrible tiredness took so many women to doctors in the 1950's that one decided to investigate it. He found, surprisingly, that his patients suffering from "housewife's fatigue" slept more than an adult needed to sleep—as much as ten hours a day—and that the actual energy they expended on housework did not tax their capacity. The real problem must be something else, he decided—perhaps boredom. Some doctors told their women patients they must get out of the house for a day, treat themselves to a movie in town. Others prescribed tranquilizers. Many suburban housewives were taking tranquilizers like cough drops. "You wake up in the morning, and you feel as if there's no point in going on another day like this. So you take a tranquilizer because it makes you not care so much that it's pointless."

It is easy to see the concrete details that trap the suburban housewife, the continual demands on her time. But the chains that bind her in her trap are chains in her own mind and spirit. They are chains made up of mistaken ideas and misinterpreted facts, of incomplete truths and unreal choices. They are not easily seen and not easily shaken off.

How can any woman see the whole truth within the bounds of her own life? How can she believe that voice inside herself, when it denies the conventional, accepted truths by which she has been living? And yet the women I have talked to, who are finally listening to that inner voice, seem in some incredible way to be groping through to a truth that has defied the experts.

I think the experts in a great many fields have been holding pieces of that truth under their microscopes for a long time without realizing it. I found pieces of it in certain new research and theoretical developments in psychological, social and biological science whose implications for women seem never to have been examined. I found many clues by talking to suburban doctors, gynecologists, obstetricians, child-guidance clinicians, pediatricians, high-school guidance counselors, college professors, marriage counselors, psychiatrists and ministers—questioning them not on their theories, but on their actual experience in treating American women. I became aware of a growing body of evidence, much of whch has not been reported publicly because it does not fit current modes of thought about women—evidence which throws into question the standards of feminine normality, feminine adjustment, feminine fulfillment, and feminine maturity by which most women are still trying to live.

I began to see in a strange new light the American return to early marriage and the large families that are causing the population explosion; the recent movement to natural childbirth and breastfeeding; suburban conformity, and the new neuroses, character pathologies and sexual problems being reported by the doctors. I began to see new dimensions to old problems that have long been taken for granted among women: menstrual difficulties, sexual frigidity, promiscuity, pregnancy fears, childbirth depression, the high incidence of emotional breakdown and suicide among women in their twenties and thirties, the menopause crises, the so-called passivity and immaturity of American men, the discrepancy between women's tested intellectual abilities in childhood and their adult achievement, the changing incidence of adult sexual orgasm in American women, and persistent problems in psychotherapy and in women's education.

If I am right, the problem that has no name stirring in the minds of so many American women today is not a matter of loss of femininity or too much education, or the demands of domesticity. It is far more important than anyone recognizes. It is the key to these other new and old problems which have been torturing women and their husbands and children, and puzzling their doctors and educators for years. It may well be the key to our future as a nation and a culture. We can no longer ignore that voice within women that says: "I want something more than my husband and my children and my home."

NOTES

1. See the Seventy-fifth Anniversary Issue of *Good Housekeeping*, May, 1960, "The Gift of Self," a symposium by Margaret Mead, Jessamyn West, *et al.*
2. Lee Rainwater, Richard P. Coleman, and Gerald Handel, *Workingman's Wife*, New York, 1959.
3. Betty Friedan, "If One Generation Can Ever Tell Another," *Smith Alumnae Quarterly*, Northampton, Mass., Winter, 1961. I first became aware of "the problem that has no name" and its possible relationship to what I finally called "the feminine mystique" in 1957, when I prepared an intensive questionnaire and conducted a survey of my own Smith College classmates fifteen years after graduation. This questionnaire was later used by alumnae classes of Radcliffe and other women's colleges with similar results.
4. Jhan and June Robbins, "Why Young Mothers Feel Trapped," *Redbook*, September, 1960.
5. Marian Freda Poverman, "Alumnae on Parade," *Barnard Alumnae Magazine*, July, 1957.

from *Main Street*

Sinclair Lewis

Sinclair Lewis' novel Main Street *(1920) depicts the soul-destroying life in a small midwestern town where dullness has become God. The heroine of the book is a modestly intelligent woman who determines in college that she will do something useful with her life. After graduation, she works as a librarian for a few years, then falls in love with and marries Will Kennicott, a small-town doctor from Gopher Prairie, Minnesota. Carol's life with Will is a struggle to fulfill her girlhood dream of making life more beautiful and meaningful in a small town. She tries numerous civic improvement projects, such as attempting to instill an appreciation for literature in the Thanatopsis Club, soliciting funds for a new town hall, or establishing a community dramatic society. All of her efforts, feeble and sometimes misdirected as they are, meet with failure, including her attempt to be satisfied with the roles of admiring wife and loving mother. The following excerpts from* Main Street *show the quality (or lack of quality) of Carol's life and her analysis of "the problem that has no name."*

1

The economic subservience of women is the subject of the following scene, when Carol goes to ask her husband for money to buy groceries.

Carol was extravagant, but at least she did not try to clear herself of blame by going about whimpering. "I know I'm terribly extravagant but I don't seem to be able to help it."

Kennicott had never thought of giving her an allowance. His mother had never had one! As a wage-earning spinster Carol had asserted to her fellow librarians that when she was married, she was going to have an allowance and be business-like and modern. But it was too much trouble to explain to Kennicott's kindly stubbornness that she was a practical housekeeper as well as a flighty playmate. She bought a budget-plan account book and made her budgets as exact as budgets are likely to be when they lack budgets.

For the first month it was a honeymoon jest to beg prettily, to confess. "I haven't a cent in the house, dear," and to be told. "You're an extravagant little rabbit." But the budget book made her realize how inexact were her finances. She became self-conscious; occasionally she was indignant that she should always have to petition him for the money with which to buy his food. She caught herself criticizing his belief that, since his joke about trying to keep her out of the poorhouse had once been accepted as admirable humor, it should continue to be his daily *bon mot*. It was a nuisance to have to run down the street after him because she had forgotten to ask him for money at breakfast.

But she couldn't "hurt his feelings," she reflected. He liked the lordliness of giving largess.

She tried to reduce the frequency of begging by opening accounts and having the bills sent to him. She had found that staple groceries, sugar, flour, could be most cheaply purchased at Axel Egge's rustic general store. She said sweetly to Axel:

"I think I'd better open a charge account here."

"I don't do no business except for cash," grunted Axel.

She flared, "Do you know who I am?"

"Yuh, sure, I know. The doc is good for it. But that's yoost a rule I made. I make low prices. I do business for cash."

She stared at his red impassive face, and her fingers had the undignified desire to slap him, but her reason agreed with him. "You're quite right. You shouldn't break your rule for me."

Her rage had not been lost. It had been transferred to her husband. She wanted ten pounds of sugar in a hurry, but she had no money. She ran up the stairs to Kennicott's office. On the door was a sign advertising a headache cure and stating, "The doctor is out, back at——" Naturally, the blank space was not filled out. She stamped her foot. She ran down to the drug store—the doctor's club.

As she entered she heard Mrs. Dyer demanding, "Dave, I've got to have some money."

Carol saw that her husband was there, and two other men, all listening in amusement.

Dave Dyer snapped, "How much do you want? Dollar be enough?"

"No, it won't! I've got to get some underclothes for the kids."

"Why, good Lord, they got enough now to fill the closet so I couldn't find my hunting boots, last time I wanted them."

"I don't care. They're all in rags. You got to give me ten dollars——"

Carol perceived that Mrs. Dyer was accustomed to this indignity. She perceived that the men, particularly Dave, regarded it as an excellent jest. She waited—she knew what would come—it did. Dave yelped, "Where's that ten dollars I gave you last year?" and he looked to the other men to laugh. They laughed.

Cold and still, Carol walked up to Kennicott and commanded, "I want to see you upstairs."

"Why—something the matter?"

"Yes!"

He clumped after her, up the stairs, into his barren office. Before he could get out a query she stated:

"Yesterday, in front of a saloon, I heard a German farmwife beg her husband for a quarter, to get a toy for the baby—and he refused. Just now I've heard Mrs. Dyer going through the same humiliation. And I— I'm in the same position! I have to beg you for money. Daily! I have just been informed that I couldn't have any sugar because I hadn't the money to pay for it!"

"Who said that? By God, I'll kill any———"

"Tut. It wasn't his fault. It was yours. And mine. I now humbly beg you to give me the money with which to buy meals for you to eat. And hereafter to remember it. The next time, I shan't beg. I shall simply starve. Do you understand? I can't go on being a slave———"

Her defiance, her enjoyment of the role, ran out. She was sobbing against his overcoat, "How can you shame me so?" and he was blubbering, "Dog-gone it, I meant to give you some, and I forgot it. I swear I won't again. By golly I won't!"

He pressed fifty dollars upon her, and after that he remembered to give her money regularly.... sometimes.

Daily she determined, "But I must have a stated amount—be business-like. System. I must do something about it." And daily she didn't do anything about it.

2

Guy Pollock is a Gopher Prairie lawyer, whom Carol seeks out as one "of the brethren in the faith" (in books, art, music—in intellect). Here she explains her dissatisfaction with life to Guy, who then gives her the standard conservative answer.

She longed to see Guy Pollock, for the confirming of the brethren in the faith. But Kennicott's dominance was heavy upon her. She could not determine whether she was checked by fear of him, or by inertia— by dislike of the emotional labor of the "scenes" which would be involved in asserting independence. She was like the revolutionist at fifty: not afraid of death, but bored by the probability of bad steaks and bad breaths and sitting up all night on windy barricades.

The second evening after the movies she impulsively summoned Vida Sherwin and Guy to the house for pop-corn and cider. In the living-room Vida and Kennicott debated "the value of manual training in grades below the eighth," while Carol sat beside Guy at the dining table, buttering pop-corn. She was quickened by the speculation in his eyes. She murmured:

"Guy, do you want to help me?"

"My dear! How?"

"I don't know!"

He waited.

"I think I want you to help me find out what has made the darkness of the women. Gray darkness and shadowy trees. We're all in it, ten million women, young married women with good prosperous husbands, and business women in linen collars, and grandmothers that gad out to teas, and wives of underpaid miners, and farmwives who really like to make butter and go to church. What is it we want—and need? Will Kennicott there would say that we need lots of children and hard work. But it isn't that. There's the same discontent in women with eight children and one more coming—always one more coming! And you find it in stenographers and wives who scrub, just as much as in girl college-graduates who wonder how they can escape their kind parents. What do we want?"

"Essentially, I think, you are like myself. Carol; you want to go back to an age of tranquility and charming manners. You want to enthrone good taste again."

"Just good taste? Fastidious people? Oh—no! I believe all of us want the same things—we're all together, the industrial workers and the women and the farmers and the Negro race and the Asiatic colonies, and even a few of the Respectables. It's all the same revolt, in all the classes that have waited and taken advice. I think perhaps we want a more conscious life. We're tired of drudging and sleeping and dying. We're tired of seeing just a few people able to be individualists. We're tired of always deferring hope till the next generation. We're tired of hearing the politicians and priests and cautious reformers (and the husbands!) coax us, 'Be calm! Be patient! Wait! We have the plans for a Utopia already made; just give us a bit more time and we'll produce it; trust us; we're wiser than you.' For ten thousand years they've said that. We want our Utopia *now*—and we're going to try our hands at it. All we want is—everything for all of us! For every housewife and every long-shoreman and every Hindu nationalist and every teacher. We want everything. We sha'n't get it. So we sha'n't ever be content————"

She wondered why he was wincing. He broke in:

"See here, my dear, I certainly hope you don't class yourself with a lot of trouble-making labor-leaders! Democracy is all right theoretically, and I'll admit there are industrial injustices, but I'd rather have them than see the world reduced to a dead level of mediocrity. I refuse to believe that you have anything in common with a lot of laboring men rowing for bigger wages so that they can buy wretched flivvers and hideous player-pianos and————"

At this second, in Buenos Aires, a newspaper editor broke his routine of being bored by exchanges to assert, "Any injustice is better than seeing the world reduced to a gray level of scientific dullness." At this second a clerk standing at the bar of a New York saloon stopped milling his secret fear of his nagging office-manager long enough to growl at the chauffeur beside him, "Aw, you socialists make me sick! I'm an individualist. I ain't going to be nagged by no bureaus and take orders off labor-leaders. And mean to say a hobo's as good as you and me?"

At this second Carol realized that for all Guy's love of dead elegances his timidity was as depressing to her as the bulkiness of Sam Clark. She realized that he was not a mystery, as she had excitedly believed; not a romantic messenger from the World Outside on whom she could count for escape. He belonged to Gopher Prairie, absolutely. She was snatched back from a dream of far countries, and found herself on Main Street.

He was completing his protest. "You don't want to be mixed up in all this orgy of meaningless discontent?"

She soothed him. "No, I don't. I'm not heroic. I'm scared by all the fighting that's going on in the world. I want nobility and adventure, but perhaps I want still more to curl on the hearth with some one I love."

"Would you————"

He did not finish it. He picked up a handful of pop-corn, let it run through his fingers, looked at her wistfully.

With the loneliness of one who has put away a possible love Carol saw that he was a stranger. She saw that he had never been anything but a frame on which she had hung shining garments. If she had let him diffidently make love to her, it was not because she cared, but because she did not care, because it did not matter.

She smiled at him with the exasperating tactfulness of a woman checking a flirtation; a smile like an airy pat on the arm. She sighed, "You're a dear to let me tell you my imaginary troubles." She bounced up, and trilled, "Shall we take the pop-corn in to them now?"

Guy looked after her desolately.

While she teased Vida and Kennicott she was repeating, "I must go on."

3

Carol finds herself envying a woman who seems contented with her traditional role of housewife.

The greatest mystery about a human being is not his reaction to sex or praise, but the manner in which he contrives to put in twenty-four hours a day. It is this which puzzles the longshoreman about the clerk, the Londoner about the bushman. It was this which puzzled Carol in regard to the married Vida. Carol herself had the baby, a larger house to care for, all the telephone calls for Kennicott when he was away; and she read everything, while Vida was satisfied with newspaper headlines.

But after detached brown years in boarding-houses, Vida was hungry for housework, for the most pottering detail of it. She had no maid, nor wanted one. She cooked, baked, swept, washed supper-cloths, with the triumph of a chemist in a new laboratory. To her the hearth was veritably the altar. When she went shopping she hugged the cans of soup, and she bought a mop or a side of bacon as though she were preparing for a reception. She knelt beside a bean sprout and crooned. "I raised this with my own hands—I brought this new life into the world."

"I love her for being so happy," Carol brooded. "I ought to be that way. I worship the baby, but the housework——Oh, I suppose I'm fortunate; so much better off than farmwomen on a new clearing, or people in a slum."

It has not yet been recorded that any human being has gained a very large or permanent contentment from meditation upon the fact that he is better off than others.

In Carol's own twenty-four hours a day she got up, dressed the baby, had breakfast, talked to Oscarina about the day's shopping, put the baby on the porch to play, went to the butcher's to choose between steak and pork chops, bathed the baby, nailed up a shelf, had dinner, put the baby to bed for a nap, paid the iceman, read for an hour, took the baby out for a walk, called on Vida, had supper, put the baby to bed, darned socks, listened to Kennicott's yawning comment on what a fool Dr. McGanum was to try to use that cheap X-ray outfit of his on an epithelioma, repaired a frock, drowsily heard Kennicott stoke the furnace, tried to read a page of Thorstein Veblen—and the day was gone.

Except when Hugh was vigorously naughty, or whiney, or laughing, or saying "I like my chair" with thrilling maturity, she was always enfeebled by loneliness. She no longer felt superior about that misfortune. She would gladly have been converted to Vida's satisfaction in Gopher Prairie and mopping the floor.

4

When Carol encounters Mrs. Julius Flickerbaugh on the street one day, she realizes in panic that she may herself become an eccentric and embittered woman. It is this realization as well as her determination to pursue an "ardent quest" for "something" that make Carol eventually move toward liberation.

Her most positive experience was the revelation of Mrs. Flickerbaugh, the tall, thin, twitchy wife of the attorney. Carol encountered her at the drug store.

"Walking?" snapped Mrs. Flickerbaugh.

"Why, yes."

"Humph. Guess you're the only female in this town that retains the use of her legs. Come home and have a cup o' tea with me."

Because she had nothing else to do, Carol went. But she was uncomfortable in the presence of the amused stares which Mrs. Flickerbaugh's raiment drew. Today, in reeking early August, she wore a man's cap, a skinny fur like a dead cat, a necklace of imitation pearls, a scabrous satin blouse, and a thick cloth skirt hiked up in front.

"Come in. Sit down. Stick the baby in that rocker. Hope you don't mind the house looking like a rat's nest. You don't like this town. Neither do I," said Mrs. Flickerbaugh.

"Why——"

"Course you don't!"

"Well then, I don't! But I'm sure that some day I'll find some solution. Probably I'm a hexagonal peg. Solution: find the hexagonal hole." Carol was very brisk.

"How do you know you ever will find it?"

"There's Mrs. Westlake. She's naturally a big-city woman—she ought to have a lovely old house in Philadelphia or Boston—but she escapes by being absorbed in reading."

"You be satisfied to never do anything but read?"

"No, but—— Heavens, one can't go on hating a town always!"

"Why not? I can! I've hated it for thirty-two years. I'll die here—and I'll hate it till I die. I ought to have been a business woman. I had a good deal of talent for tending to figures. All gone now. Some folks think I'm crazy. Guess I am. Sit and grouch. Go to church and sing hymns. Folks think I'm religious. Tut! Trying to forget washing and ironing and mending socks. Want an office of my own, and sell things. Julius never hear of it. Too late."

Carol sat on the gritty couch, and sank into fear. Could this drabness of life keep up forever, then? Would she some day so despise herself and her neighbors that she too would walk Main Street an old skinny

eccentric woman in a mangy cat's-fur? As she crept home she felt that
the trap had finally closed. She went into the house, a frail small woman,
still winsome but hopeless of eye as she staggered with the weight of
the drowsy boy in her arms.

She sat alone on the porch, that evening. It seemed that Kennicott
had to make a professional call on Mrs. Dave Dyer.

Under the stilly boughs and the black gauze of dusk the street was
meshed in silence. There was but the hum of motor tires crunching the
road, the creak of a rocker on the Howlands' porch, the slap of a hand
attacking a mosquito, a heat-weary conversation starting and dying,
the precise rhythm of crickets, the thud of moths against the screen—
sounds that were a distilled silence. It was a street beyond the end of
the world, beyond the boundaries of hope. Though she should sit here
forever, no brave procession, no one who was interesting, would be
coming by. It was tediousness made tangible, a street builded of lassi-
tude and of futility.

Myrtle Cass appeared, with Cy Bogart. She giggled and bounced
when Cy tickled her ear in village love. They strolled with the half-
dancing gait of lovers, kicking their feet out sideways or shuffling a
dragging jig, and the concrete walk sounded to the broken two-four
rhythm. Their voices had a dusky turbulence. Suddenly, to the woman
rocking on the porch of the doctor's house, the night came alive, and
she felt that everywhere in the darkness panted an ardent quest which
she was missing as she sank back to wait for—— There must be something.

To Room Nineteen

Doris Lessing

*Doris Lessing was born in Persia of British parents in 1919,
moved to Southern Rhodesia in 1924, and to England in 1949,
where she is now living and writing. She has become something*

From *A Man and Two Women* by Doris Lessing. Copyright © 1958, 1962,
1963 by Doris Lessing. Reprinted by permission of Simon & Schuster, Inc.

*of a heroine to Women's Liberation because she is one of the
first significant writers to describe in detail and sensitive accuracy the character of women in the mid-twentieth century. She
portrays the search by frustrated women for meaningful lives in
a technological world that no longer requires all their resources
for husband and children—the problems of leisure and the problems of waste. She describes the human view of women who
desire, like their men, a worthy existence, but who are often
torn by guilt and fear when they strike out from their traditional
role. Susan Rawlings is one such woman. Anna in* The Golden
Notebook *and Martha Quest in* Children of Violence *(a five-
novel sequence) are more extensive studies.*

This is a story, I suppose, about a failure in intelligence: the Rawlings'
marriage was grounded in intelligence.

They were older when they married than most of their married
friends: in their well-seasoned late twenties. Both had had a number of
affairs, sweet rather than bitter; and when they fell in love—for they did
fall in love—had known each other for some time. They joked that they
had saved each other "for the real thing." That they had waited so long
(but not too long) for this real thing was to them a proof of their sensible
discrimination. A good many of their friends had married young, and
now (they felt) probably regretted lost opportunities; while others, still
unmarried, seemed to them arid, self-doubting, and likely to make
desperate or romantic marriages.

Not only they, but others, felt they were well matched; their friends'
delight was an additional proof of their happiness. They had played the
same roles, male and female, in this group or set, if such a wide, loosely
connected, constantly changing constellation of people could be called
a set. They had both become, by virtue of their moderation, their humour, and their abstinence from painful experience, people to whom
others came for advice. They could be, and were, relied on. It was one
of those cases of a man and a woman linking themselves whom no one
else had ever thought of linking, probably because of their similarities.
But then everyone exclaimed: Of course! How right! How was it we
never thought of it before!

And so they married amid general rejoicing, and because of their
foresight and their sense for what was probable, nothing was a surprise
to them.

Both had well-paid jobs. Matthew was a subeditor on a large London
newspaper, and Susan worked in an advertising firm. He was not the
stuff of which editors or publicised journalists are made, but he was

much more than "a subeditor," being one of the essential background people who in fact steady, inspire and make possible the people in the limelight. He was content with this position. Susan had a talent for commercial drawing. She was humorous about the advertisements she was responsible for, but she did not feel strongly about them one way or the other.

Both, before they married, had had pleasant flats, but they felt it unwise to base a marriage on either flat, because it might seem like a submission of personality on the part of the one whose flat it was not. They moved into a new flat in South Kensington on the clear understanding that when their marriage had settled down (a process they knew would not take long, and was in fact more a humorous concession to popular wisdom than what was due to themselves) they would buy a house and start a family.

And this is what happened. They lived in their charming flat for two years, giving parties and going to them, being a popular young married couple, and then Susan became pregnant, she gave up her job, and they bought a house in Richmond. It was typical of this couple that they had a son first, then a daughter, then twins, son and daughter. Everything right, appropriate, and what everyone would wish for, if they could choose. But people did feel these two had chosen; this balanced and sensible family was no more than what was due to them because of their infallible sense of *choosing* right.

And so they lived with their four children in their gardened house in Richmond and were happy. They had everything they had wanted and had planned for.

And yet . . .

Their life seemed to be like a snake biting its tail. Matthew's job for the sake of Susan, children, house, and garden—which caravanserai needed a well-paid job to maintain it. And Susan's practical intelligence for the sake of Matthew, the children, the house and the garden—which unit would have collapsed in a week without her.

But there was no point about which either could say: "For the sake of *this* is all the rest." Children? But children can't be a centre of life and a reason for being. They can be a thousand things that are delightful, interesting, satisfying, but they can't be a wellspring to live from. Or they shouldn't be. Susan and Matthew knew that well enough.

Matthew's job? Ridiculous. It was an interesting job, but scarcely a reason for living. Matthew took pride in doing it well; but he could hardly be expected to be proud of the newspaper: the newspaper he read, *his* newspaper, was not the one he worked for.

Their love for each other? Well, that was nearest it. If this wasn't a centre, what was? Yes, it was around this point, their love, that the whole extraordinary structure revolved. For extraordinary it certainly was. Both Susan and Matthew had moments of thinking so, of looking in secret disbelief at this thing they had created: marriage, four children, big house, garden, charwomen, friends, cars . . . and this *thing*, this entity, all of it had come into existence, been blown into being out of nowhere, because Susan loved Matthew and Matthew loved Susan. Extraordinary. So that was the central point, the wellspring.

And if one felt that it simply was not strong enough, important enough, to support it all, well whose fault was that? Certainly neither Susan's nor Matthew's. It was in the nature of things. And they sensibly blamed neither themselves nor each other.

On the contrary, they used their intelligence to preserve what they had created from a painful and explosive world: they looked around them, and took lessons. All around them, marriages collapsing, or breaking, or rubbing along (even worse, they felt). They must not make the same mistakes, they must not.

They had avoided the pitfall so many of their friends had fallen into—of buying a house in the country *for the sake of the children;* so that the husband became a weekend husband, a weekend father, and the wife always careful not to ask what went on in the town flat which they called (in joke) a bachelor flat. No, Matthew was a full-time husband, a full-time father, and at nights, in the big married bed in the big married bedroom (which had an attractive view of the river) they lay beside each other talking and he told her about his day, and what he had done, and whom he had met; and she told him about her day (not as interesting, but that was not her fault) for both knew of the hidden resentments and deprivations of the woman who has lived her own life —and is now dependent on a husband for outside interests and money.

Nor did Susan make the mistake of taking a job for the sake of her independence, which she might very well have done, since her old firm, missing her qualities of humour, balance, and sense, invited her often to go back. Children needed their mother to a certain age, that both parents knew and agreed on; and when these four healthy wisely brought-up children were of the right age, Susan would work again, because she knew, and so did he, what happened to women of fifty at the height of their energy and ability, with grownup children who no longer needed their full devotion.

So there was this couple, testing their marriage, looking after it, treating it like a small boat full of helpless people in a very stormy sea. Well, of course, so it was. . . . The storms of the world were bad, but not too close—which is not to say they were selfishly felt: Susan and Matthew were both well-informed and responsible people. And the inner storms and quicksands were understood and charted. So everything was all right. Everything was in order. Yes, things were under control.

So what did it matter if they felt dry, flat? People like themselves, fed on a hundred books (psychological, anthropological, sociological) could scarcely be unprepared for the dry, controlled wistfulness which is the distinguishing mark of the intelligent marriage. Two people, endowed with education, with discrimination, with judgement, linked together voluntarily from their will to be happy together and to be of use to others—one sees them everywhere, one knows them, one even is that thing oneself: sadness because so much is after all so little. These two, unsurprised, turned towards each other with even more courtesy and gentle love: this was life, that two people, no matter how carefully chosen, could not be everything to each other. In fact, even to say so, to think in such a way, was banal, they were ashamed to do it.

It was banal, too, when one night Matthew came home late and confessed he had been to a party, taken a girl home and slept with her. Susan forgave him, of course. Except that forgiveness is hardly the word. Understanding, yes. But if you understand something, you don't forgive it, you are the thing itself: forgiveness is for what you *don't* understand. Nor had he *confessed*—what sort of word is that?

The whole thing was not important. After all, years ago they had joked: Of course I'm not going to be faithful to you, no one can be faithful to one other person for a whole lifetime. (And there was the word *faithful*—stupid, all these words, stupid, belonging to a savage old world.) But the incident left both of them irritable. Strange, but they were both bad-tempered, annoyed. There was something unassimilable about it.

Making love splendidly after he had come home that night, both had felt that the idea that Myra Jenkins, a pretty girl met at a party, could be even relevant was ridiculous. They had loved each other for over a decade, would love each other for years more. Who, then, was Myra Jenkins?

Except, thought Susan, unaccountably bad-tempered, she was (is) the first. In ten years. So either the ten years' fidelity was not important, or she isn't. (No, no, there is something wrong with this way of thinking, there must be.) But if she isn't important, presumably it wasn't important either when Matthew and I first went to bed with each other that afternoon whose delight even now (like a very long shadow at sundown) lays a long, wandlike finger over us. (Why did I say sundown?) Well, if what we felt that afternoon was not important, nothing is important, because if it hadn't been for what we felt, we wouldn't be Mr. and Mrs. Rawlings with four children, etc., etc. The whole thing is *absurd*—for him to have come home and told me was absurd. For him not to have told me was absurd. For me to care, or for that matter not to care, is absurd . . . and who is Myra Jenkins? Why, no one at all.

There was only one thing to do, and of course these sensible people did it: they put the thing behind them, and consciously, knowing what they were doing, moving forward into a different phase of their marriage, giving thanks for past good fortune as they did so.

For it was inevitable that the handsome, blond, attractive, manly man, Matthew Rawlings, should be at times tempted (oh, what a word!) by the attractive girls at parties she could not attend because of the four children; and that sometimes he would succumb (a word even more repulsive, if possible) and that she, a good-looking woman in the big well-tended garden at Richmond, would sometimes be pierced as by an arrow from the sky with bitterness. Except that bitterness was not in order, it was out of court. Did the casual girls touch the marriage? They did not. Rather it was they who knew defeat because of the handsome Matthew Rawlings' marriage body and soul to Susan Rawlings.

In that case why did Susan feel (though luckily not for longer than a few seconds at a time) as if life had become a desert, and that nothing mattered, and that her children were not her own?

Meanwhile her intelligence continued to assert that all was well. What if her Matthew did have an occasional sweet afternoon, the odd affair? For she knew quite well, except in her moments of aridity, that they were very happy, that the affairs were not important.

Perhaps that was the trouble? It was in the nature of things that the adventures and delights could no longer be hers, because of the four children and the big house that needed so much attention. But perhaps she was secretly wishing, and even knowing that she did, that the wildness and the beauty could be his. But he was married to her. She was married to him. They were married inextricably. And therefore the gods could not strike him with the real magic, not really. Well, was it Susan's fault that after he came home from an adventure he looked harassed rather than fulfilled? (In fact, that was how she knew he had been *unfaithful*, because of his sullen air, and his glances at her, similar to hers at him: What is it that I share with this person that shields all delight from me?) But none of it by anybody's fault. (But what did they feel ought to be somebody's fault?) Nobody's fault, nothing to be at fault, no one to blame, no one to offer or to take it . . . and nothing wrong, either, except that Matthew never was really struck, as he wanted to be, by joy; and that Susan was more and more often threatened by emptiness. (It was usually in the garden that she was invaded by this feeling: she was coming to avoid the garden, unless the children or

Matthew were with her.) There was no need to use the dramatic words, unfaithful, forgive, and the rest: intelligence forbade them. Intelligence barred, too, quarrelling, sulking, anger, silences of withdrawal, accusations and tears. Above all, intelligence forbids tears.

A high price has to be paid for the happy marriage with the four healthy children in the large white gardened house.

And they were paying it, willingly, knowing what they were doing. When they lay side by side or breast to breast in the big civilised bedroom overlooking the wild sullied river, they laughed, often, for no particular reason; but they knew it was really because of these two small people, Susan and Matthew, supporting such an edifice on their intelligent love. The laugh comforted them; it saved them both, though from what, they did not know.

They were now both fortyish. The older children, boy and girl, were ten and eight, at school. The twins, six, were still at home. Susan did not have nurses or girls to help her: childhood is short; and she did not regret the hard work. Often enough she was bored, since small children can be boring; she was often very tired; but she regretted nothing. In another decade, she would turn herself back into being a woman with a life of her own.

Soon the twins would go to school, and they would be away from home from nine until four. These hours, so Susan saw it, would be the preparation for her own slow emancipation away from the role of hub-of-the-family into woman-with-her-own-life. She was already planning for the hours of freedom when all the children would be "off her hands." That was the phrase used by Matthew and by Susan and by their friends, for the moment when the youngest child went off to school. "They'll be off your hands, darling Susan, and you'll have time to yourself." So said Matthew, the intelligent husband, who had often enough commended and consoled Susan, standing by her in spirit during the years when her soul was not her own, as she said, but her children's.

What it amounted to was that Susan saw herself as she had been at twenty-eight, unmarried; and then again somewhere about fifty, blossoming from the root of what she had been twenty years before. As if the essential Susan were in abeyance, as if she were in cold storage. Matthew said something like this to Susan one night: and she agreed that it was true—she did feel something like that. What, then, was this essential Susan? She did not know. Put like that it sounded ridiculous, and she did not really feel it. Anyway, they had a long discussion about the whole thing before going off to sleep in each other's arms.

So the twins went off to their school, two bright affectionate children who had no problems about it, since their older brother and sister had trodden this path so successfully before them. And now Susan was going to be alone in the big house, every day of the school term, except for the daily woman who came in to clean.

It was now, for the first time in this marriage, that something happened which neither of them had foreseen.

This is what happened. She returned, at nine-thirty, from taking the twins to the school by car, looking forward to seven blissful hours of freedom. On the first morning she was simply restless, worrying about the twins "naturally enough" since this was their first day away at school. She was hardly able to contain herself until they came back. Which they did happily, excited by the world of school, looking forward to the next day. And the next day Susan took them, dropped them, came back, and found herself reluctant to enter her big and beautiful home because it was as if something was waiting for her there that she did not wish to confront. Sensibly, however, she parked the car in the garage, entered the house, spoke to Mrs. Parkes the daily woman about her duties, and went up to her bedroom. She was possessed by a fever which drove her out again, downstairs, into the kitchen, where Mrs. Parkes was making cake and did not need her, and into the garden. There she sat on a bench and tried to calm herself, looking at trees, at a brown glimpse of the river. But she was filled with tension, like a panic: as if an enemy was in the garden with her. She spoke to herself severely, thus: All this is quite natural. First, I spent twelve years of my adult life working, *living my own life*. Then I married, and from the moment I became pregnant for the first time I signed myself over, so to speak, to other people. To the children. Not for one moment in twelve years have I been alone, had time to myself. So now I have to learn to be myself again. That's all.

And she went indoors to help Mrs. Parkes cook and clean, and found some sewing to do for the children. She kept herself occupied every day. At the end of the first term she understood she felt two contrary emotions. First: secret astonishment and dismay that during those weeks when the house was empty of children she had in fact been more occupied (had been careful to keep herself occupied) than ever she had been when the children were around her needing her continual attention. Second: that now she knew the house would be full of them, and for five weeks, she resented the fact she would never be alone. She was already looking back at those hours of sewing, cooking (but by herself), as at a lost freedom which would not be hers for five long weeks. And the two months of term which would succeed the five weeks stretched alluringly open ɩo her—freedom. But what freedom—when in fact she had been so careful *not* to be free of small duties during the last weeks? She looked at herself, Susan Rawlings, sitting in a big chair by the window in the bedroom, sewing shirts or dresses, which she might just as well have bought. She saw herself making cakes for hours at a time in the big family kitchen: yet usually she bought cakes. What she saw was a woman alone, that was true, but she had not felt alone. For instance, Mrs. Parkes was always somewhere in the house. And she did not like being in the garden at all, because of the closeness there of the enemy—irritation, restlessness, emptiness, whatever it was, which keeping her hands occupied made less dangerous for some reason.

Susan did not tell Matthew of these thoughts. They were not sensible. She did not recognize herself in them. What should she say to her dear friend and husband Matthew? "When I go into the garden, that is, if the children are not there, I feel as if there is an enemy there waiting to invade me." "What enemy, Susan darling?" "Well I don't know, really. . . ." "Perhaps you should see a doctor?"

No, clearly this conversation should not take place. The holidays began and Susan welcomed them. Four children, lively, energetic, intelligent, demanding: she was never, not for a moment of her day, alone. If she was in a room, they would be in the next room, or waiting for her to do something for them; or it would soon be time for lunch or tea, or to take one of them to the dentist. Something to do: five weeks of it, thank goodness.

On the fourth day of these so welcome holidays, she found she was storming with anger at the twins, two shrinking beautiful children who (and this is what checked her) stood hand in hand looking at her with sheer dismayed disbelief. This was their calm mother, shouting at them. And for what? They had come to her with some game, some bit of nonsense. They looked at each other, moved closer for support, and went off hand in hand, leaving Susan holding on to the windowsill of the living room, breathing deep, feeling sick. She went to lie down, telling the older children she had a headache. She heard the boy Harry telling the little ones: "It's all right, Mother's got a headache." She heard that *It's all right* with pain.

That night she said to her husband: "Today I shouted at the twins, quite unfairly." She sounded miserable, and he said gently: "Well, what of it?"

"It's more of an adjustment than I thought, their going to school."

"But Susie, Susie darling. . . ." For she was crouched weeping on the bed. He comforted her: "Susan, what is all this about? You shouted at them? What of it? If you shouted at them fifty times a day it wouldn't be more than the little devils deserve." But she wouldn't laugh. She wept. Soon he comforted her with his body. She became calm. Calm, she wondered what was wrong with her, and why she should mind so much that she might, just once, have behaved unjustly with the children. What did it matter? They had forgotten it all long ago: Mother had a headache and everything was all right.

It was a long time later that Susan understood that that night, when she had wept and Matthew had driven the misery out of her with his big solid body, was the last time, ever in their married life, that they had been—to use their mutual language—with each other. And even that was a lie, because she had not told him of her real fears at all.

The five weeks passed, and Susan was in control of herself, and good and kind, and she looked forward to the holidays with a mixture of fear and longing. She did not know what to expect. She took the twins off to school (the elder children took themselves to school) and she returned to the house determined to face the enemy wherever he was, in the house, or the garden or—where?

She was again restless, she was possessed by restlessness. She cooked and sewed and worked as before, day after day, while Mrs. Parkes remonstrated: "Mrs. Rawlings, what's the need for it? I can do that, it's what you pay me for."

And it was so irrational that she checked herself. She would put the car into the garage, go up to her bedroom, and sit, hands in her lap, forcing herself to be quiet. She listened to Mrs. Parkes moving around the house. She looked out into the garden and saw the branches shake the trees. She sat defeating the enemy, restlessness. Emptiness. She ought to be thinking about her life, about herself. But she did not. Or perhaps she could not. As soon as she forced her mind to think about Susan (for what else did she want to be alone for?) it skipped off to thoughts of butter or school clothes. Or it thought of Mrs. Parkes. She realised that she sat listening for the movements of the cleaning woman, following her every turn, bend, thought. She followed her in her mind from kitchen to bathroom, from table to oven, and it was as if the duster, the cleaning cloth, the saucepan, were in her own hand. She would hear herself saying: No, not like that, don't put that there. . . . Yet she did not give a damn what Mrs. Parkes did, or if she did it at all. Yet she could not prevent herself from being conscious of her, every minute. Yes, this was what was wrong with her: she needed, when she was alone, to be really alone, with no one near. She could not endure the knowledge that in ten minutes or in half an hour Mrs. Parkes would call up the stairs: "Mrs. Rawlings, there's no silver polish. Madam, we're out of flour."

So she left the house and went to sit in the garden where she was screened from the house by trees. She waited for the demon to appear and claim her, but he did not.

She was planning how to be somewhere where Mrs. Parkes would not come after her with a cup of tea, or a demand to be allowed to tele-phone (always irritating since Susan did not care who she telephoned or how often), or just a nice talk about something. Yes, she needed a place, or a state of affairs, where it would not be necessary to keep reminding herself: In ten minutes I must telephone Matthew about . . . and at half past three I must leave early for the children because the car needs cleaning. And at ten o'clock tomorrow I must remember. . . . She was possessed with resentment that the seven hours of freedom in every day (during weekdays in the school term) were not free, that never, not for one second, ever, was she free from the pressure of time, from having to remember this or that. She could never forget herself; never really let herself go into forgetfulness.

Resentment. It was poisoning her. (She looked at this emotion and thought it was absurd. Yet she felt it.) She was a prisoner. (She looked at this thought too, and it was no good telling herself it was a ridiculous one.) She must tell Matthew—but what? She was filled with emotions that were utterly ridiculous, that she despised, yet that nevertheless she was feeling so strongly she could not shake them off.

The school holidays came round, and this time they were for nearly two months, and she behaved with a conscious controlled decency that nearly drove her crazy. She would lock herself in the bathroom, and sit on the edge of the bath, breathing deep, trying to let go into some kind of calm. Or she went up into the spare room, usually empty, where no one would expect her to be. She heard the children calling "Mother, Mother," and kept silent, feeling guilty. Or she went to the very end of the garden, by herself, and looked at the slow-moving brown river; she looked at the river and closed her eyes and breathed slow and deep, taking it into her being, into her veins.

Then she returned to the family, wife and mother, smiling and responsible, feeling as if the pressure of these people—four lively children and her husband—were a painful pressure on the surface of her skin, a hand pressing on her brain. She did not once break down into irritation during these holidays, but it was like living out a prison sentence, and when the children went back to school, she sat on a white stone seat near the flowing river, and she thought: It is not even a year since the twins went to school, since *they were off my hands* (What on earth did I think I meant when I used that stupid phase?) and yet I'm a different person. I'm simply not myself. I don't understand it.

Yet she had to understand it. For she knew that this structure—big white house, on which the mortgage still cost four hundred a year, a husband, so good and kind and insightful, four children, all doing so nicely, and the garden where she sat, and yet she could not understand why, or even what it was she contributed to it.

She said to Matthew in their bedroom: "I think there must be something wrong with me."

And he said: "Surely not Susan? You look marvellous—you're as lovely as ever."

She looked at the handsome blond man, with his clear, intelligent, blue-eyed face, and thought: Why is it I can't tell him? Why not? And she said: "I need to be alone more than I am."

At which he swung his slow blue gaze at her, and she saw what she had been dreading: Incredulity. Disbelief. And fear. An incredulous blue stare from a stranger who was her husband, as close to her as her own breath.

He said: "But the children are at school and off your hands."

She said to herself: I've got to force myself to say: Yes, but do you realize that I never feel free? There's never a moment I can say to myself: There's nothing I have to remind myself about, nothing I have to do in half an hour, or an hour, or two hours. . . .

But she said: "I don't feel well."

He said: "Perhaps you need a holiday."

She said, appalled: "But not without you, surely?" For she could not imagine herself going off without him. Yet that was what he meant. Seeing her face, he laughed, and opened his arms, and she went into them, thinking: Yes, yes, but why can't I say it? And what is it I have to say?

She tried to tell him, about never being free. And he listened and said: "But Susan, what sort of freedom can you possibly want—short of being dead! Am I ever free? I go to the office, and I have to be there at ten—all right, half past ten, sometimes. And I have to do this or that, don't I? Then I've got to come home at a certain time—I don't mean it, you know I don't—but if I'm not going to be back home at six I telephone you. When can I ever say to myself: I have nothing to be responsible for in the next six hours?"

Susan, hearing this, was remorseful. Because it was true. The good marriage, the house, the children, depended just as much on his voluntary bondage as it did on hers. But why did he not feel bound? Why didn't he chafe and become restless? No, there was something really wrong with her and this proved it.

And that word *bondage*—why had she used it? She had never felt marriage, or the children, as bondage. Neither had he, or surely they wouldn't be together lying in each other's arms content after twelve years of marriage.

No, her state (whatever it was) was irrelevant, nothing to do with her real good life with her family. She had to accept the fact that after all, she was an irrational person and to live with it. Some people had to live with crippled arms, or stammers, or being deaf. She would have to live knowing she was subject to a state of mind she could not own.

Nevertheless, as a result of this conversation with her husband, there was a new regime next holidays.

The spare room at the top of the house now had a cardboard sign saying: PRIVATE! DO NOT DISTURB! on it. (This sign had been drawn in coloured chalks by the children, after a discussion between the parents in which it was decided this was psychologically the right thing.) The family and Mrs. Parkes knew this was "Mother's Room" and that she was entitled to her privacy. Many serious conversations took place between Matthew and the children about not taking Mother for granted. Susan overheard the first, between father and Harry, the older boy, and was surprised at her irritation over it. Surely she could have a room somewhere in that big house and retire into it without such a fuss being made? Without it being so solemnly discussed? Why couldn't she simply have announced: "I'm going to fit out the little top room for myself, and when I'm in it I'm not to be disturbed for anything short of fire"? Just that, and finished; instead of long earnest discussions. When she heard Harry and Matthew explaining it to the twins with Mrs. Parkes coming in—"Yes, well, a family sometimes gets on top of a woman"—she had to go right away to the bottom of the garden until the devils of exasperation had finished their dance in her blood.

But now there was a room, and she could go there when she liked, she used it seldom: she felt even more caged there than in her bedroom. One day she had gone up there after a lunch for ten children she had cooked and served because Mrs. Parkes was not there, and had sat alone for a while looking into the garden. She saw the children stream out from the kitchen and stand looking up at the window where she sat behind the curtains. They were all—her children and their friends —discussing Mother's Room. A few minutes later, the chase of children in some game came pounding up the stairs, but ended as abruptly as if they had fallen over a ravine, so sudden was the silence. They had remembered she was there, and had gone silent in a great gale of "Hush! Shhhhh! Quiet, you'll disturb her. . . ." And they went tiptoeing downstairs like criminal conspirators. When she came down to make tea for them, they all apologised. The twins put their arms around her, from front and back, making a human cage of loving limbs, and promised it would never occur again. "We forgot, Mummy, we forgot all about it!"

What it amounted to was that Mother's Room, and her need for privacy, had become a valuable lesson in respect for other people's rights. Quite soon Susan was going up to the room only because it was a lesson it was a pity to drop. Then she took sewing up there, and the children and Mrs. Parkes came in and out: it had become another family room.

She sighed, and smiled, and resigned herself—she made jokes at her own expense with Matthew over the room. That is, she did from the self she liked, she respected. But at the same time, something inside her howled with impatience, with rage. . . . And she was frightened. One day she found herself kneeling by her bed and praying: "Dear God, keep it away from me, keep him away from me." She meant the devil, for she now thought of it, not caring if she were irrational, as some sort of demon. She imagined him, or it, as a youngish man, or perhaps a middle-aged man pretending to be young. Or a man young-looking from immaturity? At any rate, she saw the young-looking face which, when she drew closer, had dry lines about mouth and eyes. He was thinnish, meagre in build. And he had a reddish complexion, and ginger hair. That was he—a gingery, energetic man, and he wore a reddish hairy jacket, unpleasant to the touch.

Well, one day she saw him. She was standing at the bottom of the garden, watching the river ebb past, when she raised her eyes and saw this person, or being, sitting on the white stone bench. He was looking at her, and grinning. In his hands was a long crooked stick, which he had picked off the ground, or broken off the tree above him. He was absent-mindedly, out of an absent-minded or freakish impulse of spite, using the stick to stir around in the coils of a blindworm or a grass snake (or some kind of snakelike creature: it was whitish and unhealthy to look at, unpleasant). The snake was twisting about, flinging its coils from side to side in a kind of dance of protest against the teasing prodding stick.

Susan looked at him thinking: Who is the stranger? What is he doing in our garden? Then she recognised the man around whom her terrors had crystallised. As she did so, he vanished. She made herself walk over to the bench. A shadow from a branch lay across thin emerald grass, moving jerkily over its roughness, and she could see why she had taken it for a snake, lashing and twisting. She went back to the house thinking: Right, then, so I've seen him with my own eyes, so I'm not crazy after all —there *is* a danger because I've seen him. He is lurking in the garden and sometimes even in the house, and he wants *to get into me and to take me over*.

She dreamed of having a room or a place, anywhere, where she could go and sit, by herself, no one knowing where she was.

Once, near Victoria, she found herself outside a news agent that had Rooms to Let advertised. She decided to rent a room, telling no one. Sometimes she could take the train in to Richmond and sit alone in it for an hour or two. Yet how could she? A room would cost three or four pounds a week, and she earned no money, and how could she explain to Matthew that she needed such a sum? What for? It did not occur to her that she was taking it for granted she wasn't going to tell him about the room.

Well, it was out of the question, having a room; yet she knew she must.

One day, when a school term was well established, and none of the children had measles or other ailments, and everything seemed in order, she did the shopping early, explained to Mrs. Parkes she was meeting an old school friend, took the train to Victoria, searched until she found a small quiet hotel, and asked for a room for the day. They did not let rooms by the day, the manageress said, looking doubtful, since Susan so obviously was not the kind of woman who needed a room for unrespectable reasons. Susan made a long explanation about not being well, being unable to shop without frequent rests for lying down. At last she was allowed to rent the room provided she paid a full night's price for it. She was taken up by the manageress and a maid, both concerned over the state of her health ... which must be pretty bad if, living at Richmond (she had signed her name and address in the register), she needed a shelter at Victoria. The room was ordinary and anonymous, and was just what Susan needed. She put a shilling in the gas fire, and sat, eyes shut, in a dingy armchair with her back to a dingy window. She was alone. She was alone. She was alone. She could feel pressures lifting off her. First the sounds of traffic came very loud; then they seemed to vanish; she might even have slept a little. A knock on the door: it was Miss Townsend the manageress, bringing her a cup of tea with her own hands, so concerned was she over Susan's long silence and possible illness.

Miss Townsend was a lonely woman of fifty, running this hotel with all the rectitude expected of her, and she sensed in Susan the possibility of understanding companionship. She stayed to talk. Susan found herself in the middle of a fantastic story about her illness, which got more and more improbable as she tried to make it tally with the large house at Richmond, well-off husband, and four children. Suppose she said instead: Miss Townsend, I'm here in your hotel because I need to be alone for a few hours, above all *alone and with no one knowing where I am*. She said it mentally, and saw, mentally, the look that would inevitably come on Miss Townsend's elderly maiden's face. "Miss Townsend, my four children and my husband are driving me insane, do you understand that? Yes, I can see from the gleam of hysteria in your eyes that comes from loneliness controlled but only just contained that I've got everything in the world you've ever longed for. Well, Miss Townsend, I don't want any of it. You can have it, Miss Townsend. I wish I was absolutely alone in the world, like you. Miss Townsend, I'm besieged by seven devils, Miss Townsend, Miss Townsend, let me stay here in your hotel where the devils can't get me...." Instead of saying all this, she described her anemia, agreed to try Miss Townsend's remedy for it, which was raw liver, minced, between whole-meal bread, and said yes, perhaps it would be better if she stayed at home and let a friend do shopping for her. She paid her bill and left the hotel, defeated.

At home Mrs. Parkes said she didn't really like it, no, not really, when Mrs. Rawlings was away from nine in the morning until five. The teacher had telephoned from school to say Joan's teeth were paining her, and she hadn't known what to say; and what was she to make for the children's tea, Mrs. Rawlings hadn't said.

All this was nonsense, of course. Mrs. Parkes's complaint was that Susan had withdrawn herself spiritually, leaving the burden of the big house on her.

Susan looked back at her day of "freedom" which had resulted in her becoming a friend to the lonely Miss Townsend, and in Mrs. Parkes's remonstrances. Yet she remembered the short blissful hour of being alone, really alone. She was determined to arrange her life, no matter what it cost, so that she could have that solitude more often. An absolute solitude, where no one knew her or cared about her.

But how? She thought of saying to her old employer: I want to back you up in a story with Matthew that I am doing part-time work for you. The truth is that . . . but she would have to tell him a lie too, and which lie? She could not say: I want to sit by myself three or four times a week in a rented room. And besides, he knew Matthew, and she could not really ask him to tell lies on her behalf, apart from his being bound to think it meant a lover.

Suppose she really took a part-time job, which she could get through fast and efficiently, leaving time for herself. What job? Addressing envelopes? Canvassing?

And there was Mrs. Parkes, working widow, who knew exactly what she was prepared to give to the house, who knew by instinct when her mistress withdrew in spirit from her responsibilities. Mrs. Parkes was one of the servers of this world, but she needed someone to serve. She had to have Mrs. Rawlings, her madam, at the top of the house or in the garden, so that she could come and get support from her: "Yes, the bread's not what it was when I was a girl. . . . Yes, Harry's got a wonderful appetite, I wonder where he puts it all. . . . Yes, it's lucky the twins are so much of a size, they can wear each other's shoes, that's a saving in these hard times.. . . Yes, the cherry jam from Switzerland is not a patch on the jam from Poland, and three times the price. . . ." And so on. That sort of talk Mrs. Parkes must have, every day, or she would leave, not knowing herself why she left.

Susan Rawlings, thinking these thoughts, found that she was prowling through the great thicketed garden like a wild cat: she was walking up the stairs, down the stairs, through the rooms, into the garden, along the brown running river, back, up through the house, down again. . . . It was a wonder Mrs. Parkes did not think it strange. But on the contrary, Mrs. Rawlings could do what she liked, she could stand on her head if she wanted, provided she was *there*. Susan Rawlings prowled and muttered through her house, hating Mrs. Parkes, hating poor Miss Townsend, dreaming of her hour of solitude in the dingy respectability of Miss Townsend's hotel bedroom, and she knew quite well she was mad. Yes, she was mad.

She said to Matthew that she must have a holiday. Matthew agreed with her. This was not as things had been once—how they had talked in each other's arms in the marriage bed. He had, she knew, diagnosed her finally as *unreasonable*. She had become someone outside himself that he had to manage. They were living side by side in this house like two tolerably friendly strangers.

Having told Mrs. Parkes, or rather, asked for her permission, she went off on a walking holiday in Wales. She chose the remotest place she knew of. Every morning the children telephoned her before they went off to school, to encourage and support her, just as they had over Mother's Room. Every evening she telephoned them, spoke to each child in turn, and then to Matthew. Mrs. Parkes, given permission to telephone for instructions or advice, did so every day at lunchtime. When, as happened three times, Mrs. Rawlings was out on the mountainside. Mrs. Parkes asked that she should ring back at such and such a time, for she would not be happy in what she was doing without Mrs. Rawlings' blessing.

Susan prowled over wild country with the telephone wire holding her to her duty like a leash. The next time she must telephone, or wait to be telephoned, nailed her to her cross. The mountains themselves seemed trammelled by her unfreedom. Everywhere on the mountains, where she met no one at all, from breakfast time to dusk, excepting sheep, or a shepherd, she came face to face with her own craziness which might attack her in the broadest valleys, so that they seemed too small; or on a mountaintop from which she could see a hundred other mountains and valleys, so that they seemed too low, too small, with the sky pressing down too close. She would stand gazing at a hillside brilliant with ferns and bracken, jewelled with running water, and see nothing but her devil, who lifted inhuman eyes at her from where he leaned negligently on a rock, switching at his ugly yellow boots with a leafy twig.

She returned to her home and family, with the Welsh emptiness at the back of her mind like a promise of freedom.

She told her husband she wanted to have an *au pair* girl.

They were in their bedroom, it was late at night, the children slept. He sat, shirted and slippered, in a chair by the window, looking out. She sat brushing her hair and watching him in the mirror. A time-hallowed scene in the connubial bedroom. He said nothing, while she heard the arguments coming into his mind, only to be rejected because every one was *reasonable*.

"It seems strange to get one now, after all, the children are in school most of the day. Surely the time for you to have help was when you were stuck with them day and night. Why don't you ask Mrs. Parkes to cook for you? She's even offered to—I can understand if you are tired of cooking for six people. But you know that an *au pair* girl means all kinds of problems, it's not like having an ordinary char in during the day. . . ."

Finally he said carefully: "Are you thinking of going back to work?"

"No," she said, "no, not really." She made herself sound vague, rather stupid. She went on brushing her black hair and peering at herself so as to be oblivious of the short uneasy glances her Matthew kept giving her. "Do you think we can't afford it?" she went on vaguely, not at all the old efficient Susan who knew exactly what they could afford.

"It's not that," he said, looking out of the window at dark trees, so as not to look at her. Meanwhile she examined a round, candid, pleasant face with clear dark brows and clear grey eyes. A sensible face. She brushed thick healthy black hair and thought: Yet that's the reflection of a madwoman. How very strange! Much more to the point if what looked back at me was the gingery green-eyed demon with his dry meagre smile. . . . Why wasn't Matthew agreeing? After all, what else could he do? She was breaking her part of the bargain and there was no way of forcing her to keep it: that her spirit, her soul, should live in this house, so that the people in it could grow like plants in water, and Mrs. Parkes remain content in their service. In return for this, he would be a good loving husband, and responsible towards the children. Well, nothing like this had been true of either of them for a long time. He did his duty, perfunctorily; she did not even pretend to do hers. And he had become like other hubsands, with his real life in his work and the people he met there, and very likely a serious affair. All this was her fault.

At last he drew heavy curtains, blotting out the trees, and turned to force her attention: "Susan, are you really sure we need a girl?" But she would not meet his appeal at all. She was running the brush over her hair again and again, lifting fine black clouds in a small hiss of electricity. She was peering in and smiling as if she was amused at the clinging hissing hair that followed the brush.

"Yes, I think it would be a good idea on the whole," she said, with the cunning of a madwoman evading the real point.

In the mirror she could see her Matthew lying on his back, his hands behind his head, staring upwards, his face sad and hard. She felt her heart (the old heart of Susan Rawlings) soften and call out to him. But she set it to be indifferent.

He said: "Susan, the children?" It was an appeal that *almost* reached her. He opened his arms, lifting them from where they had lain by his sides, palms up, empty. She had only to run across and fling herself into them, onto his hard, warm chest, and melt into herself, into Susan. But she could not. She would not see his lifted arms. She said vaguely: "Well, surely it'll be even better for them? We'll get a French or a German girl and they'll learn the language."

In the dark she lay beside him, feeling frozen, a stranger. She felt as if Susan had been spirited away. She disliked very much this woman who lay there, cold and indifferent beside a suffering man, but she could not change her.

Next morning she set about getting a girl, and very soon came Sophie Traub from Hamburg, a girl of twenty, laughing, healthy, blue-eyed, intending to learn English. Indeed, she already spoke a good deal. In return for a room—"Mother's Room"—and her food, she undertook to do some light cooking, and to be with the children when Mrs. Rawlings asked. She was an intelligent girl and understood perfectly what was needed. Susan said "I go off sometimes, for the morning or for the day— well, sometimes the children run home from school, or they ring up, or a teacher rings up. I should be here, really. And there's the daily woman...." And Sophie laughed her deep fruity *Fräulein's* laugh, showed her fine white teeth and her dimples, and said: "You want some person to play mistress of the house sometimes, not so?"

"Yes, that is just so," said Susan, a bit dry, despite herself, thinking in secret fear how easy it was, how much nearer to the end she was than she thought. Healthy *Fräulein* Traub's instant understanding of their position proved this to be true.

The *au pair* girl, because of her own common sense, or (as Susan said to herself with her new inward shudder) because she had been *chosen* so well by Susan, was a success with everyone, the children liking her, Mrs. Parkes forgetting almost at once that she was German, and Matthew finding her "nice to have around the house." For he was now taking things as they came, from the surface of life, withdrawn both as a husband and a father from the household.

One day Susan saw how Sophie and Mrs. Parkes were talking and laughing in the kitchen, and she announced that she would be away until teatime. She knew exactly where to go and what she must look for. She took the District Line to South Kensington, changed to the Circle, got off at Paddington, and walked around looking at the smaller hotels until she was satisfied with one which had FRED'S HOTEL painted on windowpanes that needed cleaning. The façade was a faded shiny yellow, like unhealthy skin. A door at the end of a passage said she must knock; she did, and Fred appeared. He was not at all attractive, not in any way, being fattish, and run-down, and wearing a tasteless striped suit. He had small sharp eyes in a white creased face, and was quite prepared to let Mrs. Jones (she chose the farcical name deliberately, staring him out) have a room three days a week from ten until six. Provided of course that she paid in advance each time she came? Susan produced fifteen shillings (no price had been set by him) and held it out, still fixing him with a bold unblinking challenge she had not known until then she could use at will. Looking at her still, he took up a ten-shilling note from her palm between thumb and forefinger, fingered it; then shuffled up two half crowns, held out his own palm with these bits of money displayed thereon, and let his gaze lower broodingly at them. They were standing in the passage, a red-shaded light above, bare boards beneath, and a strong smell of floor polish rising about them. He shot his gaze up at her over the still-extended palm, and smiled as if to say: What do you take me for? "I shan't," said Susan, "be using this room for the purposes of making money." He still waited. She added another five shillings, at which he nodded and said: "You pay, and I ask no questions." "Good," said Susan. He now went past her to the stairs, and there waited a moment: the light from the street door being in her eyes, she lost sight of him momentarily. Then she saw a sober-suited, white-faced, white-balding little man trotting up the stairs like a waiter, and she went after him. They proceeded in utter silence up the stairs of this house where no questions were asked—Fred's Hotel, which could afford the freedom for its visitors that poor Miss Townsend's hotel could not. The room was hideous. It had a single window, with thin green brocade curtains, a three-quarter bed that had a cheap green satin bedspread on it, a fireplace with a gas fire and a shilling meter by it, a chest of drawers, and a green wicker armchair.

"Thank you," said Susan, knowing that Fred (if this was Fred, and not George, or Herbert or Charlie) was looking at her, not so much with curiosity, an emotion he would not own to, for professional reasons, but with a philosophical sense of what was appropriate. Having taken her money and shown her up and agreed to everything, he was clearly disapproving of her for coming here. She did not belong here at all, so his look said. (But she knew, already, how very much she did belong: the room had been waiting for her to join it.) "Would you have me called at five o'clock, please?" and he nodded and went downstairs.

It was twelve in the morning. She was free. She sat in the armchair, she simply sat, she closed her eyes and sat and let herself be alone. She was alone and no one knew where she was. When a knock came on the door she was annoyed, and prepared to show it: but it was Fred himself, it was five o'clock and he was calling her as ordered. He flicked his sharp little eyes over the room—bed, first. It was undisturbed. She might never have been in the room at all. She thanked him, said she would be returning the day after tomorrow, and left. She was back home in time to cook supper, to put the children to bed, to cook a second supper for her husband and herself later. And to welcome Sophie back from the pictures where she had gone with a friend. All these things she did cheerfully, willingly. But she was thinking all the time of the hotel room, she was longing for it with her whole being.

Three times a week, She arrived promptly at ten, looked Fred in the eyes, gave him twenty shillings, followed him up the stairs, went into the room, and shut the door on him with gentle firmness. For Fred, disapproving of her being here at all, was quite ready to let friendship, or at least acquaintanceship, follow his disapproval, if only she would let him. But he was content to go off on her dismissing nod, with the twenty shillings in his hand.

She sat in the armchair and shut her eyes.

What did she *do* in the room? Why, nothing at all. From the chair, when it had rested her, she went to the window, stretching her arms, smiling, treasuring her anonymity, to look out. She was no longer Susan Rawlings, mother of four, wife of Matthew, employer of Mrs. Parkes and of Sophie Traub, with these and those relations with friends, schoolteachers, tradesmen. She no longer was mistress of the big white house and garden, owning clothes suitable for this and that activity or occasion. She was Mrs. Jones, and she was alone, and she had no past and no future. Here I am, she thought, after all these years of being married and having children and playing those roles of responsibility—and I'm just the same. Yet there have been times I thought that nothing existed of me except the roles that went with being Mrs. Matthew Rawlings. Yes, here I am, and if I never saw any of my family again, here I would still be . . . how very strange that is! And she leaned on the sill, and looked into the street, loving the men and women who passed, because she did not know them. She looked at the downtrodden buildings over the street, and at the sky, wet and dingy, or sometimes blue, and she felt she had never seen buildings or sky before. And then she went back to the chair, empty, her mind a blank. Sometimes she talked aloud, saying nothing—an exclamation, meaningless, followed by a comment about the floral pattern on the thin rug, or a stain on the green satin coverlet. For the most part, she woolgathered—what word is there for it?—brooded, wandered, simply went dark, feeling emptiness run deliciously through her veins like the movement of her blood.

This room had become more her own than the house she lived in. One morning she found Fred taking her a flight higher than usual. She stopped, refusing to go up, and demanded her usual room, Number 19. "Well, you'll have to wait half an hour then," he said. Willingly she descended to the dark disinfectant-smelling hall, and sat waiting until the two, man and woman, came down the stairs, giving her swift indifferent glances before they hurried out into the street, separating at the door. She went up to the room, *her* room, which they had just vacated. It was no less hers, though the windows were set wide open, and a maid was straightening the bed as she came in.

After these days of solitude, it was both easy to play her part as mother and wife, and difficult—because it was so easy: she felt an impostor. She felt as if her shell moved here, with her family, answering to Mummy, Mother, Susan, Mrs. Rawlings. She was surprised no one saw through her, that she wasn't turned out of doors, as a fake. On the contrary, it seemed the children loved her more; Matthew and she "got on" pleasantly, and Mrs. Parkes was happy in her work under (for the most part, it must be confessed) Sophie Traub. At night she lay beside her husband, and they made love again, apparently just as they used to, when they were really married. But she, Susan, or the being who answered so readily and improbably to the name of Susan, was not there: she was in Fred's Hotel, in Paddington, waiting for the easing hours of solitude to begin.

Soon she made a new arrangement with Fred and with Sophie. It was for five days a week. As for the money, five pounds, she simply asked Matthew for it. She saw that she was not even frightened he might ask what for: he would give it to her, she knew that, and yet it was terrifying it could be so, for this close couple, these partners, had once known the destination of every shilling they must spend. He agreed to give her five pounds a week. She asked for just so much, not a penny more. He sounded indifferent about it. It was as if he were paying her, she thought: *paying her off*—yes, that was it. Terror came back for a moment, when she understood this, but she stilled it: things had gone too far for that. Now, every week, on Sunday nights, he gave her five pounds, turning away from her before their eyes could meet on the transaction. As for Sophie Traub, she was to be somewhere in or near the house until six at night, after which she was free. She was not to cook, or to clean, she was simply to be there. So she gardened or sewed, and asked friends in, being a person who was bound to have a lot of friends. If the children were sick, she nursed them. If teachers telephoned, she answered them sensibly. For the five daytimes in the school week, she was altogether the mistress of the house.

One night in the bedroom, Matthew asked: "Susan, I don't want to interfere—don't think that, please—but are you sure you are well?"

She was brushing her hair at the mirror. She made two more strokes on either side of her head, before she replied: "Yes, dear, I am sure I am well."

He was again lying on his back, his big blond head on his hands, his elbows angled up and part-concealing his face. He said: "Then Susan, I have to ask you this question, though you must understand, I'm not putting any sort of pressure on you." (Susan heard the word pressure with dismay, because this was inevitable, of course she could not go on like this.) "Are things going to go on like this?"

"Well," she said, going vague and bright and idiotic again, so as to escape: "Well, I don't see why not."

He was jerking his elbows up and down, in annoyance or in pain, and, looking at him, she saw he had got thin, even gaunt; and restless angry movements were not what she remembered of him. He said: "Do you want a divorce, is that it?"

At this, Susan only with the greatest difficulty stopped herself from laughing: she could hear the bright bubbling laughter she *would* have emitted, had she let herself. He could only mean one thing: she had a lover, and that was why she spent her days in London, as lost to him as if she had vanished to another continent.

Then the small panic set in again: she understood that he hoped she did have a lover, he was begging her to say so, because otherwise it would be too terrifying.

She thought this out, as she brushed her hair, watching the fine black stuff fly up to make its little clouds of electricity, hiss, hiss, hiss. Behind her head, across the room, was a blue wall. She realised she was absorbed in watching the black hair making shapes against the blue. She should be answering him. "Do *you* want a divorce, Matthew?"

He said: "That surely isn't the point, is it?"

"You brought it up, I didn't," she said, brightly, suppressing meaningless tinkling laughter.

Next day she asked Fred: "Have enquiries been made for me?"

He hesitated, and she said: "I've been coming here a year now. I've made no trouble, and you've been paid every day. I have a right to be told."

"As a matter of fact, Mrs. Jones, a man did come asking."

"A man from a detective agency?"

"Well, he could have been, couldn't he?"

"I was asking you . . . well, what did you tell him?"

"I told him a Mrs. Jones came every weekday from ten until five or six and stayed in Number Nineteen by herself."

"Describing me?"

"Well Mrs. Jones, I had no alternative. Put yourself in my place."

"By rights I should deduct what that man gave you for the information."

He raised shocked eyes: she was not the sort of person to make jokes like this! Then he chose to laugh: a pinkish wet slit appeared across his white crinkled face: his eyes positively begged her to laugh, otherwise he might lose some money. She remained grave, looking at him.

He stopped laughing and said: "You want to go up now?"—returning to the familiarity, the comradeship, of the country where no questions are asked, on which (and he knew it) she depended completely.

She went up to sit in her wicker chair. But it was not the same. Her husband had searched her out. (The world had searched her out.) The pressures were on her. She was here with his connivance. He might walk in at any moment, here, into Room 19. She imagined the report from the detective agency: "A woman calling herself Mrs. Jones, fitting the description of your wife (etc., etc., etc.), stays alone all day in Room No. 19. She insists on this room, waits for it if it is engaged. As far as the proprietor knows, she receives no visitors there, male or female." A report something on these lines, Matthew must have received.

Well of course he was right: things couldn't go on like this. He had put an end to it all simply by sending the detective after her.

She tried to shrink herself back into the shelter of the room, a snail pecked out of its shell and trying to squirm back. But the peace of the room had gone. She was trying consciously to revive it, trying to let go into the dark creative trance (or whatever it was) that she had found there. It was no use, yet she craved for it, she was as ill as a suddenly deprived addict.

Several times she returned to the room, to look for herself there, but instead she found the unnamed spirit of restlessness, a prickling fevered hunger for movement, an irritable self-consciousness that made her brain feel as if it had coloured lights going on and off inside it. Instead of the soft dark that had been the room's air, were now waiting for her demons that made her dash blindly about, muttering words of hate; she was impelling herself from point to point like a moth dashing itself against a windowpane, sliding to the bottom, fluttering off on broken wings, then crashing into the invisible barrier again. And again and again. Soon she was exhausted, and she told Fred that for a while she would not be needing the room, she was going on holiday. Home she went, to the big white house by the river. The middle of a weekday, and she felt guilty at returning to her own home when not expected. She stood unseen, looking in at the kitchen window. Mrs. Parkes, wearing a discarded floral overall of Susan's, was stooping to slide something into the oven. Sophie, arms folded, was leaning her back against a cupboard and laughing at some joke made by a girl not seen before by Susan—a dark foreign girl, Sophie's visitor. In an armchair Molly, one of the twins, lay curled, sucking her thumb and watching the grownups. She must have some sickness, to be kept from school. The child's listless face, the dark circles under her eyes, hurt Susan: Molly was looking at the three grownups working and talking in exactly the same way Susan looked at the four through the kitchen window: she was remote, shut off from them.

But then, just as Susan imagined herself going in, picking up the little girl, and sitting in an armchair with her, stroking her probably heated forehead, Sophie did just that: she had been standing on one leg, the other knee flexed, its foot set against the wall. Now she let her foot in its ribbon-tied red shoe slide down the wall, stood solid on two feet, clapping her hands before and behind her, and sang a couple of lines in German, so that the child lifted her heavy eyes at her and began to smile. Then she walked, or rather skipped, over to the child, swung her up, and let her fall into her lap at the same moment she sat herself. She said "Hopla! Hopla! Molly . . ." and began stroking the dark untidy young head that Molly laid on her shoulder for comfort.

Well. . . . Susan blinked the tears of farewell out of her eyes, and went quietly up the house to her bedroom. There she sat looking at the river through the trees. She felt at peace, but in a way that was new to her. She had no desire to move, to talk, to do anything at all. The devils that had haunted the house, the garden, were not there; but she knew it was because her soul was in Room 19 in Fred's Hotel; she was not really here at all. It was a sensation that should have been frightening: to sit at her own bedroom window, listening to Sophie's rich young voice sing German nursery songs to her child, listening to Mrs. Parkes clatter and move below, and to know that all this had nothing to do with her: she was already out of it.

Later, she made herself go down and say she was home: it was unfair to be here unannounced. She took lunch with Mrs. Parkes, Sophie, Sophie's Italian friend Maria, and her daughter Molly, and felt like a visitor.

A few days later, at bedtime, Matthew said: "Here's your five pounds," and pushed them over at her. Yet he must have known she had not been leaving the house at all.

She shook her head, gave it back to him, and said, in explanation, not in accusation: "As soon as you knew where I was, there was no point."

He nodded, not looking at her. He was turned away from her: thinking, she knew, how best to handle this wife who terrified him.

He said: "I wasn't trying to . . . it's just that I was worried."

"Yes, I know."

"I must confess that I was beginning to wonder . . ."

"You thought I had a lover?"

"Yes, I am afraid I did."

She knew that he wished she had. She sat wondering how to say: "For a year now I've been spending all my days in a very sordid hotel

room. It's the place where I'm happy. In fact, without it I don't exist."
She heard herself saying this, and understood how terrified he was that
she might. So instead she said: "Well you're not far wrong."

Probably Matthew would think the hotel proprietor lied: he would
want to think so.

"Well," he said, and she could hear his voice spring up, so to speak,
with relief: "in that case I must confess I've got a bit of an affair on
myself."

She said, detached and interested: "Really? Who is she?" and saw
Matthew's startled look because of this reaction.

"It's Phil. Phil Hunt."

She had known Phil Hunt well in the old unmarried days. She was
thinking: No, she won't do, she's too neurotic and difficult. She's never
been happy yet. Sophie's much better: Well Matthew will see that himself, as sensible as he is.

This line of thought went on in silence, while she said aloud: "It's
no point telling you about mine, because you don't know him."

Quick, quick, invent, she thought. Remember how you invented all
that nonsense for Miss Townsend.

She began slowly, careful not to contradict herself: "His name is
Michael"—(*Michael What?*)—"Michael Plant." (What a silly name!)
"He's rather like you—in looks, I mean." And indeed, she could imagine
herself being touched by no one but Matthew himself. "He's a publisher."
(Really? Why?) "He's got a wife already and two children."

She brought out this fantasy, proud of herself.

Matthew said: "Are you two thinking of marrying?"

She said, before she could stop herself: "Good God, *no!*"

She realised, if Matthew wanted to marry Phil Hunt, that this was too
emphatic, but apparently it was all right, for his voice sounded relieved
as he said: "It is a bit impossible to imagine oneself married to anyone
else, isn't it?" With which he pulled her to him, so that her head lay on
his shoulder. She turned her face into the dark of his flesh, and listened
to the blood pounding through her ears saying: I am alone, I am alone,
I am alone.

In the morning Susan lay in bed while he dressed.

He had been thinking things out in the night, because now he said:
"Susan, why don't we make a foursome?"

Of course, she said to herself, of course he would be bound to say
that. If one is sensible, if one is reasonable, if one never allows oneself
a base thought or an envious emotion, naturally one says: Let's make a
foursome!

"Why not?" she said.

"We could all meet for lunch. I mean, it's ridiculous, you sneaking off to filthy hotels, and me staying late at the office, and all the lies everyone has to tell."

What on earth did I say his name was?—she panicked, then said: "I think it's a good idea, but Michael is away at the moment. When he comes back though—and I'm sure you two would like each other."

"He's away, is he? So that's why you've been . . ." Her husband put his hand to the knot of his tie in a gesture of male coquetry she would not before have associated with him; and he bent to kiss her cheek with the expression that goes with the words: Oh you naughty little puss! And she felt its answering look, naughty and coy, come onto her face.

Inside she was dissolving in horror at them both, at how far they had both sunk from honesty of emotion.

So now she was saddled with a lover, and he had a mistress! How ordinary, how reassuring, how jolly! And now they would make a foursome of it, and go about to theatres and restaurants. After all, the Rawlings could well afford that sort of thing, and presumably the publisher Michael Plant could afford to do himself and his mistress quite well. No, there was nothing to stop the four of them developing the most intricate relationship of civilised tolerance, all enveloped in a charming afterglow of autumnal passion. Perhaps they would all go off on holidays together? She had known people who did. Or perhaps Matthew would draw the line there? Why should he, though, if he was capable of talking about "foursomes" at all?

She lay in the empty bedroom, listening to the car drive off with Matthew in it, off to work. Then she heard the children clattering off to school to the accompaniment of Sophie's cheerfully ringing voice. She slid down into the hollow of the bed, for shelter against her own irrelevance. And she stretched out her hand to the hollow where her husband's body had lain, but found no comfort there: he was not her husband. She curled herself up in a small tight ball under the clothes: she could stay here all day, all week, indeed, all her life.

But in a few days she must produce Michael Plant, and—but how? She must presumably find some agreeable man prepared to impersonate a publisher called Michael Plant. And in return for which she would—what? Well, for one thing they would make love. The idea made her want to cry with sheer exhaustion. Oh no, she had finished with all that—the proof of it was that the words "make love," or even imagining it, trying hard to revive no more than the pleasures of sensuality, let alone affection, or love, made her want to run away and hide from the sheer effort of the thing. . . . Good Lord, why make love at all? Why make love with anyone? Or if you are going to make love, what does it matter who with? Why shouldn't she simply walk into the street, pick up a man and have a roaring sexual affair with him? Why not? Or even with Fred? What difference did it make?

But she had let herself in for it—an interminable stretch of time with a lover, called Michael, as part of a gallant civilised foursome. Well, she could not, and she would not.

She got up, dressed, went down to find Mrs. Parkes, and asked her for the loan of a pound, since Matthew, she said, had forgotten to leave her money. She exchanged with Mrs. Parkes variations on the theme that husbands are all the same, they don't think, and without saying a word to Sophie, whose voice could be heard upstairs from the telephone, walked to the underground, travelled to South Kensington, changed to the Inner Circle, got out at Paddington, and walked to Fred's Hotel. There she told Fred that she wasn't going on holiday after all, she needed the room. She would have to wait an hour, Fred said. She went to a busy tea-room-cum-restaurant around the corner, and sat watching the people flow in and out the door that kept swinging open and shut, watched them mingle and merge and separate, felt her being flow into them, into their movement. When the hour was up she left a half crown for her pot of tea, and left the place without looking back at it, just as she had left her house, the big, beautiful white house, without another look, but silently dedicating it to Sophie. She returned to Fred, received the key of No. 19, now free, and ascended the grimy stairs slowly, letting floor after floor fall away below her, keeping her eyes lifted, so that floor after floor descended jerkily to her level of vision, and fell away out of sight.

No. 19 was the same. She saw everything with an acute, narrow, checking glance: the cheap shine of the satin spread, which had been replaced carelessly after the two bodies had finished their convulsions under it; a trace of powder on the glass that topped the chest of drawers; an intense green shade in a fold of the curtain. She stood at the window, looking down, watching people pass and pass and pass until her mind went dark from the constant movement. Then she sat in the wicker chair, letting herself go slack. But she had to be careful, because she did not want, today, to be surprised by Fred's knock at five o'clock.

The demons were not here. They had gone forever, because she was buying her freedom from them. She was slipping already into the dark fructifying dream that seemed to caress her inwardly, like the movement of her blood . . . but she had to think about Matthew first. Should she write a letter for the coroner? But what should she say? She would like to leave him with the look on his face she had seen this morning— banal, admittedly, but at least confidently healthy. Well, that was impossible, one did not look like that with a wife dead from suicide. But how to leave him believing she was dying because of a man—because of the fascinating publisher Michael Plant? Oh, how ridiculous! How absurd! How humiliating! But she decided not to trouble about it, simply not to think about the living. If he wanted to believe she had a lover, he would believe it. And he *did* want to believe it. Even when he had found out that there was no publisher in London called Michael Plant, he would think: Oh poor Susan, she was afraid to give me his real name.

And what did it matter whether he married Phil Hunt or Sophie? Though it ought to be Sophie, who was already the mother of those children . . . and what hypocrisy to sit here worrying about the children, when she was going to leave them because she had not got the energy to stay.

She had about four hours. She spent them delightfully, darkly, sweetly, letting herself slide gently, gently, to the edge of the river. Then, with hardly a break in her consciousness, she got up, pushed the thin rug against the door, made sure the windows were tight shut, put two shillings in the meter, and turned on the gas. For the first time since she had been in the room she lay on the hard bed that smelled stale, that smelled of sweat and sex.

She lay on her back on the green satin cover, but her legs were chilly. She got up, found a blanket folded in the bottom of the chest of drawers, and carefully covered her legs with it. She was quite content lying there, listening to the faint soft hiss of the gas that poured into the room, into her lungs, into her brain, as she drifted off into the dark river.

The Mother

Gwendolyn Brooks

This poem by the black poet Gwendolyn Brooks is a poignant lament of a woman for her aborted children—an expression of regret, pain, and love. Here is a woman who would willingly have fulfilled the traditional role of mother in another, and better, society.

Abortions will not let you forget.
You remember the children you got that you did not get,
The damp small pulps with a little or with no hair,
The singers and workers that never handled the air.
You will never neglect or beat
Them, or silence or buy with a sweet.
You will never wind up the sucking-thumb
Or scuttle off ghosts that come.
You will never leave them, controlling your luscious sigh,
Return for a snack of them, with gobbling mother-eye.

I have heard in the voices of the wind the voices of my dim
    killed children.
I have contracted. I have eased
My dim dears at the breasts they could never suck.
I have said, Sweets, if I sinned, if I seized
Your luck
And your lives from your unfinished reach,
If I stole your births and your names,
Your straight baby tears and your games,
Your stilted or lovely loves, your tumults, your marriages,
    aches, and your deaths,
If I poisoned the beginnings of your breaths,
Believe that even in my deliberateness I was not deliberate.
Though why should I whine,
Whine that the crime was other than mine?—
Since anyhow you are dead.
Or rather, or instead,
You were never made.
But that too, I am afraid,
Is faulty: oh, what shall I say, how is the truth to be said?
You were born, you had body, you died.
It is just that you never giggled or planned or cried.

Believe me, I loved you all.
Believe me, I knew you, though faintly, and I loved, I loved you
All.

Man and Wife

Anne Sexton

The speaker of this poem addresses her (his?) spouse, comparing
their estrangement with that of a "pair who came to the suburbs by mistake." Notice particularly the images of alienation,
pain, and ugliness.

Anne Sexton grew up in Wellesley, Massachusetts, married,
and became a fashion model in Boston. When her second
daughter was born, she had a mental breakdown. After recover-
ing, she attended the Radcliffe Institute for Independent Study,
working with Robert Lowell. Her books include: To Bedlam and
Part Way Back (1960); All My Pretty Ones (1962); Live or Die
(1966), and Love Poems (1969).

To speke of wo
that is in mariage . . .

We are not lovers.
We do not even know each other.
We look alike
but we have nothing to say.
We are like pigeons . . .
that pair who came to the suburbs
by mistake,
forsaking Boston where they bumped
their small heads against a blind wall,
having worn out the fruit stalls in the North End,
the amethyst windows of Louisburg Square,
the seats on the Common
And the traffic that kept stamping
and stamping.

Now there is green rain for everyone
as common as eyewash.

Now they are together
like strangers in a two-seater outhouse,
eating and squatting together.
They have teeth and knees
but they do not speak.
A soldier is forced to stay with a soldier
because they share the same dirt
and the same blows.

They are exiles
soiled by the same sweat and the drunkard's dream.
As it is they can only hang on,
their red claws wound like bracelets
around the same limb.
Even their song is not a sure thing.
It is not a language;
it is a kind of breathing.
They are two asthmatics
whose breath sobs in and out
through a small fuzzy pipe.

Like them
we neither talk nor clear our throats.
Oh darling,
we gasp in unison beside our window pane,
drunk on the drunkard's dream.
Like them
we can only hang on.

But they would pierce our heart
if they could only fly the distance.

Communes:
A Footnote for the Future

Mary Louise Briscoe

In a recent interview, Margaret Mead talks about changing sex roles
in our culture (*McCall's*, June 1970). Recognizing that industrialized
society has needed and encouraged women to work outside the home,

she is concerned about the "domestication" of men. No previous civilization has promoted child-rearing as a single role for men, she notes. Women's Liberation suggests that neither sex have child-rearing as a single role, but that men share in the domestic activities which, as Margaret Mead notes, are a drain on creativity. Civilization at this stage needs all the creativity it can find, and the current waste of female creativity is appalling. Margaret Mead does not suggest communal living as an alternative, but she does believe that new social forms must be invented so that neither parent need be tied to the home. Many young people are experimenting in communal living, which, like Utopia, is a perennial visitor in times of social upheaval. While most communes prove to be temporary and some even reactionary, they are now being tried more widely than ever before.

Rosabeth Moss Kanter ("Communes," *Psychology Today*, July 1970) studied twenty contemporary communes and thirty nineteenth-century American ones, looking for criteria which seemed to make some of them lasting. Most of the successful nineteenth-century communes were based on a set of values, usually religious (like Amana or Oneida). In the twentieth century there are some of these, but two new kinds have emerged, those based around personal growth centers (like Esalen), and small anarchistic communes. The latter are the most frequent, the most temporary, and the least workable or satisfying to the members. Nevertheless, the large numbers of people interested in such experiments indicate a restless satisfaction with traditional social patterns.

Another article in the same issue of *Psychology Today* reports the results of a survey taken on sex (Robert Athanasiou, Phillip Shaver and Carol Tavris, "Sex"). 20,000 responses from a mostly moderate-to-liberal, college educated, middle class group, 77% under the age of 34, showed that 33% of the males and 17 of the females expressed some interest in the possibility of group marriage. 9% of the group were strongly in favor, and many others added that they were interested, though culturally conditioned to the conventional pattern. But another question on swapping partners showed that one third of the group might participate, indicating a rather prominent sign of dissatisfaction with the conventional pattern. These are only signs, to be sure, but add to them statistics on divorce and sequence marriage, and the need to change conventional patterns of marriage and the family becomes even clearer.

In one sense, the Women's Liberation movement is a symptom of the need for change, but the changes have been in process at least since the industrial age began, and have been accelerated since World War II. The current movement for freedom offers women and men the opportunity of actively participate in the study and development of new sexual roles and family patterns.

The Working Woman

Women in the Labor Force

The following tables and chart are from the Handbook on
Women Workers, published in 1969 by the Women's Bureau of
the United States Department of Labor. For those who are scep-
tical about the economic exploitation of women in our society,
these statistics about the kinds of work done by women and the
comparative wages of women and men should end all doubts.
The tables and chart reveal this descending order on the economic scale: white men, nonwhite men, white women, non-
white women.

Reprinted by permission of The United States Government Printing Office,
Division of Public Documents, Washington, D. C.

**Table 1.—Detailed Occupations in Which 100,000 or More
Women Were Employed, 1960[1]**

(Women 14 years of age and over)

Occupation	Number	As percent of total employed
Secretaries	1,423,352	97
Sales women (retail trade)	1,397,364	54
Private household workers (n.e.c.)	1,162,683	96
Teachers (elementary school)	860,413	86
Bookkeepers	764,054	84
Waitresses	714,827	87
Nurses (professional)	567,884	98
Sewers and stitchers (mfg.)	534,258	94
Typists	496,735	95
Cashiers	367,954	78
Cooks (except private household)	361,772	64
Telephone operators	341,797	96
Babysitters	319,735	98
Attendants (hospitals and other institutions)	288,268	74
Laundry and drycleaning operatives	277,396	72
Assemblers	270,769	44
Operatives (apparel and accessories)	270,619	75
Hairdressers and cosmetologists	267,050	89
Packers and wrappers (n.e.c.)	262,935	60
Stenographers	258,554	96
Teachers (secondary school)	243,452	47
Office machine operators	227,849	74
Checkers, examiners, and inspectors (mfg.)	215,066	45
Practical nurses	197,115	96
Kitchen workers (n.e.c.) (except private household)	179,796	59
Chambermaids and maids (except private household)	162,433	98
Housekeepers (private household)	143,290	99
Operatives (electrical machinery, equipment and supplies)	138,001	48
Receptionists	131,142	98
Charwomen and cleaners	122,728	68
Housekeepers and stewardesses (except private household)	117,693	81
Dressmakers and seamstresses (except factory)	115,252	97
Counter and fountain workers	112,547	71
File clerks	112,323	86
Musicians and music teachers	109,638	57
Operatives (yarn, thread, and fabric mills)	103,399	44

Source: U.S. Department of Commerce, Bureau of the Census: "U.S. Census of Population: 1960. Detailed Characteristics, U.S. Summary, PC(1)–ID." 1963.

---

[1]From "Women in the Labor Force," *Handbook on Women Workers*, p. 96.

Chart 2—A Larger Proportion of Nonwhite than White Women are in Service Work

(Employed Women, by Color and Type of Work, April 1968)

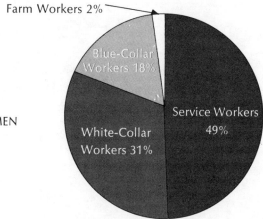

NONWHITE WOMEN

Farm Workers 2%

Blue-Collar Workers 18%

Service Workers 49%

White-Collar Workers 31%

3,439,000

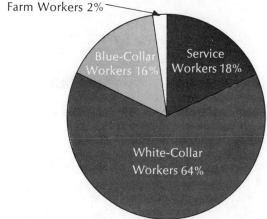

WHITE WOMEN

Farm Workers 2%

Blue-Collar Workers 16%

Service Workers 18%

White-Collar Workers 64%

Source: U.S. Department of Labor, Bureau of Labor Statistics

24,056,000

[2]For further information on the occupations of nonwhite women workers, see "Negro Women in the Population and in the Labor Force." Women's Bureau, Wage and Labor Standards Administration, U.S. Department of Labor, 1967.

Table 2.—Median Wage or Salary Income of Year-Round Full-Time Workers, by Sex and Color, 1939 and 1956–66[3]

(Persons 14 years of age and over)

Year	Median wage or salary income		Nonwhite income as percent of white income
	White	Nonwhite	
women			
1966	$4,152	$2,949	71.0
1965	3,991	2,816	70.6
1964	3,859	2,674	69.3
1963	3,723	2,368	63.6
1962	3,601	2,279	63.3
1961	3,480	2,325	66.8
1960	3,410	2,372	69.6
1959	3,306	2,196	66.4
1958	3,225	1,988	61.6
1957	3,107	1,866	60.1
1956	2,958	1,637	55.3
1939	863	327	37.9
men			
1966	$7,164	$4,528	63.2
1965	6,704	4,277	63.8
1964	6,497	4,285	66.0
1963	6,277	4,104	65.4
1962	6,025	3,799	63.1
1961	5,880	3,883	66.0
1960	5,662	3,789	66.9
1959	5,456	3,339	61.2
1958	5,186	3,368	64.9
1957	4,950	3,137	63.4
1956	4,710	2,912	61.8
1939	1,419	639	45.0

Source: U.S. Department of Commerce, Bureau of the Census: Current Population Reports, P-60, Nos. 53, 51, 47, 43, 41, 39, 37, 35, 33, 30, and 27.

[3]From "Women in the Labor Force," *Handbook on Women Workers*, p. 137.

Table 3.—Median Wage or Salary Income of Year-Round Full-Time Workers, by Major Occupation Group and Sex, 1966[4]

(Persons 14 years of age and over)

Major occupation group	Women	Men
Professional, technical workers	$5,826	$8,945
Managers, officials, proprietors (except farm) ..	4,919	9,103
Clerical workers	4,316	6,487
Sales workers	3,103	7,569
Craftsmen, foremen	4,345	7,197
Operatives	3,416	6,112
Nonfarm laborers	([1])	4,946
Private household workers	1,297	([1])
Service workers (except private household)	2,815	5,078
Farmers, farm managers	([1])	1,229
Farm laborers, foremen	([1])	2,489

[1]Median not shown where base is less than 75,000.

Source: U.S. Department of Commerce, Bureau of the Census: Current Population Reports, P-60, No. 53.

Table 4.—Median Income in 1966 of Persons, by Educational Attainment, Sex, and Color[5]

(Persons 25 years of age and over)

Educational attainment	Women			Men		
	Total	White	Non-white	Total	White	Non-white
Total	$1,926	$1,988	$1,561	$6,128	$6,390	$3,665
Elementary school ...	1,190	1,236	993	3,488	3,731	2,632
Less than 8 years .	1,009	1,055	932	2,784	2,945	2,376
8 years	1,404	1,416	1,303	4,518	4,611	3,681
High school	2,368	2,421	2,057	6,576	6,736	4,725
1 to 3 years	1,913	1,960	1,698	5,982	6,189	4,278
4 years	2,673	2,700	2,475	6,924	7,068	5,188
College	3,569	3,519	3,964	8,779	9,023	5,928
1 to 3 years	2,827	([1])	([1])	7,709	([1])	([1])
4 years	4,165	([1])	([1])	9,728	([1])	([1])
5 years or more ..	6,114	([1])	([1])	10,041	([1])	([1])

[1]Not available.

Source: U.S. Department of Commerce, Bureau of the Census: Current Population Reports, P-60, No. 53.

---

[4]From "Women in the Labor Force," *Handbook on Women Workers*, p. 139.

[5]From "Women in the Labor Force," *Handbook on Women Workers*, p. 141.

On Day Care

Louise Gross and Phyllis MacEwan

Given the great number of women in the working force in the United States, four million of them with pre-school children, the need for adequate day care for their children is obvious. Furthermore, day care centers are needed to free women to educate themselves, so that they may have not just jobs but good jobs. The New University Conference (NUC) Women's Caucus is one of many groups which is demanding day care centers which will not only free women but will also act as liberating forces for the children attending them. A day care center has a "radical potential" in that it can challenge traditional views of women through education of children.

Day Care has become one of the central issues of the Women's Liberation Movement. It is quite clear that free and public day care centers would be an important means for liberating women from the traditional tasks of child rearing. It has been suggested—and in some places carried out—that women should demand day care services from the institutions in which they work or study and from the large corporations which profit from and expand into the communities in which they live.

The authors of this discussion paper think it is a mistake to view day care solely as an issue of Women's Liberation. We would like to assert that day care centers in which children are raised in groups by men and women could be as important for the liberation of children as it would be for the liberation of women. Group child care—if well conceived—has a radical potential through the impact it could have on children's early development. It is therefore necessary that people in the movement gain a deeper understanding of the day care center as an environment for child rearing.

We consider this paper to be an introduction to the problems of existing day care centers and the possibilities for future centers. Although we have pointed out some specific areas for radicalizing a day care

From *Women: A Journal of Liberation* (Winter 1970). Reprinted by courtesy of the New University Conference Women's Caucus.

center, we certainly have not developed a comprehensive model describing what an ideal day care program would look like.

We hope to develop this paper into a more thorough pamphlet and we welcome groups that are presently organizing day care centers or teachers who are working in centers to send us their ideas and suggestions.

Why Day Care Has Existed in the U.S.

Historically in the United States full-day care programs, as contrasted to half-day nursery schools, have been provided in periods of economic stress—during World War II and the depression—when women were required in the work force.[1] These programs were created primarily as a service to the corporations which needed woman-power, not as an educational and social opportunity for children. Although wartime day care centers often became educational opportunities for children, their rapid closing following World War II was a clear indication that these centers had not been organized primarily to benefit children or even to liberate women. Rather they had been organized to facilitate the carrying out of needed production.

In the past few years there has been an upsurge of state and national government interest in developing day care facilities for welfare mothers. This current interest parallels the expansion of day care during earlier periods of economic crisis. Today the main impetus behind the new drive for day care is the goal of lowering welfare costs by channeling welfare recipients into "desirable" occupations (like key punch operating). In both periods the official drive for day care has been motivated by the "needs" of the economy rather than by a concern for the welfare of either women or children.

Why Day Care Has Not Developed in the U.S.

The underlying reason for the failure of day care programs to develop in this country exists in the traditional ideology that young children and their mothers belong in the home. Even today a strong bias exists against the concept that day care is potentially good for children and mothers. That women should *have* to work and therefore *have* to put their children in day care centers are circumstances which are generally considered to be necessary evils in this society.[2]

The Demand for Day Care of the Women's Liberation Movement

The current demand for day care by the Women's Liberation Movement springs from a rejection of the ideology which says that women belong in the home. Yet the Movement's present demand parallels the historical attitude toward day care in its non child-centered approach. The primary reason for demanding day care is the liberation of women. While recognizing that day care is essential for women's liberation, the authors want the movement to further recognize that day care is essential for the liberation of children. Group child care, in contrast to the more isolating private home environment, has the potential of providing an environment in which children will have more opportunity to develop social sensitivity and responsibility, emotional autonomy and trust, and a wider range of intellectual interests.

The struggle for day care centers must be considered a people's liberation issue, not just a women's issue, because children are people. Both men and women who are concerned with children's development must demand day care.

What Is a Day Care Center Like Today?

The majority of existing U.S. day care centers, which are run as profit-making enterprises, are glorified baby sitting services—dumping grounds—where children are bored most of the time. In these centers children are emotionally brutalized; they learn the values of obedience and passivity. They are programmed through a daily routine in which opportunities for personal choice and meaningful social relationships with adults and other children are minimal. Eating and naptime are managed in a mass production style which values efficiency over dignity. The adults as well as the children become routinized and enslaved to the daily schedule.

In contrast, there are a few day care centers where children have meaningful social and educational experiences, and where they participate in non-alienating play/work activities. In these centers self-directed learning and discovery are valued, and curriculum is developed in terms of the children's interests. Social cooperation is based on a rational group-problem-solving approach, rather than on rules impersonally established. Eating and resting activities are designed to be responsive to children's individual and group needs, rather than to meet the efficiency goals of the day care operation.

Why We Must Demand Space and Money and Not the Day Care Centers Themselves

We feel the differences among existing day care centers reflect a conflict in values and attitudes toward human development. This conflict in the care and education of young children is directly related to conflicting values and attitudes expressed in the economic and political behavior of adults. Values in competitive enterprise and individual rather than social achievement, respect for private property, adoration of the nuclear family—are attitudes that are nurtured in childhood and expressed in adult society.

As radicals we must understand that *our* goals for children are in conflict with those of the institutions—corporations and universities— from whom we will be demanding day care services. This implies that when we make demands for day care they should be solely in terms of money and space. The corporations and universities should have no control.

The Hidden Curriculum

In organizing day care centers, we need to become aware of how values and attitudes are translated into programs for young children. We need to be aware of the existence of the day care center curriculum —hidden or explicit—and how it affects children's development.

It is well documented that attitudes toward work, race, sex (including male/female roles), initiative, and cooperation are being formed during the first five years of life. It follows that as radicals, concerned with developing a radical consciousness on these issues, we need to be seriously concerned with what happens inside the day care center.

The kind of interaction that takes place between the child and the human and physical environment (be it a home or a day care center) affects the kind of capacities that the child will have as an adult. The capacity to feel deeply and be sensitive toward other people, the capacity to trust oneself and use one's initiative, the capacity to solve problems in a creative and collective way—these are all capacities that can be given their foundation or stifled in the first five years.

By the age of 4, children are assimilating the idea that a woman's place is in the home. Three- and four-year-old children are already learning that it's better to be white. They are learning to follow directions and rules without asking why. They are learning how to deny their own feelings and needs in order to win approval from adults.

These are examples of learnings that most commonly result from early childhood experiences. These are elements of the hidden curriculum that usually characterize the child's environment in our society.

The Child's Perspective

To a young child curriculum in a day care center is everything that he or she experiences: painting a picture, having to take a nap, experi-

menting with sand and water, wetting your pants or making it there
on time, listening to an interesting story, eating lunch, riding a trike,
being socked in the nose and having it bleed, observing one teacher
being bossed by the other teacher, being told that blue is called blue,
figuring out a hard puzzle, being hugged by the teacher, watching a
building be demolished, seeing the mother guinea pig give birth, having
everyone sing happy birthday to you, hammering a nail hard, and
waiting to be picked up.

Although as adults we can place these events into categories of
social, intellectual, emotional and physical experiences, for the young
child each event is experienced in a total way. That is, the experience
of painting a picture simultaneously involves emotional, intellectual,
physical, and even social capacities. Emotionally a child may be using
paint to express feelings of anger, loneliness, contentment, or boredom.
Intellectually a child may be using the paint to discover what happens
when different colors are mixed or learning how to write different letters.
Physically, the child uses the paint brush to explore her/his own coordination, movement, and rhythm. Socially, painting can give the child
an opportunity to be alone, with a friend, or in a group—depending on
how the teacher has structured the painting experience.

The adult can seldom know the value that a particular experience
has for a particular child. The same experience (e.g., painting a picture)
will have a different value for different children, a different value to
the same child at different times.

The Teacher's Ideology

The teacher's values and attitudes form the base from which the
structure and therefore the style of the group are formed. A single
activity such as "juice time" illustrates how a teacher's goals and attitudes affect the way the situation is structured. One teacher might have
three year olds pour their own juice from a pitcher, whereas another
would have the children take already filled cups from a tray. What
underlies the difference? Presumably both teachers know that three
year olds are in the process of developing muscle as well as eye-hand
coordination. Also, three year olds are usually concerned with becoming
independent and self-sufficient. By letting children pour their own juice
the teacher is structuring the situation to allow for growth—however
groping—in the areas of self reliance and manual dexterity. By filling
cups for the children, the other teacher is structuring the situation for
maximum efficiency and neatness: to keep the routine running smoothly.
One teacher uses juice time as an opportunity for children to gain some
control over their activity, while the other teacher uses juice time to

take control. In the first case the child gets to act upon the environment, while in the second case the child is treated as a passive recipient.

The traditional "housekeeping corner" of the nursery school and day care center is another dramatic illustration of how the teacher's values expressed in actions can have impact.

Let us take two teachers who have undergone similar training in early childhood education and have learned that the housekeeping corner provides an opportunity for children to "act out" adult roles, thus contributing to their "ego growth" and "sex identification." One of the teachers sets up a housekeeping corner which encourages girls to be Mommy, the Housewife, and boys to be Daddy, the Worker. The other teacher sets up an area in the classroom in which both boys and girls are given opportunities to cook, play with dolls and trucks, sew, hammer, build with blocks, wash clothes and dishes, dress up as doctors, firemen and firewomen, construction workers, and other interesting occupations. In other words, one teacher uses the housekeeping corner to promote the learning of traditional stereotyped roles, while the other transforms the housekeeping corner into an area where children can explore and test out various adult activities.

Men in the Day Care Center/Work in the Day Care Center

Another way that children learn the traditional stereotyped roles is through observing that almost all day care teachers are women. The children quickly comprehend the concept that there is "women's work" and "men's work." This in itself would be sufficient argument for us to insist that men be included at all levels in the day care staff.

Furthermore, without including men in the day care program, the demand for day care runs the risk of contradicting the goals of women's liberation. Women should not demand simply that there be special institutions for child care, but also that men take an equal role in child care.

There is another good reason that *both* men and women should be involved in the day care center. Teaching/working/playing with children can be an extraordinarily creative and non-alienating job. What often makes the caretakers of young children—teachers and mothers— feel apologetic about their occupation and what deprives men the opportunity of working with children is the fact that our society considers child care "women's work"—a low-status/cheap labor occupation biologically relegated to the weaker, "sensitive" sex.

A day care program which had a sexually integrated staff—and salaries in keeping with the value of this work—would make child-rearing a desirable and rewarding occupation. Finally, it seems self-evident that it's best for children—emotionally, socially and politically—that they be cared for equally by both men and women.

Some Conclusions

Day care is a people's liberation issue. Women, of course, will gain from a good day care program, but in the final analysis women's liberation depends on an entire transformation of society, not just on one institution. However, that one institution, if radically structured, can help obtain that transformation of society. The way children develop is part of that transformation.

In order to develop a radically structured day care program we must not allow any control to be in the hands of the universities and corporations. Our demand to these institutions for day care must be a demand solely for space and money. Control must rest with those who struggle for and use the day care center.

One of our prime tasks in that struggle is to develop an awareness of what a good day care program can be. We have simply attempted to make clear in this paper that day care is a complex issue.[3] The self-education which the movement must undergo on day care should be as thorough as on more obviously political issues.

NOTES

1. For example, the Kaiser Child Service Centers in Portland, Oregon, which served more than 4,000 children from Nov. 8, 1943 to Sept. 1, 1945.
2. Today in the U.S. there are 4 million working women who have children under the age of 6 years, out of a total of 30 million working women. There presently are enough day care facilities to take care of 500,000 children. Compared to a number of other Western industrialized countries the U.S. is backward in the field of day care. (Figures from *New York Times*, Oct. 16, 1969)
3. There are numerous implications of day care organizing which we have not included in this paper such as the questions of developing the day care center as a base for community political action, the day care center as a place to organize parents around their children's rights in the public school system, and the whole issue of day care for infants and collective child-rearing.

SUGGESTED READINGS & SOURCES OF LITERATURE RELATED TO DAY CARE

Boguslawski, Dorothy. *Guide for Establishing & Operating Day Care Centers for Young Children.* N.Y. Child Welfare League of America, Inc.: N.Y., N.Y., 1968.

Burgess, Evangeline. *Values in Early Childhood Education.* Department of Elementary-Kindergarten-Nursery Education, National Education Association, 1965.

Dittman, Laura (Ed.). *Early Child Care: The New Perspective.* N.Y.: Atherton Press, 1968.

Federal Panel on Early Childhood, *Good References on Day Care,* U.S. Department of Health, Education & Welfare, (Social & Rehabilitation Service; Children's Bureau), July, 1968.

Hartley, Ruth et al. *Understanding Children's Play.* N.Y.: Columbia University Press, 1952.

Hunt, J. McV. *Intelligence and Experience.* N.Y.: Ronald Publishing Company, 1961.

Hymes, J. L. *Teaching the Child Under 6.* N.Y.: Prentice-Hall, 1963.

Jones, Betty & Elizabeth Prescott. *Group Day Care as a Child-Rearing Environment: An Observational Study of Day Care Program.* Pasadena, Calif.: Children's Bureau, Social Security Administration, U.S. Department of Health, Education, & Welfare, 1967.

Kritchevsky, Sybil & Prescott, Elizabeth. *Planning Environments for Young Children.* National Association for the Education of Young Children, Washington, D.C., 1969.

Moustakas, Clark. *The Authentic Teacher.* Cambridge, Mass.: Doyle Publishing Company, 1966.

Piaget, Jean. *The Language & Thought of the Child.* N.Y.: Meridian Books, 1955.

U.S. Department of Labor, Women's Bureau. *Report of a Consultation on Working Women and Day Care Needs,* 1968 (free) and *Working Mothers and the Need for Day Care Services,* 1968 (free).

Warner, Sylvia Ashton. *Teacher.* N.Y.: Bantam Books, 1963.

The Morning Half-life Blues

Marge Piercy

Women being wasted by a commercial society is the theme of the following blues song for working girls.

In addition to poetry, Marge Piercy also writes essays for Women's Liberation. She is a founder of Movement for a Democratic Society.

Girls buck the wind in the grooves toward work
in fuzzy coats promised to be warm as fur.
The shop windows snicker
flashing them hurrying over dresses they cannot afford:
you are not pretty enough, not pretty enough.

Blown with yesterday's papers through the boiled coffee morning
they dream of the stop on the subway without a name,
the door in the heart of the grove of skyscrapers,
that garden where we nestle to the teats of a furry world,
lie in mounds of peony eating grapes,
and need barter ourselves for nothing,
not by the hour, not by the pound, not by the skinful
that party to which no one will give or sell them the key
though we have all thought briefly we had found it
drunk or in bed.

Black girls with thin legs and high necks stalking like herons,
plump girls with blue legs and green eyelids and strawberry breasts,
swept off to be frozen in fluorescent cubes,
the vacuum of your jobs sucks your brains dry
and fills you with the ooze of melted comics.
Living is later. This is your rented death.
You grasp at specific commodities and vague lusts
to make up, to pay for each day
which opens like a can and is empty, and then another,
afternoons like dinosaur eggs stuffed with glue.

Girls of the dirty morning, ticketed and spent,
you will be less at forty than at twenty.
Your living is a waste product of somebody's mill.
I would fix you like buds to a city where people work
to make and do things necessary and good,
where work is real as bread and babies and trees in parks
and you would blossom slowly and ripen to sound fruit.

from *Mrs. Warren's Profession*

Bernard Shaw

In Mrs. Warren's Profession, Shaw comments on the plight of woman in an exploitative economic system. In her justification of her life as a prostitute, Mrs. Warren outlines the alternatives that society offered her as a poor uneducated girl. She willingly chose prostitution over work in a white lead factory, which killed one of her sisters, and over the role of laborer's wife, which kept another sister in poverty and misery. In the play, Shaw makes it clear that he is not defending prostitution as a profession but is instead condemning a system which offers a poor woman only evil choices.

In this excerpt from the play, Mrs. Warren is talking to her daughter, Vivie, who is college-educated, self-assured, and scornful of her mother and her mother's friends, such as the prosperous businessman, Sir George Crofts.

Your way of life will be what I please, so it will. [*another pause.*] Ive been noticing these airs in you ever since you got that tripos or whatever you call it. If you think I'm going to put up with them youre mistaken; and the sooner you find it out, the better. [*Muttering*] All I have to say on the subject, indeed! [*Again raising her voice angrily*] Do you know who youre speaking to, Miss?

VIVIE [*looking across at her without raising her head from her book*] No. Who are you? What are you?

MRS WARREN [*rising breathless*] You young imp!

VIVIE. Everybody knows my reputation, my social standing, and the profession I intend to pursue. I know nothing about you. What is that way of life which you invite me to share with you and Sir George Crofts, pray?

MRS WARREN. Take care. I shall do something I'll be sorry for after, and you too.

Reprinted by permission of The Society of Authors; for the Bernard Shaw Estate.

VIVIE [*putting aside her books with cool decision*] Well, let us drop the subject until you are better able to face it. [*Looking critically at her mother*] You want some good walks and a little lawn tennis to set you up. You are shockingly out of condition: you were not able to manage twenty yards uphill today without stopping to pant; and your wrists are mere rolls of fat. Look at mine. [*She holds out her wrists.*]

MRS WARREN [*after looking at her helplessly, begins to whimper*] Vivie—

VIVIE [*springing up sharply*] Now pray dont begin to cry. Anything but that. I really cannot stand whimpering. I will go out of the room if you do.

MRS WARREN [*piteously*] Oh, my darling, how can you be so hard on me? Have I no rights over you as your mother?

VIVIE. Are you my mother?

MRS WARREN [*appalled*] Am I your mother! Oh, Vivie!

VIVIE. Then where are our relatives? my father? our family friends? You claim the rights of a mother: the right to call me fool and child; to speak to me as no woman in authority over me at college dare speak to me; to dictate my way of life; and to force on me the acquaintance of a brute whom anyone can see to be the most vicious sort of London man about town. Before I give myself the trouble to resist such claims, I may as well find out whether they have any real existence.

MRS WARREN [*distracted, throwing herself on her knees*] Oh no, no. Stop, stop. I am your mother: I swear it. Oh, you cant mean to turn on me—my own child! it's not natural. You believe me, dont you? Say you believe me.

VIVIE. Who was my father?

MRS WARREN. You dont know what youre asking. I cant tell you.

VIVIE [*determinedly*] Oh yes you can, if you like. I have a right to know; and you know very well that I have that right. You can refuse to tell me, if you please; but if you do, you will see the last of me tomorrow morning.

MRS WARREN. Oh, it's too horrible to hear you talk like that. You wouldnt—you couldnt leave me.

VIVIE [*ruthlessly*] Yes, without a moment's hesitation, if you trifle with me about this. [*Shivering with disgust*] How can I feel sure that I may not have the contaminated blood of that brutal waster in my veins?

MRS WARREN. No, no. On my oath it's not he, nor any of the rest that you have ever met. I'm certain of that, at least.

Vivie's eyes fasten sternly on her mother as the significance of this flashes on her.

VIVIE [*slowly*] You are certain of that, at least. Ah! You mean that

that is all you are certain of. [*Thoughtfully*] I see. [*Mrs Warren buries her face in her hands*]. Dont do that, mother: you know you dont feel it a bit. [*Mrs Warren takes down her hands and looks up deplorably at Vivie, who takes out her watch and says*] Well, that is enough for tonight. At what hour would you like breakfast? Is half-past eight too early for you?

MRS WARREN [*wildly*] My God, what sort of woman are you?

VIVIE [*coolly*] The sort the world is mostly made of, I should hope. Otherwise I dont understand how it gets its business done. Come [*taking her mother by the wrist, and pulling her up pretty resolutely*]: pull yourself together. Thats right.

MRS WARREN [*querulously*] Youre very rough with me, Vivie.

VIVIE. Nonsense. What about bed? It's past ten.

MRS WARREN [*passionately*] Whats the use of my going to bed? Do you think I could sleep?

VIVIE. Why not? I shall.

MRS WARREN. You! youve no heart. [*She suddenly breaks out vehemently in her natural tongue—the dialect of a woman of the people—with all her affectations of maternal authority and conventional manners gone, and an overwhelming inspiration of true conviction and scorn in her*] Oh, I wont bear it: I wont put up with the injustice of it. What right have you to set yourself up above me like this? You boast of what you are to me—to me, who gave you the chance of being what you are. What chance had I? Shame on you for a bad daughter and a stuck-up prude!

VIVIE [*sitting down with a shrug, no longer confident; for her replies, which have sounded sensible and strong to her so far, now begin to ring rather woodenly and even priggishly against the new tone of her mother*] Dont think for a moment I set myself above you in any way. You attacked me with the conventional authority of a mother: I defended myself with the conventional superiority of a respectable woman. Frankly, I am not going to stand any of your nonsense; and when you drop it I shall not expect you to stand any of mine. I shall always respect your right to your own opinions and your own way of life.

MRS WARREN. My own opinions and my own way of life! Listen to her talking! Do you think I was brought up like you? able to pick and choose my own way of life? Do you think I did what I did because I liked it, or thought it right, or wouldnt rather have gone to college and been a lady if I'd had the chance?

VIVIE. Everybody has some choice, mother. The poorest girl alive may not be able to choose between being Queen of England or Principal of Newnham; but she can choose between ragpicking and flowerselling, according to her taste. People are always blaming their circumstances for what they are. I dont believe in circumstances. The people who get on in this world are the people who get up and look for the circumstances they want, and, if they cant find them, make them.

MRS WARREN. Oh, it's easy to talk, very easy, isnt it? Here! would you like to know what my circumstances were?

VIVIE. Yes: you had better tell me. Wont you sit down?

MRS WARREN. Oh, I'll sit down: dont you be afraid. [*She plants her chair farther forward with brazen energy, and sits down. Vivie is impressed in spite of herself*]. D'you know what your gran'mother was?

VIVIE. No.

MRS WARREN. No you dont. I do. She called herself a widow and had a fried-fish shop down by the Mint, and kept herself and four daughters out of it. Two of us were sisters: that was me and Liz; and we were both good-looking and well made. I suppose our father was a well-fed man: mother pretended he was a gentleman; but I dont know. The other two were only half sisters: undersized, ugly, starved looking, hard working, honest poor creatures: Liz and I would have half-murdered them if mother hadnt half-murdered us to keep our hands off them. They were the respectable ones. Well, what did they get by their respectability? I'll tell you. One of them worked in a whitelead factory twelve hours a day for nine shillings a week until she died of lead poisoning. She only expected to get her hands a little paralyzed; but she died. The other was always held up to us as a model because she married a Government laborer in the Deptford victualling yard, and kept his room and the three children neat and tidy on eighteen shillings a week—until he took to drink. That was worth being respectable for, wasn't it?

VIVIE [*now thoughtfully attentive*] Did you and your sister think so?

MRS WARREN. Liz didnt, I can tell you: she had more spirit. We both went to a church school—that was part of the ladylike airs we gave ourselves to be superior to the children that knew nothing and went nowhere—and we stayed there until Liz went out one night and never came back. I know the schoolmistress thought I'd soon follow her example; for the clergyman was always warning me that Lizzie'd end up by jumping off Waterloo Bridge. Poor fool: that was all he knew about it! But I was more afraid of the whitelead factory than I was of the river; and so would you have been in my place. That clergyman got me a situation as scullery maid in a temperance restaurant where they sent out for anything you liked. Then I was waitress; and then I went to the bar at Waterloo station: fourteen hours a day serving drinks and washing glasses for four shillings a week and my board. That was considered a great promotion for me. Well, one cold, wretched night, when I was so tired and I could hardly keep myself awake, who should come up for a half of Scotch but Lizzie, in a long fur cloak, elegant and comfortable, with a lot of sovereigns in her purse.

VIVIE [*grimly*] My aunt Lizzie!

MRS WARREN. Yes; and a very good aunt to have, too. She's living down at Winchester now, close to the cathedral, one of the most respectable ladies there. Chaperones girls at the county ball, if you please. No river for Liz, thank you! You remind me of Liz a little: she was a first-rate business woman—saved money from the beginning—never let herself look too like what she was—never lost her head or threw away a chance. When she saw I'd grown up good-looking she said to me across the bar "What are you doing there, you little fool? wearing out your health and your appearance for other people's profit!" Liz was saving money then to take a house for herself in Brussels; and she thought we two could save faster than one. So she lent me some money and gave me a start; and I saved steadily and first paid her back, and then went into business with her as her partner. Why shouldnt I have done it? The house in Brussels was real high class: a much better place for a woman to be in than the factory where Anne Jane got poisoned. None of our girls were ever treated as I was treated in the scullery of that temperance place, or at the Waterloo bar, or at home. Would you have had me stay in them and become a worn out old drudge before I was forty?

VIVIE [*intensely interested by this time*] No; but why did you choose that business? Saving money and good management will succeed in any business.

MRS WARREN. Yes, saving money. But where can a woman get the money to save in any other business? Could you save out of four shillings a week and keep yourself dressed as well? Not you. Of course, if youre a plain woman and cant earn anything more; or if you have a turn for music, or the stage, or newspaper-writing: thats different. But neither Liz nor I had any turn for such things: all we had was our appearance and our turn for pleasing men. Do you think we were such fools as to let other people trade in our good looks by employing us as shopgirls, or barmaids, or waitresses, when we could trade in them ourselves and get all the profits instead of starvation wages? Not likely.

VIVIE. You were certainly quite justified—from the business point of view.

MRS WARREN. Yes; or any other point of view. What is any respectable girl brought up to do but to catch some rich man's fancy and get the benefit of his money by marrying him?—as if a marriage ceremony could make any difference in the right or wrong of the thing! Oh, the hypocrisy of the world makes me sick! Liz and I had to work and save and calculate just like other people; elseways we should be as poor as any good-for-nothing drunken waster of a woman that thinks her luck will last for ever. [*With great energy*] I despise such people: theyve no character; and if theres a thing I hate in a woman, it's want of character.

VIVIE. Come now, mother: frankly! Isnt it part of what you call character in a woman that she should greatly dislike such a way of making money?

MRS WARREN. Why, of course. Everybody dislikes having to work and make money; but they have to do it all the same. I'm sure Ive often pitied a poor girl, tired out and in low spirits, having to try to please some man that she doesnt care two straws for—some half-drunken fool that thinks he's making himself agreeable when he's teasing and worrying and disgusting a woman so that hardly any money could pay her for putting up with it. But she has to bear with disagreeables and take the rough with the smooth, just like a nurse in a hospital or anyone else. It's not work that any woman would do for pleasure, goodness knows; though to hear the pious people talk you would suppose it was a bed of roses.

VIVIE. Still, you consider it worth while. It pays.

MRS WARREN. Of course it's worth while to a poor girl, if she can resist temptation and is good-looking and well conducted and sensible. It's far better than any other employment open to her. I always thought that oughtnt to be. It cant be right, Vivie, that there shouldnt be better opportunities for women. I stick to that: it's wrong. But it's so, right or wrong; and a girl must make the best of it. But of course it's not worth while for a lady. If you took to it youd be a fool; but I should have been a fool if I'd taken to anything else.

VIVIE [*more and more deeply moved*] Mother: suppose we were both as poor as you were in those wretched old days, are you quite sure that you wouldnt advise me to try the Waterloo bar, or marry a laborer, or even go into the factory?

MRS WARREN [*indignantly*] Of course not. What sort of mother do you take me for! How could you keep your self-respect in such starvation and slavery? And whats a woman worth? whats life worth? without self-respect! Why am I independent and able to give my daughter a first-rate education, when other women that had just as good opportunities are in the gutter? Because I always knew how to respect myself and control myself. Why is Liz looked up to in a cathedral town? The same reason. Where would we be now if we'd minded the clergyman's foolishness? Scrubbing floors for one and sixpence a day and nothing to look forward to but the workhouse infirmary. Dont you be led astray by people who dont know the world, my girl. The only way for a woman to provide for herself decently is for her to be good to some man that can afford to be good to her. If she's in his own station of life, let her make him marry her; but if she's far beneath him she cant expect it: why should she? it wouldnt be for her own happiness. Ask any lady in London society that has daughters; and she'll tell you the same, except that I tell you straight and she'll tell you crooked. Thats all the difference.

VIVIE [*fascinated, gazing at her*] My dear mother: you are a wonderful woman: you are stronger than all England. And are you really and truly not one wee bit doubtful—or—or—ashamed?

MRS WARREN. Well, of course, dearie, it's only good manners to be ashamed of it: it's expected from a woman. Women have to pretend to feel a great deal that they dont feel. Liz used to be angry with me for plumping out the truth about it. She used to say that when every woman could learn enough from what was going on in the world before her eyes, there was no need to talk about it to her. But then Liz was such a perfect lady! She had the true instinct of it; while I was always a bit of a vulgarian. I used to be so pleased when you sent me your photos to see that you were growing up like Liz: youve just her ladylike, deter-mined way. But I cant stand saying one thing when everyone knows I mean another. Whats the use in such hypocrisy? If people arrange the world that way for women, theres no good pretending it's arranged the other way. No: I never was a bit ashamed really. I consider I had a right to be proud of how we managed everything so respectably, and never had a word against us, and how the girls were so well taken care of. Some of them did very well: one of them married an ambassador. But of course now I darent talk about such things: whatever would they think of us! [*She yawns*]. Oh dear! I do believe I'm getting sleepy after all. [*She stretches herself lazily, thoroughly relieved by her explosion, and placidly ready for her night's rest*].

VIVIE. I believe it is I who will not be able to sleep now. [*She goes to the dresser and lights the candle. Then she extinguishes the lamp, dark-ening the room a good deal*]. Better let in some fresh air before locking up. [*She opens the cottage door, and finds that it is broad moonlight*]. What a beautiful night! Look! [*She draws aside the curtains of the win-dow. The landscape is seen bathed in the radiance of the harvest moon rising over Blackdown*].

MRS WARREN [*with a perfunctory glance at the scene*] Yes, dear; but take care you dont catch your death of cold from the night air.

VIVIE [*contemptuously*] Nonsense.

MRS WARREN [querulously] Oh yes: everything I say is nonsense, according to you.

VIVIE [*turning to her quickly*] No: really that is not so, mother. You have got completely the better of me tonight, though I intended it to be the other way. Let us be good friends now.

MRS WARREN [*shaking her head a little ruefully*] So it has been the other way. But I suppose I must give in to it. I always got the worst of it from Liz; and now I suppose it'll be the same with you.

VIVIE. Well, never mind. Come: goodnight, dear old mother. [*She takes her mother in her arms*].

MRS WARREN [*fondly*] I brought you up well, didnt I, dearie?

VIVIE. You did.

MRS WARREN. And youll be good to your poor old mother for it, wont you?

VIVIE. I will, dear. [*Kissing her*] Goodnight.

MRS WARREN [*with unction*] Blessings on my own dearie darling! a mother's blessing!

She embraces her daughter protectingly, instinctively looking upward for divine sanction.

The Invisible Bar

Caroline Bird

A woman is systematically discouraged from pursuing a career. It begins in her babyhood, when she is dressed differently from boy babies to emphasize her "prettiness" (though the sex of most babies in diapers is difficult to distinguish). It continues in her childhood (e.g., she gets as presents dishes, stoves, vacuum sweepers, ironing boards and irons, dolls and doll cribs), and is firmly established in high school when she realizes that attracting men and, eventually, a husband, is her life's business. In a status-oriented culture, she rarely succeeds in the business and professional world and, if she does, pays a heavy emotional price. The following chapter from Caroline Bird's Born Female *discusses the problems confronting the ambitious and intelligent woman who desires such success.*

A young wife carrying her first unborn child may privately hope for a boy, since traditionally the world has honored the mothers of men. But if her baby turns out to be a girl, she adjusts very fast. An infant girl can be a lot of fun. You tie a pink bow in her hair—if she has anything more than a fuzz to tie it on—and ruffle and beribbon her pretty bassinet. When she starts to toddle, you put her in filmy dresses and flowery aprons. You brush her hair until it gleams like silk and buy her soft dolls so that she can play Mother. When she grows up, she will marry and have babies of her own to cherish, perhaps more pleasures and happinesses than you, and more luxuries, too, because the man she marries will . . .

But our girl baby must first grow up. Despite her mother's leanings to frills and ruffles, the toddler packs mud pies side-by-side with boys, and pumps on swings as zestfully as boys, and fights boys stubbornly for the vacant swing when she must. She pedals her tricycle as fast as she can, just like the boys, and she may organize the neighborhood group that includes both boys and girls. She wears shorts, like boys, although more brightly colored, and snowsuits and jeans, like boys. She climbs trees and bruises her knees, like boys.

A small girl learns by the time she is two or three that she is a girl. The nursery books that mother reads her tell what girls are like and what they do. Girls are mommies. Girls are nurses. Mommies care for children. Nurses are helpers. They help men, and doctors are men. The books do not show girl scientists. They don't show sisters leading brothers. They don't show girls making discoveries, creating inventions, making important decisions that others of both sexes follow. Experts tell us children live up to the unspoken expectations of parents. Girls are encouraged to be clean, neat, tender little charmers, while boys are expected to be physically active, exploratory, rebellious, and noisy. Boys must be physically competent. They don't have to be talkers.

But from nursery school on up, we educate girls equally with boys. Girls sit in the same classes and learn the same subjects at the same time from the same teachers. And until almost the end of high school, girls make better grades than boys and respond at least as enthusiastically to challenges. At ten a girl may outswim a boy her age and dream of scubadiving to the bottom of the sea, paradiving through space, and penetrating the heavens as an astronomer.

Sometime in high school a girl learns, often poignantly, that class honors are fine, but attracting the boys is what counts with her peers. The message comes over from other girls even more loudly and clearly than it does from boys. Many girls read it and cash in their aspirations. They may go on to college for more education "for oneself," but the real business of life is attracting a desirable husband. "I've never talked vocation to Mary," the mother of a pretty high-school senior said. "Her father wants a four-year education for her, not an eight- or twelve-year one he'll have to pay for. And as a mother," she added feelingly, "I believe the real vocation for a woman is marriage."

Even if a girl tries for a professional career she may be actively discouraged. Educators hold vocational guidance counselors responsible for the scandalous waste of talent, and they indignantly circulate anecdotes to prove it. One story alleges that the first woman engineering student to enroll at Detroit's Institute of Technology in ten years arrived because of a clerical error. When Thelma Lowe, an attractive Negro, was in eighth grade she was assigned to a drafting class by mistake. She did so well at it, however, that her guidance counselor then guided her into a pre-engineering course. Later, her younger sister studied mechanical engineering at Wayne State University.

In the 1960s guidance counselors were urged to encourage adolescent girls toward careers. The counselors were told to be positive. Instead of saying, "Have you thought how you would manage to do that if you had children?" they were instructed to say, "Veterinary practice is a good field for a woman, because she can carry it on near her home." A girl who had a reasonably enlightened high-school counselor might not even realize that she had to get much higher marks than a boy to get into a coed college. But the closer she approached paying work, the more she was slowed by the unspoken assumption that a woman really could not be serious about a vocation but must be working to mark time, earn a little money, or if she were obviously gifted, "just for fun." This is the Invisible Bar that keeps women down.

The Invisible Bar is unofficial. It is effective because almost everyone accepts it. Officially, graduate and professional schools invite women to apply. In private, their administrators deplore wasting facilities on women who marry and do not use their educations, but "throw it away to get married and have babies." Dr. Milton Eisenhower, President of Johns Hopkins University, once figured that it cost $200,000 to train every practicing woman biologist. He arrived at this high figure by charging the cost of educating all female biologists against those few who went on to lifetime careers.

In 1966, the dean of a leading Eastern law school confided to a nationally known woman leader that his school would admit more women if the big law firms would hire them. The story puzzled Seth Taft, who recruits law school graduates for the leading law firm in Cleveland. "I don't think we're biased against women," he said. "It's just that we don't see very many who come even close to our standards."

Girls who go to women's colleges sometimes crash unexpectedly on the Invisible Bar when they look for their first jobs. "Men don't have to type and take dictation to earn a chance to begin learning!" a Vassar graduate wrote her English professor after making the rounds of employment offices in New York. Employers seem equally dismayed. They don't always know what to do with college girls. Big companies give a Princeton senior who has majored in English an aptitude test to see where he might fit, but give a Vassar senior who has majored in English a typing test. If she demurs, they complain that liberal arts colleges simply don't prepare girls for business. "Show me the girl with a bachelor's degree in engineering from M.I.T. and a master's in business administration from Harvard, and I'll show you how much discrimination there is against women!" Bennett Kline, a management consultant, challenged a 1966 symposium, sponsored by Teachers College, Columbia, on opportunities for women executives.

Pursuing Mr. Kline's suggestion, we talked with a half-dozen women Harvard MBAs. None of them wished to be quoted. "The company recruiters were as surprised to see us as your Mr. Kline," one of them said. In 1963, women were admitted directly to the Harvard Business School in equal competition with men applicants for the first time. Before that, a few had been allowed to take the second year of the course at Harvard after completing a Radcliffe course especially designed for women. When the company recruiters came shopping for talent in 1965, they found eleven women among the hardy survivors of the two-year "B School" obstacle course.

The B School makes no compromises. It proudly avoids teaching students how to do any job below that of president of a big company. And like such a president, the students learn the hard way. They are given long, noncommittal fact-packed accounts of real companies. With no clue from the teacher, they diagnose the problems they see and recommend action. They dig for answers in books, talk out ideas with each other, and work at devising solutions until the small hours of the morning. In class, each student tries to sell his recommendation in a two-minute talk to a hundred fellow students.

"At Wellesley, the pressure came from the teachers," one of the pioneer women MBAs said. "At Harvard, it came from your fellow students." The girls reported that classroom discussions were conducted with the sharp, impersonal, but courteous manners of the best big-business executives. All the women said that they were scrupulously treated as equals in the nonstop "bull" sessions which are a B School tradition. They got their trial by fire from the company recruiters. But they gave as good as they got.

"Harvard makes the recruiters see any member of the graduating class who requests an interview," one of the pioneer women MBAs of 1965 pointed out. "We took the chance to probe the policies of companies which notoriously don't hire women who can't type. No one could say we were not prepared. No one could say we were not serious about business. Some of us had borrowed to meet the $8,000 cost of the course. So we were a perfect test case for sex discrimination. One recruiter finally broke down and blurted out that his company did not have any woman higher than a secretary, and furthermore his management didn't *want* any woman higher than a secretary."

The girls compared notes on their interviews in order to rate companies on their attitudes toward women executives. They were offered jobs, but they did not average as many offers as the men in the class, and they had trouble getting the jobs they wanted. Marketing majors wanted to be product managers, the executives who have responsibility for the success of a product. Some recruiters frankly told them to forget it.

"You'd have to get out in the field to become a product manager," one of them objected.

The girl he was interviewing said she was willing to travel.

"But you'd have to lug heavy cartons around!" the recruiter argued. She reluctantly settled for the only job he offered—research.

Another girl took a job market-testing brassieres and quickly moved up to brassiere product manager. "The idea was that I would have a big advantage because I could march into a fitting room with a tape measure over my shoulder," she said. "But when you get into management, you sort of lose the consumer point of view."

When a representative from an advertising agency tried to sell one of the girls on a job in market research, she coolly asked him why the job was open. "The woman we had in it left," the recruiter told her. "She wanted to do account work and we don't feel our clients will accept a woman account executive." The girl didn't take the job.

Recruiters wanted to know whether the girls planned to marry. "They'd never have believed me if I had said 'No,' " one attractive young graduate told us. "So I always told them 'Of course,' even though I had no plans at the time. Then they'd want to know if I was planning to have children, and I'd say, 'Not immediately.' " Several of the girls married fellow B School graduates. Most of them got to do "men's jobs" in leading companies, and their record of return to work after babies has been good. These girls demonstrated that a well-prepared, self-confident young woman didn't really have to start out in business as a secretary.

Jane Johnson, Director of Vassar's Vocational Bureau, advises girls not to learn shorthand. She warns that a bright girl who can take dictation is such a rare treasure that she may never get to do anything else. In order to get a start in merchandising, for instance, Mildred Custin, President of Bonwit Teller, ran a Christmas gift department while continuing to do the secretarial work of an officer of the store.

Other successful women have taken equally heroic measures to get out of the secretarial rut. Some of them have quietly taken on extra work until they have created a job that obviously required a title. Twenty years ago Virginia Culver was a secretary helping her boss keep tabs on the credit cards Signal Oil and Gas Company sometimes issued. Now that credit has become away of life, the Credit Card Department of the company is a sizable outfit, and she's its Collection Manager. Jan Knoop, Director of Research at the Colorado Association of Commerce and Industry in Denver, made her present job by digging out information to help her boss answer complicated questions from association members when she was his secretary.

Women assistants often get valuable professional experience. The first magazine article the author ever wrote for print appeared in *Fortune* magazine where she was an editorial researcher. When the writer for whom she was researching a story quit in the middle of it, the editor of the issue asked her to try her hand at writing it. She did, and it ran. The editor happened to be John Kenneth Galbraith. Years later, she wrote an unashamedly adoring profile of him for *Esquire*.

But hard work and real contribution haven't always been enough. The moment comes when a woman has to refuse a dead-end job. Kay Moore, a successful stockbroker in Cleveland, once bargained with a boss who wanted her to learn how to run a Teletype machine. "I'll learn to run that machine," she offered, "provided you let me hire all the people who will ever use it." The deal gave her experience in personnel work and left her free to advance.

In order to get ahead women have frequently had to quit secretarial jobs, conceal their talent for shorthand, and start out all over again, often at lower pay. Roberta J. Berkel, one of the first women branch managers of a major New York City bank, took a cut in salary to become a platform assistant at Chemical Bank New York Trust in 1959. Mary Stewart of San Francisco stuck it out as a secretary for twelve years. Then she took the examination for Certified Professional Secretary given by the National Secretaries Association. Notification that she had passed was sent to her boss, Chief Estimator in a construction company. "I suppose this means you want more money," he said.

"No, I've never asked for a raise and I'm not going to start now," she said. She was already getting top pay for a secretary and knew she could not do any other job in that organization. But she was able to use her

"CPS" (Certified Professional Secretary) in lieu of a master's degree in business education to get a job with International Business Machines helping set up customer-training programs.

Women in high-level jobs advertise their lack of secretarial skills to avoid being pressed into secretarial service. The fear is not groundless. Once a woman is cornered, heroic defense measures may be needed. "They tried it only once," a fiery Irish woman engineer in a West Coast space research company told us. "They asked me to take notes at a conference—and I did!" Instead of transcribing the long-winded and inconclusive discussion, she wrote an analysis of the meeting with critical comments of her own, such as "Target Date: None" and "Action Required: Policy Definition." None of the men involved was willing ever to risk letting her take the minutes of a meeting again. A gentler woman, now vice-president of a Los Angeles bank, confided that the president sometimes forgot her present title and asked her to do the little chores she used to do in the days when she was a secretary. She does them, but she sometimes signs her covering notes, "Your Slave."

Many high career hopes are shot down by a dead-end first job, but women encounter far more frustration of this sort than men. "If we had wanted a woman, we would have advertised for a woman," a girl was told when she tried to apply for a job listed in the Help Wanted, Male column of the newspaper. She explained she had applied under the impression that Title VII required employers to consider applicants of either sex. But even women who have managed to get jobs leading to promotion find that it is hard to realize the potential.

It takes training and experience to move out of the bull pen, and big companies have just begun to open these essential areas to women. After Title VII, some management training squads accepted women, but they were still rare enough to warrant newspaper attention. Women were more likely to teach trainees than to be trainees. We found women who were skilled in processing claims against insurance companies forced to train young men for the management jobs they should have had. Some of these teachers had "brought up" several of their own bosses. In one telephone company, customer service representatives drew an extra fifty cents a day for "having a student," but none could recall a management trainee "student" who was born female.

Ambitious men get experience and a chance to show what they can do by taking on extra work, but if it requires a trip outside the office or staying after hours, an employer often hesitates to ask a young woman to do it. In 1966, a 25-year-old customer service representative charged the Southern Bell Telephone Company with discrimination for refusing to let her sell coin-operated phones in commercial locations even though she had come out first on the tests for the job. The company contended that the work wasn't suitable for a woman because it required going into "all kinds of places." The EEOC disagreed. "The respondent's arguments sound like those used by Arabs to keep their women indoors or behind veils," the investigator snapped.

But the principal reason women aren't considered for promotion is that managers assume they aren't serious about working. If a woman wants to advance, she has to ask for a better job, and she has to ask in a way that won't arouse antagonism—or ridicule. There is something irresistibly funny to men about a woman doing a "man's job." Newspapers endlessly feature women in unexpected jobs under cute headlines:

YOUNG WOMAN FINDS HER PLACE IN BARBER SHOP.
PHONE GIRL SUITS UP FOR A MAN'S JOB.
SHE'S ALL ALONE IN MAN'S WORLD OF TOOLS AND DIES.

A girl who asks for a "man's job" can expect ribbing along this line in her office. During World War II, a woman who was actually supervising a bull pen of layout artists asked for the title of Director. Her boss just laughed. "We can't have a lady pitcher on the ball team," he told her.

Women aren't brought up to assert themselves, but a man expects to fight his way to the top. The system is designed to fit his reproductive cycle, not hers. During his career-building twenties and thirties a man's career and sex drive reinforce each other, but a career-committed woman has to be aggressive in her work just at the time of her life when she is engaged in finding a mate and bearing and raising young children. Moreover, everywhere she turns she sees sex portrayed as a woman's only value. The questions raised are how much she wants it, whether she looks as if she enjoys it. Career ambitions figure as a side issue, an extra: some men like the idea that the girl of their dreams is smart "too."

In 1967, newspaper columnist Flora Lewis got a man to define "femininity." "It's looking pretty and elegant," he began. "And it's being nice, not arguing with men or nagging or complaining, or having different opinions. Not pushing them, or interfering or anything, not wanting to get their own way instead of doing what they're told. I would say it's wanting to please a man all the time." A girl who wants to get out of the bull pen has to be assertive in the office and seductively submissive when husband-hunting after five. It can be done, but it isn't as easy as television, films, advertising, and women's magazines airily pretend.

When a girl marries, the problem simply takes another form. The energy that used to go into dating now goes into building a marriage around two careers, while back at the office it is necessary to convince the boss that her husband isn't going to move her out of town. Will she have a baby? The office waits to see before giving her more responsibility, even though she is ready for it. The women Harvard MBAs reported that their employers stopped worrying once they had had a baby and come back. Some didn't think a girl should wait too long. Others said it depended on the boss and the job.

In the past, women who had their babies and their jobs too were resented with special vehemence by spinsters who grew up at a time when marriage and career were mutually exclusive. Young women sometimes return to work after having a baby only to find that their employers don't treat them seriously as career workers any more.

A career woman who has survived the hurdle of marriage and maternity encounters a new obstacle: the hostility of men. When she was younger, men in the office liked to help her: a bright girl is usually attractive and fun to have around. But as she grows older, and particularly as she begins to exercise authority, she mobilizes the resentment men harbor against the women who disciplined them when they were boys. Sometimes they strike out against a woman colleague on the basis of her sex. Some men claim that they can tell when a woman colleague is having a menstrual period. One actually boasted that he kept a calendar to avoid riling a key woman "on those days." And if a woman is beyond "those days," she can be accused of causing trouble because she is "going through the change."

A woman who presses her case for promotion risks reprisal. "She's an aggressive woman, and I don't like to deal with aggressive women," an executive told an EEOC investigator in 1966. A secretary who wanted a chance at a technical writing job had filed a charge of discrimination under Title VII when she wasn't considered for it.

"How do you feel about aggressive men?" the mediator asked the company executive.

"That's okay," he answered. In his book, men could be aggressive but women couldn't.

When Garda Bowman, now a personnel consultant, was interviewing executives for her doctoral dissertation on the business image of a promotable person, she uncovered a great deal of hostility against women in business. "Some women are married to their jobs instead of their husbands," a bank officer told her.

"A woman's emotions take over," another man said, adding that when responsibilities pile up, the most ferocious "female kitten of management" reverts to the role of "purring, whimpering kitten, who seeks the protection of her male master." Most of the male executives Dr. Bowman queried told her that women were "temperamentally unfit for management," but three-quarters of the women in executive positions whom she interviewed disagreed.

The criticism troubles women executives. "You have to walk on eggs," one of them told us. Some of them deliberately throttle their emotions. "When I started working on a newspaper, we had a man who used to get so mad at people he was interviewing that he once tore the telephone right out of the wall and threw it across the room," said Llewellyn Miller, a magazine writer, recalling the time when she was a drama critic for a Los Angeles newspaper. "Everybody admired his manly anger. But I used to wonder what would happen if I had tried anything like that. In order to avoid criticism, I was careful never to raise my voice."

Fear of looking aggressive deters many women from seeking promotions due them. "I suppose I could be a branch manager if I really wanted the job," Kay Lewis, assistant vice president for personnel at the Crocker National Bank in San Francisco, told us. "But then I would have to call up perfectly strange men and invite them to lunch." Women in public relations in New York City, where expense accounts are common, have no such inhibitions, but in other fields and other cities it is not so easy for a woman to do. Some arrange with the headwaiter to hold the bill, or use credit cards. But even where women are accustomed to taking the initiative, they are not expected to run up the expense accounts permitted men in the same jobs. It is notoriously cheaper to maintain a woman on the road than a man, and economy is one reason why women have an easier time getting jobs requiring travel in small and marginal enterprises.

Women in executive positions try to ward off hostility by phrasing their orders as suggestions and "planting" ideas in the heads of associates in the hope that they will accept them as their own. They talk a great deal about maintaining their "femininity" and never forgetting that they are women. Many women sign their business letters with initials to avoid calling attention to their sex.

A retiring manner may disarm hostility, but it does not always ward off criticism. A woman who deliberately cultivated a quiet style complained to us that a man who was assigned to her department assured associates that she was "too reticent to toot her own horn." He made it sound like loyal defense, but the president of the company got the message: "This woman is too reticent to toot the company's horn in public."

Really successful women say that it doesn't always pay to pussyfoot— at least all the time. Women bank officers, stockbrokers, lawyers, doctors, engineers, and executives all recall confrontations with men bosses or associates. Men test each other's intentions all the time. It is the "game." If a woman shows she is willing to play it, they accept her. Bea Hicks, president of her own Newark Controls Company, realized this when she went to work, during World War II, as an engineer at Western Electric, an organization which had not theretofore employed women in that capacity. An associate was frankly skeptical. He gave her an electronic part with which they were having difficulty, and asked to redesign it.

"The design's no good," he grunted when she brought him her solution to the problem.

"Try it," she challenged. He did, and it worked. "That broke the ice," she recalls. "From then on out, I think he actually thought I was better than I was."

Women who survive the competition for positions of authority face new problems. Every responsible manager, man or woman, needs support from above and below, access to information, broad experience outside the immediate organization, and the self-confidence to make decisions. Leaders must be recognized as leaders so that others will follow them. To that end, the Army puts bars on a lieutenant's shoulders. Civilian organizations label leaders by giving them titles, decorated offices, secretarial help, pay, and above all, authentic information. All organizations resist giving these perquisites to women. Almost every sizable organization has some women exercising authority on an informal and undefined basis.

It is much harder for a woman to get the title than the work. When women were promoted during World War II, they were generally called "acting manager" or "acting head." This form is still used to identify a woman's role for a specific occasion without conferring a permanent rank. Secretaries who take on projects of their own are sometimes allowed to sign as "assistants," so that they can engage in direct correspondence with outsiders. A woman who has written many letters to collect past-due accounts was allowed to sign as "collection manager" for years on an unofficial basis. She was given the title formally only when an outside job evaluation of the entire organization disclosed that she was, in fact, carrying the responsibility that warranted the title.

"When I applied for my present job, I was told that I would be an assistant bookkeeper," a California woman told us. "I didn't want to work directly under anyone, so I asked whom I would assist. The man interviewing me couldn't think who it would be. He just looked embarrassed. I took the job, managed the books, and got raises, but it would have been easier to deal with outsiders if I had been able to identify myself as the bookkeeper in charge, which of course I really was."

Because most women work in subordinate positions, those who have responsibility need status symbols to mark their authority more urgently than men. If a woman is at all young and unassuming, she runs the risk of being taken for an assistant with no authority of her own. "Most people around here are used to me by now," Anita Best, personnel services representative of Chrysler Corporation, Chemical Division, told

The Detroit News in 1967, "but there are still times when an employee I approach thinks I'm a secretary and wants to talk to my boss."

In retailing, where there are many women at all levels, executives sometimes signal their status by wearing hats. In journalism it sometimes works the other way: when *Fortune* magazine formally requested women researchers to wear hats when interviewing business leaders, the order was quietly defied. "If you wear a hat, they'll think you are somebody's secretary," one of the researchers complained.

Women sometimes find it hard to get their names on company letterheads, or to obtain business cards of their own. In some big companies with several lunchrooms, women promoted to executive rank are discouraged from using the executive dining room unless they have visitors to entertain. At one automobile company, the first woman engineer was asked not to have herself paged over the public address system because secretaries hearing a woman's name might think that a secretary had been granted this privilege and demand it for themselves. In another company, women were not allowed to park as near the building as the men.

Women are not assigned secretaries as readily as men doing the same work, and for the sake of appearances some fake secretarial initials on the lower left margin of the letters they type themselves. "They think that because you are a woman, of course you can type," one woman told us. More than status is at stake when a professional woman is expected to serve as her own secretary. She loses time, as well as prestige.

Women notoriously resent working for women, but even when the relationship is pleasant, a woman seldom gets as much help from her secretary as a man gets from his. She isn't as willing to do personal errands for a woman boss as for a supposedly helpless man. Older women sometimes think that girls prefer to work for men because they have more chance to meet eligible bachelors, but the situation is more involved. Girls resent the discipline of their mothers even more than boys, and perhaps are less willing than men to accept women supervisors. Young secretaries sometimes think their women bosses are jealous of their youth and looks, but the problem often stems from the older woman's sense of sex betrayal: "I suffer because you are flighty," she thinks to herself. The office politics of women working for women is further complicated by the attitude of the men. Many of them expect women to bicker with each other.

Hostility and denial of status are trying to an ambitious woman, but denial of office information is fatal. In our culture, men come to women for personal sympathy, but they do not talk shop with them because they think women "would not understand." Men flout rules of the organization chart and bypass women bosses as a matter of natural right. Sometimes a woman boss is frankly told that it would be humiliating for a man to report to her. Usually she isn't told. Some time ago a woman public relations director was authorized to hire a man to assist her. When she resigned from her job to start her own business, her male assistant took her out to lunch to celebrate. After a few drinks he became confidential. "Now that you are leaving, I am going to tell you something that I know but that you don't," he said. "I know your salary, but you don't know mine." When he correctly quoted hers at $10,000 a year and claimed his own was $12,000, she realized that he was right. Although she knew the salaries of all the women working for her she had never been told his.

Home economists in business complain that the men in their companies expect them to promote products to women by implying that women have had a hand in developing them, when in fact they often have not been told about them in time to influence their design.

In some companies, women vice presidents are either not invited to meetings attended by all the men vice presidents, or they are expected to confine their advice to issues affecting women customers or employees. "They go to lunch to tell the men about a change in policy," a woman promotion director complained, "but they send me memos. When you get a memo, you can't answer back. And you don't like to run in to someone else's office to ask questions, so if you don't understand it, you just sit and wonder what it means." A highly placed woman executive in a nonprofit organization, who should have been in on board meetings, confessed that she was forced to listen through a ventilator to find out what was being planned at these sessions from which she was excluded only "because women had never attended."

Some men hate to fire a woman, so they freeze her out with silence. An art director once sat without work for months. Finally she was told there was no room for her and she was moved with her drawing board to the accounting department. All this time the other artists in the bull pen were working day and night. Every once in a while she would tiptoe in and ask them if there wasn't something she could do to help. They would always say, "No, nothing." She stuck it out until a change in the organization put her in charge of the young men who had tried to scare her into quitting.

The technique was used with more success on a woman who worked for a travel agency. She discovered, by accident, that her reports to headquarters were being thrown in the wastebasket, unread, by a man who had been told that she would soon be replaced. Her letters were not answered. She was not invited to meetings. She was given no assignments. After sticking it out for a few months, she quit and started a travel agency of her own.

There are, of course, exceptional cases. Most men have been taught as boys that it is wrong to take advantage of the weakness of a rival, particularly if the rival is a woman. The silent treatment is one of the few weapons most men feel comfortable using against her. More commonly, men simply leave out the women in the organization as a matter of course. Like waiters in a restaurant, they are present but not recognized. "I might as well be a walnut desk," a woman invited to committee meetings in a civic organization complained. "They don't want to hear what I say, so I don't speak."

Women so rarely attend some meetings that their presence is often ignored both socially and physically. Some have been roomed in with men or mistaken for wives. Virginia Sink, an engineer at Chrysler, had to ask men colleagues to stand watch at the men's room that was provided for engineering meetings, while she used it, because there was no ladies' room.

Policy is literally made in rooms officially closed to women. In law and brokerage firms, important decisions such as bonus allocations may be made at lunch in a men's club to which a woman with the rank to attend has to be admitted by a side door or up a back stairway.

Women may even be separated from their work. Before 1965, women reporters who had to cover press conferences at the stag National Press Club in Washington were seated in the balcony, where it was harder to hear and ask questions than on the floor where the men sat. The Economic Club of Detroit has barred women from high-level conferences at which national figures have made important policy announcements. The presumption that anyone important enough to attend must be a man hurts policy-making women more than missing the event itself.

Women who pioneered in certain high positions agree that the men who put them there have been nervous about the impression they would create. "My boss went to great lengths to introduce me to everyone I would need to know," one of the young Harvard women recalled. "He was particularly careful to introduce me to the secretaries as 'Mrs.' because they call the men 'Mr.', but I told them later to call me by my first name." She was, of course, a very smart girl.

Extra solicitude does not always make a woman's job easier. "They expect you to fail," an unusually well-qualified and attractive woman told us, describing her induction into a high-level job in a Detroit automobile company. "Everyone around here smokes, drinks, and swears, but they must have figured that a woman lush would have been intolerable. I told them I didn't drink, but even so, they hired a private detective to check on it." She is now one of a handful of women in the company who rank high enough to buy and run a car on favorable terms, charge gas, park in the executive lot, eat in the executive dining room, and get her hair cut (if she wishes) in the executive barbershop.

The first day on the job, her boss hovered over her. "Let me know right away if you have any trouble," he told her. Men colleagues got the idea. "During the first month I went ahead and ordered some booklets reprinted without realizing that I should have taken bids on the printing work. We needed them, and I didn't mind sticking my neck out. The man next to me asked if he could help by explaining my mistake to our boss. I told him not to bother, I'd simply cut the order to the number of booklets we needed on an emergency basis and take bids on the rest. So what did he do? He ran to the head of the department anyway and told him that *he* had thought of this way to help me out of my embarrassment. With friends like that you don't need enemies!"

Work went well, but the tension did not abate. When it came time for personnel reviews, her boss called her in, closed the door, brewed a cup of coffee, and started telling her how hard it was for him to rate people. "I thought at first he was leading up to firing me, and I couldn't imagine why," she told us. "But the trouble was the other way around. I deserved a rating of excellent, but, according to company rules, that rating would entitle me to consideration for the next opening above me. Rather than take the responsibility for forcing a woman on upper management, he had taken the unusual step of asking a vice president whether company policy on equal opportunity for Negroes also applied to women. He had been told to stick to the rules, whatever that meant. So he was going to give me the rating, but he wanted me to know that if I failed on the job in the future, he'd be ruined! Frankly, I hadn't expected such male insecurity in the rough-and-tough automobile industry. But then, I'm not bucking for vice president."

Women who get high enough to buck for vice president of a major organization face so many problems that they frequently decline to run. They know that they will be resented much more deeply than before, and they often have less to gain. The title may not mean as much to a women as to a man. Then, too, women are more likely than men to be gifted people who are working for the stimulation of the work itself. Whatever the explanation, the fact is that many professional women really prefer writing advertising copy to running an advertising agency or working on a research project to the game of grantsmanship that wins the funds for it. Many women would rather teach children than direct other teachers. Many would rather research legal briefs than drum up law business. "We don't want the top," eight well-known journalists and business women chorused cheerfully on the "Today" show of January 10, 1967. "We just want to be near the top and have the fun."

Society doesn't push a woman to succeed as hard as it pushes a man, so it is only natural that women drop out of the rat race more frequently. But even if a woman doesn't try as hard as a man to be a vice president, the fact remains that she encounters a new handicap attributable to her sex if she does try. She has no bargaining power. Unlike the promising men, it isn't as easy for her to back a demand for promotion by threatening to get a job elsewhere. Maude Lennox, one of the most-respected executive recruiters, said that there isn't enough call for women executives to warrant setting up a "Women's Department" in her service. William A. Hertan, President of Executive Manpower Corporation, told a 1966 meeting of American Women in Radio & Television that he had not been asked to fill a single executive job for a woman in ten years. He warned his audience that a woman has to rely on personal friends when she changes jobs, and that most moves by women are lateral, to similar jobs in other organizations, rather than better ones.

Sex prejudice alone does not fully account for the absence of a market for women executives. Women are older than men when they are ready for high-level jobs, simply because their promotions come more slowly. They have fewer years before retirement during which they are eligible for important positions. And while a few gray hairs might enhance the prestige of an impressive man, they seldom improve the business image of a woman. Most women in high-level jobs color their hair.

An equally important handicap is that the experience of most successful women is not transferable because they have so often risen as a result of circumstances peculiar to one organization. A woman lawyer in a city that shall remain nameless rose in her firm as an assistant to a senior partner who had become mentally ill. Although her unusual duties were extremely valuable to this particular firm, her relatively small compensation undoubtedly reflected the narrow market for lawyers who are also psychiatric nurses. The point of this story is that most women are much more valuable to the organizations in which they have risen than they could be anywhere else, so that they find it unprofitable to move even when their employers underpay them.

Successful women have fewer jobs than men who stay in the same field, but in his study of the careers of educated women, Dr. Eli Ginzberg, Hepburn Professor of Economics at the Graduate School of Business, Columbia University, found that women were more apt to change their fields than men. Teachers have done very well in business. Business machine companies hire them for their training programs, and schools are increasingly important to big companies because they are a public relations "audience" which has to be kept informed. Dr. Dorothy Gregg went from the Economics Department of Columbia University to a job promoting "economic education" in the public relations department of U.S. Steel, where she was one of the nine or ten highest-ranking women in the company. Marion Corwell, formerly Associate Director of School Relations in the Dearborn Public Schools, became Educational Affairs Representative on the Public Relations Staff of the Ford Motor Company.

In academic life as elsewhere, rules against nepotism limit professional women and sometimes deprive them of the opportunity to work at all. Men and women meet at work and marry. For a while, both may continue to work on the newspaper or in the same department of a university or on the same hospital staff. But as they rise to positions of power the situation becomes uncomfortable, even if it does not violate specific rules, and it is always the wife who withdraws. Dr. Ginzberg points out that anti-nepotism rules prevent husbands and wives working together as a team. They also work grievous injustice on talented women. Dr. Maria Goeppert Mayer, the only woman since Dr. Marie Curie to win the Nobel Prize in Physics, once worked as a "volunteer associate" at Johns Hopkins in order to keep on doing physics. She could not be paid, because her husband was on the faculty, but the University didn't object to getting her free. "I sensed the resentment of the role of women in American academic life," she says, "so I learned to be inconspicuous."

Women have less bargaining power for top management for another reason, too. They are less secure than men in the jobs they hold. A New York radio station revamping its program schedule started cutting down by firing a woman commentator. "You're the first to go because it's easier to fire a woman than a man," the manager of the station told her pleasantly. They thought they were right to protect the jobs of men. Employers are proud of this policy. In one communications company, every woman above the secretarial level was fired in a general budget cut while men were dropped or retained on the basis of their individual records.

Close to the top, the nature of the competition for advancement changes. No longer can a woman rise on competence alone. A woman can't expect to be "twice as good" as the superior men who are also competing for the top spot, because they're all good. And mere competence is less important. "Face validity"—looking the part of boss—counts more than it does at lower levels. Credibility—the ability to persuade outsiders—counts for more. Self-confidence is more important and much harder to fake. The captain dines alone. Emotional support can no longer come from within the organization. If it is needed, it has to come from home.

All these requirements for a chief executive are harder for women to fulfill than men. Take credibility, for example; it has been proved that most people simply don't believe a woman knows what she is talking about. Jessie Bernard set up an experiment in the Speech Department of Penn State University, where she was teaching sociology, to test it. A man and a woman who were equally good speakers memorized the same lectures and delivered them to different sections of the same course. One of the lectures was on politics, a "masculine" subject, the other on sex differences, a supposedly "feminine" subject. Then students were tested on the contents of the lectures. Both teachers got the information across. Students reproduced the facts equally well. But analysis of semantic clues in the examination papers of the two sections disclosed that the students believed the man more than the woman on both subjects. Student papers contained more "she saids" than "he saids," indicating that they did not necessarily accept the woman's statement. And in class discussions the students indicated that they were more aroused by the man's comments and ideas.

Finally, women are disqualified for many top jobs because they don't have wives. David Riesman, the Harvard sociologist, has said that it is hard to find a woman who can take on the presidency of a college because a president needs a wife to help him. This is true of elective office, most visibly the office of the President of the United States. Professional men, ministers, and ambassadors require home settings that need the services of wives, and they are judged in part on the performance of their wives.

More important even than the services wives render is the climate of acceptance they provide for their husbands. Women need approval as much as men. Those who have real careers are apt to be either single or married to men who are proud of them. But very few men can make a career out of providing an encouraging climate for a woman, and very few women will admit they want such a man. As Riesman has complained, "Our society really isn't set up to be very helpful to women who want to pursue careers rather than jobs."

Fail: Bright Women

Matina Horner

*Matina Horner's article, based on her study at the University of
Michigan, is frightening for several reasons. First, it reveals that
women usually fear and avoid intellectual success, particularly
when that success means competing against men. Men, on the
other hand, thrive on competition, but regard women who succeed as exceptional, over-achievers. Further, it is startling to see
these results, worthy of Victorian attitudes 100 years ago, from a
test conceived and administered in 1969.*

Consider Phil, a bright young college sophomore. He has always done
well in school, he is in the honors program, he has wanted to be a
doctor as long as he can remember. We ask him to tell us a story based
on one clue: "*After first-term finals, John finds himself at the top of
his medical-school class.*" Phil writes:

> John is a conscientious young man who worked hard. He is pleased
> with himself. John has always wanted to go into medicine and is very
> dedicated . . . John continues working hard and eventually graduates
> at the top of his class.

Now consider Monica, another honors student. She too has always
done well and she too has visions of a flourishing career. We give her
the same clue, but with "Anne" as the successful student—*after first-
term finals, Anne finds herself at the top of her medical-school class.*
Instead of identifying with Anne's triumph, Monica tells a bizarre tale:

> Anne starts proclaiming her surprise and joy. Her fellow classmates are
> so disgusted with her behavior that they jump on her in a body and
> beat her. She is maimed for life.

Condensed from *Fail: Bright Women*, PSYCHOLOGY TODAY Magazine, November 1969. Copyright © Communications/Research/Machines, Inc. An expanded version of this article appears in *Feminine Personality* published by
Brooks/Cole Publishing Co., Belmont, California.

Next we ask Monica and Phil to work on a series of achievement tests by themselves. Monica scores higher than Phil. Finally we get them together, competing against each other on the same kind of tests. Phil performs magnificently, but Monica dissolves into a bundle of nerves.

The glaring contrast between the two stories and the dramatic changes in performance in competitive situations illustrate important differences between men and women in reacting to achievement.

In 1953, David McClelland, John Atkinson and colleagues published the first major work on the "achievement motive." Through the use of the Thematic Apperception Test (TAT), they were able to isolate the psychological characteristic of a *need to achieve*. This seemed to be an internalized standard of excellence, motivating the individual to do well in any achievement-oriented situation involving intelligence and leadership ability. Subsequent investigators studied innumerable facets of achievement motivation: how it is instilled in children, how it is expressed, how it relates to social class, even how it is connected to the rise and fall of civilizations. The result of all this research is an impressive and a theoretically consistent body of data about the achievement motive—in men.

Women, however, are conspicuously absent from almost all of the studies. In the few cases where the ladies were included, the results were contradictory or confusing. So women were eventually left out altogether. The predominantly male researchers apparently decided, as Freud had before them, that the only way to understand woman was to turn to the poets. Atkinson's 1958 book, *Motives in Fantasy, Action and Society*, is an 800-page compilation of all of the theories and facts on achievement motivation in men. Women got a footnote, reflecting the state of the science.

To help remedy this lopsided state of affairs, I undertook to explore the basis for sex differences in achievement motivation. But where to begin?

My first clue came from the one consistent finding on the women: they get higher test-anxiety scores than do the men. Eleanor Maccoby has suggested that the girl who is motivated to achieve is defying conventions of what girls "should" do. As a result, the intellectual woman pays a price in anxiety. Margaret Mead concurs, noting that intense intellectual striving can be viewed as "competitively aggressive behavior." And of course Freud thought that the whole essence of femininity lay in repressing aggressiveness (and hence intellectuality).

Thus consciously or unconsciously the girl equates intellectual achievement with loss of femininity. A bright woman is caught in a double bind. In testing and other achievement-oriented situations she worries not only about failure, but also about success. If she fails, she is not living up to her own standards of performance; if she succeeds she is not living up to societal expectations about the female role. Men in our society do not experience this kind of ambivalence, because they are not only permitted but actively encouraged to do well.

For women, then, the desire to achieve is often contaminated by what I call the *motive to avoid success*. I define it as the fear that success in competitive achievement situations will lead to negative consequences, such as unpopularity and loss of femininity. This motive, like the achievement motive itself, is a stable disposition within the person, acquired early in life along with other sex-role standards. When fear of success conflicts with a desire to be successful, the result is an inhibition of achievement motivation.

I began my study with several hypotheses about the motive to avoid success:

1) Of course, it would be far more characteristic of women than of men.

2) It would be more characteristic of women who are capable of success and who are career-oriented than of women not so motivated. Women who are not seeking success should not, after all, be threatened by it.

3) I anticipated that the anxiety over success would be greater in competitive situations (when one's intellectual performance is evaluated against someone else's) than in noncompetitive ones (when one works alone). The aggressive, masculine aspects of achievement striving are certainly more pronounced in competitive settings, particularly when the opponent is male. Women's anxiety should therefore be greatest when they compete with men.

I administered the standard TAT achievement motivation measures to a sample of 90 girls and 88 boys, all undergraduates at the University of Michigan. In addition, I asked each to tell a story based on the clue described before: *After first-term finals, John (Anne) finds himself (herself) at the top of his (her) medical-school class.* The girls wrote about Anne, the boys about John.

Their stories were scored for "motive to avoid success" if they expressed any negative imagery that reflected concern about doing well. Generally, such imagery fell into three categories:

1) The most frequent Anne story reflected strong fears of social rejection as a result of success. The girls in this group showed anxiety about becoming unpopular, unmarriageable and lonely.

Anne is an acne-faced bookworm. She runs to the bulletin board and finds she's at the top. As usual she smarts off. A chorus of groans is the rest of the class's reply. . . . She studies 12 hours a day, and lives at home to save money. "Well it certainly paid off. All the Friday and Saturday nights without dates, fun—I'll be the best woman doctor alive." And yet a twinge of sadness comes thru—she wonders what she really has . . .

Although Anne is happy with her success she fears what will happen to her social life. The male med. students don't seem to think very highly of a female who has beaten them in their field . . . She will be a proud and successful but alas a very *lonely* doctor.

Anne doesn't want to be number one in her class . . . she feels she shouldn't rank so high because of social reasons. She drops down to ninth in the class and then marries the boy who graduates number one.

Anne is pretty darn proud of herself, but everyone hates and envies her.

2) Girls in the second category were less concerned with issues of social approval or disapproval; they were more worried about definitions of womanhood. Their stories expressed guilt and despair over success, and doubts about their femininity or normality.

Unfortunately Anne no longer feels so certain that she really wants to be a doctor. She is worried about herself and wonders if perhaps she isn't normal . . . Anne decides not to continue with her medical work but to take courses that have a deeper personal meaning for her.

Anne feels guilty . . . She will finally have a nervous breakdown and quit medical school and marry a successful young doctor.

Anne is pleased. She had worked extraordinarily hard and her grades showed it. "It is not enough," Anne thinks. "I am not happy." She didn't even what to be a doctor. She is not sure what she wants. Anne says to hell with the whole business and goes into social work—not hardly as glamorous, prestigious or lucrative; but she is happy.

3) The third group of stories did not even try to confront the ambivalence about doing well. Girls in this category simply denied the possibility that any mere woman could be so successful. Some of them completely changed the content of the clue, or distorted it, or refused to believe it, or absolved Anne of responsibility for her success. These stories were remarkable for their psychological ingenuity:

Anne is a *code name* for a nonexistent person created by a group of med. students. They take turns writing exams for Anne . . .

Anne is really happy she's on top, though *Tom is higher than she*—though that's as it should be . . . Anne doesn't mind Tom winning.

Anne is talking to her counselor. Counselor says she will make a fine *nurse*.

It was *luck* that Anne came out on top because she didn't want to go to medical school anyway.

Fifty-nine girls—over 65 per cent—told stories that fell into one or another of the above categories. But only eight boys, fewer than 10 per cent, showed evidence of the motive to avoid success. (These differences are significant at better than the .0005 level.) In fact, sometimes I think that most of the young men in the sample were incipient Horatio Algers. They expressed unequivocal delight at John's success (clearly John had worked hard for it), and projected a grand and glorious future for him. There was none of the hostility, bitterness and ambivalence that the girls felt for Anne. In short, the differences between male and female stories based on essentially the same clue were enormous.

Two of the stories are particularly revealing examples of this male-female contrast. The girls insisted that Anne give up her career for marriage:

> Anne has a boyfriend, Carl, in the same class and they are quite serious . . . She wants him to be scholastically higher than she is. Anne will deliberately lower her academic standing the next term, while she does all she subtly can to help Carl. His grades come up and Anne soon drops out of medical school. They marry and he goes on in school while she raises their family.

But of course the boys would ask John to do no such thing:

> John has worked very hard and his long hours of study have paid off . . . He is thinking about his girl, Cheri, whom he will marry at the end of med. school. He realizes he can give her all the things she desires after he becomes established. He will go on in med. school and be successful in the long run.

Success inhibits social life for the girls; it enhances social life for the boys.

Earlier I suggested that the motive to avoid success is especially aroused in competitive situations. In the second part of this study I wanted to see whether the aggressive overtones of competition against men scared the girls away. Would competition raise their anxiety about success and thus lower their performance?

First I put all of the students together in a large competitive group, and gave them a series of achievement tests (verbal and arithmetic). I then assigned them randomly to one of three other experimental conditions. One-third worked on a similar set of tests, each in competition with a member of the same sex. One-third competed against a member of the opposite sex. The last third worked by themselves, a non-competitive condition.

Ability is an important factor in achievement motivation research. If you want to compare two persons on the strength of their *motivation* to succeed, how do you know that any differences in performance are not due to initial differences in *ability* to succeed? One way of avoiding this problem is to use each subject as his own control; that is, the performance of an individual working alone can be compared with his score in competition. Ability thus remains constant; any change in score must be due to motivational factors. This control over ability was, of course, possible only for the last third of my subjects: the 30 girls and 30 boys who had worked alone *and* in the large group competition. I decided to look at their scores first.

Performance changed dramatically over the two situations. A large number of the men did far better when they were in competition than when they worked alone. For the women the reverse was true. Fewer than one-third of the women, but more than two-thirds of the men, got significantly higher scores in competition.

When we looked at just the girls in terms of the motive to avoid success, the comparisons were even more striking. As predicted, the students who felt ambivalent or anxious about doing well turned in their best scores when they worked by themselves. Seventy-seven per cent of the girls who feared success did better alone than in competition. Women who were low on the motive, however, behaved more like the men: 93 per cent of them got higher scores in competition. (Results significant at the .005.)

Female Fear of Success & Performance		
	perform better working alone	perform better in competition
high fear of success	13	4
low fear of success	1	12

As a final test of motivational differences, I asked the students to indicate on a scale from 1 to 100 "How important was it for you to do well in this situation?" The high-fear-of-success girls said that it was much more important for them to do well when they worked alone than when they worked in either kind of competition. For the low-fear girls, such differences were not statistically significant. Their test scores were higher in competition, as we saw, and they thought that it was important to succeed so matter what the setting. And in all experimental conditions—working alone, or in competition against males or females—high-fear women consistently lagged behind their fearless comrades on the importance of doing well.

These findings suggest that most women will fully explore their intellectual potential only when they do not need to compete—and least of all when they are competing with me. This was most true of women with a strong anxiety about success. Unfortunately, these are often the same women who could be very successful if they were free from that anxiety. The girls in my sample who feared success also tended to have high intellectual ability and histories of academic success. (It is interesting to note that all but two of these girls were majoring in the humanities and in spite of very high grade points aspired to traditional female careers: housewife, mother, nurse, schoolteacher. Girls who did not fear success, however, were aspiring to graduate degrees and careers in such scientific areas as math, physics and chemistry.)

We can see from this small study that achievement motivation in women is much more complex than the same drive in men. Most men do not find many inhibiting forces in their path if they are able and motivated to succeed. As a result, they are not threatened by competition; in fact, surpassing an opponent is a source of pride and enhanced masculinity.

If a woman sets out to do well, however, she bumps into a number of obstacles. She learns that it really isn't ladylike to be too intellectual. She is warned that men will treat her with distrustful tolerance at best, and outright prejudice at worst, if she pursues a career. She learns the truth of Samuel Johnson's comment, "A man is in general better pleased when he has a good dinner upon his table, than when his wife talks Greek." So she doesn't learn Greek, and the motive to avoid success is born.

In recent years many legal and educational barriers to female achievement have been removed; but it is clear that a psychological barrier remains. The motive to avoid success has an all-too-important influence on the intellectual and professional lives of women in our society. But perhaps there is cause for optimism. Monica may have seen Anne maimed for life, but a few of the girls forecast a happier future for our medical student. Said one:

> Anne is quite a lady—not only is she tops academically, but she is liked and admired by her fellow students—quite a trick in a man-dominated field. She is brilliant—but she is also a woman. She will continue to be at or near the top. And . . . always a lady.

Her Story

Naomi Long Madgett

Matina Horner explains that in our society an intelligent and ambitious woman is likely to fail or, at the least, is not encouraged to succeed. When a woman is intelligent, ambitious, and black, the chances of failure multiply. Her Story *tells of one such failure.*

Naomi Long Madgett is Associate Professor of English at Eastern Michigan University (Ypsilanti). She received a B.A. from Virginia State College and an M.A. from Wayne State University and, in 1965-66, won the first $10,000 Mott Fellowship in English at Oakland University. In 1967, she received the Distinguished English Teacher of the Year Award from the Metropolitan Detroit English Club. The author of an English textbook and three volumes of poetry: Songs to a Phantom Nightingale *(1941);* One and the Many *(1956); and* Star by Star *(1965), she lives in Detroit with her daughter. Her poetry has appeared in "about 27 anthologies, including several in four foreign countries."*

They gave me the wrong name, in the first place.
They named me Grace and waited for a light and agile dancer.
But some trick of the genes mixed me up
And instead I turned out big and black and burly.

In the second place, I fashioned the wrong dreams.
I wanted to dress like Juliet and act
Before applauding audiences on Broadway.
I learned more about Shakespeare than he knew about himself.
But of course, all that was impossible.
"Talent, yes," they would tell me,
"But an actress has to look the part."
So I ended up waiting on tables in Harlem

From *Star by Star* by Naomi Long Madgett. Detroit, Harlo Press, 1965.

And hearing uncouth men yell at me:
"Hey, momma, you can cancel that hamburger
And come up on up to 102."

In the third place, I tried the wrong solution.
The stuff I drank made me deathly sick
And someone called a doctor.
Next time I'll try a gun.

from *A Room of One's Own*

Virginia Woolf

In A Room of One's Own *(1928), the British novelist Virginia
Woolf takes as her subject women and fiction. Why is it, she
asks, are there so few examples of literature produced by
women? The answer, she says, lies in the great number of obstacles placed by a male-oriented society in the woman writer's
path: she has no money of her own, no place of her own, no
time of her own; above all, she has no tradition in which to
write, and no encouragement to create such a tradition. In
Chapter III, reprinted below, Virginia Woolf traces what would
have happened to a gifted woman genius of Shakespeare's day—
say, Shakespeare's sister.*

It was disappointing not to have brought back in the evening some
important statement, some authentic fact. Women are poorer than men
because—this or that. Perhaps now it would be better to give up seeking
for the truth, and receiving on one's head an avalanche of opinion hot
as lava, discoloured as dish-water. It would be better to draw the cur-

tains; to shut out distractions; to light the lamp; to narrow the enquiry and to ask the historian, who records not opinions but facts, to describe under what conditions women lived, not throughout the ages, but in England, say in the time of Elizabeth.

For it is a perennial puzzle why no woman wrote a word of that extraordinary literature when every other man, it seemed, was capable of song or sonnet. What were the conditions in which women lived, I asked myself; for fiction, imaginative work that is, is not dropped like a pebble upon the ground, as science may be; fiction is like a spider's web, attached ever so lightly perhaps, but still attached to life at all four corners. Often the attachment is scarcely perceptible; Shakespeare's plays, for instance, seem to hang there complete by themselves. But when the web is pulled askew, hooked up at the edge, torn in the middle, one remembers that these webs are not spun in mid-air by incorporeal creatures, but are the work of suffering human beings, and are attached to grossly material things like health and money and the houses we live in.

I went, therefore, to the shelf where the histories stand and took down one of the latest, Professor Trevelyan's *History of England*. Once more I looked up Women, found "position of," and turned to the pages indicated. "Wife-beating," I read, "was a recognised right of man, and was practised without shame by high as well as low. . . . Similarly," the historian goes on, "the daughter who refused to marry the gentleman of her parents' choice was liable to be locked up, beaten and flung about the room, without any shock being inflicted on public opinion. Marriage was not an affair of personal affection, but of family avarice, particularly in the 'chivalrous' upper classes. . . . Betrothal often took place while one or both of the parties was in the cradle, and marriage when they were scarcely out of the nurses' charge." That was about 1470, soon after Chaucer's time. The next reference to the position of women is some two hundred years later, in the time of the Stuarts. "It was still the exception for women of the upper and middle class to choose their own husbands, and when the husband had been assigned, he was lord and master, so far at least as law and custom could make him. Yet even so," Professor Trevelyan concludes, "neither Shakespeare's women nor those of authentic seventeenth-century memoirs, like the Verneys and the Hutchinsons, seem wanting in personality and character." Certainly, if we consider it, Cleopatra must have had a way with her; Lady Macbeth, one would suppose, had a will of her own; Rosalind, one might conclude, was an attractive girl. Professor Trevelyan is speaking no more than the truth when he remarks that Shakespeare's women do not seem wanting in personality and character. Not being a historian, one might go even further and say that women have burnt like beacons in all the works of

all the poets from the beginning of time—Clytemnestra, Antigone, Cleopatra, Lady Macbeth, Phèdre, Cressida, Rosalind, Desdemona, the
Duchess of Malfi, among the dramatists; then among the prose writers:
Millamant, Clarissa, Becky Sharp, Anna Karenine, Emma Bovary,
Madame de Guermantes—the names flock to mind, nor do they recall
women "lacking in personality and character." Indeed, if woman had no
existence save in the fiction written by men, one would imagine her a
person of the utmost importance; very various; heroic and mean; splendid and sordid; infinitely beautiful and hideous in the extreme; as great
as a man, some think even greater.[1] But this is woman in fiction. In fact,
as Professor Trevelyan points out, she was locked up, beaten and flung
about the room.

A very queer, composite being thus emerges. Imaginatively she is of
the highest importance; practically she is completely insignificant. She
pervades poetry from cover to cover; she is all but absent from history.
She dominates the lives of kings and conquerors in fiction; in fact she
was the slave of any boy whose parents forced a ring upon her finger.
Some of the most inspired words, some of the most profound thoughts
in literature fall from her lips; in real life she could hardly read, could
scarcely spell, and was the property of her husband.

It was certainly an odd monster that one made up by reading the historians first and the poets afterwards—a worm winged like an eagle; the
spirit of life and beauty in a kitchen chopping up suet. But these mon-
sters, however amusing to the imagination, have no existence in fact.
What one must do to bring her to life is to think poetically and pro-
saically at one and the same moment, thus keeping in touch with fact—
that she is Mrs. Martin, aged thirty-six, dressed in blue, wearing a black
hat and brown shoes; but not losing sight of fiction either—that she is a

---

[1]"It remains a strange and almost inexplicable fact that in Athena's city, where
women were kept in almost Oriental suppression as odalisques or drudges,
the stage should yet have produced figures like Clytemnestra and Cassandra Atossa and Antigone, Phèdre and Medea, and all the other heroines
who dominate play after play of the 'misogynist' Euripides. But the paradox
of this world where in real life a respectable woman could hardly show her
face alone in the street, and yet on the stage woman equals or surpasses man,
has never been satisfactorily explained. In modern tragedy the same pre-
dominance exists. At all events, a very cursory survey of Shakespeare's work
(similarly with Webster, though not with Marlowe or Jonson) suffices to
reveal how this dominance, this initiative of women, persists from Rosalind
to Lady Macbeth. So too in Racine; six of his tragedies bear their heroines'
names; and what male characters of his shall we set against Hermione and
Andromaque, Bérénice and Roxane, Phèdre and Athalie? So again with
Ibsen; what men shall we match with Solveig and Nora, Hedda and Hilda
Wangel and Rebecca West?"—F. L. Lucas, *Tragedy*, pp. 114-15.

vessel in which all sorts of spirits and forces are coursing and flashing perpetually. The moment, however, that one tries this method with the Elizabethan woman, one branch of illumination fails; one is held up by the scarcity of facts. One knows nothing detailed, nothing perfectly true and substantial about her. History scarcely mentions her. And I turned to Professor Trevelyan again to see what history meant to him. I found by looking at his chapter headings that it meant—

"The Manor Court and the Methods of Open-field Agriculture . . . The Cistercians and Sheep-farming . . . The Crusades . . . The University . . . The House of Commons . . . The Hundred Years' War . . . The Wars of the Roses . . . The Renaissance Scholars . . . The Dissolution of the Monasteries . . . Agrarian and Religious Strife . . . The Origin of English Seapower . . . The Armada . . ." and so on. Occasionally an individual woman is mentioned, an Elizabeth, or a Mary; a queen or a great lady. But by no possible means could middle-class women with nothing but brains and character at their command have taken part in any one of the great movements which, brought together, constitute the historian's view of the past. Nor shall we find her in any collection of anecdotes. Aubrey hardly mentions her. She never writes her own life and scarcely keeps a diary; there are only a handful of her letters in existence. She left no plays or poems by which we can judge her. What one wants, I thought— and why does not some brilliant student at Newnham or Girton supply it?—is a mass of information; at what age did she marry; how many children had she as a rule; what was her house like; had she a room to herself; did she do the cooking; would she be likely to have a servant? All these facts lie somewhere, presumably, in parish registers and account books; the life of the average Elizabethan woman must be scattered about somewhere, could one collect it and make a book of it. It would be ambitious beyond my daring, I thought, looking about the shelves for books that were not there, to suggest to the students of those famous colleges that they should re-write history, though I own that it often seems a little queer as it is, unreal, lopsided; but why should they not add a supplement to history? calling it, of course, by some inconspicuous name so that women might figure there without impropriety? For one often catches a glimpse of them in the lives of the great, whisking away into the background, concealing, I sometimes think, a wink, a laugh, perhaps a tear. And, after all, we have lives enough of Jane Austen; it scarcely seems necessary to consider again the influence of the tragedies of Joanna Baillie upon the poetry of Edgar Allan Poe; as for myself, I should not mind if the homes and haunts of Mary Russell Mitford were closed to the public for a century at least. But what I find deplorable, I continued, looking about the bookshelves again, is that nothing is known about women before the eighteenth century. I have no model in my mind to turn about this way and that. Here am I asking why women did not write poetry in the Elizabethan age, and I am not sure how they were educated; whether they were taught to write; whether they had sitting-rooms to themselves; how many women had children before they were twenty-one; what, in short, they did from eight in the morning till eight at night. They had no money evidently; according to Professor Trevelyan they were married whether they liked it or not before they were out of the nursery, at fifteen or sixteen very likely. It would have been extremely odd, even upon this showing, had one of them suddenly written the plays of Shakespeare, I concluded, and I thought of that old gentleman, who is dead now, but was a bishop, I think, who declared that it was impossible for any woman, past, present, or to come, to have the genius of Shakespeare. He wrote to the papers about it. He also told a lady who applied to him for information that cats do not as a matter of fact go to heaven, though they have, he added, souls of a sort. How much thinking those old gentlemen used to save one! How the borders of ignorance shrank back at their approach! Cats do not go to heaven. Women cannot write the plays of Shakespeare.

Be that as it may, I could not help thinking, as I looked at the works of Shakespeare on the shelf, that the bishop was right at least in this; it would have been impossible, completely and entirely, for any woman to have written the plays of Shakespeare in the age of Shakespeare. Let me imagine, since facts are so hard to come by, what would have happened had Shakespeare had a wonderfully gifted sister, called Judith, let us say. Shakespeare himself went, very probably—his mother was an heiress—to the grammar school, where he may have learnt Latin—Ovid, Virgil and Horace—and the elements of grammar and logic. He was, it is well known, a wild boy who poached rabbits, perhaps shot a deer, and had, rather sooner than he should have done, to marry a woman in the neighbourhood, who bore him a child rather quicker than was right. That escapade sent him to seek his fortune in London. He had, it seemed, a taste for the theatre; he began by holding horses at the stage door. Very soon he got work in the theatre, became a successful actor, and lived at the hub of the universe, meeting everybody, knowing everybody, practising his art on the boards, exercising his wits in the streets, and even getting access to the palace of the queen. Meanwhile his extraordinarily gifted sister, let us suppose, remained at home. She was as adventurous, as imaginative, as agog to see the world as he was. But she was not sent to school. She had no chance of learning grammar and logic, let alone of reading Horace and Virgil. She picked up a book now and then, one of her brother's perhaps, and read a few pages. But then her parents came in and told her to mend the stockings or mind the stew and not moon about with books and papers. They would have spoken sharply but kindly, for they were substantial people who knew the conditions of life for a woman and loved their daughter—indeed, more likely than not she was the apple of her father's eye. Perhaps she scribbled some pages up in an apple loft on the sly, but was careful to hide them or set fire to them. Soon, however, before she was out of her teens, she was to be betrothed to the son of a neighbouring wool-stapler. She cried out that marriage was hateful to her, and for that she was severely beaten by her father. Then he ceased to scold her. He begged her instead not to hurt him, not to shame him in this matter of her marriage. He would give her a chain of beads or a fine petticoat, he said; and there were tears in his eyes. How could she disobey him? How could she break his heart? The force of her own gift alone drove her to it. She made up a small parcel of her belongings, let herself down by a rope one summer's night and took the road to London. She was not seventeen. The birds that sang in the hedge were not more musical than she was. She had the quickest fancy, a gift like her brother's, for the tune of words. Like him, she had a taste for the theatre. She stood at the stage door; she wanted to act, she said. Men laughed in her face. The manager—a fat, loose-lipped man—guffawed. He bellowed something about poodles dancing and women acting—no woman, he said, could possibly be an actress. He hinted—you can imagine what. She could get no training in her craft. Could she even seek her dinner in a tavern or roam the streets at midnight? Yet her genius was for fiction and lusted to feed abundantly upon the lives of men and women and the study of their ways. At last— for she was very young, oddly like Shakespeare the poet in her face, with the same grey eyes and rounded brows—at last Nick Greene the actor-manager took pity on her; she found herself with child by that gentleman and so—who shall measure the heat and violence of the poet's heart when caught and tangled in a woman's body?—killed herself one winter's night and lies buried at some cross-roads where the omnibuses now stop outside the Elephant and Castle.

That, more or less, is how the story would run, I think, if a woman in Shakespeare's day had had Shakespeare's genius. But for my part, I agree with the deceased bishop, if such he was—it is unthinkable that any woman in Shakespeare's day should have had Shakespeare's genius. For genius like Shakespeare's is not born among labouring, uneducated, servile people. It was not born in England among the Saxons and the Britons. It is not born today among the working classes. How, then, could it have been born among women whose work began, according to Professor Trevelyan, almost before they were out of the nursery, who were forced to it by their parents and held to it by all the power of law and custom? Yet genius of a sort must have existed among women as it must have existed among the working classes. Now and again an Emily

Brontë or a Robert Burns blazes out and proves its presence. But certainly it never got itself on to paper. When, however, one reads of a witch being ducked, of a woman possessed by devils, of a wise woman selling herbs, or even of a very remarkable man who had a mother, then I think we are on the track of a lost novelist, a suppressed poet, of some mute and inglorious Jane Austen, some Emily Brontë who dashed her brains out on the moor or mopped and mowed about the highways crazed with the torture that her gift had put her to. Indeed, I would venture to guess that Anon, who wrote so many poems without signing them, was often a woman. It was a woman Edward Fitzgerald, I think, suggested who made the ballads and the folk-songs, crooning them to her children, beguiling her spinning with them, or the length of the winter's night.

This may be true or it may be false—who can say?—but what is true in it, so it seemed to me, reviewing the story of Shakespeare's sister as I had made it, is that any woman born with a great gift in the sixteenth century would certainly have gone crazed, shot herself, or ended her days in some lonely cottage outside the village, half-witch, half-wizard, feared and mocked at. For it needs little skill in psychology to be sure that a highly gifted girl who had tried to use her gift for poetry would have been so thwarted and hindered by other people, so tortured and pulled asunder by her own contrary instincts, that she must have lost her health and sanity to a certainty. No girl could have walked to London and stood at a stage door and forced her way into the presence of actor-managers without doing herself a violence and suffering an anguish which may have been irrational—for chastity may be a fetish invented by certain societies for unknown reasons—but was none the less inevitable. Chastity had then, as it has even now, a religious importance in a woman's life, and has so wrapped itself round with nerves and instincts that to cut it free and bring it to the light of day demands courage of the rarest. To have lived a free life in London in the sixteenth century would have meant for a woman who was poet and playwright a nervous stress and dilemma which might well have killed her. Had she survived, whatever she had written would have been twisted and deformed, issuing from a strained and morbid imagination. And undoubtedly, I thought, looking at the shelf where there are no plays by women, her work would have gone unsigned. That refuge she would have sought certainly. It was the relic of the sense of chastity that dictated anonymity to women even so late as the nineteenth century. Currer Bell, George Eliot, George Sand, all the victims of inner strife as their writings prove, sought ineffectively to veil themselves by using the name of a man. Thus they did homage to the convention, which if not implanted by the other sex was liberally encouraged by them (the chief glory of a woman is not to be talked of, said Pericles, himself a much-talked-of man), that publicity in women is detestable. Anonymity runs in their blood. The desire to be veiled still possesses them. They are not even now as concerned about the health of their fame as men are, and, speaking generally, will pass a tombstone or a signpost without feeling an irresistible desire to cut their names on it, as Alf, Bert or Chas. must do in obedience to their instinct, which murmurs if it sees a fine woman go by, or even a dog, *Ce chien est à moi*. And, of course, it may not be a dog, I thought, remembering Parliament Square, the Sieges Allee and other avenues; it may be a piece of land or a man with curly black hair. It is one of the great advantages of being a woman that one can pass even a very fine negress without wishing to make an Englishwoman of her.

That woman, then, who was born with a gift of poetry in the sixteenth century, was an unhappy woman, a woman at strife against herself. All the conditions of her life, all her own instincts, were hostile to the state of mind which is needed to set free whatever is in the brain. But what is the state of mind that is most propitious to the act of creation, I asked? Can one come by any notion of the state that furthers and makes possible that strange activity? Here I opened the volume containing the Tragedies of Shakespeare. What was Shakespeare's state of mind, for instance, when he wrote *Lear* and *Antony and Cleopatra*? It was certainly the state of mind most favourable to poetry that there has ever existed. But Shakespeare himself said nothing about it. We only know casually and by chance that he "never blotted a line." Nothing indeed was ever said by the artist himself about his state of mind until the eighteenth century. Rousseau perhaps began it. At any rate, by the nineteenth century selfconsciousness had developed so far that it was the habit for men of letters to describe their minds in confessions and autobiographies. Their lives also were written, and their letters were printed after their deaths. Thus, though we do not know what Shakespeare went through when he wrote *Lear*, we do know what Carlyle went through when he wrote the *French Revolution;* what Flaubert went through when he wrote *Madame Bovary;* what Keats was going through when he tried to write poetry against the coming of death and the indifference of the world.

And one gathers from this enormous modern literature of confession and self-analysis that to write a work of genius is almost always a feat of prodigious difficulty. Everything is against the likelihood that it will come from the writer's mind whole and entire. Generally material circumstances are against it. Dogs will bark; people will interrupt; money must be made; health will break down. Further, accentuating all these difficulties and making them harder to bear is the world's notorious indifference. It does not ask people to write poems and novels and histories; it does not need them. It does not care whether Flaubert finds the right word or whether Carlyle scrupulously verifies this or that fact. Naturally, it will not pay for what it does not want. And so the writer, Keats, Flaubert, Carlyle, suffers, especially in the creative years of youth, every form of distraction and discouragement. A curse, a cry of agony, rises from those books of analysis and confession. "Mighty poets in their misery dead"—that is the burden of their song. If anything comes through in spite of all this, it is a miracle, and probably no book is born entire and uncrippled as it was conceived.

But for women, I thought, looking at the empty shelves, these difficulties were infinitely more formidable. In the first place, to have a room of her own, let alone a quiet room or a sound-proof room, was out of the question, unless her parents were exceptionally rich or very noble, even up to the beginning of the nineteenth century. Since her pin money, which depended on the good will of her father, was only enough to keep her clothed, she was debarred from such alleviations as came even to Keats or Tennyson or Carlyle, all poor men, from a walking tour, a little journey to France, from the separate lodging which, even if it were miserable enough, sheltered them from the claims and tyrannies of their families. Such material difficulties were formidable; but much worse were the immaterial. The indifference of the world which Keats and Flaubert and other men of genius have found so hard to bear was in her case not indifference but hostility. The world did not say to her as it said to them, Write if you choose; it makes no difference to me. The world said with a guffaw, Write? What's the good of your writing? Here the psychologists of Newnham and Girton might come to our help, I thought, looking again at the blank spaces on the shelves. For surely it is time that the effect of discouragement upon the mind of the artist should be measured, as I have seen a dairy company measure the effect of ordinary milk and Grade A milk upon the body of the rat. They set two rats in cages side by side, and of the two one was furtive, timid and small, and the other was glossy, bold and big. Now what food do we feed women as artists upon? I asked, remembering, I suppose, that dinner of prunes and custard. To answer that question I had only to open the evening paper and to read that Lord Birkenhead is of opinion— but really I am not going to trouble to copy out Lord Birkenhead's opinion upon the writing of women. What Dean Inge says I will leave in peace. The Harley Street specialist may be allowed to rouse the echoes of Harley Street with his vociferations without raising a hair on my head. I will quote, however, Mr. Oscar Browning, because Mr. Oscar

Browning was a great figure in Cambridge at one time, and used to examine the students at Girton and Newnham. Mr. Oscar Browning was wont to declare "that the impression left on his mind, after looking over any set of examination papers, was that, irrespective of the marks he might give, the best woman was intellectually the inferior of the worst man." After saying that Mr. Browning went back to his rooms—and it is this sequel that endears him and makes him a human figure of some bulk and majesty—he went back to his rooms and found a stable-boy lying on the sofa—"a mere skeleton, his cheeks were cavernous and sallow, his teeth were black, and he did not appear to have the full use of his limbs.... 'That's Arthur' [said Mr. Browning]. 'He's a dear boy really and most high-minded.'" The two pictures always seem to me to complete each other. And happily in this age of biography the two pictures often do complete each other, so that we are able to interpret the opinions of great men not only by what they say, but by what they do.

But though this is possible now, such opinions coming from the lips of important people must have been formidable enough even fifty years ago. Let us suppose that a father from the highest motives did not wish his daughter to leave home and become writer, painter or scholar. "See what Mr. Oscar Browning says," he would say; and there was not only Mr. Oscar Browning; there was the *Saturday Review;* there was Mr. Greg—the "essentials of a woman's being," said Mr. Greg emphatically, "are that *they are supported by, and they minister to, men*"—there was an enormous body of masculine opinion to the effect that nothing could be expected of women intellectually. Even if her father did not read out loud these opinions, any girl could read them for herself; and the reading, even in the nineteenth century, must have lowered her vitality, and told profoundly upon her work. There would always have been that assertion—you cannot do this, you are incapable of doing that—to protest against, to overcome. Probably for a novelist this germ is no longer of much effect; for there have been women novelists of merit. But for painters it must still have some sting in it; and for musicians, I imagine, is even now active and poisonous in the extreme. The woman composer stands where the actress stood in the time of Shakespeare. Nick Greene, I thought, remembering the story I had made about Shakespeare's sister, said that a woman acting put him in mind of a dog dancing. Johnson repeated the phrase two hundred years later of women preaching. And here, I said, opening a book about music, we have the very words used again in this year of grace, 1928, of women who try to write music. "Of Mlle. Germaine Tailleferre one can only repeat Dr. Johnson's dictum concerning a woman preacher, transposed into terms of music. 'Sir, a woman's composing is like a dog's walking on his hind legs. It is not done well, but you are surprised to find it done at all.' "[2] So accurately does history repeat itself.

Thus, I concluded, shutting Mr. Oscar Browning's life and pushing away the rest, it is fairly evident that even in the nineteenth century a woman was not encouraged to be an artist. On the contrary, she was snubbed, slapped, lectured and exhorted. Her mind must have been strained and her vitality lowered by the need of opposing this, of disproving that. For here again we come within range of that very interesting and obscure masculine complex which has had so much influence upon the woman's movement; that deep-seated desire, not so much that *she* shall be inferior as that *he* shall be superior, which plants him wherever one looks, not only in front of the arts, but barring the way to politics too, even when the risk to himself seems infinitesimal and the suppliant humble and devoted. Even Lady Bessborough, I remembered, with all her passion for politics, must humbly bow herself and write to Lord Granville Leveson-Gower: "... notwithstanding all my violence in politics and talking so much on that subject, I perfectly agree with you that no woman has any business to meddle with that or any other serious business, farther than giving her opinion (if she is ask'd)." And so she goes on to spend her enthusiasm where it meets with no obstacle whatsoever upon that immensely important subject, Lord Granville's maiden speech in the House of Commons. The spectacle is certainly a strange one, I thought. The history of men's opposition to women's emancipation is more interesting perhaps than the story of that emancipation itself. An amusing book might be made of it if some young student at Girton or Newnham would collect examples and deduce a theory—but she would need thick gloves on her hands, and bars to protect her of solid gold.

But what is amusing now, I recollected, shutting Lady Bessborough, had to be taken in desperate earnest once. Opinions that one now pastes in a book labelled cock-a-doodle-dum and keeps for reading to select audiences on summer nights once drew tears, I can assure you. Among your grandmothers and great-grandmothers there were many that wept their eyes out. Florence Nightingale shrieked aloud in her agony.[3] Moreover, it is all very well for you, who have got yourselves to college and enjoy sitting-rooms—or it is only bed-sitting-rooms?—of your own to say that genius should disregard such opinions; that genius should

---

[2] *A Survey of Contemporary Music*, Cecil Gray, p. 246.

[3] See *Cassandra*, by Florence Nightingale, printed in *The Cause*, by R. Strachey.

be above caring what is said of it. Unfortunately, it is precisely the men or women of genius who mind most what is said of them. Remember Keats. Remember the words he had cut on his tombstone. Think of Tennyson; think—but I need hardly multiply instances of the undeniable, if very unfortunate, fact that it is the nature of the artist to mind excessively what is said about him. Literature is strewn with the wreckage of men who have minded beyond reason the opinions of others.

And this susceptibility of theirs is doubly unfortunate, I thought, returning again to my original enquiry into what state of mind is most propitious for creative work, because the mind of an artist, in order to achieve the prodigious effort of freeing whole and entire the work that is in him, must be incandescent, like Shakespeare's mind, I conjectured, looking at the book which lay open at *Antony and Cleopatra*. There must be no obstacle in it, no foreign matter unconsumed.

For though we say that we know nothing about Shakespeare's state of mind, even as we say that, we are saying something about Shakespeare's state of mind. The reason perhaps why we know so little of Shakespeare —compared with Donne or Ben Jonson or Milton—is that his grudges and spites and antipathies are hidden from us. We are not held up by some "revelation" which reminds us of the writer. All desire to protest, to preach, to proclaim an injury, to pay off a score, to make the world the witness of some hardship or grievance was fired out of him and consumed. Therefore his poetry flows from him free and unimpeded. If ever a human being got his work expressed completely, it was Shakespeare. If ever a mind was incandescent, unimpeded, I thought, turning again to the bookcase, it was Shakespeare's mind.

The first step toward freedom comes with recognition of what really exists. Artists have always been able to shape our concept of reality by providing us with glimpses of the world which we accept as the real thing. In the case of women, too often artists have offered only stereotyped views, portraying women as models of physical beauty, ethereal grace, patient endurance, or gentle maternity.

In the following pictorial section, the artists show us women who contradict the traditional views. We see women oppressed by poverty and women dehumanized by commercial exploitation of their beauty. We also see women breaking free from stereotyped roles—moving toward freedom.

Daumier. *Third-Class Carriage.* c. 1862.
Steichen. *Homeless Women: The Depression.* 1932.
Honoré Daumier's study of poor women traveling in a third-class carriage reveals a characteristic sympathy with those oppressed by social injustice. The mood, posture, and facial expression of the women can be compared with Edward Steichen's study of women in the depression which was made for the Travelers Aid Society.

Kanaga. *Black Mother and Two Children.*
The photographer, Consuelo Kanaga, in describing this picture, writes, "She is a tree of life to them" (Proverbs III:18).

Lange. *Migrant Mother*. 1936.
Dorothea Lange was among the first to use photography as social criticism for the WPA during the depression. The woman in *Migrant Mother* (the mother of seven children) is one of the destitute peapickers in California. She is 32 years old.

Dali. *Project of Interior Decoration for a Stable-Library*. 1942.
In this study by Salvador Dali, a woman takes her place among the sheep as a part of the artificial interior decor of a room which bears the trappings of modern civilization.

Warhol. *Marilyn Monroe.* 1967.
This detail from one of Andy Warhol's studies of Marilyn Monroe comments on
the exploitation of a modern sex goddess. The nine images of Marilyn in the
complete painting show her face distorted by apparent superimposition of one
image on another. The effect is of a beautiful woman mangled by commercial
processing.

Delacroix. *Liberty Leading the People.* 1830.
Eugène Delacroix uses an idealized image of woman to personify the abstract idea of liberty. With breasts bare, holding a flag in one hand and a bayoneted rifle in the other, she inspires and leads the people in the French Revolution.

May Day Parade in New York City. 1918.
Women Teamsters. 1970.
These pictures show women who have entered the labor force and have become
active in agitation for their rights as workers.

Unpaid Labor. 1970.
A pregnant woman protests "Unpaid Labor" in a march organized in New York. Society shows the value it places on "woman's work" by paying low—or in the case of the housewife-mother—no wages.

Miss Montana
The Miss America pageant has reinforced an "ideal" model for women in America: the body beautiful equipped with brainless innocence and plastic sex appeal. Miss America's job is to be pretty, to sell products, and to retire after a year into a quiet life of motherhood. But, increasingly, more women are rejecting this "ideal." This year Kathy Huppe, Miss Montana, refused to give up her political commitment and insisted on her right to take part in anti-war demonstrations. She was therefore barred from Atlantic City.

Weathergirl. 1969.
Vietnamese Freedom Fighter.
In their struggle for equal human rights women in the mid-twentieth century are sometimes forced into extreme positions. In Chicago, a Weathergirl wears a helmet for protection and symbol of her militant political beliefs, and, in Vietnam, a young woman joins the fight for her political freedom.

Flax Hermes/THE MILITANT

New Haven March, 1969.
Here New Haven Women's Liberation is in the forefront of one of the marches
protesting the jailing of fourteen members of the Black Panther Party in 1969.

Part Four:

Toward Freedom

Sojourner Truth:
On Women's Rights

Frances D. Gage

During the nineteenth century, women active in the cause of abolition of slavery, arguing for human rights, began to claim the same rights for themselves. After the first Women's Rights Convention at Seneca Falls, New York, in July 1848, women in other states began holding similar conventions, issuing appeals and passing resolutions. One of these conventions was held in Akron, Ohio, on May 28-29, 1851; presiding was Frances D. Gage, who is the source of the following reminiscences. At the Akron convention a black woman, Sojourner Truth, spoke—over the objections of racists in the audience—on women's rights. A former slave, she was described by leaders of the women's movement as "a woman of rare intelligence and common-sense on all subjects" who had doubly suffered as black and as woman.

The leaders of the movement trembled on seeing a tall, gaunt black woman in a gray dress and white turban, surmounted with an uncouth sun-bonnet, march deliberately into the church, walk with the air of a queen up the aisle, and take her seat upon the pulpit steps. A buzz of disapprobation was heard all over the house, and there fell on the listening ear, "An abolition affair!" "Woman's rights and niggers!" "I told you so!" "Go it, darkey!"

I chanced on that occasion to wear my first laurels in public life as president of the meeting. At my request order was restored, and the business of the Convention went on. Morning, afternoon, and evening exercises came and went. Through all these sessions old Sojourner, quiet and reticent as the "Lybian Statue," sat crouched against the wall on the corner of the pulpit stairs, her sun-bonnet shading her eyes,

From *History of Woman Suffrage*, eds. Elizabeth Cady Stanton, Susan B. Anthony, and Matilda Joslyn Gage. New York: Fowler & Wells, 1881. Vol. I (of two vols.).

her elbows on her knees, her chin resting upon her broad, hard palms. At intermission she was busy selling the "Life of Sojourner Truth," a narrative of her own strange and adventurous life. Again and again, timorous and trembling ones came to me and said, with earnestness, "Don't let her speak, Mrs. Gage, it will ruin us. Every newspaper in the land will have our cause mixed up with abolition and niggers, and we shall be utterly denounced." My only answer was, "We shall see when the time comes."

The second day the work waxed warm. Methodist, Baptist, Episcopal, Presbyterian, and Universalist ministers came in to hear and discuss the resolutions presented. One claimed superior rights and privileges for man, on the ground of "superior intellect"; another, because of the "manhood of Christ; if God had desired the equality of woman, He would have given some token of His will through the birth, life, and death of the Saviour." Another gave us a theological view of the "sin of our first mother."

There were very few women in those days who dared to "speak in meeting"; and the august teachers of the people were seemingly getting the better of us, while the boys in the galleries, and the sneerers among the pews, were hugely enjoying the discomfiture, as they supposed, of the "strong-minded." Some of the tender-skinned friends were on the point of losing dignity, and the atmosphere betokened a storm. When, slowly from her seat in the corner rose Sojourner Truth, who, till now, had scarcely lifted her head. "Don't let her speak!" gasped half a dozen in my ear. She moved slowly and solemnly to the front, laid her old bonnet at her feet, and turned her great speaking eyes to me. There was a hissing sound of disapprobation above and below. I rose and announced "Sojourner Truth," and begged the audience to keep silence for a few moments.

The tumult subsided at once, and every eye was fixed on this almost Amazon form, which stood nearly six feet high, head erect, and eyes piercing the upper air like one in a dream. At her first word there was a profound hush. She spoke in deep tones, which, though not loud, reached every ear in the house, and away through the throng at the doors and windows.

"Wall, chilern, whar dar is so much racket dar must be somethin' out o' kilter. I tink dat 'twixt de niggers of de Souf and de womin at de Norf, all talkin' 'bout rights, de white men will be in a fix pretty soon. But what's all dis here talkin' 'bout?

"Dat man ober dar say dat womin needs to be helped into carriages, and lifted ober ditches, and to hab de best place everywhar. Nobody eber helps me into carriages, or ober mud-puddles, or gibs me any best place!" And raising herself to her full height, and her voice to a pitch like rolling thunder, she asked, "And a'n't I a woman? Look at me! Look at my arm! (and she bared her right arm to the shoulder, showing her tremendous muscular power). I have ploughed, and planted, and gathered into barns, and no man could head me! And a'n't I a woman? I could work as much and eat as much as a man—when I could get it—and bear de lash as well! And a'n't I a woman? I have borne thirteen chilern, and seen 'em mos' all sold off to slavery, and when I cried out with my mother's grief, none but Jesus heard me! And a'n't I a woman?

"Den dey talks 'bout dis ting in de head; what dis dey call it?" ("Intellect," whispered some one near.) "Dat's it, honey. What's dat got to do wid womin's rights or nigger's rights? If my cup won't hold but a pint, and yourn holds a quart, wouldn't ye be mean not to let me have my little half-measure full?" And she pointed her significant finger, and sent a keen glance at the minister who had made the argument. The cheering was long and loud.

"Den dat little man in black dar, he say women can't have as much rights as men, 'cause Christ wan't a woman! Whar did your Christ come from?" Rolling thunder couldn't have stilled that crowd, as did those deep, wonderful tones, as she stood there with outstretched arms and eyes of fire. Raising her voice still louder, she repeated, "Whar did your Christ come from? From God and a woman! Man had nothin' to do wid Him." Oh, what a rebuke that was to that little man.

Turning again to another objector, she took up the defense of Mother Eve. I can not follow her through it all. It was pointed, and witty, and solemn; eliciting at almost every sentence deafening applause; and she ended by asserting: "If de fust woman God ever made was strong enough to turn de world upside down all alone, dese women togedder (and she glanced her eye over the platform) ought to be able to turn it back, and get it right side up again! And now dey is asking to do it, de men better let 'em." Long-continued cheering greeted this. " 'Bleeged to ye for hearin' on me, and now ole Sojourner han't got nothin' more to say."

Amid roars of applause, she returned to her corner, leaving more than one of us with streaming eyes, and hearts beating with gratitude. She had taken us up in her strong arms and carried us safely over the slough of difficulty turning the whole tide in our favor. I have never in my life seen anything like the magical influence that subdued the mobbish spirit of the day, and turned the sneers and jeers of an excited crowd into notes of respect and admiration. Hundreds rushed up to shake hands with her, and congratulate the glorious old mother, and bid her God-speed on her mission of "testifyin' again concerning the wickedness of this 'ere people."

from *A Doll's House*

—*Henrik Ibsen*
translated by R. Farquarson Sharp

A Doll's House shows a woman's gradual realization that she leads a totally useless life. Just before the final scene of the play, Nora has returned from a party where she has costumed herself and danced for company as a pretty Capri girl (fulfilling the function of Woman-as-Object). On arriving home, her husband, Torvald Helmer, discovers through a letter that she has been guilty of contracting a debt without his knowledge and of forging her father's name to a note; she has expected Helmer to sacrifice himself for her sake (in accord with the protective male role he has been playing) but, instead, he blames her for wrecking his good name and calls her an unfit wife and mother. When he discovers that the note has been cancelled and his reputation is safe, he offers to forgive and forget. But Nora has had it with Helmer and the doll's house.

For a contemporary analysis of the social significance and the results of Nora's move toward liberation, read Eve Merriam's After Nora Slammed the Door *(1964), a portion of which appears on pages 213-222.*

HELMER. You have loved me as a wife ought to love her husband. Only you had not sufficient knowledge to judge of the means you used. But do you suppose you are any the less dear to me, because you don't understand how to act on your own responsibility? No, no; only lean on me; I will advise you and direct you. I should not be a man if this womanly helplessness did not just give you a double attractiveness in my eyes. You must not think any more about the hard things I said in my first moment of consternation, when I thought everything was going to overwhelm me. I have forgiven you. Nora; I swear to you I have forgiven you.

NORA. Thank you for your forgiveness. (*She goes out through the door to the right.*)

HELMER. No, don't go—. (*Looks in.*) What are you doing in there?

NORA. (*from within*). Taking off my fancy dress.

HELMER (*standing at the open door*). Yes, do. Try and calm yourself, and make your mind easy again, my frightened little singing-bird. Be at rest, and feel secure; I have broad wings to shelter you under. (*Walks up and down by the door.*) How warm and cosy our home is, Nora. Here is shelter for you; here I will protect you like a hunted dove that I have saved from a hawk's claws; I will bring peace to your poor beating heart. It will come, little by little, Nora, believe me. To-morrow morning you will look upon it all quite differently; soon everything will be just as it was before. Very soon you won't need me to assure you that I have forgiven. you; you will yourself feel the certainty that I have done so. Can you suppose I should ever think of such a thing as repudiating you, or even reproaching you? You have no idea what a true man's heart is like, Nora. There is something so indescribably sweet and satisfying, to a man, in the knowledge that he has forgiven his wife—forgiven her freely, and with all his heart. It seems as if that had made her, as it were, doubly his own; he has given her a new life, so to speak; and she has in a way become both wife and child to him. So you shall be for me after this, my little scared, helpless darling. Have no anxiety about anything, Nora; only be frank and open with me, and I will serve as will and conscience both to you—. What is this? Not gone to bed? Have you changed your things?

NORA (*in everyday dress*). Yes, Torvald, I have changed my things now.

HELMER. But what for?—so late as this.

NORA. I shall not sleep to-night.

HELMER. But, my dear Nora—

NORA (*looking at her watch*). It is not so very late. Sit down here, Torvald. You and I have much to say to one another. (*She sits down at one side of the table.*)

HELMER. Nora—what is this?—this cold, set face?

NORA. Sit down. It will take some time; I have a lot to talk over with you.

HELMER (*sits down at the opposite side of the table*). You alarm me, Nora!—and I don't understand you.

NORA. No, that is just it. You don't understand me, and I have never understood you either—before to-night. No, you mustn't interrupt me. You must simply listen to what I say. Torvald, this is a settling of accounts.

HELMER. What do you mean by that?

NORA (*after a short silence*). Isn't there one thing that strikes you as strange in our sitting here like this?

HELMER. What is that?

NORA. We have been married now eight years. Does it not occur to you that this is the first time we two, you and I, husband and wife, have had a serious conversation?

HELMER. What do you mean by serious?

NORA. In all these eight years—longer than that—from the very beginning of our acquaintance, we have never exchanged a word on any serious subject.

HELMER. Was it likely that I would be continually and for ever telling you about worries that you could not help me to bear?

NORA. I am not speaking about business matters. I say that we have never sat down in earnest together to try and get at the bottom of anything.

HELMER. But, dearest Nora, would it have been any good to you?

NORA. That is just it; you have never understood me. I have been greatly wronged, Torvald—first by papa and then by you.

HELMER. What! By us two—by us two, who have loved you better than anyone else in the world?

NORA (*shaking her head*). You have never loved me. You have only thought it pleasant to be in love with me.

HELMER. Nora, what do I hear you saying?

NORA. It is perfectly true, Torvald. When I was at home with papa, he told me his opinion about everything, and so I had the same opinions; and if I differed from him I concealed the fact, because he would not have liked it. He called me his doll-child, and he played with me just as I used to play with my dolls. And when I came to live with you—

HELMER. What sort of an expression is that to use about our marriage?

NORA (*undisturbed*). I mean that I was simply transferred from papa's hands into yours. You arranged everything according to your own taste, and so I got the same tastes as you—or else I pretended to, I am really not quite sure which—I think sometimes the one and sometimes the other. When I look back on it, it seems to me as if I had been living here like a poor woman—just from hand to mouth. I have existed merely to perform tricks for you, Torvald. But you would have it so. You and papa have committed a great sin against me. It is your fault that I have made nothing of my life.

HELMER. How unreasonable and how ungrateful you are, Nora! Have you not been happy here?

NORA. No, I have never been happy. I thought I was, but it has never really been so.

HELMER. Not—not happy!

NORA. No, only merry. And you have always been so kind to me. But our home has been nothing but a playroom. I have been your doll-wife, just as at home I was a papa's doll-child; and here the children have been my dolls. I thought it great fun when you played with me, just as they thought it great fun when I played with them. That is what our marriage has been, Torvald.

HELMER. There is some truth in what you say—exaggerated and strained as your view of it is. But for the future it shall be different. Play-time shall be over, and lesson-time shall begin.

NORA. Whose lessons? Mine, or the children's?

HELMER. Both yours and the children's, my darling Nora.

NORA. Alas, Torvald, you are not the man to educate me into being a proper wife for you.

HELMER. And you can say that!

NORA. And I—how am I fitted to bring up the children?

HELMER. Nora!

NORA. Didn't you say so yourself a little while ago—that you dare not trust me to bring them up?

HELMER. In a moment of anger! Why do you pay any heed to that?

NORA. Indeed, you were perfectly right. I am not fit for the task. There is another task I must undertake first. I must try and educate myself—you are not the man to help me in that. I must do that for myself. And that is why I am going to leave you now.

HELMER (*springing up*). What do you say?

NORA. I must stand quite alone, if I am to understand myself and everything about me. It is for that reason that I cannot remain with you any longer.

HELMER. Nora, Nora!

NORA. I am going away from here now, at once. I am sure Christine will take me in for the night—

HELMER. You are out of your mind! I won't allow it! I forbid you!

NORA. It is no use forbidding me anything any longer. I will take with me what belongs to myself. I will take nothing from you, either now or later.

HELMER. What sort of madness is this!

NORA. To-morrow I shall go home—I mean, to my old home. It will be easiest for me to find something to do there.

HELMER. You blind, foolish woman!

NORA. I must try and get some sense, Torvald.

HELMER. To desert your home, your husband and your children! And you don't consider what people will say!

NORA. I cannot consider that at all. I only know that it is necessary for me.

HELMER. It's shocking. This is how you would neglect your most sacred duties.

NORA. What do you consider my most sacred duties?

HELMER. Do I need to tell you that? Are they not your duties to your husband and your children?

NORA. I have other duties just as sacred.

HELMER. That you have not. What duties could those be?

NORA. Duties to myself.

HELMER. Before all else, you are a wife and a mother.

NORA. I don't believe that any longer. I believe that before all else I am a reasonable human being, just as you are—or, at all events, that I must try and become one. I know quite well, Torvald, that most people would think you right, and that views of that kind are to be found in books; but I can no longer content myself with what most people say, or with what is found in books. I must think over things for myself and get to understand them.

HELMER. Can you not understand your place in your own home? Have you not a reliable guide in such matters as that?—have you no religion?

NORA. I am afraid, Torvald, I do not exactly know what religion is.

HELMER. What are you saying?

NORA. I know nothing but what the clergyman said, when I went to be confirmed. He told us that religion was this, and that and the other. When I am away from all this, and am alone, I will look into that matter too. I will see if what the clergyman said is true, or at all events if it is true for me.

HELMER. This is unheard of in a girl of your age! But if religion cannot lead you aright, let me try and awaken your conscience. I suppose you have some moral sense? Or—answer me—am I to think you have none?

NORA. I assure you, Torvald, that is not an easy question to answer. I really don't know. The thing perplexes me altogether. I only know that you and I look at it in quite a different light. I am learning, too, that the law is quite another thing from what I supposed; but I find it impossible to convince myself that the law is right. According to it a woman has no right to spare her old dying father, or to save her husband's life. I can't believe that.

HELMER. You talk like a child. You don't understand the conditions of the world in which you live.

NORA. No, I don't. But now I am going to try. I am going to see if I can make out who is right, the world or I.

HELMER. You are ill, Nora; you are delirious; I almost think you are out of your mind.

NORA. I have never felt my mind so clear and certain as to-night.

HELMER. And is it with a clear and certain mind that you forsake your husband and your children?

NORA. Yes, it is.

HELMER. Then there is only one possible explanation.

NORA. What is that?

HELMER. You do not love me any more.

NORA. No, that is just it.

HELMER. Nora!—and you can say that?

NORA. It gives me great pain, Torvald, for you have always been so kind to me, but I cannot help it. I do not love you any more.

HELMER (*regaining his composure*). Is that a clear and certain conviction too?

NORA. Yes, absolutely clear and certain. That is the reason why I will not stay here any longer.

HELMER. And can you tell me what I have done to forfeit your love?

NORA. Yes, indeed I can. It was to-night, when the wonderful thing did not happen; then I saw you were not the man I had thought you.

HELMER. Explain yourself better. I don't understand you.

NORA. I have waited so patiently for eight years; for, goodness knows, I knew very well that wonderful things don't happen every day. Then this horrible misfortune came upon me; and then I felt quite certain that the wonderful thing was going to happen at last. When Krogstad's letter was lying out there, never for a moment did I imagine that you would consent to accept this man's conditions. I was so absolutely certain that you would say to him: Publish the thing to the whole world. And when that was done—

HELMER. Yes, what then?—when I had exposed my wife to shame and disgrace?

NORA. When that was done, I was so absolutely certain, you would come forward and take everything upon yourself, and say: I am the guilty one.

HELMER. Nora—!

NORA. You mean that I would never have accepted such a sacrifice on your part? No, of course not. But what would my assurances have been worth against yours? That was the wonderful thing which I hoped for and feared; and it was to prevent that, that I wanted to kill myself.

HELMER. I would gladly work night and day for you. Nora—bear sorrow and want for your sake. But no man would sacrifice his honour for the one he loves.

NORA. It is a thing hundreds of thousands of women have done.

HELMER. Oh, you think and talk like a heedless child.

NORA. Maybe. But you neither think nor talk like the man I could bind myself to. As soon as your fear was over—and it was not fear for what threatened me, but for what might happen to you—when the whole thing was past, as far as you were concerned it was exactly as if nothing at all had happened. Exactly as before, I was your little skylark, your doll, which you would in future treat with doubly gentle care, because it was so brittle and fragile. (*Getting up.*) Torvald—it was then it dawned upon me that for eight years I had been living here with a strange man, and had borne him three children—. Oh, I can't bear to think of it! I could tear myself into little bits!

HELMER (*sadly*). I see, I see. An abyss has opened between us—there is no denying it. But, Nora, would it not be possible to fill it up?

NORA. As I am now, I am no wife for you.

HELMER. I have it in me to become a different man.

NORA. Perhaps—if your doll is taken away from you.

HELMER. But to part!—to part from you! No, no, Nora, I can't understand that idea.

NORA (*going out to the right*). That makes it all the more certain that it must be done. (*She comes back with her cloak and hat and a small bag which she puts on a chair by the table.*)

HELMER. Nora, Nora, not now! Wait till to-morrow.

NORA (*putting on her cloak*). I cannot spend the night in a strange man's room.

HELMER. But can't we live here like brother and sister—?

NORA (*putting on her hat*). You know very well that would not last long. (*Puts the shawl around her.*) Good-bye, Torvald. I won't see the little ones. I know they are in better hands than mine. As I am now, I can be of no use to them.

HELMER. But some day, Nora—some day?

NORA. How can I tell? I have no idea what is going to become of me.

HELMER. But you are my wife, whatever becomes of you.

NORA. Listen, Torvald. I have heard that when a wife deserts her husband's house, as I am doing now, he is legally freed from all obligations toward her. In any case I set you free from all your obligations. You are not to feel yourself bound in the slightest way, any more than I shall. There must be perfect freedom on both sides. See, here is your ring back. Give me mine.

HELMER. That too?

NORA. That too.

HELMER. Here it is.

NORA. That's right. Now it is all over. I have put the keys here. The maids know all about everything in the house—better than I do. To-morrow, after I have left her, Christine will come here and pack my own things that I brought with me from home. I will have them sent after me.

HELMER. All over! All over!—Nora, shall you never think of me again?

NORA. I know I shall often think of you and the children and this house.

HELMER. May I write to you, Nora?

NORA. No—never. You must not do that.

HELMER. But at least let me send you—

NORA. Nothing—nothing—

HELMER. Let me help you if you are in want.

NORA. No. I can receive nothing from a stranger.

HELMER. Nor—can I never be anything more than a stranger to you?

NORA (*taking her bag*). Ah, Torvald, the most wonderful thing of all would have to happen.

HELMER. Tell me what that would be!

NORA. Both you and I would have to be so changed that—. Oh, Torvald, I don't believe any longer in wonderful things happening.

HELMER. But I will believe in it. Tell me! So changed that—?

NORA. That our life together would be a real wedlock. Good-bye. (*She goes out through the hall.*)

HELMER (*sinks down on a chair at the door and buries his face in his hands*). Nora! Nora! (*Looks round, and rises.*) Empty. She is gone. (*A hope flashes across his mind.*) The most wonderful thing of all—?

(*The sound of a door shutting is heard from below.*)

The Changing Women

Stan Steiner

Perhaps nowhere is the pernicious effect of male chauvinism so apparent as in the effect of white politics on Indian tribal life. Unable to comprehend a society where women were influential in the decision-making processes of government, the white government ignored Indian women and taught Indian men to imitate the white man. Indian women are now, however, re-asserting their leadership qualities, drawing on the strength of

their Indian heritage. Consider the militancy of this statement
by a young Assiniboin woman who plans to be tribal chairman
in five years: "I am a mean and savage Indian, so watch out.
Mother, you are too old-fashioned; if you are too polite the
white man will walk all over you. And the Indian men will never
elect you. The young Indian girls are different. We're modern."

In this chapter from The New Indians, *Stan Steiner traces the*
Indian woman's past and present roles, ending with a series of
vignettes dramatizing the modern Indian woman's combination
of white and Indian cultures.

"We are full-blooded Assiniboins, my daughters and I," the mother
said with pride.

The eldest daughter had a tense and hard laugh. "I am a mean
savage," she said. She was not joking; there was a severity in her face.
"My sister, on the other hand," and she indicated a young girl who was
quietly sitting in the corner of the kitchen, with long, light hair and a
calm face, "... my sister runs with the whites! I run with the Indians!
And my mother, she runs ..."

"Where does your mother run?" the mother asked.

It was the late afternoon of a cool and lucid summer day in northern
Montana. The quiet was brittle. In the tall grasses of the high prairie
the wind blew autumn from the Canadian border, through the fields of
the Fort Peck Reservation. The horses in the corrals kicked up a whirlwind of dust. The horses snorted; the wind in their nostrils had excited
them and they had to be tied up.

The women sat around the kitchen table and talked politics.

"Where does your mother run?" the mother repeated.

"You run for tribal office. But where does that get you?"

"It is true. Sometimes I think I am running in circles."

When women led by being women, they held together the tribe and
family by their act of being. Unobtrusive, soft-spoken, quiet women
did not have to act like men. In those days women did not have to be
elected to leadership that was theirs by virtue of their existence as the
core of the kinship family. When the men of the tribe were away to hunt,
or to war, women held things together.

But the old tribal way no longer held together. In the governments
of parliamentary men, the position of women had been usurped by elections and the laws of the white man that came outside of tribal life.

"Whoever heard of a tribal chairwoman?" the mother said.

The mother had been recognized for her political leadership as a vice
president of the National Congress of American Indians; but she had

not been recognized by her own tribe. She had run for the tribal council
and lost.

"Now they say I should run for tribal chairman," the mother said,
her hands in her apron knotted at the thought. What should she do? Her
uncle, "a medicine man, as you say," had told her that two men would
stand in her way in the last election. That had happened. "I lost by two
votes," she said, "so I better ask my uncle before I run again. My daughters do not believe these things; they do not understand the old things."

"There is nothing wrong with medicine men," said the eldest daughter, who had been to college for two years. "Psychologically they are
quite perceptive sometimes. But there is something wrong with tribal
politics."

"What?" the mother said.

"Men!" said the eldest daughter. "For too long tribal politics have
been the refuge for yes men. For self-seeking men. For weak men. I
think we need women running things once more."

"Like you, I suppose?" the younger daughter scoffed. "You hate
everybody."

"Just white Indians."

"Whites are no different than Indians."

"Why do you always side with them?"

"Because you think you are better than they are."

"I am better! I am Indian!"

The squall of words subsided as abruptly as it had begun. The mother
smiled at both. Her daughters were strong-spoken; she liked that.
Women ought to be strong.

"Mother, if you run for tribal chairman," the eldest daughter said, "I
will run against you."

"As long as it is in the family," the mother responded.

The Assiniboins are rural people, ranchers and farmers most of them.
On the Fort Peck Reservation they keep to themselves. When the tumult
of the outside world enters their lives they like to keep it a family affair,
within the tribe.

"If you're so Indian, how come you left home?" the younger daughter
chided.

The eldest daughter's eyes flared: "It's the psychology of the whites
that I want to learn. To be inside of their psychology. That's something
we Indians can do. But they can't learn to be inside our psychology.
None of the girls in the army believe I am Indian. They say to me, 'You
must be Greek or Spanish or Italian. You are too smart to be Indian.'
But I tell them I am a savage. I tell them I am a mean and savage Indian,
so watch out. Mother, you are too old-fashioned; if you are too polite
the white men will walk all over you. And the Indian men will never

elect you. The young Indian girls are different. We're modern." She frowned, biting her lips. "Except, that is, my sister. But, you'll see, in five years I will be tribal chairman."

On the kitchen table lay the shadows of the late afternoon sun that slanted through the window. The three women sat quietly. Listening to the silence that separated them, they were thoughtful. "We live in three different worlds," the mother said.

The men of the family had galloped off, as was fitting, to hunt for stray cows, and the women of the family had stayed home to discuss the social structure of the family, in the modern kitchen of the ranch house. The Assiniboin family had simply modernized the traditional division of tribal labor.

Women had tilled the earth, sown the seeds, and harvested the crops. Women had preserved the tribal unity and maintained the family. In fact, the women had often been what modern man somewhat enviously had termed "the decision makers." In the matriarchal clans that ruled many of the tribes barely a few generations ago—in some tribes they still do—the women were not merely the titular heads of the families, with the inheritance of tribal leadership and family name being given by them. These women were often the de facto powers of government.

That this was but a few generations ago may account for the modernized and traduced form in which it had persisted. Even if only around the kitchen table.

"Someone had to do it," the eldest daughter said. "Those anthropologists say we had a matrilineal family. Actually, all we had was common sense. Someone had to run things while the boys were being boys, and shooting the countryside full of arrows and making widows, instead of babies. Someone had to keep the home fires burning. You know, a buffalo hide was no Social Security system. That matrilineal family talk was about the only survivor's insurance we had.

"Oh, all that Earth Mother nonsense. Those anthropologists ought to write mysteries." She laughed. "Women were just being practical."

The power of women within Indian beliefs may nonetheless have corresponded with their importance in tribal life. In the myriad theories of tribal religions about the creation of human beings—the creation myths, as the scientific mythology referred to tribal theories—there was one recurring theme: the sacredness of the Earth Mother.

The Earth Mother was thought to have created human beings. The theory varied with the teller and the tribe, but it was told that the Spirit of the Sky, or the Grandfather Sky, or the Father Rock, or the Father Sun, or whatever name was given to the Supreme Being, who was male, may have guided the Earth Mother in her act of creation. However, she, not he, was the creator. The female origin of humanity was self-evident to tribal man. It was woman's work. She was the Creator, the Source, the Womb.

So there were: The Grandmother Cedar, of the Arikara Tribe of the Plains, who was the "Grandmother of life," and who "Led the people out of the Underworld." The Mother Corn of the Pueblo Indians, who "gave" life and led "the people to the surface of the earth." The Mother Corn of the Pawnees, who "taught the tasks of mankind," and who "gave the breath of life," and speech itself. The Grandmother Earth of the Winnebagos, who, like the creator God of the Sioux, was feminine and who was the symbol of women. "Our Grandmother Earth is a woman, and in abusing your wife you will be abusing her," an old Winnebago man told Paul Radin. "She it is who takes care of us."

The Zuñis had a prayer:

> Mother Corn caused movement.
> She gave life.
> Life being given we came.
> Out of the Underground.

It was the Navajo Goddess of Creation who was, however, the most vivid. The Changing Woman, said the Navajo religion, created the Diné—the people—by molding them from the skin of the underneath of her breasts, the tenderest and most sensitive part of a woman's skin, it was said. Human beings were the only creatures created from the breasts of the Changing Woman, it was said.

Whichever way she created life, and whatever her form was, the Earth Mother was not merely a holy woman. She was thought of as a living deity. She was an earthy goddess, indeed, for she was the biological, as well as the agricultural, as well as the spiritual giver of life.

In a time when the power of women in tribal life had diminished, and the attitudes of men toward these women had demeaned them, why resurrect the belief in the Earth Mother? The historic and religious background of tribal women is of importance in understanding the self-image of the modern young Indian girls, and the source of the strengths that they draw upon to become the contemporary Changing Woman.

Nowhere was the power of women in tribal life more dramatically shown than in the shaping of the Iroquois Confederation of Nations. It was the women of the Iroquois tribes who fought what may have been the first successful feminist rebellion in the New World. The year was 1600, or thereabouts, when these tribal feminists decided that they had had enough of unregulated warfare by their men. Lysistratas among the Indian women proclaimed a boycott on love-making and childbearing. Until the men conceded to them the power to decide upon war and peace, there would be no more warriors. Since the Iroquois men believed that women alone knew the secret of birth, the feminist rebellion was instantly successful.

In the Constitution of Deganawidah the founder of the Iroquois Confederation of Nations had said: "He caused the body of our mother, the woman, to be of a great worth and honor. He purposed that she shall be endowed and entrusted with the birth and upbringing of men, and that she shall have the care of all that is planted by which life is sustained and supported and the power to breathe is fortified: *and moreover that the warriors shall be her assistants.*"

The footnote of history was curiously supplied when Susan B. Anthony began her "Votes for Women" movement two and a half centuries later. Unknowingly the feminists chose to hold their founding convention of latter-day suffragettes in the town of Seneca, New York. The site was just a stone's throw from the old council house where the Iroquois women had plotted their feminist rebellion.

But, as the white women were gaining power, the Indian women were losing theirs.

Ironically, it was the very power of women within tribal life that led to their powerlessness in modern society. The women were trapped within the confines of the kinship families and tribes. In political affairs their influence was limited to the tribal world and went no further. The white man was ignorant of the tribal women, or ignored them.

Because of this ignorance, or because of the masculine conceits of "Western Man," the government in its official dealings with Indians did not recognize the power of the tribal women. The matriarchs of the tribes were not invited to sign the treaties of peace, though it may have been they who had decided upon the peace. It was a disastrous oversight. The headmen, or the heads of the warrior bands, were summoned to these X-signing ceremonies, but never the women.

One observer knowingly noted: "The Indian Service has made the mistake of dealing exclusively with the men, only to wonder or to be annoyed when agreements reached with men are not carried out."

Women were as conspicuously absent from the hundreds of tribal delegations brought to Washington by the government in the late 1800's. Perhaps the government could not comprehend a society where women held the power to influence peace and war so decisively.

It was a moot question. The U.S. Army in that period had reflected the attitude of white men toward Indian women by naming the sitting target on their shooting ranges "The Kneeling Squaw."

When the power of the tribes began to disintegrate in the nineteenth century, so did that of the women. The men were confined to the reservations and could no longer hunt in the old way or do things that men

did. In frustration they turned their energies inward to tribal affairs.
And the tribal councils of men and tribal chairmen that were established
by the government to carry on official business further diminished the
older tribal ways of governing and the political role of the women. The
men then began to adopt some of. the white man's attitudes toward
their women.

Mrs. Anne Wauneka, of the Navajo Tribe, who has seen three generations of changing attitudes, said: "In the Navajo way of thinking, leadership is really a man's business. The men say that a woman's place is
in the hogan, not in the council."

Once dislodged from their traditional role the women withdrew
deeper into the remnants of tribal life. Commissioner of Indian Affairs
Hiram Price perceived the sorrowful result when he reported, in 1882,
that "The intelligent, decent Indian girl is a problem." His annual report
to the Congress quoted the remarks of the principal of the Hampton
Normal School for Indians, General S. C. Armstrong, who wrote:
"There is absolutely no position of dignity to which an Indian girl, after
three years of training, can look forward with reasonable confidence.
There is nothing for her but to enjoy or suffer in the present state as
best she may."

"The Kneeling Squaw" was expendable. Her life on the reservations
was not only confining but crippling, for she was to be usually ignored
by the dominant society. She was rarely elected to tribal leadership.
She was not selected for schooling. She was burdened with her traditional role in tribal life but was denied any official voice in tribal
decisions.

"It is understandable that the superficial white observer concludes
that the Navajo woman is little better than a chattel of her husband,"
wrote one anthropologist.

The heritage of tribal women was not that easily obliterated. It had
merely withdrawn into the kinship family so deeply that it was not
visible to outsiders.

Symbols of the power of women are preserved in different ways by
different tribes:

Among the Mescalero and White Mountain Apaches, that symbol
is the ceremony of puberty rites for young girls. It is one of a few of the
old religious rituals that is strictly adhered to and widely celebrated in
the traditional way by these tribes.

Among the Navajos, that symbol, one of many, has been built into
the very structure of the hogan; for to this day the hogan is built upon
four poles—the east pole named after the Earth Woman; the south pole
after the Mountain Woman; the west pole after the Water Woman;
and the north pole after the Corn Woman. Literally the homes of the

Navajos are supported by their women—and would collapse without them.

In everyday life the tribal women often have more than symbolic influence. Where they are heard and to the degree that they are listened to, it is by the guiles and wiles that are more traditional to white women than to Indian women. "By vigorous use of their tongues [they] frequently nullify decisions made by their men," it has been said of Navajo women. It is pathetic evidence of the external powerlessness to which tribal women in a once matriarchal society have been reduced.

Some women have been elected to tribal councils. But they have been few. Like Mrs. Wauneka of the Navajos, they have been exceptions, or exceptional.

However there has never been an Indian tribe that elected a woman as tribal chairman. Several women have made the attempt. None of them has won. One bold tribal lady, who had seemingly been elected at the polls, promptly had her election invalidated by the tribal council of men. In itself this would hardly be extraordinary were it not that in every crisis that has faced the Indians in the last generation women have been recognized as leaders.

In the Fish-Ins in Washington State one of the undaunted spokesmen for the fishermen was Janet McCloud of the Nisqually Tribe. Of the three young Indians who organized the Washington State Project, Sandy Johnson, a young college girl of the Makah Tribe, was one of the staunchest. When the Urban American Indian Protest Committee was formed in Minneapolis, one of the two organizers was a young Indian girl, Mary Thunder.

When the Dakota Sioux successfully fought the State Jurisdiction Law over their lands, several Sioux women were leaders of the campaign, though no tribal women held a top position on any Dakota Sioux reservation.

When the end of World War II brought demands for intertribal unity and the National Congress of American Indians was founded, it was a Sioux young woman, Helen Peterson, who was chosen its executive director. The "United Nations of the tribes" has had women in many of its leading positions: Georgeann Robinson, of the Osage, is first vice president, and Helen Mitchell, of the Quinault, is secretary. While of its regional vice presidents three are women: Elsie Ricklefs, of the Hoopa Valley Tribe, Agnes Savilla of the Mohave, and Alvina Grey Bear of the Standing Rock Sioux.

And when ten young Indians founded the National Indian Youth Council five were college girls. Of the three top officers of that youth movement two were young women: Shirley Witt, of the Mohawks (first vice president) and Joan Noble, of the Utes (second vice-president). It is not unusual for young women to be prominent in youthful politics, but this emphasis on femininity cannot be equaled by the leadership of any non-Indian collegiate group.

None of these women who are national Indian leaders held positions of equal importance within their own tribes. Why the seemingly strange double standard? It is more than an expression of the baffling peculiarity of tribal politics.

These women have had to go outside of their tribes to be recognized as leaders. Within tribal life they were trapped by the confines of their own history. Once unburdened by the weight of obligations that no longer functioned, they were freer to reassert themselves and to draw upon their heritage as women.

Tens of thousands of Indian women have come into the cities. For the last decade they have been leaving the reservations in growing numbers, not to seek their fortunes—few have any expectation of finding any—but to find a fuller, freer life for themselves. Many have made the trek to the cities simply to find the meagerest of jobs.

More often than the tribal men, these tribal women have been able to cross the cultural divide from rural to urban life without losing their way. One survey of the Indian community of Chicago indicated that half of the Indian women in that city were not living with their husbands. The husbands had left, unnerved by the hectic momentum of urban life, the ghettos of crowded rooms, the smoggy sky, and the humiliation of unemployment lines. Or they had sought solace in the nearest bar, or had hitchhiked back to the reservation where *they* felt freer.

In the cities, the power of the women has been recognized by the extratribal communities. Election of tribal women to the leadership of these urban Indian centers has been a phenomenon in modern Indian life. The San Francisco Indian Center during the winter of 1966-67, for instance, had four women on its board of directors and one man. Of the seven officers of the California group, three were women. The Indian Center of Chicago had three women on its board of directors.

Los Angeles, Minneapolis, and New York City clubs of urban Indians all have women among their leaders. So do the Indian centers in other cities, almost without exception.

"We adapt like crazy," said Mary Lou Payne of the young Indian women. The women, especially the younger women, are more resilient and flexible, more accepted and accepting, more capable of outward change and inner stability than their husbands are at times. "No one adapts like an Indian, if given half a chance. I'm schizophrenic myself," the Cherokee girl said.

The older and traditional Navajo woman, Mrs. Anne Wauneka, thought there was a more profoundly Indian way to explain the staying power of the young women. She said: "I see a lot of these educated Navajo girls typing. They went to school. As secretaries they have been taught to use shorthand, they have been taught to use typewriters. This is the way an office should be run. This person is using what she has been taught. And she has been paid. And this is done for economy reasons.

"And she has been taught to live in a nice house where you just touch the walls and the lights come on. Where you touch a certain metal, turn it, and the water is running. Yet she is an Indian. Her belief is within her. Her heritage is within her. She is just an image in the office, who copied what the white man has taught her to do, for economy reasons. But she is a Navajo and will always remain an Indian.

"An Indian is an Indian," Mrs. Wauneka said. "She may have a dark complexion. She may have a light complexion. She may have blue eyes. She may not have. But she is an Indian."

On the Rosebud Sioux reservation of South Dakota, the tribal newspaper, *Eyapaha*, told of one such—a Crow Creek girl, Marlene Bearheels—who has journeyed, it said, "from the jobless reservation world to the world of the machine that seems to be replacing man." This descendant of the warriors of Spotted Tail and Red Cloud was studying data-processing machines and office automation at Rocky Mountain College.

"This is a good field to get into, especially for Sioux students," said Miss Bearheels. She cheerfully added, "I hope to get a job in Florida."

There is a newspaper column in the *Navajo Times,* "The Law and You," that offers tribesmen legal advice. One day the law columnist talked about the legality of love and the illegality of children. And for weeks and weeks after Navajo women laughed at the advice offered.

Love is not legal to the white man unless you "buy marriage licenses," the tribal newspaper informed its readers. "A little piece of paper may not make a man and his wife better people in the eyes of God, but it sure helps in keeping the 'paper work' straight."

The "white man's law" was odd. It was even said that if a wife's husband died, and she didn't have that "little piece of paper," the justices in the white man's courts "might even say the children were not of [her] husband." But that was not to be believed. No matter how powerful the white man thought a "little piece of paper" was, he could not really think that babies could be made that way.

Humor the "white man's law," the tribal newspaper concluded, by obeying it. It was even said that without that "little piece of paper," children, as well as love, were not legal. If the readers had been married in the religious ceremony of the tribe, they would be well advised to "buy marriage licenses."

"Make it easier for your children to live in the white man's world. Don't brand them as 'illegitimate' in the white man's world."

Wahleah Lujan, the demure Taos Pueblo beauty, who was Miss Indian America for 1967, was standing in the lobby of a hotel in Denver. She had left her courses in sociology at Fort Lewis College to tour the country and plead the cause of her people.

The young woman in the resplendent robes of her pueblo, pure alabaster cloth embroidered with brilliant designs, stood there in confusion. For the whirlwind public-relations tour had taken her into a strange world of urban madness, from the calm of her muted adobe.

A Denver matron murmured in the politest tones, "Tell me, what foreign country do you come from?"

"What did you say?"

"I said to her," Wahleah Lujan said smiling, "that I came from Taos."

Sitting in the living room of her suburban home in Window Rock, the Navajo capital, on a sofa bright with Navajo rugs as upon a throne, Mrs. Anne Wauneka talked of these changing women. In the room several men of the tribe sat about her as her court would about a queen.

Her clothes were regal. The subtle brown velvets of the traditional Navajo woman's gown flowed to her feet. Her breast was adorned with splashes of silver and turquoise jewelry, which encircled her fingers as well.

If there were a queen in the United States, it would have to be this woman, the most honored and most powerful of Indian women leaders in modern times, the daughter of the last of the great chiefs of the Navajos. Her crown, however, was a knot of white sheep's wool that bound her black hair in the ancient way.

She talked of those who had said a woman's place was in the hogan:

"We are all human beings. To me it doesn't really matter whether it's a woman, or whether it's a man. Their structure is the same. They have a brain to think with. This is what I always base my opinion on in dealing with people. And the problems are the same. And the teaching is the same. And the house they live in is the same. And the food that is placed on the table is the same. When you serve to the people you don't say that a man eats this kind of food so they go to another place. And the language is the same. And the subject to be discussed is about the same.

"So everything points to a human being. Whether it's a man or a woman. To my way of thinking there should be woman leadership as there should be man. Because the problem remains. And the problem affects both sex. If a leader is needed, although it is a woman, I would say it should be used."

Combining the qualities of Mary Lou Payne and Anne Wauneka, resilience and inheritance, the ability to change and yet retain and draw upon the traditional sources of the power of tribal women, the image of the contemporary Indian woman is being created. She is no longer the shy Indian maid of romantic legend. She is no longer "The Kneeling Squaw." She wears a bouffant hairdo, has a diploma in her purse, and dances the Twist, but in her heart is the rediscovery of her strength as an Indian, and a pride in the unique beauty of her Indianness.

In the town of Whiteriver on the Apache Reservation of White Mountain, there is an old trading post that has been modernized into a supermarket. Hanging above the checkout counters was a display of cradleboards. And the young Apache girls who worked the office machines in the tribal office across the road came in with mini-skirts to shop; their eyes were amused as they saw the portable baby carriages in which they themselves had been carried—they had seen plastic imitations in the drugstores of Phoenix that were not half as comfortable.

The old Hopi grandmother told of her grandson who visited her in Oraibi for the summer, but could not sleep at night in the ancient village because "it is too quiet." Her daughter was a schoolteacher in Tucson, who lived in a suburb near an Air Force base. "Quiet is frightening, if you come from a city of jet planes," the grandmother said.

Oraibi is high on a mesa, a parched pueblo, dry as dust, in the midst of the desert where there has never been any running water. The Hopis have lived there for one thousand years. Now, the young women of Oraibi carry their clothes to a newly built self-service laundromat.

In a little café on the Navajo reservation, a young girl was reading her book. She was seated on a worn stool beside a holey screen door through which the desert sands sifted, as they have for an eternity.

"What are you reading?" she was asked.

"Russian."

"It looks like Navajo."

"Navajo?" the girl laughed. "These days, if you study science you have to read Russian."

Within the barbaric beauty of Monument Valley an Indian mother and her little son were herding sheep. The mother, Mrs. Rose Greyeyes, her son too, were suddenly thrown by the horses, frightened by an explosion in the sky where a jet plane had broken the sound barrier. The mother and son were both injured. Laconically, a tribal newspaper commented: It is "a type of accident nonexistent a few years back."

In the old Southwestern-style Hotel Adams in Phoenix, Arizona, a project of the Federal Development and Training Act was under way. The goal: "To convert shy Indian girls into scintillating waitresses" and "motel housekeepers."

At Window Rock a young mother patiently wheeled her newly bought baby carriage back and forth on the narrow strip of cement sidewalk outside the lodge. It was one of the few bits of paved sidewalk on the sixteen-million-acre reservation. And she had to show off her prized purchase. But the baby carriage was empty. The infant was in the arms of his father, who was inside the lodge, watching television.

There was a "cooking column" in the *Navajo Times*. In it Sarah Twomey asked the ladies of the tribe, "How many of you remember when your rooftops were.covered with apples drying in the sun?"

Well, she said, that's "old-fashioned."

If an up-to-date Navajo housewife dries fruit nowadays, wrote Mrs. Twomey, in her recipe for dried cantaloupe Indian-style, she "pops them into an electric oven" and then stores the fruit, not on the roof of her hogan, but in plastic bags.

The Mohawks of the Caughnawaga Tribe, whose muscular men have been famed for their daring as high structural steel workers, had a most articulate and beautiful spokeswoman. She was a high-fashion model. Kahn Tineta Horn, in her twenties, educated in Montreal, New York, and Paris, had been elected to the National Council of Indians of Canada. Her voice in behalf of her people has been heard in the Parliament in Ottawa, and in the political arenas of Washington.

Before becoming an Indian leader, the young Mohawk girl had been "Princess Canada," the counterpart of "Miss America."

"My people were disturbed when I left the reservation," Kahn Tineta recalled. "They acted as if they thought I was betraying them. But I knew I would suffocate if I stayed there.

"It was a difficult thing. My mother thought I should marry and raise children the way other Mohawk girls do. My family thought I would lose my identity, or something. They had real anxieties about it. And a lot of them still look at me funny when I visit my family on weekends."

On the reservation at the Oglala Sioux, Mrs. Irving, who said she was a direct descendant of the warrior Crazy Horse, was elected mayor of the town of Pine Ridge.

Laura Peshlakai, a young Navajo girl, came home to her reservation town of Crystal, New Mexico, population 250, after visiting New York City. She had been feted at the Waldorf-Astoria and had attended youth conferences throughout the urban East.

Her thoughts on coming home?

"We feel very strongly that we do not want to be used as showpieces or our homes as tourist attractions. It is about time that people saw us as we really are, not as the colorful vanishing primitives, but as alert, responsible citizens of the United States.

"We have realized that we can have the best of our culture, the best of the White Man's culture, and apply it to our lives. In this way we will play our part in bringing sanity and unity back to the world."

In the woods of Minnesota, on the Leech Lake Reservation of the Chippewa, a young girl said: "The American Indians are a very proud people, no matter what tribe they are from. But so are most of the white people.

"Though nowadays we are told we are all a defeated nation, our parents still teach us to be proud we are Indians and never to be ashamed, no matter what some white people tell us. Some of the whites sure like to push us around, or try to, but if we fight back, they soon enough leave us alone. My folks always tell me to stick up for myself and fight back, and then when I do, they say it's the old Indian in me, always fighting.

"The American Indian today, though he is supposed to be civilized, conformed, etc., still has a lot of the old ways in him. He does things the way some of his ancestors did. So we Indians of today really aren't too much different from Indians of before. We are supposed to be more civilized and educated today. But then, weren't we, before the white man came? Maybe not in his way, but in ours, very much so."

One Woman's Lib

Joan Jones

The dialog between a man and a woman in One Woman's Lib *alludes to a love that has resulted in frustration for both. As the man wonders what has gone wrong, the woman declares her independence.*

Joan Jones, who graduated from the State University of New York at Buffalo in 1968, has recently become active in Women's Liberation. She has published poems in underground papers and little magazines.

I loved one once
over by the oak there.
God she was really laid
in that rush
with such ecstatic mumblings
I could have been old Zeus himself
if I'd had feathers.
But now . . . a regular harpy!
Diana sicking her dogs on me,
The maenad after my very blood!

> Angry now and sullen . . .
> We'll drink no blood,
> but might consider cutting down
> that oak.

Take time and it'll all come right;
I'll give a week of Sundays
and you'll see,
you can come back
and stay with me.

> No, bitter now.
> Not up to
> follow you and cart your tail
> from one tree to another.

I'll give you a song to sing
and labor long into the night
to bring
it about
and make
it right.

> I make my own song . . .
> hack it out in that clover there:

"I dream I am a woman kept
all her unspent days
hanging from that horrible tree,
picking juniper berries for your gin."
"And we meet once a week
in winter
and perhaps more often in spring."

I am rested
to sing a longer song than yours.
It rests me.

On Sisterhood

Dana Densmore

*One of the greatest dangers in Women's Liberation is that
college-educated women presently active in the movement will
forget the fact that no revolution can succeed unless it is supported by the people. And "the people" in Women's Liberation
are women everywhere—housewives and career girls, rich and
poor, nonwhite and white—all sisters, united in their common
oppression by a male-run society. Dana Densmore, addressing
herself to women who have moved toward self-liberation
pleads for a recognition of the sisterhood of all women. Densmore is active in female liberation in Boston; this essay, as well
as her essay On Celibacy, originally appeared in the Women's
Liberation journal, No More Fun and Games.*

Do you see yourself stronger, more able to resist or reject conditioning,
more real than other women? Are you better able to act in this society as
an individual rather than relating solely to the stereotypes of feminine
behavior and the woman's place?

It is because you were fortunate enough to have some countervailing
influences that others didn't have to counteract all that propaganda to
some degree.

You were, perhaps, more trusted by your parents in your youth and
learned to trust yourself and your own instincts. Or you were taught
straight out that certain things were vanity, or silly, or unworthy. You
were taught that individual action was honorable when others were
taught only that inaction, womanly passivity, was honorable.

Now you both carry out what you have learned, both doing what you were taught was the honorable thing, and you look down on the others and say you have no sympathy for their suffering or the slights they incur, because they "ask for it," they "like it."

There is nothing male society succeeds in so well as Divide and Conquer. We have all fallen for it, so there can be no pointing the finger, but it is a shameful thing nonetheless.

"You are different," they say, and how eagerly we agree.

We are not like those other women who sit at home all day reading magazines and gossiping. We are not like those silly bunnies using their bodies and the padding of torturedly sleek bunny costumes to get big tips from silly men.

We are not like those empty headed girls who spend all their money on clothes and all their ingenuity on snagging men into marriage and get together to giggle over nothing for hours. We are not like those nagging possessive wives who have nothing to offer but sap the life out of their husbands. We are not like those bitter dried up women of whatever age who hate sex and are desperately afraid that someone somewhere may be having a good time.

"You are different," the men say, and justify the most vicious prejudice and discrimination and cruelty by inviting us into their select little club (or rather by giving us the false illusion that we are in).

They make us accomplices; eager for respect and acceptance, we insist that we too are prejudiced; we agree eagerly that women are contemptible indeed—most women, that is, the masses of women, not *me* of course, but most women.

This is a strange but very widespread schizophrenia which results among women who have been not entirely ruined by the womanhood conditioning. They see that men are free and respected and identify with them, rejecting their own sex in horror, pretending that it is some kind of moral failing, convincing themselves of it even, saying the women like it because they are lazy and selfish.

In fact only a low self image could produce that kind of self-destructive conduct, a low self image and general despair.

They have been taught that it is immoral and selfish to try to make something of yourself, to care about yourself, not to devote yourself to your family and home. But it isn't easy to devote yourself to your family and all their faults are but symptoms of their unhappiness.

The kind of "moral strength" it takes to stand up and fight the world for the right to be an authentic person, a functioning individual rather than an undifferentiated function (housekeeper, mother) comes only from training and encouragement. The ego can be hopelessly crippled and it is at a very young age in American Indians, blacks, and women.

So you pulled yourself up by your bootstraps, did you? Despite the disadvantage of being a woman, and tainted with the laziness and un- reliability and stupidity of other women, and subject to the very natural prejudice against women, you succeeded. This proves that any woman with ambitions could succeed too if she works hard enough to prove that she's different. Men will be glad to accept her as an equal if she only proves that she's different. Or at least most men will.

But the bootstrap theory is false. Those women are where they are because that's what they've been conditioned for.

They have been taught that to do otherwise is wrong, and enormous pressures are immediately brought against them if they try. And suppose they aren't intelligent enough to get your glamorous jobs even with the healthiest egos in the world? Do you then write them off?

You have no sympathy for women who "like" playing the feminine role. They "enjoy" the discrimination, they "ask for it." But they've been conditioned, programmed, even traumatized to shun "unfeminine" behavior.

If they do enjoy the attention a good job of femininity brings them, you are cruel to feel contemptuous of them for enjoying the one pleasure they're allowed, the one honor in all that degradation. They're too ruined to assert themselves the way you do, demanding attention as an indi- vidual; that requires self-respect and they have none; they were taught to believe fully in their inferiority.

We are all one. All the same influences have acted on us. If you have somehow escaped the consequences of your conditioning you are lucky, not superior, not different. We are all sisters.

We all work within the same constraints. The prostitute, the married woman, the model, the bunny, and the career woman who makes herself glamorous are all using their bodies to get what they want or need from men. We all play the role to one extent or another and in one style or an- other and the career woman who plays lends honor to the system that op- presses her less healthy, ambitious, talented, educated, intelligent sisters.

But their oppression oppresses her because she will never be a man, she will never be accepted as a man; her mind and talents are just being used; ultimately all men know she is a woman and will never completely accept her. She *is* a woman, and women, as she so eagerly agrees, are stupid, selfish, and lazy, not to be respected, clearly not the equals of men. She cannot be exempted just by imagining she is.

This elitism is rampant among the only-partially-ruined women, the golden ones who were brought up to have a strong sense of self, the intelligent educated talented ones who have "succeeded."

There is a complete identification with the ruling class, coupled not only with a rejection of their own class, but with an insistence that the pressures, influences, and conditioning that forced the women into their oppressed situation did not exist. ("They never should have HAD so many children, they should have thought ahead. They knew that marriages break up. They deserve to be in that fix. I can't have any sympathy for women with ten kids.")

This is bad faith and bad sociology. It is worse. It is an incredible lack of compassion, explainable only as a defensive rejection to avoid identification.

They are identifying with the men. To have sympathy for women is by implication to condemn the circumstances that oppress them, and those circumstances are the male power structure. But the elitist women cannot afford to criticize the male power structure even by implication because they are so busy currying favor from men to maintain their own "success."

So they must maintain an attitude of moral superiority toward those who do not succeed, and avoid at any cost analysis of why they "chose" their oppression.

It is an appalling snobbery for a golden career girl to brush off impatiently as irrelevant the plight of the masses of women who don't identify with the men, who have been convinced that they are, in fact, inferior, and who are just trying to do the best they can in a miserable situation.

We are all sisters. We all work within the same constraints. If some of us are more successful or less oppressed it is because we are less crippled, not because we are superior, not because we are different.

Revised December 1968

Women of Lesbos

Martha Shelley

"She must be a dyke." If a woman believes in female liberation and the concept of sisterhood, she will inevitably be accused at some time of Lesbianism. The Women's Liberation movement is not a Lesbian movement; but, in that it is working for the freedom of all women, it is working for the freedom of Lesbians as well as their "straight sisters." In Women of Lesbos, *Martha*

Reprinted by permission of the author. This article originally appeared in COME OUT under the title of *Notes of a Radical Lesbian.*

Shelley discusses the rejection of Lesbians by women in female liberation and the male hatred and social abhorrence of Lesbianism. As Del Martin and Phyllis Lyon in The Realities of Lesbianism *say, "The Lesbian minority in America, which may run as high as ten million women, is probably the least understood of all minorities and the most downtrodden. She (the Lesbian) has two strikes on her from the start; she is a woman and she is a homosexual, a minority scorned by the vast majority of people in our country. If, in addition, she is a member of a racial minority, it is hard sometimes to understand how she survives"* (Motive, *March-April 1969, p. 61).*

Martha Shelley is currently on the staff of COME OUT.

Lesbianism is one road to freedom—freedom from oppression by men.

To see lesbianism in this context—as a mode of living neither better nor worse than others, as one which offers its own opportunities—one must abandon the notion that deviance from the norm arises from personal illness.

It is generally accepted that America is a "sick society." There is an inevitable corollary to this statement, which has not been generally accepted: that people within our society are all crippled by virtue of being forced to conform to certain norms. (Those who conform most easily can be seen as either the most healthy, because adaptable, or most sick because least spirited.) Blacks are struggling to free themselves not only from white oppression, but from the sickness of self-contempt and the sick sexual roles. It is clear that the self-abasing, suffering, shuffling black is not someone with a personal neurosis, but society's victim— and someone who has been forced to learn certain techniques for survival. Few people understand that the same is true of the self-abnegating passive housewife. Fewer understand this truth about the homosexual.

For women, as for other groups, there are several American norms. All of them have their rewards—and their penalties. The nice girl next door, virginal until her marriage—the Miss America type—is rewarded with community respect and respectability. She loses her individuality and her freedom to become a toothpaste smile and a chastity belt. The career woman gains independence and a larger margin of freedom—IF she is willing to work twice as hard as a man for less pay, and IF she can cope with emotional strains similar to those that beset the black intellectual surrounded by white colleagues. The starlet, call-girl, or bunny whose source of income is directly related to her image as a sex object, gains some financial independence and freedom from housework. She doesn't have to work as hard as the career women, but she pays through psychological degradation as a sex object, and through the insecurity of knowing that her career—based on youthful good looks—is short-lived.

The lesbian, through her ability to obtain love and sexual satisfaction from other women, is freed of dependence on men for love, sex and money. She does not have to do menial chores for them (at least at home) nor cater to their egos, nor submit to hasty and inept sexual encounters. She is freed from fear of unwanted pregnancy and the pains of childbirth, and from the drudgery of childraising.

On the other hand, she pays three penalties. The rewards of child raising are denied her. This is a great loss for some women, but not for others. Few women abandon their children, as compared with the multitudes of men who abandon both wives and children. Few men take much interest in the process of child raising. One suspects that it might not be much fun for the average person, and so the men leave it to the women.

The lesbian must compete with men in the job market, facing the same job and salary discrimination as her straight sister. On the other hand, she has more of a chance of success since her career is not interrupted by childbirth.

Finally, she faces the most severe contempt and ridicule that society can heap on a woman.

A year ago, when Women's Liberation picketed the 1968 Miss America pageant, the most terrible epithet heaped on our straight sisters was "lesbian." The sisters faced hostile audiences who called them "commies," "tramps," etc., and they faced these labels with equanimity; but they broke into tears when they were called lesbians. When a woman showed up at a feminist meeting and announced that she was a lesbian, many women avoided her. Others told her to keep her mouth shut, for fear that she would endanger the cause. They felt that men could be persuaded to accept some measure of equality for women—as long as these women would parade their devotion to heterosexuality and motherhood.

A woman who is totally independent of men—who obtains love, sex and self-esteem from other women—is a terrible threat to male supremacy. She doesn't need them, and therefore they have very little power over her.

I have met many, many feminists who were not lesbians—but I have never met a lesbian who was not a feminist. Straight women by the millions have been sold the belief that they must subordinate themselves to men, accept less pay for equal work, and do all the shit work around the house. I have met straight women who would die to pre-serve their chains. I have never met a lesbian who believed that she was innately less rational or capable than a man.

Lesbians, because they are not afraid of being abandoned by men, are less reluctant to express hostility towards the male class who are oppressors of women. Hostility towards your oppressor is healthy—but the guardians of modern morality, the psychiatrists, have interpreted this hostility as an illness, and they say this illness causes and is lesbianism.

If hostility to men causes lesbianism, then it seems to me that in a male-dominated society, lesbianism is a sign of mental health.

The psychiatrists have also forgotten that lesbianism involves love between women. Isn't love between equals healthier than sucking up to an oppressor? And when they claim we aren't capable of loving men, even if we want to—I ask you, straight man, are you capable of loving another man so deeply that you aren't afraid of his body or afraid to put your body in his hands? Are you really capable of loving women, or is your sexuality just another expression of your hostility? Is it an act of love or sexual conquest? An act of sexual imperialism?

I do not mean to condemn all males. I have found some beautiful, loving men among the revolutionaries, among the hippies, and the male homosexuals. But the average man—including the average student male radical—wants a passive sex-object cum domestic cum baby nurse to clean up after him while he does all the fun things and bosses her around—while he plays either bigshot executive or Che Guevara—and he is my oppressor and my enemy.

Society has taught most lesbians to believe that they are sick and has taught most straight women to despise and fear the lesbian as a perverted, diseased creature. It has fostered the myth that lesbians are ugly and turn to each other because they can't get that prize, that prince, a male! In this age of the new "sexual revolution," another myth has been fostered—the beautiful lesbians who play games with each other on the screen for the titillation of heterosexual males. They are not seen as serious people in love—but as performers in the "let's try a new perversion" game.

Freud founded the myth of penis envy, and men have asked me, "But what can two women do together?" As though a penis were the sine qua non of sexual pleasure! Man, we can do without it, and keep it going longer, too!

Women are afraid to be without a man's protection—because other men will assault them on the streets. And this is no accident, not an aberration performed by a few lunatics. Assaults on women are no more an accident than are lynchings of blacks in Mississippi. Men have oppressed us, and like most oppressors, they hate the oppressed and fear their wrath. Watch a white man walking in Harlem and you will see what I mean. Look at the face of a man who has accidentally wandered into a lesbian bar.

Men fear lesbians because they are less dependent, and because their hostility is less controlled.

Straight women fear lesbians because of the lesbian inside them, because we represent an alternative. They fear us for the same reason that uptight middle class people fear hip people. They are angry at us because we have a way out that they are afraid to take.

And what happens to the lesbians under all this pressure? Many of my sisters, confused by the barrage of anti-gay propaganda, have spent years begging to be allowed to live. They have come begging because they believed they were psychic cripples, and that other people were healthy and had the moral right to judge them. Many have lived in silence, burying themselves in their careers, like name-changing Jews and blacks who passed for white. Many have retreated into an apolitical domesticity, concerning themselves only with the attempt to maintain a love relationship in a society which attempts to destroy love and replace it with consumer goods—flowers, mouthwashes, diamond rings, automobiles—and which attempts to completely destroy any form of love outside the monogamous marriage.

This, by the way, is an important point for all kinds of revolutionaries. If you love your brothers and sisters you are less willing to stand by and watch them get crushed under the relentless pressures of the rat race, of the doctor bills and the furniture bills. If you love your brothers and sisters you won't try to swindle them. Restricting love to the immediate family group isolates each family from the community—each ethnic group from the others—and makes all these isolated frightened people more willing to settle for fancy furniture on the installment plan, for grudgingly bestowed respectability, because they can't get the real thing, real love.

To return to the lesbian—because LESBIAN has become such a vile epithet, we have been afraid to fight openly. We can lose our jobs— we have fewer civil rights than any other minority group. Because we have few family ties and no children, for the most part, we have been active in many causes—but always in secret, because our name contaminates any cause that we work for.

To the radical lesbian, I say that we can no longer afford to fight for everyone else's cause while ignoring our own. Ours is a life style born out of a sick society—so is everyone else's. The revolution must be fought for us, too, as well as Blacks, Indians, welfare mothers, grape pickers, SDS people, Puerto Ricans, or mine workers. We must have a revolution for human rights.

Maybe after the revolution, people will be able to love each other regardless of skin color, ethnic origin, occupation, or type of genitals. But if that's going to happen, it will only happen because we make it—starting right now.

On Celibacy

Dana Densmore

The initial response of most men to the idea of a free woman is laughter—after it has subsided, hostility. The following manifesto warns women that, if they are serious about their liberation, they must be prepared to be unattractive, even repulsive, to men. In arguing that they must also be prepared to give up the sex-game, Dana Densmore is actually demanding that they be true to themselves and refuse to conform to traditional images of woman. Apropos of this essay, Densmore wrote in June 1970, "I express myself somewhat less violently these days, although the article certainly captures the desperate lonely determination of the first months of the movement."

One hangup to liberation is a supposed "need" for sex. It is something that must be refuted, coped with, demythified, or the cause of female liberation is doomed.

Already we see girls, thoroughly liberated in their own heads, understanding their oppression with terrible clarity, trying, deliberately and a trace hysterically, to make themselves attractive to men, men for whom they have no respect, men they may even hate, because of "a basic sexual-emotional need."

Sex is not essential to life, as eating is. Some people go through their whole lives without engaging in it at all, including fine, warm, happy people. It is a myth that this makes one bitter, shriveled up, twisted.

The big stigma of life-long virginity is on women anyway, created by men because woman's purpose in life is biological and if she doesn't fulfill that she's warped and unnatural and "must be all cobwebs inside."

Men are suspected at worst of being self-centered or afraid of sex, but do not carry any stigma of being unnatural. A man's life is taken as a whole on its merits. He was busy, it may be thought, dedicated, a great man who couldn't spare the time and energy for demanding relationships with women.

The guerrillas don't screw. They eat, when they can, but they don't screw. They have important things to do, things that require all their energy.

Everyone of us must have noticed occasions when he was very involved in something, fighting, working, thinking, writing, involved to the extent that eating was haphazard, sleeping deliberately cheated. But the first thing that goes is sex. It's inconvenient, time-consuming, energy-draining, and irrelevant.

We are programmed to crave sex. It sells consumer goods. It gives a lift and promises a spark of individual self-assertion in a dull and routinized world. It is a means to power (the only means they have) for women.

It is also, conversely, a means of power for men, exercized over women, because their sexual desire is directed to men.

Few women ever are actually satisfied, of course, but they blame the particular man and nurse the myth that they can be satisfied and that this nirvana is one which a man and only a man can bring.

Moreover, sexual freedom is the first freedom a woman is awarded and she thinks it is very important because it's all she has; compared to the dullness and restrictiveness of the rest of her life it glows very brightly.

But we must come to realize that sex is actually a minor need, blown out of proportion, misunderstood (usually what passes for sexual need is actually desire to be stroked, desire for recognition or love, desire to conquer, humiliate or wield power, or desire to communicate).

We must come to realize that we don't need sex, that celibacy is not a dragon but even a state that could be desirable, in many cases preferable to sex. How repugnant it really is, after all, to make love to a man who despises you, who fears you and wants to hold you down! Doesn't screwing in an atmosphere devoid of respect get pretty grim? Why bother? You don't need it.

Erotic energy is just life energy and is quickly worked off if you are doing interesting, absorbing things. Love and affection and recognition can easily be found in comrades, a more honest and open love in which you are loved for yourself and not for how docile and cute and sexy and ego-building you are, a love in which you are always subject, never merely object, always active, never merely relative. And if despite all this genital tensions persist you can still masturbate. Isn't that a lot easier anyway?

This is a call not for celibacy but for an acceptance of celibacy as an honorable alternative, one preferable to the degradation of most male-female sexual relationships. But it is only when we accept the idea of celibacy completely that we will ever be able to liberate ourselves.

Until we accept it completely, until we say "I control my own body and I don't need any insolent male with an overbearing presumptuous prick to come and clean out my pipes," men will always have over us the devastating threat of withdrawing their sexual attentions and worse, the threat of our ceasing even to be sexually attractive.

And that devastating rejection is absolutely inevitable. If you are serious, and men realize it, they will cease being attracted to you.

If you don't play the game, the role, you are not a woman and they will NOT be attracted. You will be sexless and worse, unnatural and threatening.

You will be feared and despised and viciously maligned, all by men you know perfectly well you could charm utterly and wrap around your finger just by falling into the female role, even by men who have worshipped you in the past.

How is that possible? Obviously, because they never were worshipping you. That's the bitter truth, and you'd better catch on now.

Whenever they're nice to us, it isn't us they're being nice to but their own solipsistic creations, the versions of us they manufacture for their own amusement and pleasure and purposes. How presumptuous it is of us to accept the love and admiration, to crave it even, as if it were meant for us!

It's their female ideal they adore and they will be resentful and angry if you mar that image and will turn against you to a man if you try to destroy it.

Unless you accept the idea that you don't need them, don't need sex from them, it will be utterly impossible for you to carry through, it will be absolutely necessary to lead a double life, pretending with men to be something other than what you know you are. The strain of this would be unimaginable and could end in any number of disastrous ways.

You, who have had such heady power to charm and arouse and win men's total admiration and respect, must be willing to give it up. You must be willing that they cease to be attracted to you, even find you repulsive, that they cease to respect you, even despise you, that they cease to admire you, even find you unnatural and warped and perverted sexually.

These men who were so tenderly protective will try to destroy you, to stab you in the back, to use any underhanded means to get back at you for posing this threat to them. You have done them the incalculable offense of not deferring to their sex, of daring to be yourself (putting your needs ahead of theirs), of stepping out of your role, of rejecting the phony sexual differentiations that make each of them feel like a man.

If you don't act like a woman he doesn't see himself as a man, since his sexual identity depends on the differences, and so he feels actually castrated. Expect no love, no desire, no mercy from this man.

You have to be prepared, then, to be not just unattractive but actually sexually repulsive to most men, perhaps including all the men you currently admire.

We've spent many years learning to be appealing to men, to all men, whether we are specifically interested in them or not. We dress, we walk, we laugh, we talk, we move our hands and our heads, we sit, we speak, all in a way carefully cultivated to be feminine and charming.

We need to be thought charming and appealing even by men who bore us or repulse us, by strangers who may be trying to pick us up; we have a horror of appearing vulgar and repulsive even to the most nauseating creep. The creeps must all be brushed off gracefully, in a way that leaves their egos intact and consequently leaves them with a friendly impression of us.

It's so important that our image be favorable, we are willing to put up with the fact that it is false, distorted, that we are being loved for our weaknesses, or for qualities we don't have at all, and our strengths are denied or ridiculed.

If we are going to be liberated we must reject the false image that makes men love us, and this will make men cease to love us.

Unless we can accept this we will crumble under the first look of fear and disgust; or certainly under the first such look from a man we love and admire.

Ultimately, of course, we will cease to love and admire such men. We will have contempt for men who show that they cannot love us for ourselves, men whose egos demand and require falsehoods.

It will be a less friendly world, but there will be no unrequited longing. What we're really after is to be loved for ourselves and if that's impossible, why should we care about love at all? Friends and enemies will be clearly lined up, and the friends will be real friends and the enemies unable to hide behind phony benevolence—nor will we have to toady to them.

An end to this constant remaking of ourselves according to what the male ego demands! Let us be ourselves and good riddance to those who are then repulsed by us!

August 1968

Abortion: Women, Men
and the Law

William Lafferty

William Lafferty received his Ph.D. in 1969 from the University of Wisconsin where he did his major work on Joseph Conrad. He is currently attending the University of Wisconsin Law School while on leave from his teaching position at Wisconsin State University—Whitewater.

If you have always thought the proscription against abortion is based on widespread belief that abortion involves the destruction of human life rather than on the sexist oppression of women, consider what the abortion laws would be like, if, overnight, men got pregnant instead of women. It is unthinkable that men would be much solaced by womanly assurances that the joys of "motherhood" would compensate for interrupting their work and other activities, keeping them at home and giving them the primary responsibility for child care during the next eighteen years. Naturally, in this hypothetical world where men rather than women bear children, some men would want to carry their pregnancies to term, but certainly others would insist on their right to abort pregnancies on the grounds that they have the right to control their bodies and their lives. Men have always enjoyed personal control over their lives and it seems unlikely that many would be put off by religious rhetoric or want to jeopardize their careers, risking professional supplantation by women. Since men make the laws, there would probably be a sudden lifting of the ban on abortion, the emergence of laws forbidding doctors to refuse to perform abortions on request, and the establishment of abortion clinics at every local shopping center. Law probably would not require pregnant men to get the consent of their wives before having abortions[1] and men in general probably would not talk so much about the advisability of those who want abortions first consulting with clergymen or submitting to examination by psychiatrists to make sure that they were doing the right thing.

Reprinted by permission of the author.

This hypothetical situation is ludicrous only to those who believe that people of both sexes should not be accorded equal treatment under law and social custom. Admittedly, the term "equal" is ambiguous when it is applied to any suppressed group because of differences between that group and the suppressors. Women bear children and men don't; Blacks attend ghetto schools and suburban whites don't; Indians have cultural traditions that the rest of us don't. But the ambiguity of "equality" is not absolute and can be at least partially resolved by recognizing the principle that, regardless of differences, people ought to be given the opportunity to know what all of the possibilities of their lives are, to prepare and educate themselves within their abilities as they see fit, and to exercise the right to choose freely the nature of their employment and the direction of their lives. At present, only men are able to make these choices. White men.

The simplistic antagonist will hold up examples of female school teachers he has known and Black medical doctors he has read about, failing to see that it is general patterns, not occasional exceptions that matter. To say that the general pattern of American life is for women to be housewives and mothers (or school teachers when the kids get old enough to go to school), but that all women are free to diverge from this pattern, is to fail to recognize the chilling effect that general patterns have on an individual woman's desire to be different. Being different means that she risks being called "unfeminine" and "castrating" and "masculine."

The point of all this is that proscription against abortion is motivated by male sexist oppression of women just as is male exclusion of women from the professions and male preference for women who are housewives and mothers. The predominant male vision of "Woman" and of the good life is that women remain subordinate, allowing men to protect them, be polite to them, provide for them, write laws for them which will be as religious and chivalrous as possible and which women must obey, fight wars for them and be heroes for them; and, in return, women will "always be there" to bolster their men's egos. It is in man's interest to keep saying that the woman's place is in the home, for not only is this necessary to his moral vision of the world, but also to his job security—it eliminates female competition. What "feminine" girl would want to do anything in college but study the art of teaching second grade? She knows that this is the way to be feminine because this is what her culture (including her mother) tells her, and her culture, of course, has been shaped by men.

Activist women aside, most American women are forced into roles not of their own choosing that are perpetuated by men, and men design the role of women so as to enhance their own egos, to maintain their

psychological, political and financial power over women, and more specifically, to continuously reinforce their sexual prowess. Dr. R. B. White,
commenting on physicians' determined reluctance to permit abortions,
questions:

> Is it possible that the pregnant woman symbolizes the proof of male
> potency and that if we loosen our rule over women and grant them the
> right to dispose of that proof when *they* want to, we men then feel
> terribly threatened lest women can at will rob us of the proof of our
> potency and masculinity?[2]

It is depressing to think that women might actually be suppressed by
this sort of male fear, but it is equally depressing to think of oneself as
a man with this sort of fear-potential. Dr. White's analysis, that our use
of legal restraint and professional pressures to discourage abortions is
motivated not only by our desire to keep women subservient, but also
by our desire to assert our own masculinity, suggests that the women's
liberation movement, if it is to succeed, will someday become a women's
and men's liberation movement.

Dr. Allan Barnes adds another dimension to our consideration of the
secret forces behind the proscription against abortion in suggesting that
we are afraid of abortion because we are afraid of sex:

> I think we have to face the fact that if you got pregnant by rubbing
> a cloth across your cheek, there would be no abortion act or bill in the
> law and there would be no concern about terminating a pregnancy. . . .
> It's the fact that you get pregnant through sexual intercourse, and sex
> is different, sex is worrisome to some people, sex bothers them. . . .[3]

The gist of this statement and of the above argument in general is that
laws against abortion have remained in force because of certain myths
that we have decided we want to perpetuate, certain views of what the
good life is, which include ideas about the sanctity of fetal life, the religiosity of motherhood, the submissive and essentially maternal nature
of women, the essentially shameful nature of sex and sexual intercourse,
and the natural superiority (physical and intellectual) of men. Such
ideas are ludicrous in 1970. They are, in fact, culturally insane in light
of the suffering which they have caused and the greater suffering that
is threatened unless there is drastic change.

But how serious is the suffering that is caused by abortion proscription? Well, not everyone suffers. Crime syndicates are estimated to make
more than $350,000,000 yearly on illegal abortions,[4] and it is common
knowledge that doctors who are willing to take the risk make from $500

to $2000 for "therapeutic" abortions. One source reports that an abortion ring in the East which is staffed by four doctors makes about $25,000,000 a year.[5] On the other hand, the women who experience the one-to-two million illegal abortions annually don't fare so well. Many die from infection or other complications that result from the abortionist's inexpertise or carelessness about sanitation: 8,000 die every year, probably more.[6] The number is impossible to determine exactly because of the reluctance of coroners to certify death from abortion. The women who survive often end up in hospitals for post-abortive care or find that they are sterile because of the carelessness of the abortionist's methods. Even the women who suffer no ill after-effects physically suffer resentment against the society which made them "criminals."

Some doctors also suffer. The doctor who performs an abortion for a woman who really does not want her child but to whom the law will not grant an abortion is sometimes prosecuted as a felon. And the women who cannot get abortions, usually poor women, suffer. If a woman is on relief, unmarried, the mother of four children and pregnant, the birth of this fifth child only makes her plight more hopeless and contributes to the repetition of the welfare cycle. Her daughters become mothers at an early age, usually unmarried, and her sons grow up in a family overcrowded with children, poverty stricken, without a father, and with experiences and values which are at best unhappy and at worst criminal.

Middle-class women suffer too. 80% of all criminal abortions, according to some investigators,[7] 90%, according to the American Law Institute, are performed on married women, many of whom already have other children.[8] There are any number of obvious reasons why a married woman may not want to carry the embryo to term, and it seems clear that the one-to-two million women who get illegal abortions every year feel that these reasons are compelling enough to risk death, sickness and sterilization, to associate themselves with the frightening world of criminals and to commit with intent a criminal act.

In addition to individual, psychological and physical suffering, there is also the large social problem of over-population to consider. Even if it should be shown that all of the unwanted babies who are born suffer no lasting harmful effects and that all of the mothers who seek abortions likewise suffer neither grave nor permanent injury from carrying the unwanted pregnancy to term, we are left with the staggering fact that within 40 years the population of the world, at its present rate of growth, will double.[9] The good life as we idealize it—where there is love and attention for each child, where each child can be educated, find satisfactory work, and enjoy the world in which he lives—may become an unrealizable dream unless the growth rate is diminished. The obvious answer is birth control, but there is no time to perfect a totally effective method. The Federal Government has now issued warnings about the danger of blood clotting which can occur from the pill, and other methods are notoriously unreliable. Faced with a population crisis, it seems only natural—were there not emotional factors involved—to supplement ordinary methods of birth control with abortion. More than 200 Nobel laureates have issued a joint statement calling for immediate reduction of the population growth rate and predicting that otherwise we risk misery, famine, and social disaster on a global scale that may explode into world wars of survival.[10]

I have already suggested that sexist oppression of women—which includes economic and social suppression, the reinforcement of male sexual prowess that comes from being able to deny women abortions, and a Victorian embarrassment about sex and its association with pregnancy—is what lies behind our proscription against abortion. No one in the establishment will admit this, of course, for no one likes to see himself as "the oppressor." Consequently, the establishment puts forth reasons of its own that are designed to obscure its oppressive nature. These include the appeal to religious authority, to legal precedent, to the fear of moral degeneration that might result from liberalized abortion laws, and to public opinion, which, it is argued, is opposed to abortion reform.

The Roman Catholic Church has been perhaps the most militant opponent of liberal abortion laws. Wooden-cross-wielding Catholics wearing red berets, brown shirts, and rosaries smashed their way into George Washington University Hospital on June 6, 1970 chanting *Viva Cristo Rey* [Long live Christ the King] and insisting that the hospital call a moratorium on abortions, that it become "a place for honoring the sanctity of human life."[11] Not all Roman Catholics, of course, insist that abortion is wrong, but the fact remains that the official teaching of the Church condemns abortion except to save the life of the mother and that the Church uses all its considerable influence to forestall changes in abortion laws. It is interesting, however, that in Colorado, which has a moderately liberal abortion law and a population 22% of which is Catholic, since 1967 17% of those applying for legal abortion have been Roman Catholic.[12] This reveals dissent even within the powerful Roman Church, but the main argument against religious beliefs which prohibit abortion is not internal dissent, but the fact that religion cannot be legislated in the United States. Roman Catholics at this point in history choose to advocate the overpopulation of the world. At some point in the near future, such advocacy will be recognized as a danger to the state and a threat to the continued existence of mankind, but, in the meantime, others need not be bound by Roman dogma.

The legal argument is that since the fetus can inherit property, be protected by the courts from failure of the father to support the pregnant mother, and recover damages for injuries inflicted on it before its birth, it has the same legal right to protection from death as any citizen.[13] The fourteenth amendment, which provides that no state shall "deprive any person of life, liberty, or property without due process of law" is sometimes used to support this position. In addition it is argued that judicial history supports the view that abortion is a crime against the fetus and not merely an attempt to protect pregnant women from dangerous surgery.[14]

In answer to the property argument, the majority decision in *People v. Belous*, the case in which the California Supreme Court ruled that state's abortion law unconstitutional, cites Civil Code 29 as follows:

> A child conceived, but not yet born, is to be deemed an existing person, so far as may be necessary for its interests in the event of its subsequent birth . . .

and points out that the rights of property afforded a fetus ". . . require a live birth or reflect the interest of the parents."[15] In other words, that a fetus may have property rights which it realizes after it is born does necessitate that it must be born. Abortion, therefore, does not violate property rights that have been established. Protection of the fourteenth amendment is of dubious applicability because of the uncertainty of the fetus's legal status: "The dearth of case law on the constitutionality of present abortion statutes itself implies that a fetus has no constitutional rights."[16] As for damages which the fetus may recover for injury, it seems clear that the courts, in awarding such damages, are more interested in providing redress for a wrong than in deciding the question of the fetus's right to protection from abortion.[17]

Concerning the argument based on judicial history, which can be supported by infinite quotations from 19th century courts and legislators who are scandalized by the "barbarity" of abortion, it can only be answered that because the conditions of living change from one century to the next, legal and social precedent cannot be our only guide. In *Belous* the California Supreme Court points out that a law which may have been constitutional in 1850 is not necessarily constitutional now.[18] Surgical dangers that were present in 1850 are not problematic today; the social and personal consequences of abortion in 1850 are not the consequences of today; and reasons for the states' exercising abortion police powers that would have been acceptable in 1850 are either irrelevant or unacceptable today.

The last two objections—fear of moral degeneration and reliance on public opinion—are closely related. "The public" fears that abortion-on-request would result in moral degeneration and destruction of the bonds which hold society together, and this view, again, can be liberally documented using 19th and early 20th century legislative, judicial and clerical comments on the subject. It is precisely because there has been this heritage of fear of moral degeneracy that the public is opposed to abortion. But it is unwise to be too confident in public opinion, for public opinion has, on occasion, tended to undercut the legal and moral foundations of our country. In an Associated Press news release that was carried in papers across the nation on July 5, 1970, it was reported that 49 out of 50 people in Miami refused to sign a typed copy of the Declaration of Independence. The document was called "Commie junk" and the work of hippie, revolutionist, anti-government forces. The one man who signed charged a quarter for his signature.[19]

Another thing wrong with this reasoning is that there has been very little effort made to acquaint the public with the horrors of our present abortion laws. The Roman Chuch is still the most effective propagandist. Political leaders have avoided accepting the responsibility of leadership in abortion reform because, for the most part, it's too hot an issue. Thus the public at large is at the mercy of religious leaders and its own psychology which, as explained above, is culturally attuned to the suppression of women in favor of "greater" ends like religiosity and the sanctity of fetal life. In a fairly typical survey, 83% of people interviewed felt that women who are married but who want no more children should be denied legal abortions; 80% felt that an unmarried woman who will not marry the father of her fetus should be denied an abortion; 77% felt that women from families with low incomes who cannot afford another child should be denied an abortion.[20] Perhaps few of those interviewed know that many countries—Sweden, Denmark, Norway, China, Japan, Hungary, Bulgaria, the Soviet Uunon, England, Poland, Czechoslovakia and Yugoslavia—have all escaped moral decay in spite of their liberal abortion laws, even though some of them, including the Soviet Union, give abortions upon request.[21] Far from being an indication of immorality, Dr. R. E. Hall contends that the number of abortions performed in any given culture is relatively constant and is a function of the availability of contraception and the desire for a certain family size.[22] If Hall is right, and recent history of abortion here and in countries that have liberalized laws indicate that he is, we will continue to have between one and two million abortions annually whether it is legal or not.

Opposed to establishment arguments are a host of legal, sociological, philosophical and ethical arguments that favor liberalized abortion. Besides the fact that abortion is based on sexist dominance, a few specific considerations in favor of abortion are that all people ought to be able to maintain control over their own bodies and their own lives, that laws which are violated by large numbers of ordinary citizens are unworkable, and that original legislative motivation to protect women's lives from the dangers of abortion no longer pertain.

In March 1970, a three-judge federal court struck down parts of Wisconsin's abortion statutes and bolstered its decision with an impressive series of judicial quotations that took note of one's right to personal freedom in matters of sex, the family, marriage and, in general, the right "to be let alone."[23] The Wisconsin court begins its argument with a quote from a case in 1891:

> No right is held more sacred, or is more carefully guarded by the common law, than the right of every individual to the possession and control of his own person, free from all restraint or interference of others, unless by clear and unquestionable authority of law.[24]

The court also notes that in *Griswold v. Connecticut* (1965) the Connecticut ban on the use of contraceptives was struck down because specific and implied guarantees of the Bill of Rights protect persons from governmental invasion of their privacy.[25] The Wisconsin tribunal quotes the Connecticut court as follows:

> To hold that a right so basic and fundamental and so deep-rooted in our society as the right of privacy in marriage may be infringed because that right is not guaranteed in so many words by the first eight amendments to the Constitution is to ignore the Ninth Amendment and to give it no effect whatsoever.[26]

The Wisconsin court cites an article on the judicial evolution of our present concept of individual rights by Justice Tom C. Clark, who argues that the right to freedom from government interference in one's private life is an idea that underlies the framing of our Constitution,[27] and the court itself concludes:

> Under its police power, the state can regulate certain aspects of abortion. Thus, it is permissible for the state to require that abortions be conducted by qualified physicians. The police power of the state does not, however, entitle it to deny to a woman the basic right reserved to her under the ninth amendment to decide whether she should carry or reject an embryo which has not yet quickened. The challenged sections of the present Wisconsin statute suffer from an infirmity of fatal overbreadth.[28]

The California court in *People v. Belous* (1969) and the District of Columbia court in *U.S. v. Vuitch* (1969) both reached similar decisions prior to the Wisconsin decision. In *Belous*, the court writes: "The critical issue is not whether such rights exist [the right to bear children], but whether the state has a compelling interest in the regulation of a subject which is within the police powers of the state."[29] Similarly the *Vuitch* court writes:

> There has been . . . an increasing indication in decisions of the Supreme Court of the United States that as a secular matter a woman's liberty and right of privacy extends to family, marriage and sex matters and may well include the right to remove an unwanted child at least in the early stages of pregnancy. . . . Matters have certainly reached a point where a sound, informed interest of the state must affirmatively appear before the state infringes unduly on such rights.[30]

All three courts have declared unconstitutional portions of abortion laws which forbade removal of the embryo except in limited circumstances, within the first weeks of pregnancy.

The decisions of the Wisconsin and California courts also recognize that restrictive abortion laws raise the question of equal protection of the laws. The California court has noted that in subjecting doctors to prosecution for making a wrong decision when performing an abortion, the state makes it impossible for a physician to be an impartial judge; he "has a 'direct, personal, substantial, pecuniary interest in reaching a conclusion' that the woman should not have an abortion."[31] The Wisconsin court takes judicial notice of the differences in the law's effect on the rich and the poor by noting that the affluent may procure abortions outside the country and that they are likely to be able to "enjoy a longstanding, personal relationship with a well-paid physician, who might more likely be willing or able to persuade his fellow doctors to authorize a therapeutic abortion."[32]

Judicial decisions aside, it is difficult to avoid the feeling that there is something wrong with a law which is violated so frequently and which would prosecute more than two million persons every year. Criminal laws are designed to differentiate criminal from ordinary behavior, to separate the ordinary citizen from the wrongdoer, and abortion laws, in failing to do this, are anomalous. In addition to the fact that most of the abortion "criminals" are ordinary and respectable citizens, the American Law Institute has found that over half of all illegal abortions are performed by medical doctors and that the majority of hospitals they surveyed admitted that they perform "illegal" abortions.[33] Many prominent citizens and doctors[34] are now speaking out against repressive abortion laws and some of them openly offer to counsel women who seek abortions. Even the clergy is involved in a nationwide "Clergy Consultation Service (On Abortion/On Problem Pregnancies/etc.)." They have offices in more than ten large U.S. and Canadian cities and are always available by long-distance telephone.[35] Political organizations like National Organization for Women are also active in abortion reform and counseling, and there have been mass demonstrations and public outcry against restrictive abortion laws.[36] These protests can be ignored only at the risk of undermining the authority and credibility of our entire legal system.

The third consideration, that legislative intent when the abortion laws were originally written is no longer applicable, has been supported by both the *Belous* and the *Babbitz* courts. Dr. R. E. Hall has also noted that until the nineteenth century, there was no proscription anywhere in the world against abortion and that early laws in this country were designed, at least in large part, to protect women from the dangers of abortion at that time. Anesthetics and bacteria were discovered in the nineteenth century, and when the early abortion statutes were written there were no blood banks or antibiotics.[37] As the *Belous* court points out, "It is now safer for a woman to have a hospital therapeutic abortion during the first trimester than to bear a child."[38] There is, therefore, no ". . . compelling state interest in a need to protect the mother's life."[39]

These considerations and others make "strict" abortion laws untenable and call into question many aspects of so-called "liberal" laws. However, even the judicial decisions mentioned above are not comprehensive; they do not, for example, address themselves to the problem of the legality of the mother's right to request an abortion after the first trimester of pregnancy. And according to many of the "liberal" laws, as in Colorado, a married woman living with her husband must have his approval as well as that of "a special hospital board." These boards in Colorado can grant abortions only where there is danger of "serious permanent impairment" of the physical or mental health of the woman, and in the case of danger of mental impairment the woman must be examined by a psychiatrist.[40] This law and others in Arkansas, Delaware, Georgia, Kansas, Maryland, New Mexico, North Carolina and Oregon were passed following a recommendation in 1965 for abortion reform by the American Law Institute. In accord with the Institute's recommendations, most of these states allow abortion to be performed (1) where there is danger of damage to the mother's physical or mental health, (2) where the pregnancy has been caused by rape or incest, (3) where there is danger of birth defects.[41]

Methods of approval for the abortion vary from state to state; in the states which limit abortions to the three conditions listed above, the woman must usually obtain approval not only from her doctor, but also from a hospital board, and from a psychiatrist in the case of alleged danger to mental health. In New York, however, effective July 1, 1970, abortion is viewed as a private matter between the woman and her doctor when it can be performed before the twenty-fourth week.[42] In

North Carolina, two doctors besides the authorizing doctor must approve,[43] and in Washington state there can be a review in criminal proceedings of the doctor's decision to perform an abortion.[44]

Several of the states with "liberal" abortion laws, including North Carolina and Hawaii, have residence requirements of four and three months, respectively. Other states, including Colorado, have no residency requirement.

If all of this seems at least partially encouraging, it should be noted that there are still grave injustices in the most liberal of the laws passed thus far. For one thing, judicial decisions notwithstanding, no state has declared that it is a woman's *right* to have an abortion on request. England, on the other hand, has implied the right to abortion by paying for the operation and by declaring that termination of the pregnancy is permissible "where the pregnant woman's capacity as a mother will be severely overstrained by the care of a child or of another child."[45]

Among other injustices of the liberal American laws are that they still favor the affluent; that they fail to provide adequate facilities for the abortions which they legalize; that they discriminate among women on the basis of residency; that they insist on approval procedures which tend to frighten less educated women (and embarrass the victims of rape and incest into confessing that they have been raped or committed incest); and that in placing restrictions on the abortions which may be legally performed they unnecessarily restrict women's freedom.

To get an idea of how the affluent are favored, consider that in 1965 the therapeutic abortion-to-birth ratio for New York City was 1:250 but that it was 1:20,000 in the municipal hospitals.[46] A lot of people paid the extra money for treatment at private hospitals. This is not surprising, for hospital boards are notoriously conservative about abortions (if you don't have any influential doctor friends) and they are reluctant to commit hospital space to what they consider non-essential use. Admittedly there is a shortage of hospital space, but as Lucinda Cisler, a feminist abortion expert, points out, abortion is almost always a simple procedure that can be performed in a doctor's office or clinic.[47] Dr. R. E. Hall suggests that the government establish new facilities staffed by paramedical personnel to perform abortions, to give instruction in sex education and to disseminate birth-control information. He recommends further that these facilities, like those in the Soviet Union, handle abortions on an out-patient basis.[48] These centers would take the pressure off hospitals and make abortion easily accessible. Cisler mentions that some modern methods of performing abortions are exceedingly simple and safe, notably the vacuum aspiration technique. She suggests that if the performance of abortions remains restricted to physicians, the cost will remain exhorbitant, for the demand will exceed the supply of doctors, but that if paramedicals can be trained to perform abortions under the general supervision of a resident doctor, as they are now being trained to perform births, the cost would decrease significantly.[49]

The abortion problem remains with us in spite of liberalized laws and favorable judicial decisions. What is needed now is not merely a tentative withdrawal of abortion proscription but a positive program designed to assure that all women who want abortions are able to have them safely and inexpensively. Such a program would not only signal a new and healthier trend in our attitudes toward women and their rights as human beings, but also would be a significant factor in the increasingly crucial fight against overpopulation. In the end, it is unworkable to continue to endorse laws which condemn large numbers of people to unnecessary hardship, suffering and even death, which deny them the fundamental right to control over their own lives and which ultimately may constitute a danger to the survival of the state.

June 1970

NOTES

1. See Colo. Stat. Ch. 190, 40-2-50 (4) (a) (1967).
2. *Texas Reports of Biology and Medicine* (Winter 1966).
3. In a television appearance quoted in Marion K. Sanders, "The Right Not to Be Born," *Harper's*, 240 (April 1970), 98.
4. David Lowe, *Abortion and the Law* (New York, 1966), p. 6.
5. *Ibid.*
6. Figures are those of the American Law Institute quoted in Paul G. Reiter, "Trends in Abortion Legislation," *St. Louis Law Review*, 12:269 (Winter 1967).
7. David Lowe, p. 8.
8. Paul G. Reiter, p. 269.
9. *Reverence For Life* (Planned Parenthood/World Population, 515 Madison Ave., New York), no pagination.
10. *Ibid.*
11. *Washington Post* (No. 184), June 7, 1970, 1.
12. Marion K. Sanders, 98.
13. John T. Noonan, Jr., "The Constitutionality of the Regulation of Abortion," *The Hastings Law Journal*, 21:59 (Nov. 1969).
14. See Jane McGrew, "To Be or Not to Be: The Constitutional Question of the California Abortion Law," *The University of Pennsylvania Law Review*, 18:654 (Feb. 1970).
15. Cal. 2d. 458 P.2d 194, 80 *Cal Reptr.* 362 (1969).
16. Harvey L. Ziff, "Recent Abortion Law Reforms (Or Much Ado About Nothing)," *The Journal of Criminal Law, Criminology and Police Science*, 60:17 (1969).
17. "Abortion Legislation: The Need for Reform," *Vanderbilt Law Review*, 20:1317 (Nov. 1967).
18. 80 *Cal. Reptr.* (1969) at 362.
19. "To Some, Founders are 'Red'," *Milwaukee Journal* (July 5, 1970), 1.

20. "Abortion Legislation: The Need for Reform," 1314.
21. Janis Beaver, "Antiquated Abortion Laws: Sexist Oppression of Women," *Guardian* (April 4, 1970), 7.
22. Robert E. Hall, "Abortion Laws: A Call for Reform," *De Paul Law Review*, 18:587 (Summer 1969).
23. *Union Pacific Railway Co. v. Botsford* quoted in *Babbitz v. McCann*, No. 69-C-548, USDC EWis (three-judge court) 3/5/70 at 12.
24. *Ibid.* 12.
25. *Ibid.* 13.
26. *Ibid.* 13.
27. *Ibid.* 14.
28. *Ibid.* 17.
29. 80 *Cal. Reptr.* (1969) at 360.
30. *USDC DistCol; U.S. v. Vuitch* in *The United States Law Week* 38:2275 (Nov 18, 1969).
31. 80 *Cal. Reptr.* (1969) at 366.
32. *Babbitz v. McCann*, 10.
33. Paul G. Reiter, 269.
34. At this writing, the American Medical Association has just announced its support of liberal abortion laws. The new policy would permit a doctor to perform an abortion for social and economic reasons, as well as for medical considerations, in the states which permit abortions. A section of the new resolution which would have endorsed also doctors who fail to perform socio-economic abortions because their states forbid them was defeated on the grounds that it might discourage the development of liberal legislation in those states.

    The new policy was not, however, without its opponents. Dr. Gino Popola, President of the National Federation of Catholic Physicians guilds, resigned from the A.M.A. three hours after the new policy was announced. He urged all of the 6,000 doctors who are members of the Catholic Guild to resign and intimated that the 33,000 Catholic members of the A.M.A. will not be the only ones considering resignation. Popola said, "The A.M.A. has made it ethical for doctors to become paid executioners." (From Ronald Kotulak, "New Abortion Policy Threatens AMA Rift," *Chicago Tribune*, No. 177 (June 26, 1970), 1, 4.
35. The National Organization for Women lists the address of this service at 55 Washington Square South, New York City 10012. Telephone is 212-254-6314 weekdays between 9 a.m. and noon.
36. See *Guardian* (April 4, 1970) 6-7 or Judith Coburn, "Off the Pill?" *Ramparts* (June, 1970) 44-49.
37. Robert E. Hall, 585.
38. 80 *Cal. Reptr.* (1969) at 360-361.
39. *Babbitz v. McCann*, 16.
40. Colo. Stat., Ch. 190, 40-2-50 (4) (a) (i) (1967). Psychiatric letters certifying that there is a danger of mental impairment usually cost about $75 apiece.
41. Janis Beaver, p. 6.
42. *Guardian* (April 18, 1970), 7.
43. "Abortion Legislation: The Need for Reform," 1322.
44. "A Survey of Abortion Reform Legislation," *Washington Law Review*, 43:646 (March 1968).

45. *Ibid.* 652.
46. Gold, *Therapeutic Abortion in New York City: A 20-Year Review*, in Robert E. Hall, 587.
47. "On Abortion and Abortion Law," *Notes From the Second Year: Women's Liberation* (New York, 1970), p. 91.
48. Robert E. Hall, 589-590.
49. "On Abortion and Abortion Law," pp. 91-92.

Man's Role in Women's Liberation

Mary Louise Briscoe and Elsie Adams

The following essay, by the editors of this anthology, is reformist, not revolutionary, in nature. It represents what strikes us as a reasonable and moderate appeal to men to re-evaluate and then to change their attitudes toward women. It also reflects what we conceive to be the present attitude of most women in the Women's Liberation movement: optimistic, hopeful. Current history of other political movements has taught some depressing lessons about "working within the system for peaceful change"; nevertheless, at this time (December 1970), the Women's Liberation movement is non-violent and non-separatist. What women will be saying five years hence depends on their progress toward equality in the immediate future.

I

At present, very few men do anything to actively liberate women. There are those who have sacrificed traditional roles by helping to cook and clean a bit, but most of their basic attitudes about women are shrouded by historical myths. If, for example, they "instinctively" protect their women from physical or emotional threat, or if, indeed, they talk about "their women" with all the pride of ownership that derives from the cave or slave market, then they are really enacting the patterns of ancient culture in which the distinction between the sexes was dependent on physical differences only, i.e., bearing the club or the child.

It is no secret that no one is really free. The question is, how can more people obtain greater freedom? And if men must dominate women, or imagine that they must, in order to feel freer themselves, are they really free at all? The answer seems obvious. But although most people today are confronted by many problems of social sickness, the need for Women's Liberation within this society has been relegated to the bottom of the pile. The responses from men vary: "What are they so excited about? They have an easy life while we have to support them." "They're sick. They talk about freedom but what they really want is to castrate and dominate men (i.e., they want to be like us)." "All they really need is a good screw to settle them down." "If they keep it up they will destroy important sexual differences and therefore sexual attraction." "Women's Liberation is not a political issue—why don't the women spend their time on real problems?"

The fact of the matter is that women have spent their time on real problems, and their participation in political activity is the very thing that has made them cognizant of their lack of freedom. By this time most literate people know that women throughout the U.S. are getting organized to protest the denial of their basic freedoms. It has happened rapidly, spontaneously, and to such an extent that it looks like a master plan has prompted a movement. However the organizing factor is not a master plan but the idea of a master who excels and dominates his mistress. The peace movement began as a small campus voice—male or female—and was soon joined by various groups of women working actively for peace on local and national levels. The cry against war seemed "natural" to women, but young men who protested the war in those days were called cowards and thought to be unmanly. Now, after ten years, the cry for peace is heard in state as well as federal government, and the women who supported the cause, who helped convince men that it was a cause, have had some time to examine their own positions. They are joined by many young women on and off the campuses who have had their own freedom denied by their friends who claim to live for the greater freedom of all people.

If this all sounds too simple, check the news coverage—above and under ground—of any nearby peace and freedom movement. It is sometimes frightening how similar the objectives of women within these movements are. The following description of one such movement will illustrate.

II

On a Sunday evening in November 1969, a meeting was called to discuss the next Vietnam war moratorium on the Wisconsin State University-Whitewater campus. Two students (male) anxious to get started on the plans called a few other students and arranged to meet at the home of a faculty member who had worked with such plans before. He and his wife were having an informal supper on the meeting night, with two other faculty members who had also been politically active during the past months. When the invited students arrived (all male, though one brought his girl friend), the faculty wives were busy cleaning up after supper, and the meeting proceeded. One male faculty member asked why there were no women at the meeting, since many student and faculty women had been active in the organization of the past moratorium. The responses to this question were revealing, and unfortunately appear to be typical. One man explained that the meeting had been called in a hurry, and that the women he had called were really not interested. (This is the women-are-unreliable-and-therefore-belong-at-home-not-at-a-political-meeting syndrome.) Another said that he didn't seriously consider the question, since he thought the presence of women was a social consideration and not a political problem. (This is the who-are-we-going-to-screw-after-the-meeting syndrome.) Another said that women were politically ineffective anyway (or, the nobody-is-as-good-as-we-are-in-the-arena syndrome).

The men were surprised, and then abashed and annoyed when at the next meeting a group of women protested their exclusion from the planning stages. The men explained that women had been accidentally excluded from the initial planning session—a particularly offensive explanation, since it implied unthinking acceptance of the male-dominated culture by men who profess the ideal of human equality. The result of the women's protest, aside from strained relations and hurt (male) feelings, was a series of demands: (1) that women be represented on all committees planning the December and future moratoria; (2) that women not be exclusively assigned typing and mimeograph work; (3) that Women's Liberation workshops be offered at all future moratoria; and (4) that men change their attitudes toward women in and out of the movement. Out of the male-dominated peace movement on the Whitewater campus a Women's Liberation movement had been born.

Whitewater is one of hundreds of small universities (the total enrollment in 1953 was 600; in 1970, 10,000) that has grown fast and suffered what are euphemistically called "transitional problems." In addition to ROTC, the draft and the war, it had a long hard year of discontent and peaceful demonstrations about local and national issues. In late February 1970, the local problems escalated into a student strike involving over half the student body, and a student action called the Out to Lunch Movement evolved. (Administrators had been consistently "Out to lunch" when student leaders came to them with petitions.) Participating in the Out to Lunch Movement were many of the students who had organized the moratorium, including those who had responded favorably (i.e., with mixed feelings of sympathy, embarrassment, anger and defensiveness) to the women's criticism in the fall. Many had made rather elaborate professions of understanding the commitment to the women's cause.

After about three weeks of tension, including the student strike, occupation of the campus by riot police, and the suspension of four faculty members, the campus returned to a level of fairly stable agitation for the rest of the semester. And the women then had a chance to analyze the role they had played in the movement. They found, not surprisingly, that their role had been, in a word, *subordinate*. With one exception, all the leaders of the Out to Lunch Bunch were male. The exception was a woman who became chairman of the student marshals after a male had tired of the position. The typing, mimeographing, ditto work had been done mostly by women; three men and over thirty women volunteered for typing. Both women and men had, however, acted as marshals, distributed literature at tables, put out flyers and posters, and co-ordinated the mailing of letters to congressmen. During the crisis, when fear of arrests for speaking against the administration was high, women were asked and volunteered to follow the leaders around, taking notes for and about their activities. These women were called "Shadows." No men volunteered for the positions, and many of the women later admitted they did so in order to be around the centers of activity. The value judgments implicit in the term and concept of "Shadows" are depressingly obvious.

With few exceptions, the women who attended key meetings were there either as Shadows or girl friends and were notably shy about asserting their opinions. In the aftermath of the crisis, a good deal of energy was directed to raising money for federal lawsuits, which had been brought against the university administration for infringement of first amendment and procedural rights; during this period, it was suggested that women bake cakes and make flowers.

This is an appalling catalogue of subservient roles for women, one which most women as well as men in the Out to Lunch Movement did not want to contemplate, since it spoiled the exhilaration most of them felt from being involved in an important political event. But the evidence reveals all too clearly that, in this and supposedly more sophisticated circles of political action, men demand and women tend toward the traditional roles of the sexes that have culturally defined women as inferior, weak, and subordinate.

In communal hip life the situation is not much different. The desire to escape from the kind of life that is expected by society—competition, money, success and war—motivates the desire to find a life that is less complicated, less complex, and less destructive. And by turning to the more primitive social forms in which a group sustains itself by living according to need and love instead of success and exploitation, it becomes very easy to turn also to traditional sex roles. And, in fact, communal living often serves to aggrandize these roles. The desires that motivated Alice to open her Restaurant in Arlo Guthrie's biographical film seem a natural part of femininity—good food, warm kitchen, great feasts and happiness for wayward souls, i.e., the image of the Great Mother. But Alice had to close her Restaurant when she realized that her husband and all the kids were more interested in going to the beach, singing and making love than in helping with the kitchen work which sustained the commune economically. True, this is a film fiction, but it is based on and reflects the kind of problem that often breaks up a commune. Relying on one or a few, many people will not do their communal share. In Alice's restaurant the base of work is female labor. It was Alice's idea, you say, to base a commune on a kitchen. Yes, and she offered her traditional services to the community in good faith, but it took advantage of them. If she is to be blamed for the traditional nature of her offering, surely the community is to be blamed for accepting that offering in bad faith.

The film *Woodstock* offers another view of communal-folk-hip life, and it is a decidedly male view. The film is a sham, full of church camp rhetoric ("Isn't this heaven, sitting hungry in the mud—but only for three days—with 400,000 people like ourselves?") and capitalistic hypocrisy ("We don't care about our $3 million debt," said the wealthy promoters to the camera that was making their multimillion dollar movie, "it's the beautiful people that matter.") It concentrates on male creators (driving the bulldozer, building the stage, developing a hip city and making money) and male performers. The only woman performer is pregnant Joan Baez, who pats her tummy, talks about her husband, and sings a song. The rest of the music is heavy and male. The effect is that of watching one frenetic musical orgasm after another with all the male pride that usually accompanies such public rituals. The images of women at Woodstock include bare breasts (the cameramen were obviously raised on *Playboy*), breast-feeding children, spoon-feeding children, bathing nude in the lake, and huddling under plastic in the rain. A lot of men are bathing and huddling too, but the dominance of orgiastic male musicians bolsters the general male image well enough. Nothing bolsters the female image, however, and the identity this culture offers women is negligible.

In these two cultural areas—the political and communal—you expect to find more liberated people, and it is disillusioning as well as frustrating when you do not. The Black movement is, on the other hand, making some progress in its view of women. The evolution of the Black Panthers seems a necessary movement not just against white exploitation but against the old myths of black matriarchy. Now there are also sister Panthers, and the black ideology has come a long way since Stokeley Carmichael's statement that woman's place in S.N.C.C. is "prone." Recently when a reporter asked Kathleen Cleaver about woman's place in revolution, she responded: "No one ever asks what a man's place in the Revolution is." With her husband in exile, she, like women in war time, was placed in a significant position of power, and she has proved an extremely competent leader. Both Cleavers have made important statements about the need for human, not male or female, involvement in the Revolution. At least the Blacks have seen the importance of a united effort in working for their cause. Some of the same problems occur in the American Indian movement, but neither the movement nor the solutions to the problems are as far developed (see *The Changing Women,* pp. 456-469).

III

The motivation of women to change their roles, or to develop roles that are more human and less subordinate, is clear enough. But they cannot change unless society also changes, and that means that men must work toward the liberation of women as well as men in all racial groups. Fewer people are startled these days when they hear talk about the need for equal rights of blacks, reds, yellows and whites. They see that skin color does not necessarily suggest qualitative differences among races. The terms male and female should operate in a similar way: to describe the characteristics which distinguish people of different sexes who have equal rights to be human. Current studies in psychology, sociology and anthropology indicate that no one is really certain just how the sexes are different; we have until now assumed differences that are based only on inherited value judgments, not fact. Because men have been instrumental in developing and maintaining the value judgments which determine the traditional role of women, they are morally obligated to help change that role if they sincerely desire social change.

The first thing men must do is to discover and examine their own chauvinism, then try to free themselves from the need to suppress another group. This is probably the most difficult stage in the process of male liberation from male supremacist attitudes, since no one wants to admit that he is an oppressor. The process of discovery and liberation should be continual, because as in all forms of prejudice, the underlying attitudes are difficult to find and get rid of. The initial discovery is not enough. Traditional patterns of behavior are sometimes subtle and elusive to those who are pleased by them. When men feel alienated from a society they fear or distrust, they are pleased by the comforting presence they hope or imagine to have in their women. The ties of the nuclear family may seem to form a safe harbor from the ghastly business of a computerized world for many. But few men can honestly say they have this kind of comfort in any form but fantasy. They fear change in the role of women because they are afraid to lose what they probably don't even have. Psychic isolation is frightening to women as well as men, and if men realize they cannot tolerate it, they ought to realize that women's cry for greater freedom is not an attempt to destroy humane bonding among individuals but to create a more satisfactory bonding for both sexes. The defensive reaction most men have when they hear of Women's Liberation probably comes from their fear of losing their position as king of an imaginary mountain. They must examine their kingdom to see how it creates problems for both sexes. Women do not usually want to do men in, they simply want to improve their own position, which will also improve their relationship with men and other women. Women become hateful to men when their rights and recognition are continually evaded or deliberately ignored.

Once men begin to see their chauvinism they should talk seriously to other men and women about the problem and its damaging effects on both sexes. It is imperative that men take the problem seriously. There have been as many bad jokes about women as about minstrel shows, and neither are funny. Often men ask why women don't have a sense of humor about Women's Liberation—but they would not dare ask a Black or an Indian a comparable question. The answer is clear—there is nothing funny about being oppressed, and the male need for laughter usually reveals either unconscious fear of castration or blind refusal to see that the problem exists. The effect on women is the same eventually—they get more frustrated because they are not being taken seriously, and soon become more resentful, more bitter, and more militant.

Castration jokes are among the most frequent. A man who feels threatened by castration ought to read Freud again. It will become obvious, as it has to contemporary psychology, that Freud's theory of penis envy may describe his own sexual problems, but it hasn't much to do with those of little girls. In fact, the more recent studies of castration indicate that it is a ritual among men, not women. Examples of actual castration by women are rare, and usually represent women who have been mentally and physically exploited by men to such extremes that they were left with no alternative to suicide but violence against their oppressor. The fear of castration is nonetheless very real among many men who feel that women, by asking for equal human rights, want to un-man them.

Another common joke is that a liberated woman simply means free sex. The idea that freedom of spirit could be interpreted as a means to cheaper sex is hideous to women working for their liberation. One male student interviewed in *Woodstock* explained with a grin that he was going to the rockfest because there would be a lot of girls around with freer ideas about sex. Many so-called radical men profess sympathetic understanding of Women's Liberation, then expect sex as a reward for their benevolence. Many simply use Women's Liberation as a front for sexual exploitation; they pass out the latest Women's Liberation literature, and admit that they are chauvinists but can't help it. Some men have, however, taken serious steps to put aside the veil of humor and investigate its cause.

In addition to increasing self-awareness, men can take many practical steps to prevent their automatic and traditional oppression of women. In political action groups, for instance, men can learn to type and run mimeo machines and volunteer to use these skills instead of depending on women to work for them. There is often no good reason why men are chairmen and women the secretaries at movement meetings: men can volunteer to take notes. Men can learn to understand and actively support the demands of Women's Liberation groups, like the need for day-care centers, abortion reform, and equal employment rights. They can offer to help with, but not to run, the organization of women's action groups. In all social activities, men should learn to respond to women as human beings rather than merely physical objects. Hardly anyone is interested in destroying the basis of physical attraction, but to emphasize only physical qualities in women de-humanizes them and enforces a barrier between the sexes. Men should consider what women say instead of merely how they look, and not conclude automatically that what they say will be insignificant because spoken by women.

Men can learn to actively participate in home life. Since one of the real sicknesses in our society is momism, men should take more time and interest in the actual work of child rearing to give the child the benefit of a humane, sympathetic male model instead of the usually absent patriarch. They would undoubtedly learn to appreciate the responsibility of caring for children, and greatly contribute to the needed change in children's attitudes toward both parents. At the same time they could avoid the alienation from the family circle common to so many fathers which has enforced the silent matriarchy in our culture. Since more women are working outside the home than ever before, the need for parents to share the labor in the home is great. Yet most men expect working wives to fulfill the traditional housewife and mother roles while working at another job full or part time. Men can volunteer to share in the jobs that must be done regularly, like cleaning, the laundry, grocery shopping, cooking and washing dishes. When both parents are working outside the home, contributing significantly to the economic and social well being of the family, there is no viable reason for men to expect women to do all of this work themselves. Even if only the man works outside the home, his parental responsibilities are the same as the woman's, and his obligation to at least help with the housework remains.

There is also a need for men to encourage women in their pursuit of freedom. This costs men a great deal, since from their point of view they will lose a power over another segment of humanity that they have enjoyed for over 5000 years. Nevertheless, for the improvement of both sex roles, men should encourage women to evaluate their own image. Many women are afraid to demand their own freedom because they have been taught to believe in the moral value of their submission. Men should encourage women to respect themselves as individuals, to develop their talents and interests in significant ways, to develop and act on their own opinions, and to reject their traditional role as submissive women whose primary purpose in life is to fulfill and support the desires of men. Men should encourage women to become active in things that matter, and avoid the usual rationalizations that women are less capable, too temperamental, unreliable, and unavailable when needed. These phrases describe men as well as women, and men must have the courage to face this fact.

And what should women do? Plenty, but this essay is about man's responsibility. Thousands of women are actively working to liberate themselves and their sisters in order to bring about a better society. The purpose of this essay is to state what should be obvious: that no one is free as long as someone is oppressed; that those who oppress must recognize it and act responsibly to free those they oppress; that the oppressed cannot peacefully gain their freedom without responsible action by their oppressors. Peacefully. That is the key. Men have nothing to fear from Women's Liberation if they truly believe in freedom. On the contrary, they have everything to gain, because freedom provides greater happiness for everyone.

Bibliography

A cartoon in *Off Our Backs* (Apr. 25, 1970) has two magazine editors saying, "Just put a nude woman on the cover, get some chick to write an article on Women's Liberation and your sales rise 40%." Women's Liberation has suddenly become good business; the dozens of books on the subject presently in the works, and this book itself, testify to the fact. Almost every magazine in the U.S., often taking the advice of the exploitative editors in the *Off Our Backs'* cartoon, has featured special articles on Women's Liberation. Considering the deluge of articles and books on the subject, we have in the following bibliography tried to limit ourselves to works which we believe to be most useful as a place to begin reading about the Women's Liberation movement. We have not attempted to list works from the traditional point of view, but refer our readers to the entirety of Western literature, with few exceptions, for the view of woman as the Second Sex, as beautiful object, as enemy, and as the Eternal Feminine. Nor have we included any of those works reprinted or excerpted in our book. We include a list, with addresses when they were available, or organizations and presses to contact for reading materials, as well as a list of journals to subscribe to.

Organizations

Abortion Counseling Information, by National Organization of Women (NOW). Box 114, Cathedral Sta., New York, N.Y., 10025.

Association for the Study of Abortion. 120 W. 57th St., New York, N.Y., 10019.

Bay Area Radical Education Project. 491 Guerro St., San Francisco, Calif. 94410.

Black Women's Alliance. c/o St. Peter's Church, 346 W. 20th St., New York, N.Y.

Bread and Roses. A Socialist Women's Liberation organization. Box 116, Cambridge, Mass., 02138.

Female Liberation (Boston). 371 Somerville Ave., Somerville, Mass.

Female Liberation (Durham-Chapel Hill). Box 954, Chapel Hill, N.C., 27514.

Media Women. Women working in media institutions. P.O. Box 1692, New York, N.Y., 10001.

National Association For Repeal of Abortion Laws. 250 W. 57th St., Rm. 2428, New York, N.Y., 10019.

National Organization for Women (NOW). Membership and other information from Box 114, Cathedral Sta., New York, N.Y., 10025.

New Haven Women's Liberation. Harriet Wolff, 65 E. Pearl St., New Haven, Conn., 06513.

New University Conference Women's Caucus. Rm. 403A, 622 W. Diversey, Chicago, Ill., 60614.

Radical Education Project. Box 561A, Detroit, Mich., 48232.

Redstockings. For literature list and prices send stamped, self-addressed envelope to Box 748, Stuyvesant Sta., New York, N.Y., 10009.

Society for Humane Abortion, Inc. Box 1862, San Francisco, Calif., 94101. Newsletters and mailing list: $2.00 a year.

Women's Liberation—Washington, D.C. 1840 Biltmore St., N.W.

Journals, Presses and Bookstores

Aphra/Free Women, Thinking, Doing, Being. $1/issue, $3.50/4 issues; Box 355, Springtown, Pa., 18081.

Everywoman, a paper available for $2.50/10 issues, from Everywoman Bookstore. 6516 W. 83rd St., Los Angeles, Calif. Directory of Women's Liberation in L.A. available for 25 cents.

It Ain't Me Babe. Women's Liberation Basement Press Collective, Box 6323, Albany, Calif., 94706.

Lilith: Journal of Women's Liberation. 50 cents/issue; Women's Majority Union, Box 1895, Seattle, Wash. 98111.

Motive, "On the Liberation of Women: A Special Double Issue." Vol. XXIX, Nos. 6 & 7, Mar.-Apr. 1969. (See *Motive* Oct. 1969, for letter responses to the above.)

New England Free Press. 791 Tremont St., Boston, Mass. 02118. Available is a packet of materials on Women's Liberation.

New Feminist Bookstore. 5037 C. South Drexel, Chicago, Ill.

New York City Women's Liberation: A Feminist Journal. $1; Joyce Betries, 509 E. 5th St., New York, N.Y. 10009.

No More Fun and Games (Dialectics of Sexism). Issues available for $1/ea. Female Liberation, 371 Somerville Ave., Somerville, Mass.

Off Our Backs: A women's news-journal. $6/yr.; $6.50-Canada. Box 4859, Cleveland Park Sta., Washington, D.C. 20008.

Pittsburgh Women's Press. c/o Jo Ann Gardner, 726 St. James St., Pittsburgh, Pa. 15232.

Southern Female Rights Union. Rm. 3, 1024 Jackson Ave., New Orleans, La. 70130.

Tooth and Nail. $2/6 mos. San Francisco Area Women's Liberation, 1800 Prince St., Berkeley, Calif. 94703.

Up from Radicalism: A Feminist Journal. $1; Bantam, 666 Fifth Ave., New York, N.Y. 10019.

Up from Under. Edited by a collective of women. 339 Lafayette St., New York, N.Y. 10012.

Women: A Journal of Liberation. $1.25/issue, $5/5 issues; 3011 Guilford Ave., Baltimore, Md. 21218.

Women's Liberation Center. 2875 W. Cermak, Chicago, Ill. Women's Center. 1027 S. Crenshaw, Los Angeles, Calif. 90005.

Women's Liberation: Notes from the First Year. June 1968. 50c; Kathie Amatniek, 169 Sullivan St., New York, N.Y. 10012.

Women's Liberation: Notes from the Second Year. $1.50; Radical Feminism; P.O. Box 621, Chelsea Sta., New York, N.Y. 10011.

Women's Liberation Newsletter (Boston-New England). Box 116, Cambridge, Mass. 02138.

Bibliographies

Many of the books listed in the "General" section include extensive bibliographies.

Business and Professional Women's Foundation. *Sex Role Concepts: An Annotated Bibliography.* 2012 Massachusetts Ave., N.W., Washington, D.C. 20036.

Cisler, Lucinda. *Women: A Bibliography.* 25¢; 102 W. 80th St., New York, N.Y., 10024.

Farians, Elizabeth J. *Women and Religion: Writings and Bibliography.* $1; Elizabeth J. Farians, 6825 N. Sheridan Rd., Chicago, Ill., 60626. Special focus on Catholicism.

New University Women's Caucus. *A Selected Bibliography on Women.* Rm. 403A, 622 W. Diversey, Chicago, Ill. 60614.

Women's Liberation. c/o Broedel, 308 S. McComb, Tallahassee, Fla. *Bibliography of Women's Liberation.*

United Nations at UN Plaza, New York, N.Y., or UNESCO in Paris. Numerous studies of women around the world.

General Bibliography

Asimov, Isaac. *Uncertain, Coy, and Hard to Please.* Boston: New England Free Press. Also in *The Magazine of Fantasy and Science Fiction,* Feb. 1969.

Astin, Helen S. *The Woman Doctorate in America: Origins, Career, and Family.* New York: Russell Sage Foundation, 1969.

Beard, Mary R. *Woman as a Force in History.* New York: Collier Books, 1962. Contrasts conventional myths and reality of woman in history. Extensive bibliography.

Bender, Marylin. *The Beautiful People.* New York: Dell, 1967. Puts the fashion mania into a broader social context than is usual. Good implicit material on women.

Bettelheim, Bruno. *Children of the Dream: Communal Child Rearing and American Education.* New York: Macmillan, 1969. Interesting discussion of kibbutz child-rearing.

Buck, Pearl S. *Of Men and Women.* New York: John Day Company, 1941. Sections on "Monogamy," "Women as Angels," "Women and War," "Women and Freedom," etc.

Cade, Toni. *The Black Woman.* New York: New American Library, 1970. An anthology.

Chasseguet-Smirgel, J. *Female Sexuality: New Psychoanalytic Views.* Ann Arbor: Univ. of Michigan Press, 1970.

Cowley, Joyce. *Pioneers of Women's Liberation.* New York: Merit, Dec. 1969.

Dahlstrom, Edmund, ed. *The Changing Roles of Men and Women.* London: Duckworth, 1967. Collection includes a summary, in translation, of a major Scandinavian research work on effects of sex roles.

de Beauvoir Simone, *The Second Sex.* Trans. H. M. Parshley. New York: Bantam, 1961.

de Rougement, Denis. *Love Declared:* Essays on the Myth of Love. Boston, Beacon, 1964. An extension of *Love in the Western World* in a group of essays.

de Rougement, Denis. *Love in the Western World.* Fawcett, 1966. Greenwich, Conn. Especially good on the inter-relationship of love and war; but author relies too heavily on Freudian psychology.

Densmore, Dana. *Sex Roles and Female Oppression—A Collection of Articles.* Boston: New England Free Press.

Dickson, Ruth. *Marriage Is a Bad Habit.* New York: Award Books, 1969. Advertised as "a no-holds-barred approach to the real joys of being single, as well as an outspoken guide that points up the dangers of foolish romanticism, prolonged virginity, staying together because of the children, and more."

389

Dudar, Helen. 'Women's Lib: The War on 'Sexism,' " *Newsweek*, March 23, 1970, 71-78.

Dunbar, Roxanne. *Female Liberation as the Basis for Social Revolution*. Boston: New England Free Press and Southern Student Organizing Committee, Box 6403, Nashville, Tenn., 37212.

Ellis, Julie. *Revolt of the Second Sex*. New York: Lancer, 1970. A survey of movement groups, including how to contact some of them.

Ellmann, Mary. *Thinking About Women*. New York: Harcourt, 1968.

Fanon, Frantz. *Studies in a Dying Colonialism; The Wretched of the Earth*. New York: Grove, 1961.

Farber, Seymour M. and Roger H. L. Wilson. *The Potential of Woman*. New York: McGraw-Hill, 1963. A written record of papers and discussion from a symposium which was third in the "Man and Civilization" series held at Univ. of Calif. San Francisco Medical Center, Jan. 25-27, 1963.

Figes, Eva. *Patriarchal Attitudes*. New York: Stein and Day, 1970.

Firestone, Shulamith. *The Dialectic of Sex: The Case for Feminist Revolution*. New York: Morrow, 1970.

Flexnor, Eleanor. *A Century of Struggle*. Cambridge, Mass.: Harvard Univ. Press, 1966. Most complete history of the women's rights movement in the U.S. up to 1920.

Gould, Lois. *Such Good Friends*. New York: Random House, 1970. A novel about the depressed, unhappy and bitter frustrations of Julie Messinger, a suburbanite turned woman as enemy.

Gross, Amy. "Women's Lib Loves You," *Mademoiselle*, Feb. 1970, 232–233, 286–288. The same issue includes a special section on "Women: The New Sex."

Hall, Mary Harrington. "A Conversation with Masters and Johnson," *Psychology Today*, July 1969, 50–58. Good clarification of Masters and Johnson and of their work.

Hartman, Sylvia. "Should Wives Work?" *McCall's*, Feb. 1969, 57 ff. A feminist's exposition of the idea that men don't want to do any of the dirty work of "homemaking."

Herschberger, Ruth. *Adam's Rib*. New York: Pellegrini & Cudahy, 1948. On the sexual-biological nature of woman; discusses at length the frustrations of women from culturally conditioned attitudes toward sex.

Hinckle, Warren and Marianne Hinckle. "A History of the Rise of the Unusual Movement for Women Power in the United States 1961-1968," *Ramparts*, Feb. 1968, 23–31. (See "Letters" in Mar. 1968 *Ramparts* for responses to the article.)

Horney, Karen. *Female Psychology*. New York: Norton, 1967.

——————————. *New Ways in Psychoanalysis*. New York: Norton, 1939. Her chapter "Feminine Psychology" is a rejoinder to the penis-envy theory.

Howe, Florence. "The Education of Women," *Liberation*, Aug.-Sept. 1969, 49–55. A résumé of historical attitudes toward women's education, with excellent analysis of the problems facing educators of women trying to reshape women's education.

Hunt, Morton M. *The Natural History of Love*. New York: Knopf, 1959. An early study which leads into the sexual revolution and questions of woman's identity in the late 50's. Based on historical and sociological view of women, with a good bibliography of same.

Jensen, Oliver. *The Revolt of American Women*. New York: Harcourt, 1952. Subtitled a pictorial history of the century of change from bloomers to bikinis, from feminism to Freud.

Jordan, Joan. *The Place of American Women—Economic Exploitation of Women*. Boston: New England Free Press.

Kanowitz, Leo. *Women and the Law: The Unfinished Revolution*. Albuquerque: Univ. of New Mexico Press, 1969.

Kanter, Rosabeth Moss. "Communes: Why and How They Are Formed and Which Are Likely to Make It and Why," *Psychology Today*, July 1970, 53–57, 78.

Kelso, Ruth. *Doctrine for the Lady of the Renaissance*. Urbana: Univ. of Illinois Press, 1956. A thorough, scholarly study of Renaissance women, including a bibliography of 150 pp. of literature about women in this period.

Kempton, Sally. "Cutting Loose: A Private View of the Women's Uprising," *Esquire*, July 1970, 53–57.

Komisar, Lucy. "The New Feminism," *Saturday Review*, Feb. 21, 1970, 27–30, 55.

Kraditor, Aileen S., ed. *Up From the Pedestal: Selected Documents from the History of American Feminism*. New York: Quadrangle, 1968.

Krich, A. M., ed. *Women—The Variety and Meaning of Their Sexual Experience*. New York: Dell, 1953. A collection of essays by Havelock Ellis, Margaret Mead, Helene Deutsch and others.

Lanison, Peggy. *Few Are Chosen: American Women in Political Life Today*. Boston: Houghton Mifflin, 1968.

Langer, Elinor. "Inside the New York Telephone Company," *The New York Review of Books*, Mar. 12, 1970, and Mar. 19, 1970. 2-part article.

La Rue, Linda Jo. "The Black Movement and Women's Liberation," *Black Scholar* (May 1970). Single copies available for $1.25 at Box 908, Sausalito, Calif. 94965.

League for Socialist Action (Canada). *The Status of Women in Canada*. Vanguard Books, 1208 Granville St., Vancouver, B.C., Canada.

Lifton, Robert Jay, ed. *The Woman in America*. Boston: Beacon, 1967. Includes essays by Erik H. Erikson, Diana Trilling, Alice S. Rossi, and others.

"Lower Your Voice—Swallow Your Gum," *Guardian*, Mar. 7, 1970, 5, 18. On telephone operators. First of a 5-part *Guardian* series (Mar. 7-Apr. 11, 1970) on the exploitation of women.

Lutz, Alma. *Crusade for Freedom: Women in the Anti-Slavery Movement*. Boston: Beacon, 1968. Account of the first 50 years of the abolitionist and women's rights movement.

Lydon, Sue. "Understanding Orgasm," *Ramparts*, Dec. 1969, 14–28. Concise discussion of debate over female orgasm and sexual pleasure and implication of that debate.

Mead, Margaret. *Male and Female: A Study of the Sexes in a Changing*

World. New York: Morrow, 1949. Also, *Sex and Temperament in Three Savage Societies*, 1935. Studies illustrate how primitive and present cultures determine meaning of sex and roles assigned to each.

Mead, Margaret, et al. *The Peaceful Revolution: Birth Control and the Changing Status of Women*. Planned Parenthood-World Population, 1967. Women from several nations write how birth control alters women's "place."

Millett, Kate. *Sexual Politics*. New York: Doubleday, 1970.

Mitchell, Juliet. *The Longest Revolution*. Boston: New England Free Press. Also in *New Left Review*, Nov.-Dec. 1966.

Morgan, Robin. *Sisterhood Is Powerful: An Anthology of Writings from the Women's Liberation Movement*. New York: Vintage, 1970. Extensive compendium of writings by women's liberation people: psychology, education, birth control, sexuality, etc.

Myrdal, Alva and Viola Klein. *Women's Two Roles:Home and Work*. London: Routledge & Kegan Paul, 1968. Discusses working women, including "Why Married Women Seek Employment," "The Effects on Children," etc.

Myrdal, Gunnar, *An American Dilemma*. 2 vols. New York: Harper, 1941, 1944.

Neill, A. S. *Summerhill—A Radical Approach to Child Rearing*. New York: Hart, 1960. Neill was a school revolutionary 50 years ago and set up his own school to experiment in freer, more creative education. An especially good chapter on "The Unfree Child."

Novack, George. *Revolutionary Dynamics of Women's Liberation*. New York: Merit, 1969.

Parker, Elizabeth. *The Seven Ages of Woman*. New York: Bantam, 1967. Heavily based on biology and its effects on woman's psychological and social functions, but cognizant of the new freedom women desire, and its responsibility.

Piercy, Marge. "The Movement: For Men Only?"*Guardian*, Jan. 31, 1970, 8; Feb. 7, 1970, 16; Feb. 14, 1970, 15–16. 3-part series.

Plato. *The Republic*. Book 5: The Communal Rearing of Children.

Rainwater, Lee, Richard P. Coleman, and Gerald Handel. *Workingman's Wife: Her Personality, World and Life Style*. New York: Oceana, 1959. After describing the psychosocial world of the workingman's wife, the study considers consumer behavior, "blue collar aesthetics," and the strategy used to reach workingclass women through advertising. The book is remarkable as an honest disclosure of exploitation.

Reed, Evelyn. *Problems of Women's Liberation: A Marxist Approach*. New York: Merit, 1969.

Rossi, Alice. "Sex Equality: The Beginnings of Ideology," *The Humanist*, Sept./Oct. 1969. Especially useful for its discussions of models of equality.

Ruderman, Florence. *Child Care and the Working Mother*. Child Welfare League of America, 44 E. 23rd St., New York, N.Y., 10010. A study of working mothers, showing benefits of day care to the mothers and the children.

Rhys, Jean. *Good Morning, Midnight.* New York: Harper & Row, 1970. Novel of a previously married woman in her forties who is exploited by a conventional image of middle age (see also *Wide Sargasso Sea*).

Rimmer, Robert. *Proposition 31.* New York: Signet, 1969. Novel about communal marriage which suggests larger social implications.

Schur, Edwin M., ed. *The Family and the Sexual Revolution.* Bloomington: Indiana Univ. Press, 1964. Collection of essays on changing sex standards, "the woman problem," and birth control.

Sorensen, Theodore C. "A Special Report on the Woman Voter," *Redbook,* Apr. 1968, 61.

Soubiran, André. *Diary of a Woman in White.* New York: Avon. A best seller in France; this is a novel about nursing by a strong speaker for women's rights.

Spinks, Sarah. "Sugar and Spice," *This Magazine Is About Schools,* Toronto, Summer 1969. Good account of how little girls are conditioned.

Stamberg, Margie. "The New Feminism: 'You've Come a Long Way, Baby.'" *Guardian,* Mar. 22, 1969, 11; Mar. 29, 1969, 10; Apr. 19, 1969, 11. 3-part series.

Thompson, Mary Lou, ed. *Voices of the New Feminism.* Boston, Beacon, 1970.

Vogue: The Life and Looks of the American Woman 1970. June 1970. A special issue, interesting as a new direction for *Vogue,* but it's still *Vogue,* liberation in name only.

Willis, Ellen. "Women and the Myth of Consumerism." *Ramparts,* June 1970, 14–16.

The Woman Question: Selections from the Writings of Karl Marx, Frederich Engels, V. I. Lenin, Joseph Stalin. New York: International, 1951. Includes sections on "The Enslavement of Women," "The Exploitation of Women," "The Bourgeois Family," "Women in the Struggle for Socialism," etc.

Women and The Cuban Revolution. Speeches by Fidel Castro; articles by Linda Jenness. New York: Merit, 1970.

Women's Bureau, U.S. Department of Labor, Washington, D.C. Leaflet #10 lists their numerous publications on women, especially as workers. 1969 *Handbook on Women Workers,* Bulletin 294: a thorough study including a 40-page bibliography.

"Woman's Place," *Atlantic,* Mar. 1970, 81–126. A special supplement on women: includes an article on job discrimination, women and the law, women's liberation, motherhood, etc.

Woodward, Helen. *The Lady Persuaders.* New York: Aster-Honor, 1960. Over 100 years of women's magazines; their influence.